THE BALANCE BETWEEN INDUSTRY AND AGRICULTURE IN ECONOMIC DEVELOPMENT
Volume 5: FACTORS INFLUENCING CHANGE

THE BALANCE BETWEEN INDUSTRY AND AGRICULTURE IN ECONOMIC DEVELOPMENT

Volume 1 BASIC ISSUES
Kenneth J. Arrow (*editor*)

Volume 2 SECTOR PROPORTIONS
Jeffrey G. Williamson and Vadiraj R. Panchamukhi (*editors*)

Volume 3 MANPOWER AND TRANSFERS
Sukhamoy Chakravarty (*editor*)

Volume 4 SOCIAL EFFECTS
Irma Adelman and Sylvia Lane (*editors*)

Volume 5 FACTORS INFLUENCING CHANGE
Nurul Islam (*editor*)

These volumes are, respectively, nos 86–90 in the
IEA/Macmillan series

Series Standing Order

If you would like to receive future titles in this series as they are published,
you can make use of our standing order facility. To place a standing order
please contact your bookseller or, in case of difficulty, write to us at the
address below with your name and address and the name of the series.
Please state with which title you wish to begin your standing order. (If you
live outside the United Kingdom we may not have the rights for your area,
in which case we will forward your order to the publisher concerned.)

Customer Services Department, Macmillan Distribution Ltd,
Houndmills, Basingstoke, Hampshire, RG21 2XS, England.

The Balance between Industry and Agriculture in Economic Development

Proceedings of the Eighth World Congress of the
International Economic Association, Delhi, India

Volume 5
FACTORS INFLUENCING CHANGE

Edited by
Nurul Islam

Volume Rapporteur: David W. Brown

MACMILLAN
PRESS

in association with the
INTERNATIONAL ECONOMIC
ASSOCIATION

First published 1989

Published by
THE MACMILLAN PRESS LTD
Houndmills, Basingstoke, Hampshire RG21 2XS
and London
Companies and representatives
throughout the world

Printed in Hong Kong

British Library Cataloguing in Publication Data
International Economic Association, *World Congress (8th : Delhi)*
The balance between industry and agriculture
in economic development : proceedings of
the Eighth World Congress on the
International Economic Association, Delhi, India.
Vol. 5: Factors influencing change
1. Economic development—Social aspects
2. Economic development—Political aspects
I. Title II. Islam, Nurul III. International Economic
Association
330.9   HD82
ISBN 0–333–46715–9

Contents

Preface

The Eighth World Congress of the International Economic Association was held in Delhi from 1 to 5 December 1986, presided over by Professor Kenneth J. Arrow, President of the IEA from 1983 to 1986. The subject of the Congress was 'The Balance between Industry and Agriculture in Economic Development'. It was organised by the Indian Economic Association.

Participation in the Congress was broadly based in terms both of geography and of the types of economy from which participants came; market orientated and centrally planned; developed and developing; mainly agricultural and predominantly industrial.

The Congress included a number of plenary sessions, but much of the work of the Congress was undertaken in eighteen specialised meetings. The volume of papers was too large for them all to be published, but the five volumes in this group, together with a volume on the Indian economy being published separately in India, represent the major viewpoints expressed. The volumes generally contain reports on the discussions which took place during the specialised sessions.

The volumes are:

1. *Basic Issues*, edited by Kenneth J. Arrow
2. *Sector Proportions*, edited by Jeffrey G. Williamson and Vadiraj R. Panchamukhi
3. *Manpower and Transfers*, edited by Sukhamoy Chakravarty
4. *Social Effects*, edited by Irma Adelman and Sylvia Lane
5. *Factors Influencing Change*, edited by Nurul Islam

The Indian volume is edited by Professor P. R. Brahmananda and Professor S. Chakravarty under the title *The Indian Economy: Balance between Industry and Agriculture* and will be published by Macmillan (India).

This volume contains selected papers from four sessions of the Congress, as follows:

Session 8   Relative Price Movements in Agriculture and Industry, organised by Dr Nurul Islam

Session 11 World Trade and Agricultural/Industrial Balance, organised by Dr I. M. D. Little

Session 13 Protection of Agricultural and Industrial Products, organised by Professor Bela Balassa

Session 15 Industrialisation in Primary Export Economies, organised by Professor Shigeru Ishikawa

The International Economic Association

A non-profit organisation with purely scientific aims, the International Economic Association (IEA) was founded in 1950. It is in fact a federation of national economic associations and presently includes fifty-eight such professional organisations from all parts of the world. Its basic purpose is the development of economics as an intellectual discipline. Its approach recognises a diversity of problems, systems and values in the world and also takes note of methodological diversities.

The IEA has, since its creation, tried to fulfil that purpose by promoting mutual understanding of economists from the West and the East as well as from the North and the South through the organisation of scientific meetings and common research programmes and by means of publications on problems of current importance. During its thirty-seven years of existence, it has organised seventy-nine round-table conferences for specialists on topics ranging from fundamental theories to methods and tools of analysis and major problems of the present-day world. Eight triennal World Congresses have also been held, and these have regularly attracted the participation of a great many economists from all over the world. The proceedings of all these meetings are published by Macmillan.

The Association is governed by a Council, composed of representatives of all member associations, and by a fifteen-member Executive Committee which is elected by the Council. The present Executive Committee (1986–9) is composed as follows:

President:	Professor Amartya Sen, India
Vice-President:	Professor Béla Csikós-Nagy, Hungary
Treasurer:	Professor Luis Angel Rojo, Spain
Past President:	Professor Kenneth J. Arrow, USA
Other members:	Professor Edmar Lisboa Bacha, Brazil
	Professor Ragnar Bentzel, Sweden
	Professor Oleg T. Bogomolov, USSR
	Professor Silvio Borner, Switzerland
	Professor P. R. Brahmananda, India

The Association has also been fortunate in having secured the following outstanding economists to serve as President:

Gottfried Haberler (1950–3), Howard S. Ellis (1953–6), Erik Lindahl (1956–9), E. A. G. Robinson (1959–62), G. Ugo Papi (1962–5), Paul A. Samuelson (1965–8), Erik Lundberg (1968–71), Fritz Machlup (1971–4), Edmond Malinvaud (1974–7), Shigeto Tsuru (1977–80), Victor L. Urquidi (1980–3), Kenneth J. Arrow (1983–6).

The activities of the Association are mainly funded from the subscriptions of members and grants from a number of organisations, including continuing support from UNESCO.

Acknowledgements

The host for the Eighth World Congress of the International Economic Association was the Indian Economic Association and all Congress participants are in its debt for the organisation of the Congress itself and for the welcome given to economists from all over the world. The preparation for such a gathering, culminating in a week of lectures, discussions and social activities, is an enormous undertaking. The International Economic Association wishes to express its appreciation on behalf of all participants.

Both the Indian and the International Economic Associations are grateful to the large number of institutions and organisations, including many states, banks, business firms, research and trade organisations which provided funds for the Congress. They particularly wish to thank the following Indian Government Departments and other official agencies:

Ministry of Finance
Ministry of External Affairs
The Reserve Bank of India
The State Bank of India
The Industrial Development Bank of India
The Indian Council of Social Science Research
The Industrial Credit and Investment Corporation of India
The Industrial Finance Corporation of India
The National Bank for Agriculture and Rural Development
The Industrial Reconstruction Bank of India
The Punjab National Bank
The Canara Bank
Tata Group of Industries
The Government of Uttar Pradesh
The Government of Karnataka
The Government of Kerala
The Government of Madhya Pradesh

Valuable support was given by the Ford Foundation and the International Development Research Centre. The Research and Information System for Non-aligned and Other Developing Countries and the Institute of Applied Manpower Research provided valuable assistance in staffing and in the infrastructure of the Congress.

The social events of the Congress provided a useful opportunity for informal discussion as well as being a source of great enjoyment. The hospitality of the Indian Economic Association, the Export Import Bank of India, the Federation of Indian Chambers of Commerce and Industry, the Punjab Haryana and Delhi (PHD) Chambers of Commerce and Industry and the DCM Ltd created memorable occasions. Thanks go to the Indian Council for Cultural Relations, which organised a cultural evening. In addition there were many small social gatherings which stressed the international flavour of the Congress.

Lastly, and vitally important, was the contribution of the members of the IEA Organising Committee and the Indian Steering Committee listed overleaf; in particular, Dr Manmohan Singh, Chairman of the Steering Committee, Professor S. Chakravarty, President of the Indian Economic Association, and then Vice-President of the International Economic Association and Dr V. R. Panchamukhi, Convenor of the Steering Committee; the authors; the discussants; the rapporteurs and the ever-helpful students. The International Economic Association wishes to thank them all for the success of the Congress in Delhi in 1986.

Thanks are expressed to the International Social Science Council under whose auspices the publications programme is carried out, and to UNESCO for its financial support.*

* Under the auspices of the International Social Science Council and with a grant from UNESCO (1986–87/DG/7.6.2/SUB. 16 (SHS)).

The IEA Programme Committee International Economic Association Eighth World Congress

Irma Adelman
Kenneth J. Arrow
P. R. Brahmananda
Sukhamoy Chakravarty
Béla Csikós-Nagy
Shigeru Ishikawa
Nurul Islam
Bruce Johnston
Paolo Sylos–Labini

Indian Steering Committee

Dr Manmohan Singh (*Chairman*)
Professor S. Chakravarty (*President, Indian Economic Association,
then Vice-President of the International Economic Association*)
Dr V. R. Panchamukhi (*Convenor*)

Dr Malcom S. Adiseshaiah
Dr M. S. Ahluwalia
Dr D. S. Awasthi
Dr Mahesh Bhatt
Professor P. R. Brahmananda
Shri M. Dubey
Professor Alak Ghosh
Professor P. D. Hajela
Dr Bimal Jalan
Professor A. M. Khusro
Professor D. T. Lakdawala
Dr M. Madaiah
Professor Gautam Mathur
Professor M. V. Mathur
Professor Iqbal Narain
Professor D. L. Narayana
Dr D. D. Narula
Professor Kamta Prasad
Dr C. Rangarajan
Dr N. K. Sengupta
Professor Shanmugasundaram
Dr R. K. Sinha .

List of Contributors and Rapporteurs

Authors

Professor Bela Balassa, Johns Hopkins University, Baltimore, and World Bank, Washington DC, USA.

Dr Romeo M. Bautista, International Food Policy Research Institute, Washington DC, USA.

Professor Shigeru Ishikawa, School of International Politics, Economics and Business, Aoyama Gakuin University, Tokyo, Japan.

Dr Nurul Islam, International Food Policy Research Institute, Washington DC, USA.

Professor V. I. Kiselev, USSR Academy of Sciences, Central Economic Mathematical Institute, Moscow, USSR.

Professor Deepak Lal, University College, London UK and World Bank, Washington DC, USA.

Dr I. M. D. Little, Nuffield College, Oxford, UK.

Dr Montague J. Lord, Inter-American Development Bank, Washington DC, USA.

Professor Alasdair I. MacBean, Department of Economics, University of Lancaster, UK and World Bank, Washington DC, USA.

Professor Gerald M. Meier, Graduate School of Business, Stanford University, California, USA.

Professor T. Ademola Oyejide, Economics Department, University of Ibadan, Nigeria.

Professor Gustav Ranis, Economic Growth Center, Yale University, New Haven, USA.

Dr Gary P. Sampson, UNCTAD, Geneva, Switzerland.

Professor Paul Streeten, World Development Institute, Boston University, USA.

Dr Simón Teitel, Economic and Social Development Department, Inter-American Development Bank, Washington DC, USA.

Dr Lien H. Tran, Development Strategy Division, The World Bank, Washington DC, USA.

Dr Alberto Valdés, International Food Policy Research Institute, Washington DC, USA.

Professor Karl Wohlmuth, University of Bremen, FRG.

Professor Ippei Yamazawa, Hitotsubashi University, Tokyo, Japan.
Dr Joachim Zietz, Kiel Institute of World Economics, Kiel, FRG.

Rapporteurs
Dr D. D. Guru, A. N. Sinha Institute of Social Studies, Patna, Bihar, India.
Dr N. S. Iyengar, Indian Statistical Institute Ruce Po, Bangalore, India.
Dr V. S. Mahajan, Centre for Indian Economic Development Studies, Chandigarh, India.
Dr S. N. Mishra, Institute of Economic Growth, University Enclave, Delhi, India.
Dr I. N. Mukherji, School of International Studies, Jawaharlal Nehru University, New Delhi, India.
Dr K. Seeta Prabhu, Department of Economics, University of Bombay, India.
Professor V. Lakshmana Rao, Department of Economics, Andhra University, Waltair AP, India.
Professor Sunanda Sen, Centre for Economic Studies and Planning, Jawaharlal Nehru University, New Delhi, India.
Dr N. S. Siddarthan, Institute of Economic Growth, University Enclave, Delhi, India.
Dr R. Thamarajakshi, Planning Commission, Government of India, Delhi, India.

Volume Rapporteur
Dr David W. Brown, Food and Agriculture Organisation of the United Nations, Rome, Italy.

Abbreviations and Acronyms

ACP	African Caribbean and Pacific
ADLI	Agricultural demand-led industrialisation
AIC	Agro-industrial complex
APRA	Alianza Popular Revolucionaria Americana
ASEAN	Association for South East Asian Nations
CAP	Common Agricultural Policy (of the EEC)
CCCN	Customs Co-operation Council Nomenclature
CES	Constant elasticity of substitution
CPC	Catching-up product cycle
CPE	Centrally planned economy
CPSU	Communist Party of the Soviet Union
CSE	Consumer subsidy equivalents
CTA	Committee on Trade in Agriculture (of GATT)
DMEC	Developed market economy country
EEC	European Economic Community
EFTA	European Free Trade Area
EP	Export promotion
FAO	Food and Agriculture Organisation (of the UN)
GATT	General Agreement on Tariffs and Trade
GDP	Gross domestic product
GNP	Gross national product
GSP	Generalised System of Preferences
HOS	Heckscher–Ohlin–Samuelson (model)
IIASA	International Institute for Applied Systems Analysis
IC	Industrialised country
ICA	International Coffee Agreement
IFPRI	International Food Policy Research Institute
IMF	International Monetary Fund
IS	Import substitution
ISI	Import substitution-orientated industrialisation
ISIC	International Standard Industrial Classification
LDC	Less-developed country
LIC	Less-industrialised country
MFA	Multifibre Arrangement
MFN	Most favoured nation

MNC	Multinational corporation
MTN	Multilateral trade negotiation
nec	not elsewhere classified
NIC	Newly industrialising country
NIEO	New international economic order
NPC	Nominal protection coefficient
NTB	Non-tariff barrier
OECD	Organisation for Economic Co-operation and Development
OLS	Ordinary least squares
OPEC	Organisation of Petroleum Exporting Countries
PC	Product cycle
PFES	Producer-financed export subsidies
PL	Public Law (USA)
PPF	Production possibility frontier
PSE	Producer subsidy equivalent
QR	Quantity restriction
SITC	Standard International Trade Classification
SUR	Seemingly unrelated regression
TAS	Total agricultural surplus
TSLS	Two-stage least squares
TSUS(A)	Tariff Schedules of the United States (of America)
UNIDO	United Nations Industrial Development Organisation
VER	Voluntary export restriction
VPER	Vice President Economic Research

Introduction

Nurul Islam

The relative balance between agriculture and industry changes in the course of economic development in response to a combination of factors. To mention only a few – growth and changes in the composition of demand, technological progress, the external economic environment, especially international trading opportunities, domestic policies, both macroeconomic and sectoral, including exchange rate and pricing policies all influence the intersectoral allocation of resources and the changing balance between agriculture and industry.

The papers and reports on the discussions of the four sessions included in this volume cover a few selected aspects of the overall theme, that is, price relations in agriculture and industry, influence of world trade on balance between agriculture and industry, relative degrees of protection of agriculture and industry, and industrialisation of primary exporting economies.

1 PATTERNS OF DEVELOPMENT

In a closed economy, the balance between agriculture and industry is determined in the long run by the relative demand, including final demand and intersectoral demand, for the outputs of the two sectors. Any imbalance or inconsistency with the pattern or composition of demand creates surpluses or shortages, setting in motion the corrective forces. The allocation of resources between the two sectors evolves or changes over time, subject to the demand constraints mentioned above, in response to changes in technology. In an open economy, the relative balance between agriculture and industry depends, in addition to the relative domestic demand for the products of both the sectors, on comparative costs as well as on international trading opportunities. Most countries in the real world are open economies and face differential trading opportunities and comparative costs. The pattern and rate of technological progress as well as changes in demand in different countries for different commodities are among the factors affecting the shifts in intersectoral balance. Both macro and micro or sectoral policies affect the intersectoral allocation of resources.

Most developing countries start out as primary producing and exporting countries. The first stage in their economic transformation often begins with the processing of primary commodities for meeting domestic needs in substitution for imports. Frequently a spurt in export demand for primary products provides the initial push or stimulus to economic growth. Historically this was true in many instances. It increases export earnings needed to import capital goods and production inputs. The increase in the export sector income leads to the expansion of national markets for the domestically produced goods, both agricultural and manufactured. High rents obtained from the exploitation of primary exports are added to the flow of savings and accelerate the domestic capital formation.

In the course of time, as experience is gained and quality is improved, processed raw materials begin to be exported. Where primary exports are predominantly non-food commodities they provide the foreign exchange resources for food imports in addition to manufactured consumer goods. Expansion of non-food primary exports, in countries where land is abundant and labour is scarce, requires improved productivity in food production for meeting the requirements of increasing supply of labour to the export sector.

As income grows and the demand pattern changes, the relative importance of food and agricultural goods in the consumption basket declines and that of manufactured goods increases and, in response, investment in the manufacturing sector increases. Increased labour productivity in agriculture, as technological progress is accelerated, releases labour for absorption in the expanding manufacturing sector. In many countries import substituting industrialisation has been initiated on the basis of extensive domestic market and large reservoirs of cheap labour – not always using domestic raw materials but imported materials as well. With a small domestic market, but cheap labour, industrialisation is often primarily export market oriented with the help in several cases of foreign capital and entrepreneurship. The relative importance of domestic versus export market as the basis of industrialisation has varied over time and over countries.

2 OUTWARD- AND INWARD-LOOKING STRATEGIES

However, the debate on the appropriateness of import substitution or export promotion strategy or on the choice between outward- or inward-looking development strategy continues undiminished. Since, in most developing countries, the export sector is dominated by agriculture and the import competing sector is dominated by industry, the choice between import substitution and export promotion strategies affects the balance between agriculture and industry. The differences in the degree of protection and subsidy between the two sectors affect the intersectoral allocation of resources.

The debate centres on the following questions. Firstly, what exactly is the nature of the distinction between outward- or inward-looking strategy? Is the distinction as rigid or absolute as is often suggested? Secondly, how far is an outward-looking strategy of a developing country a matter solely of its own decision? In other words, how far is action by the industrialised countries crucial for the success of an export promotion or outward-looking strategy?

An outward-looking strategy is considered to be one in which incentives provided by macroeconomic and sectoral policies are neutral between import substitution and export promotion. In other words, under such a policy returns from the use of resources in the import competing sectors are not higher or lower than those derived from the export sectors. An inward-looking strategy is one in which incentives for or profitability of import substituting activities are higher than those for export activities. The success of an outward-looking strategy, which does not discriminate against exports, depends partially on the import policy of the industrialised countries and on world market conditions, which are dominated by developed countries.

The import substituting strategy of industrialisation in the postwar period as propelled by a general pessimism which was pervasive in developing countries, relating to the export prospects of primary commodities. For tropical agricultural commodities like coffee, tea and cocoa, both price and income elasticity of demand were considered to be low; the principal market for most of these commodities was in developed countries, where per capita consumption of these items was already quite high, and hence was stagnant or expanding very slowly. Also the slowing down of economic growth in the developed countries in recent years further contributed to a decline in the rate of expansion of demand for developing country exports. In commodities such as cereals, wheat, oilseeds, sugar and so on, in which developing countries compete with industrialised countries in world markets, both supply and demand factors contribute to either a declining or a stagnant share of the developing countries in the world market.

3 INSTABILITY IN WORLD MARKETS – PROTECTION AND SUBSIDIES

In many senses world agriculture is in disarray. The developed countries, with the help of high support prices and other incentives, continue to produce, far in excess of present and prospective domestic demand, large agricultural surpluses which they are only able to dispose of in the world market with the help of considerable export subsidies. The net result of insulating domestic economy from the impact of fluctuations in domestic production or in world supplies has been an increased instability in the world agricultural markets. The increased instability or fluctuations in prices and supplies of agricultural commodities in the world market has exposed developing countries to higher risks and uncertainties. This enhances the need of additional measures to achieve stability, such as international commodity arrangements to manage commodity stocks or internationally co-ordinated national stocks with a view to regulating world supply and hence stabilising world prices.

In addition to the impact which agricultural protectionism of industrialised countries has on the stability of prices and supplies of agricultural commodities, it has the effect of depressing the levels of prices in the world markets. This in turn creates disincentives for importing countries to increase domestic production, even in cases where comparative cost advantages warrant such an increase. The international allocation of resources in agriculture is thus divorced from comparative cost considerations. In situations like this, world prices can no longer serve as a guide for the allocation of resources in the agricultural sector. In the case of sugar, for example, the world prices, owing to the heavy subsidies provided by some high cost producers, mostly developed countries, are so low as to make it almost impossible for even the most efficient producers to compete in the export market.

Developing countries might however protect their food and

agriculture sector from the impact of subsidy-induced, artificially depressed world prices, by placing tariffs and quotas on their imports. Undoubtedly, any indiscriminate use of such devices may further misallocate resources in world agriculture.

Elimination or reduction of agricultural protectionism of industrial countries is likely to raise the prices in the world market. Questions have been raised as to whether this is necessarily true in all cases. Most of the analysis of the impact of trade liberalisation on world prices has been undertaken within a partial equilibrium framework and confined to individual commodities without reference to the implications of interrelationships between different countries in consumption and production. A simultaneous liberalisation of trade in more than one commodity, for example, a liberalisation of trade by the EEC in both cereals (wheat mainly) and livestock products, would reduce the domestic production of cereals in the EEC and at the same time reduce the demand for cereal as feed for animal production, since livestock production would decrease. The reduced supply of cereal would be offset by reduced demand – and hence would have no price-raising effect in the world market.

Is the rise in world prices of agricultural commodities resulting from trade liberalisation by OECD countries an unmixed blessing for developing countries? The low-income food deficit countries benefit from depressed world prices whereas the exporting countries like Argentina and Thailand suffer. However, if liberalisation is widespread enough, benefits will be widely distributed. While food importing countries will lose from higher cereal prices, they will at the same time gain from an expansion of exports, for example, of agricultural raw materials, which will enjoy a greater market access. It is hoped that reduction of agricultural protectionism will be associated as well with the liberalisation of trade in processed agricultural commodities, which suffer from 'cascading' trade restrictions in the markets of developed countries, with the intensity of restrictions increasing with the degree of processing. This will confer substantial benefits on the primary producing and exporting developed countries.

In a multisectoral framework, liberalisation of trade would affect the relative competitive position of agricultural and industrial exports in world trade for both developed and developing countries. Agricultural protectionism, which is much higher than industrial protectionism in many developed countries, increases the relative prices of their manufactured *vis-à-vis* agricultural exports in world markets. As a consequence, the competitive position of industrial exports of developing countries improves in relation to their agricultural exports. A reduction in their agricultural protectionism will tend to reverse the situation and by reducing the relative prices of their manufactured exports in world markets will provide greater competition to the developing countries. Within the developed countries a reduction in agricultural protectionism would shift resources to the industrial sector; given the lower levels of skill of agricultural workers, they are likely to move relatively more readily to the labour-intensive industries which compete with the exports of developing countries. At the same time, however, the lower world prices of manufactured relative to agricultural goods would help improve the terms of trade of low-income developing countries, which are heavily dependent upon imports of manufactures.

The foregoing analysis illustrates firstly how complex are the consequences of trade liberalisation in an individual agricultural commodity or in the agricultural sector as a whole when interactions with other commodities or sectors are considered together. Secondly, it also demonstrates that benefits of trade liberalisation are likely to be considerably greater if they are undertaken across all commodities and all countries. The benefits are not to be measured solely by their impact on world prices; they also emanate to a much greater extent from a more efficient allocation of resources between sectors within a country and among countries.

Historical evidence so far seems to indicate that agricultural protectionism is directly related to the stage of development of a country. The higher the per capita income and the higher the stage of industrialisation, the higher the degree of agricultural protectionism. As an agricultural economy progresses towards industrialisation, the discrimination against agriculture tends to diminish gradually and, at a higher level of income and industrialisation, agriculture enjoys positive and increasing degrees of protection. This seems to be the experience with NICs in East Asia and also in Latin America.

Several explanations have been offered for this phenomenon. Even though agriculture constitutes a small percentage of employment and GDP in high-income, industrialised countries, farmers constitute a well-organised pressure group strong enough to influence their commercial policy. In fact, it is argued that the smaller the group, often concentrated in specific regions of a country, the easier it is to organise to use as a pressure group especially in view of modern means of transportation and communication. In a developing country, with a large agricultural population scattered throughout the country and with poor communications system, the farmers are too widely scattered to serve as a pressure group. Furthermore, in high-income countries, while direct farming constitutes a small percentage of overall economic activity, those engaged in processing, marketing and distribution of farm output as well as of inputs, constitute a large segment of the economy and are a very well organised group. Their interests are closely linked with high prices and high-income support policies for those who are directly engaged in agriculture production. They often constitute a strong bulwark for agricultural protectionism.

What are the options for export policies of developing countries, firstly for those exports which face stagnant or very slowly increasing demand prospects, and secondly for those which face competition in the export market either from synthetics or other low-cost substitutes, or from subsidised exports of developed countries, and which face import restrictions in the domestic markets of developed countries? For countries saddled with commodities which face stagnant or weak demand prospects, the alternative suggested is diversification away from such commodities to others which face buoyant demand prospects and in which developing countries concerned have comparative cost advantage. In a broader sense, diversification is meant to include greater participation of developing countries in processing, marketing and distribution of primary commodities, so that their aggregate income from primary exports is enhanced through downstream operations adding value to these primary products. In its widest sense, diversification implies a decreasing dependence on primary products and an increase in the pace of industrialisation.

For those groups of commodities which face competition from low-cost substitutes, synthetic or otherwise, increased productivity and cost-reducing innovations will increase their competitiveness. With price-elastic world demand, both the value and quantity of exports will expand. It is important to note that while frequently the elasticity of demand for an export commodity from an individual country is high, the aggregate elasticity of world demand for the same commodity is often low. It is also true that, in a few cases, the assumption of low elasticity of demand has led to export restraint policy on the part of developing countries and consequently to the emergence of substitute crops – natural or synthetic. For commodities facing major import barriers in domestic markets of developed countries, increased price competitiveness through cost reduction will be less effective, and can even bring losses, if the import restrictions are increased to offset the reduction in costs and prices of exports. In cases where supply inelasticity is a constraint on the expansion of supplies in the export markets, increased productivity would expand domestic supply and hence the exportable surplus.

Confronted with constraint on the expansion of primary exports and hence on foreign exchange earnings to finance imports, developing countries have sought to accelerate the pace of import substitution in the industrial sector. Admittedly in many developing countries export pessimism regarding the prospects or possibilities of primary exports was exaggerated. In some cases domestic supply constraints rather than stagnant export market limited exports. In some others exchange rate policy discouraged exports. The impact of price and macroeconomic policies on intersectoral allocation of resources is discussed later in this Introduction.

Even when import substitution strategy was adopted, the possibilities of import substitution in the field of agriculture were inadequately recognised. Many countries failed to increase food production, even when they had resources and technology to produce food competitively in substitution for imports.

4 THE SELF-SUFFICIENCY ARGUMENTS

How desirable is it that the developing countries should pursue the objective of self-sufficiency in food and how efficient would they be? How important is self-sufficiency for achieving food security? What is essential for food security is a sure, stable and equitable supply of food for all at all times. It is not necessary that all food requirements should be met from domestic production. The extent to which domestic production should be relied upon depends on the comparative costs of domestic food production, on shadow price of foreign exchange which determines cost comparison with foreign import prices and perceived or real risks of reliance on international markets for meeting food requirements. Many countries, both developed and developing tend to consider dependence on imports for their entire food supplies risky or politically unacceptable. Historical reasons and experience of food shortages especially during wartime or during periods of international conflict have left an indelible impression on the minds of policy makers in many countries and, therefore, make it difficult for them to sustain a policy of extreme or total dependence on imports as a source of food supply. Many developing countries have fresh in their memories the experience of 1973–4 when they could not get access to food supply either because supplies were physically not available or because they were unable to pay the exceptionally high prices prevailing in the world market. Those among them heavily dependent on food aid are also conscious of the risks of dependence on sources which are highly political and volatile. A minimum level of domestic production, irrespective of high relative domestic costs, is thus considered politically desirable. How high this minimum is depends on the domestic interest groups and how strong and organised the interest groups are.

Given a certain degree of stability in world food markets in terms of availabilities and prices as well as access to financial resources for food imports at times of high import prices or domestic shortages, the perceived or real risks of dependence on world markets are likely to be substantially reduced and hence the drive for self-sufficiency is unlikely to be carried too far beyond what is warranted by competitive cost considerations. However, dependence on domestic production for food supplies is not completely without risks. Fluctuations in domestic production contribute as well to the instability of food supplies and shortages at times of crop failure have adverse impact on food security for the poor. To attempt to offset such food insecurity arising from fluctuations in food production by building large domestic stocks is costly, especially since in developing countries capital is scarce and the interest rates are high, with attendant high costs of holding stocks over time.

The comparison between domestic and world prices should be based upon not the nominal rate of exchange but the shadow price of foreign exchange. In many developing countries foreign exchange is overvalued so that domestic prices of imported food are lower than the domestic costs of production with consequent discouragement to domestic food production. A correction of the overvaluation through devaluation or through offsetting tariffs on imported food will increase the domestic prices of food and will make domestic food production competitive with imports.

The maintenance of an overvalued exchange rate to keep prices of food and other essential imports low is part of a general price policy discussed later. Currently world prices of food are depressed, largely due to the subsidies, especially competitive subsidies for exports provided by surplus producers in developing countries. To use such artificially depressed prices as a guide to resource allocation for food production in developing countries is not very efficient since in the long run such policies in the developed countries may be reversed and the competitive cost situation changed. It is, therefore, necessary to take more longer-run cost comparisons into account in order to decide food production policy in developing countries. Moreover there is always the possibility of keeping domestic prices of food temporarily above world prices along the lines of 'infant-industry' argument for protection for the manufacturing industry in order that it may develop experience, gain skills and absorb new technologies. A large number of developing countries have not fully exploited their comparative advantage in food production because of inadequate institutions, infrastructure, incentives, technology and so on, and in many of them, especially in Africa, a reorientation of policy to accelerate domestic food production and to reduce their dependence on imported food is still in its early stages.

The scarcity of foreign exchange or a shadow price of foreign exchange is intimately related – and necessarily so – to the domestic production possibilities and the future state of balance of payments. The feasible and sustainable degree of dependence on food imports in the long run depends on the availability of foreign exchange to purchase food either through the expansion of non-food agricultural exports or manufactured exports. Limited outlet for markets of such exports would increase the scarcity of foreign exchange and hence the shadow price of foreign exchange, making increased domestic food production competitive or economically efficient.

The case for increased self-sufficiency in food production has also been made on the ground that food production in many countries provides the most important source of income and employment for the rural poor, especially rural women and landless labourers. If this really is the case and there are very limited opportunities of alternative income and employment for the poor, there is indeed a conflict between growth and equity in the short run. In the long run the conflict can be resolved if production of non-food commodities, both agricultural and non-agricultural, expands sufficiently to allow savings, investment and technological progress to absorb the unemployed rural poor. In the short run, however, the production of non-food commodities may lead to substantial gains in overall or aggregate income, even though the poor are left out; food subsidies, made to the poor until alternative opportunities are found for them, can be considered as a necessary social cost for economic progress.

It has also been argued that increased production of food rather than cash or non-food crops for exports ensures greater nutritional status for the poor. Food produced by the small farmers, often subsistence farmers, is frequently consumed by them. However, an expansion of non-food or cash crop production for export provides foreign exchange not only to maintain the food supply at the previous level but also to expand it through additional foreign exchange earnings. Foreign exchange earnings may not be used for food imports to compensate for shortfalls in domestic food supplies. Therefore expansion of cash crop production should have no adverse effect on food supplies and consumption. Even if aggregate food supplies are maintained or even expanded through imports, this does not necessarily ensure that the food consumption on the part of those now shifted to non-food or cash production would be met. This is because additional food, even though imported, may not find its way to those newly engaged in the cash crop production due to an inadequate marketing and distribution system. Moreover expanded cash crop production, in substitution of food production by the subsistence farmers, may facilitate the extraction of surplus by state marketing boards or procurement agencies by means of price policy or otherwise, for investment elsewhere in the economy and thus reduce the disposable income of the cash crop producers and consequently their food consumption and nutritional status.

In all the instances cited above control over food production and its disposal is lost by the poor farmers whose incomes were derived previously from subsistence food production and were spent mainly on food. They become dependent market mechanisms, which are susceptible to policy interventions by the government or in which they may not effectively participate because distribution of income or endowment of resources changes against them. However, at each of the above-mentioned stages where leakages occur and the food consumption of the cash crop producers is depressed, there are possibilities of intervention by the government to correct the situation. The adverse impact on food consumption is not, therefore, an inevitable consequence of an expansion of cash crop production. In many cases, agro-ecological conditions dominate the choice of cropping pattern; in many others crops are grown together in a system of mixed farming or multiple cropping. The same group of farmers grows both export and food crops, even though some may grow predominantly cash crops. They grow food crops, even though returns are higher from cash crops, because of perceived risks of food insecurity arising from failures of food crops or rises in food prices. They are willing to pay an insurance premium. Expansion of export crops is not at the expense of a decline in food crops, when increases in productivity, improved cultivation practices and technology spread from one to the other and expand the output of both.

5 DOMESTIC INTERSECTORAL TERMS OF TRADE

The terms on which resources, inputs and outputs are interchanged between agriculture and industry determine the intersectoral allocation of resources and the magnitude and pattern of growth of each sector, as well as income distribution between and within each sector. Much has been written about the historical movements in the domestic intersectoral terms of trade and their impact on agricultural performance or on aggregate agricultural supply.

While price responsiveness of supply is high enough to matter, it is not sufficiently high to be relied upon as the sole engine of economic growth. Non-price incentives, such as inputs, infrastructure, credit and institutions are a crucial factor in stimulating agricultural growth. The absence of infrastructure, institutions, and technology in many African countries severely limits the responsiveness of agricultural supply to price incentives. On the other hand, in several developing countries lack of price incentives has inhibited the fullest utilisation or efficient exploitation of whatever infrastructure, inputs and institutions are in place. In many cases, there is a 'slack' in the existing capacity which could be harnessed, stimulating an increase in supply through the provision of price incentives in the intervening period, while institutions and infrastructures are being established or strengthened, and the supply of inputs, credit and appropriate technology is being expanded. For example, price incentives alone cannot generate new technology or lead to technological innovations, especially through research conducted in public sector research institutions, but they can and do promote rapid diffusion and optimal utilisation of new, more productive technologies.

High price incentives used to stimulate growth have in the short run adverse effects on income distribution. They benefit the large, surplus producers much more than the small farmers or the subsistence producers; they hurt the deficit farmers or landless labourers who are net purchasers of food in both the urban and rural areas. High support prices may not reach or benefit the farmers because of inadequacies or high costs of the marketing and distribution system. In extreme cases, high food prices not only reduce the income and consumption of the deficit farmer (the net purchaser of food) but also may cut down his resources to obtain purchased inputs and hence his food production capacity.

It is not only in the developing countries but also in the centrally-planned socialist countries that the role of markets and prices is being increasingly reassessed, as evidenced by recent policy changes in China, the Soviet Union and other Eastern European countries. How to combine the increasing role of markets and prices within a framework of a centrally-planned economy, is not a fully resolved issue and requires a high degree of skill and flexibility in economic management.

Turning the terms of trade against agriculture is often the most readily available way of extracting resources from agriculture in order to expand national funds for investment. Given the predominant share of agriculture in national income in the early stages of development, agriculture remains the only major source of savings; in the absence of a well-developed system of taxation such as direct taxation on income and assets, squeezing terms of trade is the most widely available means of resource mobilisation.

Resources extracted through adverse terms of trade against agriculture are one aspect; the other is the extent of public investment in agriculture in infrastructure, research and education, and extension and supply of credit and inputs. The latter can more than offset the effects of adverse terms of trade. Furthermore private savings from the non-agricultural sector could be channelled through the financial and credit institutions to the agricultural sector for investment. However this is unlikely as disincentive effects of adverse terms of trade discourage private investment.

Therefore the moot question is not so much whether resources are transferred from the agricultural sector through adverse terms of trade or otherwise; the question is rather how much, at what rate and through which mechanism such transfers take place, and for what uses resources so transferred are invested. In Côte d'Ivoire resources extracted from export crops by paying the farmers less than world export prices were reinvested in agricultural research, roads and other infrastructure as well as agricultural education and extension, leading to high rates of agricultural growth. In Sudan and Ghana, extraction of resources from wheat and cocoa were not similarly used or otherwise designed to generate growth in areas of comparative advantage or increase in the rate of overall investment. If resources are transferred from the agricultural sector and invested in ways which yield low or lower social returns than in the agricultural sector, taking into account long-run social benefits, external economies and intersectoral linkages, then efficiency in overall investment is sacrificed. Moreover, if resources are extracted in a manner and to an extent which discourage agricultural production, and provide disincentives to the generation of agricultural savings, this would be counterproductive in that it would kill the goose that lays the golden eggs and jeopardise overall growth.

6 PUBLIC INVESTMENT

The urban bias in agricultural policy expresses itself not only in macroeconomic policies including pricing policies, exchange rate, tax and credit policies which tend to discriminate against agriculture but also in inadequate allocations of public investment. On the basis of rough and broad estimates available for a sizeable number of developing countries, it appears that investment in agriculture, both public and private, averages no more than 10–15 per cent of agricultural GDP. The magnitude of investment in many countries is less than what is needed to attain a rate of growth in the food and agricultural sector which is comfortably in excess of the rate of growth of population. Experience to date emphasises that agricultural growth cannot be obtained at a relatively low cost, however labour-intensive the strategy of agricultural investment remains. Resource requirements for current inputs and capital investment for the modernisation of agriculture are substantial, not only for such purposes as irrigation, land improvement, livestock development and mechanisation, but also for such related rural investment expenditures as energy development, roads, transportation and communications infrastructure, as well as marketing and distribution, storage and processing facilities. The investment required for promoting agricultural growth cannot be totally disjointed from investment requirements for rural development, including requirements for education and health, and rural infrastructure development.

This brings into focus the question as to how the agricultural investment strategy should be designed so as to strengthen the linkages between agriculture and industry, and to promote an integrated, balanced intersectoral development. The role of 'urban centres' in close proximity to corresponding farming communities, mentioned earlier, is often critical. Investment in agriculture-related 'urban centres' or 'market towns' enhances the profitability of investment in agriculture and in promoting access to inputs, markets and services. Agricultural development with emphasis on growth and equity, and in the context of an integrated development of urban centres and the hinterlands of farming communities, requires a decentralisation of investment decisions, including investment in small-scale, labour-intensive rural industries.

The intersectoral allocation of investment resources needs to be dynamically adjusted, in response to changing sectoral requirements. As agricultural productivity and income increase, demand for non-agricultural goods and services increases, and the proportion of the labour force employed in agriculture declines. This requires a change in the pattern and magnitude of agricultural investment. The role of public investment is crucial in this respect, in directing and promoting the changing pattern of intersectoral investment. The profitability of private investment depends upon (a) public investment, especially in physical infrastructure extension and delivery services, and (b) prices and incentive policies pursued by the government, which determine the rates of return on investment in agriculture.

7 OBSERVED AND FUTURE POLICIES

In many countries in the recent past significant changes have occurred in public policies, which tend to redress the balance against agriculture. A number of factors have contributed to this phenomenon. Firstly, mounting food imports and foreign exchange constraints, which have squeezed essential imports available for meeting development needs of the economy, have increasingly turned attention towards the need for expanding food production. Agricultural development is seen as an important source of foreign exchange saving and earning. Secondly, there has been an increasing awareness about poverty alleviation, even though not much success has been achieved in many countries. However, it is recognised that most of the poor live in the rural areas, predominantly engaged in agriculture. Thirdly, the development aid agencies, both bilateral and multilateral have, in the recent past, been emphasising the merits of agriculture-based development strategy, with all the beneficial interlinkages it provides for overall development. Finally, economic analysis in recent years has contributed very substantially to an increased understanding of the role of agriculture in economic development.

The urban interest groups which dominate economic policy-making have begun in several instances to understand the need for a thriving rural economy or a prosperous agriculture to maintain the momentum of growth in the industrial sector. The import substituting industries have been faced with a limited market, in view of the stagnant domestic demand. The expanding agricultural sector provides an assured market – compared to the risks and uncertainties of our dependence on export markets, which in many cases are restricted by trade barriers or slow growth. Price incentives to increase agricultural production have been accepted as necessary, while subsidies for urban consumers have been introduced, partly with a view to keeping urban money wages down. Availability of food aid to contain the impact of rising food prices on the poor through feeding programmes and food-for-work programmes has facilitated the acceptance among policy makers of the new emphasis on the role of price and markets for stimulating agricultural growth.

Export pessimism regarding primary exports was merely one among a host of the considerations which contributed to the adoption of a strategy of rapid industrialisation in many countries. Modernisation, scientific advance, technological progress, high rates of savings, investment and economic growth have all been associated with industrialisation. While this association was not necessarily wrong, what in many instances went wrong was that the pace of industrialisation was 'forced' – beyond what was warranted by demand and cost considerations. Morover, the pattern of import substituting industrialisation policy did not always follow the dictates of comparative costs. In some cases domestic markets were too small and economies of scale could not be achieved. Not only were costs high but installed capacity was underutilised.

Frequently this was so because the balance between agriculture and industry did not keep pace with the need to forge and intensify the manifold interlinkages between agriculture and industry, that is, not only in terms of input–output relationships in production but also in consumption. Not enough attention was attached to the institutions and infrastructure such as marketing, distribution and delivery systems, as well as transport and communications systems which affected the intersectoral flows or interchanges.

Several countries, however, followed up a strategy of industrialisation through import substitution with a policy of export promotion. South Korea, for example, often cited as an outstanding case of outward-looking or export promotion strategy, started with a heavy bias towards import substitution in the industrial sector, and sustained in the process attendant inefficiencies and costs – which one may term 'costs of learning'.

The transition from import substitution to export promotion occurred not only in countries but also in individual firms and industries. Examples abound in developing countries, like Brazil and India, of import substitution industries eventually becoming successful export industries. As industries built behind protective walls gained skill and experience they were exposed to competition in the export market. Not all import substitution provides foundation for subsequent export promotion; it depends on the efficiency of import substitution. Successful industrialisation is not merely a matter of moving along the production frontier following competitive cost advantage but also one of moving from within the frontier to the production possibility frontier itself. Exposure to international environment may bring new incentives, new institutions, technology and managerial framework. Furthermore there are economies of scale and advantages of vigorous competition which a limited, narrow domestic market cannot provide. In view of these considerations, a few have argued in favour of a positive bias towards export promotion rather than a position of neutrality between domestic and export markets.

In some cases in the past export promotion efforts through subsidies and incentives were carried too far and involved inefficiencies and waste of resources. Both export promotion and import substitution strategy can be pursued inefficiently. There are risks attendant on both. For example, there are uncertainties involved in export-oriented strategy; especially when planning for the export market, one is faced with an uncertain future. It is not easy to calculate and compare high cost of import substitution with an export promotion policy in which export opportunities are lost or frustrated or not realised, resulting in additional costs of excess capacity, falling terms of trade and unsold stocks.

Much has been said about the success achieved by the Asian gang of four, that is, South Korea, Taiwan, Hong Kong and Singapore, in pursuing an industrialisation policy based on exports of labour-intensive manufactures. However, the very high rate of growth of manufactured exports which was achieved by them is unlikely to be repeated for the rest of the developing world. Experience to date indicates that protectionism in industrialised countries not only constrains the current exports of developing countries but also discourages investment in potential, new or prospective exports, because the chances are high that new exports, if successful in penetrating the markets of developed countries, would be confronted with trade barriers. It has been argued that, for example, if countries like India or China follow the examples of Taiwan or South Korea and strive to achieve the level of per capita manufactured exports which these two countries achieved in the past, they would create a glut in the market with a resultant collapse in prices, or would face, in view of their impact on the markets of industrial countries, a marked rise in protectionism.

There are, however, a number of counter arguments to this line of reasoning. Firstly, it is not likely that all developing countries would be engaged in expanding the same manufactured exports at the same time and that all developing countries would emerge simultaneously as major exporters of the same manufactured goods. Neither past history nor logical analysis predicts such a scenario. Countries differ greatly in resource endowments, levels of skills and entrepreneurial ability and capital. There is likely to be a process of graduation; those countries who have entered the race early will move out of the labour-intensive industries at a later stage as their domestic wages and levels of skills rise. They will move into more sophisticated skill- and capital-intensive products. Secondly, price elasticity of demand for manufactured exports is high and, even with a relatively slowly growing domestic market in industrialised countries, the developing countries, if they are sufficiently price-competitive, can make an inroad in their market of industrial products. Thirdly, as the more advanced among the developing countries lose their comparative advantages in labour-intensive products and move on to more sophisticated skill-intensive industries, they are likely to open up their own markets for imports from less advanced developing countries with the result that intra-developing countries trade in manufactured goods will expand. This has been happening to some extent over the past two decades. The expansion of intra-developing country manufactured exports could thus be a logical complement to the expansion of manufactured goods from developing countries to the markets of industrialised countries.

For such a pattern of industrialisation to spread amongst developing countries, each concentrating in areas of their comparative advantage which will be both acquired and resource-based and which will be shifting over time, it is necessary that all countries maintain a relatively liberal trade regime. This in turn implies that they pursue exchange rate policies which reflect relative costs and prices at home and abroad, as well as a policy of gradual structural adjustment in the domestic economy. They need to remain flexible and responsive to changing costs, technology and demand. However, the political difficulties of pursuing a policy of structural adjustment consistent with an open and liberal trade and exchange rate regime have been found to be very considerable, as the experience of developed countries indicates. At the same time, it is also true that the longer the adjustments to changes in costs and demand conditions are resisted, and the longer the changes in external trading conditions are ignored, the greater and the more painful the subsequent adjustments which are needed.

There is one redeeming feature: as developing countries advance along the path of industrialisation, discriminatory and higher tariff barriers against exports of developing countries will tend to diminish. This is because, with a higher level of industrialisation and income and the corresponding consumption patterns, the product characteristics of exports of developing countries would resemble more closely those which dominate intra-developed country trade. Under those circumstances the degree of trade restrictions on the same category of commodities would be the same in respect of imports from both developed and developing countries. However, developing country exports can still suffer from discriminatory trade restrictions if such discrimination is exercised by country rather than by commodity.

The right timing in the sequence of moving from one to the other strategy is important in designing an appropriate and a relevant policy. What is important is to minimise the cost of learning a new economic activity, be it manufacturing or agriculture, and to choose those areas where long-run cost advantages are the greatest. However, it is not always easy to perceive or quantify long-run comparative cost advantage. Technological progress changes comparative cost ratios and alters the comparative advantage of different countries. Comparative cost advantages are often the result of accumulation of experience, as well as of research and development efforts. In a dynamic world with shifting comparative advantage caused by technological progress, periodic adjustments are necessary adjustments in the structure of production and trade.

Part I

Relative Price Changes in Agriculture and Industry

Introduction to Part I

Nurul Islam
INTERNATIONAL FOOD POLICY RESEARCH
INSTITUTE, WASHINGTON

The relative price changes in agriculture and industry are affected by changes in relative demand and costs in the two sectors. They, in turn, affect the intersectoral allocation of resources, savings, investment, and relative incomes in both sectors as well as the distribution of income within and between sectors. The session of the Congress which included the papers in Part I of this volume discussed price relationships between agriculture and industry, its causes and consequences as well as the institutional and political–economic framework within which changes in relative prices take place.

1 PRICES, SUBSIDIES AND OTHER INCENTIVES

The impact of changes in the domestic intersectoral terms of trade on the agricultural performance or aggregate agricultural supply has been much discussed in the literature. Data on movements in the domestic intersectoral terms of trade are not easy to come by. The statistics, especially consistent time series, relating to producer prices, be they wholesale prices or farmgate prices, marketing margins, prices of consumer goods and inputs used by the agricultural sector and so on are woefully inadequate. No less easy is the interpretation of the movements of prices in terms of trade and their impact on growth and equity in the agricultural sector.

Since the movements in terms of trade, as well as the variations in supply and demand, are simultaneously determined, a general equilibrium approach is often, as the paper by Romeo Bautista argues, a more efficient way of identifying and quantifying the causes and consequences of changes in terms of trade. The oft-quoted estimates of price elasticity of agricultural supply are frequently the estimates for individual commodities, rather than for the aggregate agricultural supply. In addition they refer to the short-run rather than the long-run elasticities. Necessarily, the long-run supply elasticities as well as those for individual commodities are higher than those which hold in the short run or for the total agricultural supply. The various studies on the estimation of the aggregate supply elasticity have been found to be on the low side, that is, between 0.3 and 0.5. Romeo Bautista derives an elasticity of aggregate supply at about 0.7 through a simultaneous equations approach.

There seems to be an emerging consensus that while getting prices right is not the end of economic development, getting them wrong may be. What is meant by getting prices right? It is usually intended to imply that domestic price ratios between alternative crops or commodities should be the same as world price ratios. Given the appropriate or equilibrium foreign exchange rate and the absence of intervention in trade and commodity markets, domestic prices are assumed to equal world prices. World prices represent relative returns from alternative uses of resources in an open economy which takes advantage of opportunities of trade in world markets. If world prices are used as a guide, they are expected to result in an optimum and efficient allocation of resources between alternative commodities or crops. It does not mean, however, that domestic prices should continually fluctuate in response to or in conformity with short-run variations in world prices. This would imply frequent reallocation of resources between sectors or commodities and, therefore, waste and inefficiencies. But it does, however, imply that domestic prices would conform to the long-run trend of world prices.

What represents the long-run trend of world prices is not an easy question to answer and is based upon judgement about the trends in costs and demands in respective commodities across various countries. Moreover policies followed by various countries also affect the world prices. Especially the latter are often the result of policies of major actors in world markets intervening in trade flows with the help of subsidies or tariffs or other trade restrictions. In the face of such interventions in world markets they do not, therefore, represent what is called competitive equilibrium, determined solely by competitive costs and demand conditions across various commodities and countries.

Non-price incentives, such as inputs, infrastructure, credit and institutions are a crucial factor in stimulating agricultural growth. Moreover the effectiveness of price incentives is enhanced by the provision of non-price incentives. The absence of infrastructure, institutions, and technology in many African countries severely limits the responsiveness of agricultural supply to price incentives. On the other hand, in several developing countries the lack of price incentives has inhibited the fullest utilisation or efficient exploitation of whatever infrastructure, inputs and institutions are in place. The full potential of non-price factors can often be realised, or their maximum and best results obtained, by the provision of price incentives; the optimum use of fertilisers, seeds, or irrigation facilities is promoted if price incentives enhance the profitability of their use.

In the absence of non-price incentives, a considerable increase in price would be necessary to stimulate more than a very modest increase in supply. Furthermore the side effects of a substantial increase in prices in the short run on income distribution within the agricultural sector and on the levels of living and welfare of the poor or net purchasers of agricultural commodities or food, in both urban and rural areas, would be severe.

Agricultural price policies encompass pricing of outputs as well as of agricultural inputs, that is, purchased inputs such as fertiliser, pesticide, seed and agricultural machinery. They may also include subsidies on the interest rate on agricultural credit which thus expand capacity of farmers to have command over purchased inputs. Modernisation of agriculture greatly increases the use of purchased inputs in agricultural production. In developing countries domestic prices of agricultural products are below world prices whereas those for manufactured goods are above world prices. As a result there is an incentive to substitute by domestic production commodities which are cheaper to buy abroad and to discourage domestic production of commodities which they can competitively produce and sell abroad. Incentives for increased production of food and other agricultural products can, therefore, be provided by raising output prices or by lowering input prices through subsidies. Both measures improve the profitability of increased production.

Raising output prices helps the large producers more than the small producers; it affects adversely the poor consumers, both urban and rural. Lowering input prices through subsidies also benefits large producers proportionately more than the small producers since large farmers use a much greater quantity of purchased inputs in their production than do the smaller farmers. Lowering input prices, used as an incentive to expand production, does not adversely affect the poor consumers as does raising output prices. Subsidised inputs, however, encourage their wasteful and uneconomical use; distort factors proportions towards the use of more scarce inputs which foreign exchange-intensive or costly to produce and away from less expensive and abundant inputs. For example, subsidised fertilizers substitute for more intensive care or use of land and labour.

2 SUBSIDIES FOR INPUTS

The use of subsidies for inputs is justified as a temporary measure to overcome the initial costs of learning in order to introduce a new or unfamiliar technology or input. There are risks and uncertainties attendant on the use of a new technology. Its adoption, therefore, requires to be stimulated by a promise of a substantially higher level of profits or gains than are normally available in the long run for the introduction of such a new technology. For example, the expected results of the introduction of fertilisers are unlikely to be realised if they are used inappropriately or under unsuitable soil and water conditions or if they are used at an inappropriate time and in an inappropriate combination of different types of fertilisers without reference to the particular soil characteristics. The expected output may even be less than the output obtained before the introduction of the new technology if the required conditions for the optimum use of technology are not met.

It is also argued that the small farmers who are more risk-averse and/or more slow to adopt new technology than the big farmers require special stimulus or incentive. It is not, however, quite clear whether the incentives to small farmers should be given in the form of subsidised inputs or through an assurance of an adequate supply of credit at rates of interest which are competitive with those provided to big farmers. Often the farmers in the most remote and distant areas with limited transport and communication facilities pay higher prices than farmers in convenient locations. Therefore in these cases small farmers require special assistance, which may include subsidised inputs or alternatively may encompass subsidisation of transportation costs for all inputs since the latter measure does not distort factors proportions.

While the case for a temporary subsidy to compensate for risks attached to the introduction of specific input in the initial years is recognised, a note of warning is sounded. What starts as a temporary measure tends to become permanent owing to the vested interests which develop in the process. The farmers, especially the large farmers as well as the distributors, producers and importers of fertilisers lobby for its continuation long after its justification is past. Often a fertiliser subsidy has been used to build up a high cost domestic fertiliser industry so that the subsidy in fact goes to the domestic fertiliser industry and raises the price to the farmer above the world price. However it is true that at a given moment of time there are always new users in the process of expansion and diffusion of a new technology so that even though the early users may not need any more subsidy, the late-comers may still need incentives to compensate for initial risks. Until the time when the new input becomes widely used among the majority of farmers, it may be necessary to continue subsidy but at a declining rate; the early users will continue to reap excess profits for this period.

The fact that reduced input subsidy is sometimes associated with a decline in the use of input does not necessarily imply that the continuation of subsidy is warranted. First it could be that an excessive use of the input encouraged by subsidy is curbed and a more optimal use is achieved. Secondly, in the meanwhile the relative prices of other inputs might have declined, making it more profitable and efficient to use a higher proportion of other inputs.

An important area of policy reforms in the dialogue between the international donors and the developing countries has centered on appropriate price policies regarding inputs and outputs, that is, raising prices of agricultural products to the world level wherever they are depressed and eliminating subsidies on inputs. Apart from the distortions in the allocation or use of resources the continuation of subsidies has placed a heavy burden on the government budget. Keeping output prices below world prices does not result in such a direct burden on government expenditures even though it does discourage domestic production. On the other hand, if output prices are raised to the world level and consumer subsidies are introduced to reduce their adverse impact on the poor consumers, this also leads to an attendant burden on the budget. This, however, does not directly affect the allocation of resources between sectors and commodities.

Elimination or reduction of subsidies is frequently a part of overall fiscal reform. Input subsidies, when domestic revenues are unable to finance them, are often financed by deficits, which leads to a consequential rise in overall prices which, in turn, partially offsets the effect of subsidies. It is argued that savings in government expenditures obtained through reduction in subsidies for fertilisers, for example, could better be used for expenditures on education, extension and training intended to guide farmers in the efficient use of fertilisers and also in expanding and improving their marketing, distribution and transportation, especially since these activities suffer from shortage of resources. Additional expenditures on improving the distribution and marketing of fertiliser, for example, as well as in training farmers can ensure a greater and more efficient use of fertilisers than can be accomplished by subsidies.

Recent experience indicates that progressive elimination of subsidy is possible and has indeed taken place in several countries. It is, however, true that such changes or policy reforms have not been without pains and costs of transition and that they have often been associated with pressure from the international donor community with substantial resources to back up policy reforms. All policy changes affect the distribution of income. The beneficiaries who lose are expected to resist. External assistance may therefore be necessary to cushion the costs of adjustment and to compensate those who temporarily lose from policy reforms.

3 IMPLEMENTATION OF POLICY REFORM

This brings us to the problems of the implementation of policy reforms. A rise in output prices through an increase in support prices provided by the government procurement or marketing agencies may be absorbed largely by the high cost of distribution and marketing and may not reach the farmers. The costs of distribution and marketing are high either because of the inadequacy and/or the inefficiency of infrastructure or because monopoly rents are earned by some elements in the chain of the marketing and distribution system. Often the return to the farmers can be increased without raising prices to the consumer if efficiency of and competitiveness in the marketing and distribution systems can be improved. This is also relevant to the distribution of subsidised inputs. The benefits of subsidies have gone to the intermediaries because there are scarcities of supplies resulting in parallel markets, that is, the public distribution system, on the one hand, and the open market sales, on the other, for those not having any or sufficient access to the public distribution system. The rural rich and the powerful have greater access to and influence over the public distribution system. The poor pay the higher prices in the open market. The role of public investment in physical infrastructure including marketing and distribution facilities where external economies are high and social benefits exceed private ones is critical.

4 CENTRALLY-PLANNED ECONOMIES

The role of markets and prices in the centrally-planned socialist countries is being increasingly reassessed. This is shown by recent policy changes in China, the Soviet Union and other Eastern European countries. The need for increasing the efficiency of investment in agriculture in countries like the Soviet Union, which has devoted a significant proportion of its total investment to agriculture, has been a matter of intense debate. As Kiselev's paper analyses in detail, the decentralisation of detailed investment and production decisions either to the lower levels of decision-making authorities or to the productive enterprises themselves, the linking of rewards to performance for individuals as well as enterprises, and the strengthening of the role of prices as a stimulus to production and allocation of resources are some of the policy changes taking place or being seriously considered in the Soviet Union. In the Soviet Union, prices of industrial equipment and current inputs like fertiliser used by the agricultural sector have been under re-examination in recent years. Two issues are interlinked: one is pricing of industrial inputs, including incentive consumer foods used in the agricultural sector, and the second is the efficiency with which investment and current inputs are being used in the agricultural sector, that is, rate of return on investment in agriculture. The calculation of rate of return on investment is a matter also of pricing of agricultural products. The recent upward revision of agricultural prices, especially for deliveries of the surplus above compulsory quota to the pubic sector agencies and for sales in free markets, as well as an increasing use of private plots, small though they are, for the production of high value agricultural goods, have provided some stimulus to agricultural growth. This has also brought into focus the question of competition in the use of scarce resources between private plots and collective farms and hence the related questions of incentives and rewards for collective farmers.

The recent spurt in agricultural production in China, indicated by the very high rates of growth, that is, 8 to 8.5 per cent per annum within the span of 5 to 8 years, provides an important instance of price and non-price incentives acting in a process of beneficiary interaction in producing a considerable increase in production. Substantial rises in agricultural prices resulted not only from an increase in procurement prices by state procurement agencies but also from an expansion of free market sales. The introduction of the responsibility system changed the structure of incentives while the increase in prices expanded the opportunity for obtaining higher incomes. Both these factors encouraged the fullest exploitation of the existing technology and institutions, including an efficient system of irrigation and land management and an extended supply of inputs. The extraordinarily high rate of growth unleashed by new incentives was unlikely to be sustained in the long run, as indicated by a slowing down in the past 2 to 3 years. However, this example illustrates how price incentives can lead to a substantial once-and-for-all increase in output, that is, a very large movement along the supply curve. Further increases in output at a significant rate have to rely upon a shift to the right of the supply curve through the introduction of new technology and possibly new rural institutions, especially regarding the supply of inputs and accelerating investment in physical and social infrastructure.

Chinese experience also confirms that a substantial rise in food prices in the short run has to be combined with increases in consumer subsidies for food, especially in the urban areas, partly in order to relieve the distress of the poor consumers and partly because of the unfavourable political repercussions emanating from a change in the rural–urban balance. At the same time urban wages across the board were raised in order to cushion the impact of rising food prices. The combined effect of increasing food subsidies and expanding incomes or wages in the urban sector led to the problems of inflation in the economy as a whole. This illustrates how agricultural pricing policies have far-reaching repercussions outside the agricultural sector, involving problems of macroeconomic management of the economy as well.

The domestic terms of trade between agriculture and industry are affected not only by relative movements in world prices but also by a wide range of such domestic policies as exchange rate policies, protectionism in the manufacturing sector and direct interventions in agricultural prices through export taxes, public procurement policies and agricultural support prices. These policies do not necessarily act in a mutually supportive or reinforcing manner. Price incentives offered through high support prices can be offset by overvalued exchange rates through depressing returns from export crops and cheapening the prices of import-competing domestic crops. Industrial protectionism raises the prices of agricultural inputs and of consumer goods used by the farmers.

5 THE SPATIAL DIMENSION AND INTERSECTORAL LINKAGES

As Gus Ranis reminds us, a neglected aspect of agricultural development and intersectoral linkages is the spatial dimension. The location of a multiplicity of urban or semi-urban centres, serving as a hub for diverse industrial activities dispersed throughout a country in close proximity with surrounding rural areas or farming activities serving as hinterland, greatly facilitates the ease or effectiveness of institutions and infrastructure in promoting intersectoral linkages. The 'spatial' dimension has two aspects: (a) physical distance and (b) ease or cost of transportation and communication between urban centres and rural hinterlands. The physical proximity which promotes frequency and closeness of contact between urban and rural areas not only stimulates new ideas and innovations and widens the horizons of the farmers, but also promotes modernisation and transfer of technology to agriculture. There is usually a system of hierarchy of urban centres, ranging from small and medium to large. The size of the 'standard market area', with an urban centre at the core and rural populations in the surrounding hinterland, depends on the size of economies of scale and externalities, on the one hand, and the cost of transportation and communications, on the other. The larger the economies of scale and the more extensive the transportation and communications network, the larger is the effective size of 'standard market areas'.

The development of semi-urban growth centres with farming communities linked to them strengthens the growth linkages between agricultural and non-agricultural sectors through input–output relationships as well as interrelationships in consumption demand for each other's goods. Moreover, as rural income grows consumption of fisheries and livestock products as well as horticultural products increases very rapidly. These activities are usually high labour-intensive and employment/income generating for the poor and, therefore, in their turn lead to increasing demand for food and other non-agricultural items of consumption. At an early stage of development, intersectoral input–output linkages are unlikely to be substantial especially in terms of linkages between agriculture and industry. However, the consumption linkages are likely to be even stronger and these have come to attract increasing attention in recent years. As rural income grows, demand for a wide variety of non-agricultural goods and services increases, especially light consumer goods, simple household tools, utensils, and appliances as well as tools and implements for agricultural production. If they are produced in the rural areas in close proximity to where the farmers live and work, their demand is likely to be met more effectively. If there is infrastructure already in place, such as roads, communications and electricity, the incentives to start such activities for meeting the needs of the farmers are likely to be high. An analysis of expenditures and incomes of the rural families in various countries confirms that a growing proportion of farmer's income consists of non-farm sources of income, that is, income derived from the production of rural output and services in the non-agricultural sector.

The pattern and strength of intersectoral growth linkages is not unrelated to the pattern of agricultural growth itself. Is the agricultural growth strategy basically oriented to small farmers or landless labourers, or does it also include medium farmers? This affects distribution of income as well as the pattern of consumption which has its implications for the multiplier effect on non-agricultural activities in the rural areas or in the urban areas for that matter. If the overwhelming thrust of the growth strategy is on the small farmer or landless labourer, it is unlikely that demand for non-food or non-agricultural products will be greatly stimulated in the initial stages because their demand at that low level of income is basically concentrated on food items. An expansion of the income of medium farmers is likely to lead to higher growth linkages as far as non-agricultural or non-food items are concerned because the elasticity of demand for those commodities for the medium farmers is much higher. The concentration on medium farmers, however, may conflict in the short run with the need or the objective of providing for expanded employment and income for the poorest of the poor. The conflict is mitigated or resolved in the long run, as it is likely that the multiplier effect of employment generated for the poor engaged in the production of labour-intensive goods and services consumed by the medium groups increases the income and consumption of the poor. The net result in the long run depends on the particular circumstances and the relative emphasis placed on income and consumption of the medium *vis-à-vis* the small farmers or landless labourers. The latter, in turn, depends on the magnitude of poverty, on the one hand, and on the urgency which the policy makers attach to the task of relieving immediate poverty, on the other.

The development of growth linkages between agricultural and non-agricultural sectors through small market towns and service centres or decentralised growth centres depends partly upon government policies regarding decentralisation of economic functions to the local government. For efficient functioning of such services to be provided or stimulated by the public sector, the responsibility must necessarily devolve largely upon the local governments. This involves the wider issue of structure of politics and government in developing countries.

6 INSTITUTIONS AND POLITICS

Paul Streeten raises the question, often forgotten or ignored by conventional economic analysis, of the incorporation of institutional and political variables in the analysis of economic policy issues, that is, institutional or political channels through which supply and demand and markets operate or make their influence felt. In the field of pricing policy analysis, it is illuminating to examine firstly which are the interest groups/sectors of the society which gain or lose from a policy of high food prices, and secondly how the losers or gainers react to a rise in food prices. The political economic analysis of agricultural pricing policies needs to examine how these various interest groups interact with each other and how the policy decisions are eventually taken.

To view the state either as a tool in the hands of the dominant interest groups, who are engaged in competitive lobbying for the furtherance of their own interests, or as an institution which stands totally aloof from the conflicting interest groups and takes decisions on the basis of their perception of the general good is to take a very partial or extreme view. The real world is in the intermediate situation of a grey area in which policy makers or politicians are not all totally selfish maximisers of their own welfare or the welfare of whatever interest groups they represent. There are amongst them some who take a broader or national, rather than a sectoral, view.

Secondly, amongst the elite groups or dominant groups there is no continuous monolithic cohesion. The views of the urban and rural elites may not always coincide. There is a role for bureaucrats and professionals, including economists, who can take a long and broader view of national interest. They can strengthen the hands of those amongst the politicians who want to take a broader or a longer-run view. Also, the weak and the poor, who are not organised well and cannot lobby vigorously for their interests, need to be assisted in developing their organisational strength.

The role of 'normative' analysis is crucial in this context. For example, it can explain that a lobbying group may not be pursuing its own interests efficiently. The gains it may secure for itself may inflict losses on other groups which may exceed, sometimes by a wide margin, the gains accruing to it. The high food prices in many OECD countries inflict a loss on the consumers and a burden on the taxpayers (who pay for the cost of storage of surplus food commodities and export subsidies), but these costs exceed income gains which are enjoyed by the producers of food. The reform of the Common Agricultural Policy in the EEC, for example, would confer a net gain on the economy as a whole. On the other hand, in many developing countries food prices are lower than world prices, which depress production. A rise in prices would stimulate production and expand or improve income, employment and balance of payments.

The adverse effect of high food prices on urban purchasers of food can be offset by food subsidies. The burden on the poor would be moderated to the extent that the large and medium farmers who benefit from high prices expand output and employment. This, in turn, depends on whether the choice of output mix and production techniques is such that they are labour-intensive and expand employment and whether factor prices are biased towards capital-intensive techniques or not. To the extent that higher wages are associated with higher demand for labour, this will also mitigate the adverse impact of rising food prices.

The costs of compensation to the poor, if properly designed, fall short of the gains to producers. However, unless compensations are in fact paid, it is possible that the losers, who may include middle income and not-so-poor urban consumers, may muster sufficient strength to organise 'food' riots and destabilise the government and thus retard agricultural and overall economic progress. Thus, even if the costs of compensation which is extended to middle-income classes exceed the benefits to the producers, it may still be necessary in the medium term to compensate them as 'side payments' for the implementation of necessary policy reforms, until the gains in income and productivity growth which accrue from higher price incentives more than offset the temporary overall losses.

A comprehensive treatment of the political economy of relative price changes either between agriculture and industry or within the agricultural sector itself will include an examination of (a) the nature and magnitude of increase in overall efficiency in the use of resources resulting in a net increase in income and overall welfare, (b) the nature and magnitude of changes in the distribution of income and losses and gains accruing to the different income groups and (c) the feasibility of compensation to be paid to the losers and its amount as well as the appropriate mechanism through which such compensation may in fact be provided.

The objective or 'normative' analysis of a political–economic nature can extend towards wider horizons. For example, it can help evaluate whether the system of competitive lobbying by the various interest groups is the best way of arriving at decisions or whether alternative institutional arrangements for decision making are possible or preferable.

1 Domestic Terms of Trade and Agricultural Growth in Developing Countries

Romeo M. Bautista
INTERNATIONAL FOOD POLICY
RESEARCH INSTITUTE, WASHINGTON

1 INTRODUCTION

Writing twenty years ago, Raj Krishna (1967) made a distinction between *negative* agricultural price policy, in which 'the terms of trade of agriculture are deliberately depressed', and *positive* price policy 'which attempts to improve or at least maintain the terms of trade of agriculture'. He also observed that 'a negative agricultural price policy . . . has been a common feature of policy in the early phases of development in capitalist as well as socialist countries', but that there were emerging signs of 'a reluctant turn to a positive agricultural price policy' as developing country planners saw agricultural output failing to grow at a rate necessary to achieve the desired growth of the national economy.

In this paper we first present and analyse, in Section 2, the observed movements in the agricultural terms of trade, since the early 1960s, for 41 low- and middle-income developing countries. Indeed, a significantly increasing trend in domestic agricultural prices relative to non-agricultural prices is shown for a large number of developing countries, including several Sub-Saharan African economies. We then examine, in Section 3, the trends in agricultural production for the same sample of developing countries. A striking observation is the large number of countries, mostly Sub-Saharan African countries, with low or negative agricultural growth rates.

It is a standard formulation of the empirical relationship between agricultural output and relative prices in developing countries that agricultural supply is influenced by relative price changes, the latter being assumed to be independently determined. In Section 4 of this paper, we argue that the assumed exogeneity of the domestic terms of trade is inappropriate, and that it is necessary to examine the simultaneous determination of domestic supply and the relative price of agricultural products, taking demand influences systematically into account. As a special case, we also explore the hypothesis that, for the countries in Sub-Saharan Africa, domestic agricultural supply is primarily determined by non-price factors (cf Delgado and Mellor, 1984), which implies a reverse direction of causality, that is, the exogenously determined agricultural output affecting the domestic terms of trade (rather than vice-versa).

These relationships are subjected to empirical investigation (in Section 5) based on the collective experience of the developing countries in our sample during 1960–84. The results bear out the inadequacy of single-equation price elasticity estimates of aggregate agricultural supply and the need to consider the agricultural terms of trade as being determined (jointly with domestic output) by supply–demand interactions. For the Sub-Saharan African countries it may well be appropriate to assume that non-price influences had been the dominant factors in the determination of agricultural supply which in turn significantly affected the domestic terms of trade.

Finally, in Section 6, some concluding comments are given concerning directions for further empirical work, Krishna's distinction between positive and negative agricultural price policy, and the intersectoral resource transfer implicit from temporal changes in the agricultural terms of trade.

2 TERMS OF TRADE MOVEMENTS

The domestic terms of trade are represented in the present study as the ratio of agricultural prices to non-agricultural prices (Pa/Pna), calculated from annual data since the early 1960s on agricultural value added (AVA) and gross domestic product (GDP) which are available at current and constant market prices from the World Bank Data Tape (Economic Data Sheet I).[1] Both trend and variability (instability) of the terms of trade are examined in this section. The trend measure used is the coefficient estimate in the logarithmic trend regression based on the annual values of Pa/Pna, the dispersion around the logarithmic trend representing the instability measure.[2]

The developing countries included in our sample consist of all 'low-

income and middle-income economies'[3] in which the contribution of
agriculture to GDP was at least 20 per cent in the early 1970s *and*
for which data are available to compute for Pa/Pna as described
above for the time series beginning 1965 at the latest and ending
1981 at the earliest. It was possible to meet these requirements in
41 countries. The most complete time series (1960–84) was obtained
only for 17 countries.

In view of the sharp changes in the international price structure
since 1973, some interest attaches to comparing the trend and
instability values between the two subperiods 1960–72 and 1972–84.
It has been pointed out, for example, that the higher energy prices
in the 1970s 'caused macroeconomic pressures on the balance of
payments and foreign exchange rates', inducing a deterioration in
the agricultural terms of trade for the oil-importing countries and
an improvement for the oil-exporting countries (Timmer, 1984, p.
54). Also recent discussions of agricultural development and price
policy have drawn attention to the special problems of Sub-Saharan
Africa (see, for example, Delgado and Mellor, 1984). Moreover
questions on the reliability of economic data for many of these
countries are frequently raised.[4] Table 1.1 presents the calculated
values of the trend and instability measures for Pa/Pna, distinguishing
between the two subperiods and between countries in Sub-Saharan
Africa (from here on, 'Africa,' for short) and other countries in the
sample. Low-income (LI) and middle-income (MI) economies are
also identified in the table.

Consistent with Krishna's observation, a relatively large number
of developing countries – 17 out of the 41 countries in the sample
– show a significantly positive trend in the domestic terms of trade
since the early 1960s (c.f. column (1) of the table).[5] However,
significant terms of trade deterioration can also be observed for 7
countries, and no significant trend is found for the remaining 17
countries. Somewhat surprisingly, only 4 of the 19 African countries
have had a negative trend; a significant improvement in Pa/Pna is
seen for 9 countries, the rest of the African countries showing non-
negative but statistically insignificant trend values. Among the 22
non-African countries, 9 show a significantly positive trend, and 4
have had a significant terms-of-trade deterioration; these are exactly
the same numbers for the two trend categories within the Africa
group. Distinguishing by income category, a significantly positive
trend is observed for 10 low-income and 8 middle-income countries,
while 3 low-income and 5 middle-income countries have had a
significantly negative trend.

Table 1.1 Trend and variability of the domestic terms of trade

Sub-Saharan Africa	1960–84		1960–72		1972–84	
	Trend (1)	Var. (2)	Trend (3)	Var. (4)	Trend (5)	Var. (6)
1 Chad (LI)	0.81*	8.11	0.28	9.78	0.24	5.31
2 Ethiopia (LI)	1.08*	5.19	1.21*	4.95	1.73*	5.61
3 Mali (LI)	0.02	7.69	−0.84	8.87	0.69	4.92
4 Tanzania (LI)	2.64*	21.27	−2.22*	5.73	8.05	7.84
5 Uganda (LI)	6.59*	18.03	3.34*	9.54	9.93	20.92
6 Togo (LI)	2.15	36.71	11.12*	34.66	−2.66	24.91
7 Cent. African Rep. (LI)	−1.88*	12.85	−4.47*	8.59	−2.35*	9.80
8 Somalia (LI)	−4.37*	15.95	−6.48*	15.70	−4.87*	11.12
9 Kenya (LI)	2.11*	11.87	1.99	12.57	0.22	8.91
10 Sierra Leone (LI)	1.39*	11.17	0.21	3.68	0.08	12.54
11 Ghana (LI)	3.47*	20.53	2.72*	14.72	1.79	24.00
12 Sudan (LI)	0.00	0.19	−0.03	0.28	0.00	0.11
13 Senegal (LI)	0.02	11.09	−0.54	10.76	−0.71	11.01
14 Mauritania (MI)	4.99*	16.92	5.83*	15.60	1.29	14.48
15 Liberia (MI)	0.56	9.65	−2.79*	4.61	1.64	9.57
16 Ivory Coast (MI)	0.21	5.57	−0.59	5.63	0.38	3.98
17 Nigeria (MI)	−1.60*	11.87	−2.00*	8.47	1.24	9.74
18 Cameroon (MI)	2.32*	8.50	−1.61*	3.50	3.04*	7.07
19 Congo (MI)	−0.40*	6.00	−0.09	2.41	−1.23	8.10

Other Countries

20	Nepal (LI)	1.92*	10.65	1.11	5.03	1.22	8.46
21	Burma (LI)	2.42*	10.65	0.07	5.98	2.18*	9.59
22	India (LI)	−0.40	11.19	1.94*	7.62	−1.98*	8.79
23	Sri Lanka (LI)	1.27*	7.59	0.25	5.09	0.79	8.54
24	Pakistan (LI)	−0.98*	8.50	−0.95*	2.96	−2.26*	11.08
25	Bolivia (MI)	−0.53	11.06	−2.28	3.64	0.80	13.54
26	Indonesia (MI)	−2.11*	12.10	−0.88	12.75	−0.92	8.32
27	Philippines (MI)	1.04*	11.36	2.90*	3.98	−2.06*	6.66
28	Morocco (MI)	1.34*	9.62	−1.33*	5.64	2.55*	3.89
29	Honduras (MI)	−0.72*	8.59	−2.27*	2.20	−1.06	10.47
30	El Salvador (MI)	0.13	18.95	0.23	4.04	−1.84	24.27
31	Egypt (MI)	2.41*	6.41	2.93*	2.25	1.14	7.30
32	Thailand (MI)	0.55*	7.95	−0.07	6.86	−1.14*	4.17
33	Dominican Rep. (MI)	0.79*	10.15	0.65	7.73	−0.79	10.64
34	Ecuador (MI)	0.92*	8.32	−1.72*	4.02	−2.09*	8.97
35	Turkey (MI)	−0.37	12.48	−0.03	2.18	−3.63*	10.37
36	Costa Rica (MI)	0.68	11.78	−1.72*	4.41	0.68	9.11
37	Paraguay (MI)	1.08*	9.49	1.10*	5.47	−2.09*	5.61
38	Tunisia (MI)	−0.18	6.55	0.80	6.34	−1.31*	7.03
39	Colombia (MI)	−0.50	8.88	−0.01	3.10	−2.27*	10.15
40	Malaysia (MI)	−0.34	6.81	−1.81*	3.56	−0.54	6.71
41	Korea (MI)	0.57	11.70	0.52	13.82	−1.14	7.44

Notes: Trend values represent compound annual rates of change, in per cent. LI and MI denote low-income and middle-income economies, respectively.
*Significant at the 5 per cent level.

In terms of the instability measure, a wider range of values are seen among the African countries – from 0.19 for Sudan to 36.71 for Togo; the range for the group of other countries is from 6.41 for Egypt to 18.95 for El Salvador (c.f. column (2) of Table 1.1). The mean values are 12.7 for the low-income countries and 10.0 for the middle-income countries, the difference between which, using the t-test, is not significant. Therefore, it cannot be said that the middle-income countries have shown a greater capacity to deal with domestic terms of trade instability.

Distinguishing between the two subperiods, we note a reversal of trend in Pa/Pna from 1960–72 to 1972–84 for several countries (c.f. columns (3) and (5)). Thus, the significantly positive trend for India, the Philippines, and Paraguay during the first subperiod became significantly negative; these countries are all oil importers, so that the presumed favourable effect of higher oil prices on the agricultural terms of trade in the post–1972 period is not borne out. Of the three countries whose terms of trade moved from having significantly negative to positive trends from the first subperiod to the next, *viz.*, Tanzania, Morocco, and Cameroon, the last is an oil exporter – which again contradicts the expectation. Among the other middle-income oil-exporting countries, Nigeria and Malaysia also show an improvement in the trend of Pa/Pna; on the other hand, a post-1972 deterioration is seen for Indonesia, Egypt, Ecuador, and Tunisia. No blanket statement can be made, therefore, about the actual direction of terms of trade changes based solely on the distinction between oil-importing and oil-exporting countries.

Higher values of the variability measure are observed during the second subperiod for a relatively large number of countries in the sample (c.f. columns (4) and (5)), suggesting that the increased instability in the world economy was passed through to the agricultural terms of trade in those countries. Nonetheless, 6 countries each from the low- and middle-income categories show more unstable terms of trade movements during 1960–72.

3 AGRICULTURAL GROWTH RATES

Calculated values of the annual rates of change in agricultural value added at constant prices, based on logarithmic trend regression, are given in Table 1.2 for the 41 countries in our sample, distinguishing again the Sub-Saharan African countries, the two income (LI and MI) categories, and the two subperiods 1960–72 and 1972–84.

Table 1.2 Compound annual growth rates of agricultural value added (at constant prices), in per cent

Sub-Saharan Africa	1960–84	1960–72	1972–84
1 Chad (LI)	−0.69	0.91	−0.99
2 Ethiopia (LI)	1.49	2.22	1.01
3 Mali (LI)	2.92	1.72	4.43
4 Tanzania (LI)	2.84	3.16	2.53
5 Uganda (LI)	1.33	3.62	−0.52
6 Togo (LI)	1.58	2.68	1.16
7 Cent. African Rep. (LI)	1.86	1.14	2.36
8 Somalia (LI)	2.17	2.15	2.77
9 Kenya (LI)	4.20	5.41	3.07
10 Sierra Leone (LI)	1.97	1.54	2.24
11 Ghana (LI)	1.19	4.75	−0.23
12 Sudan (LI)	3.05	0.32	2.85
13 Senegal (LI)	1.36	2.25	−0.13
14 Mauritania (MI)	−0.38	−0.17	0.94
15 Liberia (MI)	4.47	6.27	2.48
16 Ivory Coast (MI)	3.76	3.92	3.38
17 Nigeria (MI)	0.60	0.64	−1.25
18 Cameroon (MI)	2.87	4.69	1.70
19 Congo (MI)	2.14	2.21	0.71
Other Countries			
20 Nepal (LI)	1.28	1.75	1.23
21 Burma (LI)	4.21	4.02	5.88
22 India (LI)	2.24	1.97	2.40
23 Sri Lanka (LI)	2.81	2.70	3.75
24 Pakistan (LI)	3.50	4.58	2.93
25 Bolivia (MI)	3.01	3.14	1.50
26 Indonesia (MI)	3.73	3.07	3.78
27 Philippines (MI)	4.21	4.11	4.02
28 Morocco (MI)	2.05	4.76	0.29
29 Honduras (MI)	2.89	4.89	2.84
30 El Salvador (MI)	2.72	3.10	1.26
31 Egypt (MI)	2.78	2.87	2.48
32 Thailand (MI)	4.69	5.18	3.95
33 Dominican Rep. (MI)	3.51	2.92	3.19
34 Ecuador (MI)	3.03	3.93	2.10
35 Turkey (MI)	2.87	2.83	3.11
36 Costa Rica (MI)	4.03	5.67	1.79
37 Paraguay (MI)	4.68	2.30	6.04
38 Tunisia (MI)	4.21	4.17	1.76
39 Colombia (MI)	3.76	3.60	3.47
40 Malaysia (MI)	4.68	4.40	4.36
41 Korea (MI)	3.23	3.94	2.03

Note: LI and MI denote low-income and middle-income economies, respectively.

Generally lower agricultural growth rates for the African economies compared to the other countries are revealed by even a cursory
examination of the table. Mauritania, Sudan, and Chad during
1960–72, and Nigeria, Chad, Uganda, Ghana, and Senegal during
1972–84, are the extreme cases. For the entire period (c.f. column
(1)), less than 2 per cent growth is seen for 10 of the 19 African
countries, versus only one (Nepal) from the larger non-African
group. Also, the latter category includes 7 countries exceeding 4
per cent growth, while the Africa group is represented by only two
countries (Kenya and Liberia). Interestingly, agricultural production
in either group of countries did not seem much affected by the
unstable conditions in the post-1972 period: the difference between
the mean growth rates observed during 1960–72 and 1972–84 is
positive but not statistically significant.

Distinguishing by income category, MI countries are found to
have posted significantly higher agricultural growth rates than LI
countries for 1960–72 and 1960–84, but not for 1972–84. Also, the
growth rates for the LI group during the two subperiods are not
significantly different. In the case of the MI countries, the 1972–84
growth rates are found to be significantly lower; drastic declines in
agricultural production are seen especially for Bolivia, Morocco, El
Salvador, Costa Rica and Tunisia.

Comparison between Tables 1.1 and 1.2 indicates no close
correspondence between the trend values for agricultural terms of
trade and output. Among the African countries, three of the four
best production performers during 1960–84 (Liberia, Kenya, Ivory
Coast, and Sudan) did not benefit from a significant improvement
in agricultural prices (Kenya being the exception). Where a positive
trend in the domestic terms of trade had been strongest (Uganda,
Mauritania, and Ghana), agricultural growth rates much less than
the average (2.04 per cent) were achieved. Two (Tanzania and
Cameroon) show both higher than average growth rates and a
significantly positive trend in the terms of trade, while one (Nigeria)
has had both low agricultural growth and significant terms of trade
deterioration. The simple correlation coefficients between the trend
values of Pa/Pna and agricultural value added among African
countries are 0.182 for the entire period, 0.023 for 1960–72, and
0.208 for 1972–84.

In the case of the other countries, 4 of the 7 with the best
agricultural growth record during 1960–84 show a significantly
positive trend in the terms of trade (Paraguay, Thailand, Burma,

and the Philippines). However, the two lowest growth countries (Nepal and Morocco) also have had a significant improvement in Pa/Pna. Among the 4 countries with a significantly negative trend in the terms of trade (Indonesia, Pakistan, Ecuador, and Honduras), the agricultural growth rate is observed to be higher than the 3.37 per cent average for the group in two cases (Indonesia and Pakistan). The calculated values of the simple correlation coefficient are 0.238 for 1960–84, 0.505 for 1960–72, and 0.191 for 1972–84.

It is remarkable that the domestic terms of trade and agricultural growth are found to be negatively correlated for either group of countries in each of the three observation periods. This would seem to suggest, following what most empirical investigators of agricultural supply response have assumed, that non-price influences have dominated the presumably positive terms-of-trade effect on agricultural output.[6] Another possibility would be that it is domestic output which affects (negatively) the agricultural terms of trade, rather than the other way around.

The conclusion that emerges from the above findings is that the relationship between domestic terms of trade changes and agricultural growth is not a simple one. Other factors influencing either or both variables must have changed concurrently, confounding the *ex post* correlation between them. These analytical issues are examined more closely in the next section.

4 RELATIONSHIP BETWEEN TERMS OF TRADE CHANGES AND AGRICULTURAL GROWTH

The agricultural terms of trade, or more generally, agricultural pricing policy, are widely regarded as an important instrument at the disposal of developing country governments that can be used to pursue growth and equity objectives. Given international prices of tradable agricultural and non-agricultural goods, government restrictions on imports and exports through trade and exchange rate policies determine the equilibrium domestic terms of trade in a small, open economy. In turn movements in the terms of trade affect the relative profitability of producing agricultural goods, encouraging or discouraging domestic supply. The direction of causality in the relationship between the domestic terms of trade and agricultural output is, therefore, widely assumed to be from the former to the latter.

It is conceivable, however, that the main line of causation is in the opposite direction, the relative agricultural price being dependent (at least in part) on exogenously determined domestic output. This could be the case, for example, if the degree of government reliance on, or access to, foreign trade in agricultural products were itself dependent on the domestic terms of trade. In addition to domestic and foreign supplies, demand factors would also influence the behaviour of the agricultural terms of trade over time in such a case. More concretely, consider the following aggregate supply, demand, and import functions for agricultural products:

$$S = S(P, X) \tag{1}$$

$$D = D(P, Y) \tag{2}$$

$$M = M(P, Z) \tag{3}$$

where, S, D and M denote domestic production, consumption, and net imports, respectively; P ($\equiv$ Pa/Pn) is the agricultural terms of trade; X represents other supply influences (for example, public inputs); Y represents other demand influences (for example, national income); and Z represents other trade influences (for example, a capacity-to-import variable). The expected signs of the partial derivatives with respect to the terms of trade are given by: s_1 ($\equiv \partial S/\partial P$) > 0, d_1 ($\equiv \partial D/\partial P$) < 0, and m_1 ($\equiv \partial M/\partial P$) > 0.

Because the domestic price of agricultural products (in particular, food) represents a politically sensitive issue in most developing countries, government intervention in agricultural markets is prevalent. Thus it is frequently the case that the government has a monopoly of the international trade in major food and other agricultural products. It is assumed above that, as the domestic terms of trade rises (falls), the government increases (decreases) net imports of agricultural products. While imports (exports) serve as a safety valve to promote stability of domestic agricultural prices, the 'trade policy function' given in equation (3) also presupposes some constraints on the actual volume of trade (in the form of Z, as additional explanatory variables). Thus, if there is a shortage in foreign exchange due to external imbalance, a food-deficit country may not be able to import sufficiently to prevent an excessive food price inflation. In this formulation, the import function (3) replaces the horizontal import supply function normally implied by the small country assumption.[7]

Changes over time among the variables included in (1)–(3) would be related as follows:

$$\dot{S} = s_1 \dot{P} + s_2 \dot{X} \qquad (4)$$

$$\dot{D} = d_1 \dot{P} + d_2 \dot{Y} \qquad (5)$$

$$\dot{M} = m_1 \dot{P} + m_2 \dot{Z} \qquad (6)$$

$$\dot{M} = \dot{D} - \dot{S} \qquad (7)$$

where $s_2 \equiv \partial S/\partial X$, $d_2 \equiv \partial D/\partial Y$, $m_2 \equiv \partial M/\partial Z$, and a dot ($\cdot$) over a variable denotes its total derivative with respect to time (for example, $\dot{P} = dP/dt$).

The equation system (4)–(7) contains 4 endogenous variables (in time rates of change), namely, P, S, D and M, each of which can be expressed in terms of the exogenous variables X, Y and Z. The reduced form equation for the terms of trade variable is given by

$$\dot{P} = (1/s_1 - d_1 + m_1)\,(-s_2 \dot{X} + d_2 \dot{Y} - m_2 \dot{Z}) \qquad (8)$$

which shows the effects on relative domestic prices of changes in the exogenous variables influencing agricultural production, consumption, and trade. The coefficient $(1/s_1 - d_1 + m_1)$ has a positive sign.

Referring back to the supply function (1), several empirical investigations have yielded (single-equation) estimates of the price elasticity of aggregate agricultural supply that are invariably near zero.[8] For this reason it is sometimes assumed that agricultural growth in developing countries is 'more a function of public policy towards research, education, and such matters than of price policy' (Mellor, 1969, p. 1414). Indeed, where agricultural technology is stagnant and rural infrastructure remains underdeveloped, it does not seem reasonable to expect that an improvement in agricultural price incentives will lead to higher output. On the other hand, technological change and infrastructure development can loosen supply constraints and result in higher agricultural production even if relative prices remain the same.

In the context of the above-specified model, the case of zero supply response to agricultural terms of trade changes would imply that $s_1 = 0$ and $\dot{S} = s_2 \dot{X}$. Equation (8) then becomes

$$\dot{P} = (1/d_1 - m_1)\,(\dot{S} - d_2 \dot{Y} + m_2 m_2 \dot{Z}) \qquad (9)$$

and S can be treated as an exogenous variable. The expected sign of the coefficient $(1/d_1 - m_1)$ is negative.

Alternatively, equation (9) can be considered as part of a complete, two-equation system which, together with equation (1), jointly determines $\dot{S}$ and $\dot{P}$ given $\dot{X}$, $\dot{Y}$ and $\dot{Z}$.

The empirical analysis in the following section makes use of the analytical framework developed above. In particular, we are interested in estimating equations (1) and (9) based on the alternative interpretations (a) that they are independent, and (b) that agricultural supply and the domestic terms of trade are jointly dependent variables.

5 ESTIMATING AND INTERPRETING THE AGRICULTURAL SUPPLY AND TERMS OF TRADE EQUATIONS

In investigating empirically the relationship between agricultural growth and terms of trade changes, our interest is in the collective experience, rather than individual experiences, of the developing countries in our sample; additionally, we are also interested in examining the special case of Sub-Saharan Africa. Furthermore, it is the medium- to long-run, rather than short-run, relationships that we want to analyse; for this reason the critical variables are expressed in average annual (compound) rates of changes (that is, the trend values) over the observation period 1960–84. In contrast to time series analysis, using this type of cross-country data enables us to abstract from dynamic considerations (for example, adjustment lags) and short-term disturbances (for example, weather). Multi-country, long-period analysis is advantageous in that it reduces the probability of gross error arising from sources peculiar to individual countries and specific short periods.

Using the simultaneous equation model formulated in the preceding section, we need to specify the explanatory variables assumed to influence domestic agricultural production, consumption, and trade. Considering first the agricultural supply equation, the domestic terms of trade – in terms of both its trend (Pa) and, as a measure of price risk, its instability (Is), together with the trend in GDP per capita (Gc), rural population density (RPD), life expectancy (LE), and the proportion of agricultural land irrigated (ALI) are hypothesised to affect the agricultural growth rate (Sa). GDP per capita can be considered, following Mundlak and Hellinghausen (1982), to represent a country's ability to finance agricultural investments, especially public expenditures on research, extension, transport, and other rural infrastructure facilities.

The three 'endowment' variables RPD, LE, and ALI have been found in recent empirical work using cross-country data (cf. Binswanger *et al.*, 1985) significantly to affect agricultural supply. Higher population density is believed to induce greater specialisation in rural production activities and to lower the per capita cost of providing rural infrastructure, conditions which favour more rapid agricultural growth (Boserup, 1965). On the other hand, a larger rural population on a given land area can also be associated with greater use of land for human settlement to the detriment of agricultural production. Life expectancy is used as a proxy measure for health, which is expected to have a positive influence on labour productivity; LE is admittedly a very imperfect measure since it pertains to the entire population rather than just the rural population (on which the required data are not available). We also considered an education variable, represented by adult literacy rate, which however turned out to be highly correlated with life expectancy.

The non-price demand factors (represented in the analytical discussion above by the vector Y) are assumed to consist only of GDP per capita and size of population (POP). While we acknowledge that demand for agricultural products is determined in part by the distribution of national income (due, for example, to the higher marginal budget share of food in lower income households), income distribution data are simply not available for the majority of developing countries in our sample. As for the trade policy function, the (non-price) capacity-to-trade variable (CT) is represented simply by the observed growth rate of each country's aggregate imports in US dollars during 1960–84. While CT is not a quantity measure, it is assumed that the same trend in the dollar price of agricultural products over the observation period applies to all developing countries in our sample; hence there is no need to introduce a world price variable in the trade policy equation. Tables 1.3a and 1.3b present the estimated equations for agricultural supply and terms of trade[9] using ordinary least squares (OLS) and two-stage least squares (TSLS) on 1960–84 data for the entire set of 41 developing countries and the subset of 19 Sub-Saharan African countries. Because the regressions are based on cross-country, rates-of-change data, we can be more liberal in the interpretation of the resulting test statistics.

Nonetheless, it is necessary to acknowledge that some relevant characteristics of LDC economies have not been taken into account (including non-quantifiable cultural and institutional factors) that must have had significant differential effects across countries on the domestic market for agricultural products.

What is most important about the regression results for present purposes is that they provide empirical support to the hypothesis raised earlier concerning the direction of causality in the relationship between agricultural growth and terms of trade changes. Single-equation (OLS) estimation of the agricultural supply function is seen from Table 1.3a to yield a negative coefficient for the terms-of-trade variable in both equations (1) and (4). Based on the two-equation model in which Sa and Pa/Pna are jointly dependent variables, estimating the supply equation by TSLS results in a positive terms-of-trade coefficient, as shown in equations (2) and (5), Table 1.3a. For the 'All countries' regression, the estimated terms-of-trade coefficient of 0.739 does not seem an unreasonable value of the aggregate supply elasticity averaged across the developing countries in our sample.

That the coefficient estimate (and its t-value) for the terms-of-trade variable in the Africa equation is lower than that for 'All countries' is not surprising, given the relatively undeveloped rural infrastructure and stagnant agricultural technology in Sub-Saharan Africa. Indeed, suppressing the Pa/Pna and Is variables tends to improve the overall fit of the Africa regression, as shown by the OLS-estimated equation (6). Consistent with the Delgado–Mellor hypothesis, non-price factors – represented particularly in growth of GDP per capita (public investments) and the health (LE) variable – appear to be the primary determinants of agricultural growth in Sub-Saharan Africa during 1960–84. A final observation on the regression results for agricultural supply is that they bear out the expected direction of the effects of Is, Gc, LE and ALI; contrary to the Boserup hypothesis, however, the coefficient of RPD turns out to be always negative.

Considering now the results of the regressions with the domestic terms of trade as dependent variable (Table 1.3b), it is striking that the signs of the coefficient estimates for the explanatory variables appearing in equations (1) – (4) are consistently correct, indicating negative effects of the supply variables Sa and CT and positive effects of the demand variables Gc and POP. The quantitative effect of domestic output on the terms of trade is seen to be larger than that of the trade variable. It is also remarkable that population shows up consistently to have a much more potent influence on the domestic terms of trade than per capita income. This is particularly so in the regression results for Sub-Saharan Africa.

In the 'All countries' regressions, the TSLS estimated terms-of-trade equation appears more acceptable than the OLS result. The opposite seems to be the case for the Africa equations, in which the TSLS result (c.f. equation 4) shows a considerable reduction in Sa coefficient estimate and its t-value.

Therefore, to the extent that the underlying data for the Sub-Saharan Africa countries are reliable, it would seem that the simultaneous equation bias in the relationship between agricultural growth and terms-of-trade changes during 1960–84 can reasonably be ignored. The direction of causality is, however, different from what is invariably assumed in most existing studies of agricultural supply response. Instead of an exogenously determined domestic terms of trade variable affecting directly agricultural output, the above results indicate that it is the terms of trade that are directly influenced by agricultural supply, which in turn is primarily determined by non-price factors (such as public investments in technology development and rural infrastructure).

More generally, our findings from the 'All countries' regressions suggest that agricultural growth and the domestic terms of trade are jointly dependent variables and that single-equation estimates of the price elasticity of aggregate agricultural supply can be grossly misleading. The empirical results call attention to the need to take systematically into account the demand-raising effects of population growth and per capita income on the domestic market for agricultural products. Analysis of the relationship between agricultural growth and terms-of-trade changes is also likely to prove inadequate unless the role of trade policy in influencing total availability is appropriately specified.

6 SOME PERSPECTIVES AND CONCLUDING REMARKS

There are obviously many ways of extending the empirical work of this study. First of all, it would be useful to verify, using independent data sources at the individual country level, the behaviour of the domestic terms of trade observed above for the 41 developing countries. The World Bank data files offer the most comprehensive

Table 1.3a: Regression results: dependent variable, S_a

Equation No.	Estimation technique	Constant	Pa/Pna	I_s	G_c	RPD	LE	ALI	Coefficient of determination
All Countries									
(1)	OLS	−0.660 (−0.59)	−0.063 (−0.69)	−0.031 (−1.08)	0.212 (2.19)	−0.244 (−0.69)	0.072 (3.12)	0.009 (0.40)	0.449
(2)	TSLS	0.078 (0.04)	0.739 (1.02)	−0.090 (−1.22)	0.384 (1.65)	−1.072 (−1.10)	0.060 (1.38)	0.046 (0.87)	0.473
(3)	OLS	−1.044 (−0.98)	—	—	0.250 (2.68)	−0.388 (−1.16)	0.071 (3.09)	0.018 (0.81)	0.447
Sub-Saharan Africa									
(4)	OLS	−9.461 (−2.12)	−0.170 (−1.39)	−0.028 (−0.75)	0.274 (1.88)	−0.795 (−0.57)	0.281 (2.57)	0.368 (0.56)	0.355
(5)	TSLS	−6.546 (−0.76)	0.139 (0.20)	−0.048 (−0.75)	0.308 (1.57)	−0.798 (−0.46)	0.209 (0.99)	0.669 (0.63)	0.360
(6)	OLS	−8.477 (−1.91)	—	—	0.321 (2.17)	−1.166 (−0.83)	0.245 (2.24)	0.777 (1.23)	0.366

Note: Numbers in parentheses are the *t*-values. Coefficient of determination is adjusted for degrees of freedom (OLS), or is the square of the correlation coefficient between actual and predicted values of the dependent variable (TSLS).

Table 1.3b: Regression results: dependent variable, P_a/P_{na}

Equation No.	Estimation technique	Constant	S_a	CT	G_c	POP	Coefficient of determination
All countries							
(1)	OLS	0.141 (0.09)	−0.456 (−1.50)	−0.170 (−1.28)	0.216 (0.81)	0.792 (1.32)	0.233
(2)	TSLS	0.197 (0.13)	−0.589 (−1.95)	−0.185 (−1.26)	0.289 (0.72)	0.885 (1.24)	0.357
Sub-Saharan Africa							
(3)	OLS	−0.968 (−0.41)	−0.723 (−1.36)	−0.263 (−1.16)	0.269 (0.64)	1.473 (1.50)	0.294
(4)	TSLS	−0.924 (−0.39)	−0.288 (−0.27)	−0.209 (−0.81)	0.103 (0.19)	1.111 (0.88)	0.403

Note: Numbers in parentheses are the t-values. Coefficient of determination is adjusted for degrees of freedom (OLS), or is the square of the correlation coefficient between actual and predicted values of the dependent variable (TSLS).

source of time series data for developing economies 'intended to be suitable for cross-country analysis'; while 'considerable effort has been made to standardise the definitions, coverage, time, valuation, and other characteristics of the basic data,' it is admitted that 'this has not been possible for all countries' (World Bank, 1983, p. vii). A particularly relevant question to investigate is how closely the implicit price deflators for value added obtained from the World Bank tapes reflect the actual prices facing agricultural and non-agricultural producers in the sample developing countries (especially countries in Sub-Saharan Africa).

We consider the results of our empirical investigation to be significant enough to warrant further examination of the relationship between terms-of-trade changes and agricultural growth based on the analytical framework developed above. It would indeed be interesting to undertake individual country analysis, using annual time series data from the *World Tables* or from any alternative sources of the various hypotheses explored above, taking into account dynamic considerations (such as intersectoral resource flows) and short-term disturbances. Such in-depth studies would also provide ample scope for incorporating individual peculiarities of, and exogenous factors impinging on, the workings of each country's market for agricultural products as they affect the terms of trade and aggregate output; this will serve to improve the statistical fit of the estimated equations. Finally, enlarging the framework of analysis so as to be able to examine the macroeconomic and income distribution effects of agricultural growth and terms-of-trade changes would also seem a useful direction for further work to take.

Government policies can significantly affect the relative domestic price of agricultural products *vis-à-vis* non-agricultural products. As recognised in the analytical framework developed above, foreign trade provides a mechanism for influencing the agricultural terms of trade, implying that trade policy is an integral part of agricultural pricing policy. A further implication is that, in the evaluation of the distortionary effects of agricultural pricing policy, what is relevant is not so much the temporal movements of the domestic terms of trade from some base year level, but the structure of domestic prices relative to foreign prices (or marginal revenues if import supply and export demand elasticities are not infinite). Past prices are an inferior reference in so far as they do not represent an alternative set of prices concurrently available to which can be related the scope for policy action.

The distinction between negative and positive agricultural price policy made by Krishna as quoted above is unclear on the reference price structure with which to compare the domestic terms of trade at a given point in time. If negative agricultural price policy means deliberately depressed terms of trade, the question arises: depressed with respect to what? Similarly, does an improvement in the terms of trade from some past period's level (which can be very 'depressed') necessarily imply a positive agricultural price policy? A rise in the terms of trade from some base year value only means that the prices paid and received by agricultural producers have improved; however, this could have been due to a favourable movement in international prices, not to an improvement in agricultural price policy.

There is a growing body of empirical evidence that government price interventions in developing countries have tended to discriminate against agricultural production (cf World Bank, 1986). The strong policy bias toward rapid industrialisation – in the 1950s via import substitution in most developing countries and since the early 1960s via industrial export expansion in an increasing number of developing countries – meant higher levels of protection to industry relative to agriculture. Such development strategy entailed the artificial lowering of the relative prices of agricultural products *vis-à-vis* industrial products, penalising farm producers in two ways: (1) they received lower than international prices for their products; and (2) they paid higher than international prices for industrial inputs such as fertiliser and pesticides.

Differences in relative prices can lead to significant resource transfers between sectors (Bautista, 1987). While the need to extract agricultural surplus to finance capital formation in the rest of the economy during development is a widely accepted proposition in development economics, one has to be concerned about the possible inefficiency with which the transferred resources are used in the non-agricultural sectors. In most developing countries where the industrial sector has been highly protected, the distortions in product and factor markets have led to the inefficient use of investment resources for non-agricultural production and the inability to compete in international markets. Unless such policy-induced distortions are corrected, and given the opportunities for rapid productivity growth in agriculture provided the capital requirements for technological change and rural infrastructure development (among other needed investments) are met,[10] there is cause for scepticism as to whether agricultural resource transfers can help accelerate the development process. An additional consideration, of course, is that the increased rural incomes due to rising agricultural productivity can provide the stimulus to the expansion of non-agricultural production. This form of 'rural growth linkage' is at the heart of some proposals for an agriculture-based development strategy (Mellor, 1976; Adelman, 1984).

Notes

Discussions with Yair Mundlak and Tshikala Tshibaka were helpful in the preparation of this paper. Valuable research assistance was provided by James Gilmartin.

1. More precisely,

$$Pa/Pna = \frac{AVA^c/AVA^k}{(GDP^c - AVA^c)/(GDP^k - AVA^k)}$$

where the superscript c and k denote, respectively, current and constant prices in domestic currency units. This terms-of-trade measure has been used in previous studies; see, for example, Timmer (1984). It should be noted that the agricultural sector is defined here broadly, as in the national accounts, to include not only crops and livestock, but also fishery and forestry.

2. Following Della Valle (1978), the instability measure (I_s) is given by

$$I_s = \frac{100 \cdot SEE}{\overline{P}} \sqrt{\frac{1 - R_a^2}{1 - R^2}}$$

where SEE is the standard error of estimate in the linear trend regression, $\overline{P}$ is the mean value of Pa/Pna, and R^2 and R_a^2 are the coefficients of determination in the linear and logarithmic trend regressions, respectively.

3. Based on the classification in the *1986 World Development Report*, per capita GNP of US $380 or lower in 1984 defines the low-income countries.

4. For instance, in the context of East African countries, Lele and Candler (1981, p. 114) state that 'although official agricultural prices are known, actual prices . . . faced by the majority of rural producers and consumers are not known'.

5. To be sure, one cannot always associate rising terms of trade with improving production incentives. For example, lengthy periods of civil disturbances (as have occurred in Uganda since the early 1970s) can lead to food scarcity due to disruption in domestic supply and impaired capacity to import. Food prices increase, to which agricultural producers

cannot respond; indeed they may be forced to leave the farms and get into some informal non-agricultural production activities. Under such conditions the domestic terms of trade improve but not agricultural production incentives.

6. A negative output response to agricultural prices is, of course, possible – if leisure is valued very highly or if agricultural producers have rigid income targets. We do not consider this possibility in the present study.

7. For an analytical discussion and application to Philippine food imports, see Bautista (1978).

8. For recent reviews, see Food and Agriculture Organization (1985) and Binswanger *et al.* (1985).

9. Dummy variables for (i) oil-exporting and (ii) low-income countries were included in the preliminary runs of terms-of-trade regression, which however did not yield significant coefficient estimates.

10. For historical evidence of relatively large investment requirements for agricultural development (in terms of the incremental capital–output ratios in agriculture and in mining and manufacturing), see Krishna (1982).

References

Adelman, I. (1984) 'Beyond Export-Led Growth', *World Development* vol. 12, pp. 937–49.

Bautista, R.M. (1978) 'Import Demand in a Small Country with Trade Restrictions', *Oxford Economic Papers* vol. 30, pp. 199–216.

Bautista, R.M. (1987) *Production Incentives in Philippine Agriculture: Effects of Trade and Exchange Rate Policies,* Research Report 59 (Washington DC: International Food Policy Research Institute).

Binswanger, H., Mundlak, Y., Yang, M.C. and Bowers, A. (1985) 'Estimation of Aggregate Agricultural Supply Response from Time Series of Cross-Country Data', Report ARU 48 (Washington, DC: The World Bank, Agriculture and Rural Development Department).

Boserup, E. (1965) *Conditions of Agricultural Growth* (Chicago: Aldine Publications).

Delgado, C.D. and Mellor, J.W. (1984) 'A Structural View of Policy Issues in African Agricultural Development', *American Journal of Agricultural Economics* vol. 66, pp. 665–70.

Della Valle, P.A. (1978) 'On the Instability Index of Time-Series Data: A Generalization', *Oxford Bulletin of Economics and Statistics* vol. 40, pp. 247–9.

Food and Agriculture Organization (1985) 'Agricultural Price Policies' (Rome, mimeographed).

Krishna, R. (1967) 'Agricultural Price Policy and Economic Development', in H.M. Southworth and B.F. Johnston (eds) *Agricultural Development and Economic Growth* (Ithaca: Cornell University Press).

Krishna, R. (1982) 'Some Aspects of Agricultural Growth, Price Policy, and Equity in Developing Countries', *Food Research Institute Studies* vol. 18, pp. 219–60.

Lele, U. and Candler W. (1981) 'Food Security: Some East African Considerations', in A. Valdés (ed.) *Food Security for Developing Countries* (Boulder: Westview Press, Inc.).

Mellor, J.W. (1969) 'Agricultural Price Policy in the Context of Economic Development', *American Journal of Agricultural Economics* vol. 51, pp. 1413–20.

Mellor, J.W. (1976) *The New Economics of Growth* (Ithaca: Cornell University Press).

Mundlak, Y. and Hellinghausen, R. (1982) 'The Intercountry Agricultural Production Function: Another View', *American Journal of Agricultural Economics* vol. 64, pp. 664–72.

Timmer, C.P. (1984) 'Energy and Structural Change in the Asia–Pacific Region: The Agricultural Sector', in R.M. Bautista and S. Naya (eds) *Energy and Structural Change in the Asia–Pacific Region* (Makati: Philippine Institute for Development Studies and Asian Development Bank).

World Bank (1983) *World Tables* (3rd edn, vol. I) (Baltimore: Johns Hopkins Press).

World Bank (1986), *World Development Report 1986* (Oxford: Oxford University Press).

2 Macro Policies, the Terms of Trade and the Spatial Dimension of Balanced Growth

Gustav Ranis*
YALE UNIVERSITY

1 INTRODUCTION

Over the past half century both theoretical analysis and policy have focused rather heavily on the impact of international trade in the context of individual LDCs' development efforts. With most of the developing countries emphasising a shift from a raw materials enclave an industrial enclave, the focus of theory and policy has been on the relations between the import substituting industrial enclave and the rest of the world. Inevitably, the discussion, especially in the 1950s and 1960s, concentrated on the promotion of that enclave in interaction with the rest of the world, while agriculture and dispersed industry and services were neglected.

In more recent years, especially since the 1970s, it is fair to say that policy makers and analysts have become increasingly aware of the need to pay more attention to the agricultural sector, but mainly as a source of food or, better, as a way of substituting for the importation of food which had resulted from the earlier neglect of that important set of activities. Given a relatively stagnant agriculture, that is, growing at less than 3 per cent a year in 42 major developing countries between 1960 and 1981, thus barely staying ahead of population growth on average, the need fully to mobilise that sector as a source of savings as well as of foreign exchange has been increasingly recognised. Included in that recognition has been the view that much of the problem resided in the price environment facing the individual farmer, that is, the terms of trade he is facing. These relative prices, of course, refer to what the typical farmer sells, whether the produce ultimately ends up in domestic or in foreign markets, relative to the prices of what he buys, whether the source is a domestic or imported product. The terms of trade represent one of the most important signals or, if one prefers, developmental instruments with which the typical mixed economy government can hope to reach millions of dispersed decision makers. If, as is often the case, those signals are distorted by government macroeconomic policy interventions of one kind or another a lot of damage can be done to the development effort. On the other hand, it is the contention of this paper that the terms of trade represent but one, albeit important, link in the chain which determines the success or failure of third-world development – and that we must seek to place it in proper perspective.

It is probably fair to say that the profession, along with policy makers, has been fascinated almost exclusively by the open economy aspects of development over the last two decades as LDCs wrestled with the industrialisation effort, first via import substitution and, later, either via more import substitution or via export promotion – with agriculture assigned an increasingly supportive role. What I believe is still missing is a development theory and strategy which encompasses the full recognition of the importance of domestic balanced growth, but without abandoning the important open economy dimensions of the problem. It is in this context that this paper is directed at the issue of macroeconomic policies, the importance of the terms of trade and the revival of domestic balanced growth. Such balanced growth, it must be emphasised, involves domestic agriculture and non-agriculture acting in a mutually reinforcing fashion, but is very much consistent with, and in fact requires, an increasingly open economy setting. In other words, this paper hopes to provide the basis for a broader understanding of the critical linkages between industrial and agricultural activities at different stages of the transition growth effort, the factors which affect the strengths and weaknesses of these linkages, and the identification of government policies, macro as well as sectoral, to strengthen those linkages where they are weak.

As is well known, in the typical import substitution mode of development the agricultural sector is basically viewed as a milch cow providing resources to help finance industrial development activity. The effort is normally made to channel resources towards the urban industrial class for both political and economic reasons, that is because governments are usually most concerned with satisfying the needs of the new elite by providing them with windfall profits and low-priced wage goods for their workers. The most effective way of achieving the necessary income transfers is by influencing the terms of trade facing farmers, for example, via the maintenance of an overvalued exchange rate, import controls and the establishment of a protective tariff.

Frequently an effort is made, in addition, to intervene directly in the domestic food crop markets by setting artificially low government procurement prices for basic cereals, by levying a 'hidden tax' via high fertiliser procurement prices and/or by using food imports (including PL480-type aided imports) to depress the price of food, at least for some urban consumers. However, given government's limited capacity to enforce price controls and prevent the spread of parallel markets, while the official terms of trade can be turned against agriculture, there are distinct limits as to what can actually be accomplished. Since the typical LDC indeed has a need to transfer resources from agriculture to non-agriculture 'on the table', for example, via trade-related agricultural taxes and land taxes, such measures are likely to be much more effective in eliciting the required supply response, that is, avoiding the danger of disincentive effects on agricultural producers.

That the burden of this tax system falls especially heavily on the spatially dispersed rural families is perhaps inevitable at the beginning of the transition growth process since agriculture is the sole productive sector which is not only preponderant in size but also contains a squeezable surplus or rent, especially in the natural resource-abundant LDCs. It is worthy of note, however, that the more successful developing countries, once they emerged from primary import substitution, began to shift from 'under the table', that is, incentive-dulling efforts generating an agricultural surplus for non-agricultural activity, to explicit 'on the table' measures. At the same time the signals facing the agriculturalist in terms of both external and internal prices gradually became more closely aligned to equilibrium prices. This has certainly been the East Asian experience. Elsewhere, in contrast, in spite of an increased recognition of the importance of agriculture, it is fair to state that there has not been the same gradual reversal in the macroeconomic policy setting. Most developing countries have persevered with earlier trends, if with oscillations, that is, occasional liberalisation followed by a return to import substitution policies. The practice of indirectly squeezing the food producing agricultural sector and, as a consequence, maintaining its basically subservient relationship to a large-scale urban industrial enclave focussed almost exclusively on international trade has generally been maintained.

The same contrast, incidentally, may be noted with respect to the pattern of government expenditures, that is, how much infrastructure goes into the agricultural sector, as opposed to the urban industrial sector, and, of course, within the agricultural sector, how infrastructure is allocated as between plantation and food crop activities. Thus, even in the best performing post-Second World War LDCs a combination of covert and overt interventions ranging from protection and overvalued exchange rates to hidden taxes and expenditure allocations distorted the domestic terms of trade and effected income transfers from agricultural to industrial interests. But it must also be noted that early on, that is, at the end of 'easy' import substitution, these situations and their negative impact on agriculture and rural industry were gradually eased through import duty rebate systems, export processing zones and so on and finally virtually eliminated in the later export orientation phase with which we are all familiar. In contrast, the more typical Latin American type of LDC has continued to rely extensively on an overvalued exchange rate as well as direct interventions depressing agricultural terms of trade in order to transfer the income of primary product exporters to the urban industrial class, a situation ameliorated only by the enhanced recognition of the importance of local and global food shortages in the early 1970s.

As developing countries in the 1960s moved into secondary import substitution, relying heavily on imported capital, this tended to further separate industrial development, urban, large-scale and often foreign dominated, from the rural agricultural development, especially from the food sub-sector. Consequently in most LDCs growth has become increasingly compartmentalised, concentrated on the modern enclave and limited in human capital participation. Externally, as is also well known, serious foreign exchange and debt problems have emerged, especially in recent years, and while this is often not accorded the most urgent consideration, it is the increasing disarticulation between the agricultural and industrial sectors, that is, the weakness of the internal balanced growth mechanism, which is as much the culprit as the 'over-borrowing' of the 1970s which has been given so much of the blame for the current crisis.

This in essence is the basic thesis of this paper. The industrial sector inevitably constitutes an ever larger and the agricultural sector an ever smaller proportion of total output and employment as development proceeds. But on this road to economic maturity productivity increase in agriculture is critical not only because of its direct effects on output and incomes but also because it generates opportunites outside agriculture, especially in the production and sale of consumer goods, agricultural implements, repair and the rest. In turn, rural industrial development is much more likely to be sustainable when based on increased local agricultural output as a source of market power as well as inputs.

All too often, in my view, agricultural performance has been viewed as the consequence of physical inputs plus technology, sometimes (increasingly in recent years) with the relative price environment or the terms of trade thrown in for good measure. The so-called organisational school of agricultural development has focussed on the way in which agricultural production is institutionally determined, for example, how alternative land tenure systems operate, but the significance of intersectoral linkages as a key factor explaining agricultural performance has rarely been reflected in the analysis. It is necessary to add the spatial or linkages dimension in determining the success or failure of a balanced growth effort. This adds, we believe, an important dimension to our usual explanatory canvas and enhances the importance of the terms of trade through what an econometrician would call the interactions effect.

Perhaps best known is the work of John Mellor and Uma Lele (1973) as well as that of Johnston and Kilby (1972). The former focused entirely on consumption linkages, the latter on production linkages. A further major effort in recent years was the work by Bell, Hazell and Slade (1982) which attempted to evaluate a given project, namely the Muda irrigation project in North Western Malaysia, in terms of the input and consumption demands generated by the project. This paper introduced income and substitution effects in response to price changes, while in the previous literature prices were fixed, as were production and consumption coefficients. Causality in the other direction has indeed been virtually left to one side since the early work of Tang (1958) and Nicholls (1969) that is, the so-called contact school at Vanderbilt, which tested Ted Schultz's proposition that the proximity of urban industrial growth reduces imperfections in both factor and product markets and hence raises farm income per capita. The agricultural production function indeed should contain not only physical inputs, technology and organisation but also the terms of trade and the locational dimension of economic activity.

2 A FUNCTIONAL APPROACH TO DOMESTIC BALANCED GROWTH

Different dimensions of the interaction between agriculture and non-agriculture assume different levels of importance at different stages of the development process. First of all it must be recognised that agricultural products and non-agricultural products are different in kind and cannot substitute fully for each other, with food an essential component of consumption while the industrial sector provides inputs for both sectors, as well as final consumption goods. Secondly, we can expect agriculture to dominate the economy in the early stages of development, as has already been pointed out, thus conditioning agricultural development possibilities such as savings, foreign exchange availabilities and markets to a substantial extent early on. Foreign trade increasingly provides a mechanism whereby industrial production can be converted into agricultural consumption over time and many of the contributory functions of the agricultural sector can be performed by the industrial sector.

In addition to intersectoral commodity and financial flows, intersectoral labour movement occurs, that is, the reallocation, over time, of a portion of the agricultural labour force to the non-agricultural sector, as non-agricultural labour through the intersectoral labour market. Intersectoral linkages or interactions at the aggregate level must be concerned with the way these various economic functions are carried out.

Particularly at an early stage of development, the total agricultural surplus represents a crucial concept in that its presence is essential for the growth of the non-agricultural sector, certainly in the closed economy. In the absence of such a surplus a shortage of food would prevent the sustained reallocation of labour from agricultural to non-agricultural activities. The surplus represents the difference between agricultural output and the consumption of agricultural output within the sector and is determined by the level of agricultural labour productivity. A sustained increase in total agricultural surplus (TAS) thus requires increases in agricultural labour productivity. In this context, we see the importance of the various approaches which help us understand agricultural performance.

The physical inputs school of thought emphasises the contribution of modern inputs from the non-agricultural sector, in conjunction with modern science and technology, as embodied in the so-called Green Revolution technology. Modern inputs permit a consistent and rapid increase in agricultural productivity, in contrast to the slow growth associated with traditional technology. Hence linkages – in the form of technology and inputs from industry into agriculture – permit growth in agricultural productivity, which, in turn, generates a demand for industrial products and a supply of agricultural products for the non-agricultural labour force.

The technological focus of this physical inputs approach often means neglecting the question as to *why* in many country situations this process of the infusion of modern inputs does not, in fact, occur on a sustained basis. Such failure may be related to adverse organisational or tenure arrangements or to terms of trade which discriminate against agricultural production. This has been increasingly recognised of late. But what remains a neglected issue is the fact that appropriate or inappropriate terms of trade, for example, will have a very different impact depending on the locational dimension of non-agricultural activity. This has to do with the proximity or ready availability of industrial incentive goods to the agricultural household as well as the terms on which they can be acquired. This dimension is crucial in determining the extension of rural people's economic horizons and their motivation for taking the inevitable risks involved in experimenting with new technology in the effort to increase agricultural productivity at its source.

A virtuous pattern of rural balanced growth depends on consumption patterns, associated technology choice and the distribution of income. But it also depends on environmental conditions such as the terms of trade and on supply conditions such as the transportation infrastructure which may prevent any such sustained interaction from occurring. While a closed economy *requires* balanced growth, in the open economy international trade permits imbalances in internal development to be offset by trade. Economies at an early stage of development are unavoidably more 'closed' in the relevant sense because, while they do export and import, their flexibility in using trade is more limited. Large economies also more closely approximate the closed economy assumption than small ones. But even in the relatively small economy case, such as historical Japan or contemporary Taiwan, the agricultural sector's surplus remains of critical importance for non-agricultural development. In the early stages of development the industrial sector is generally a heavy net user of foreign exchange, relying on imported capital goods and having little export potential. Hence the agricultural sector normally has to provide the foreign exchange as well as the food for workers in the non-agricultural sector. While export income may be supplemented by foreign savings, the latter rarely provides more than a modest portion of foreign exchange needs. As industrialisation proceeds, the industrial sector may develop its own export capacity and can begin to finance its own imports, but it generally remains dependent on domestic agriculture for the bulk of its food requirements.

In the early stages of development, there may exist only limited strategic options. All countries have to rely largely on their agricultural (or mineral) sectors for foreign exchange to finance the early stages of import substituting industrialisation. But later a wide choice emerges. Countries have options with respect to trade, and options with respect to internal development. Moreover, there are connections between the two.

The trade options have been thoroughly explored in the literature; in particular, the distinction has been drawn between an industrial strategy of secondary import substitution, and one of emphasis on labour-intensive exports. Secondary import substitution involves expansion of industrial production into capital and intermediate goods production and into 'elite' consumption tending to involve rather capital-intensive methods. Because of the continued protection required this option often means continued (or worsening) terms of trade for the agricultural sector. In contrast, a labour-intensive export strategy is more likely to be associated with improved terms of trade for agriculture and, because of the greater employment generated, a stronger demand for agricultural products.

On the internal side, the major options consist of a balanced growth strategy in which agricultural and non-agricultural growth are mutually supportive and a more lopsided development pace in which industrialisation becomes self-supporting with limited links to the agricultural sector. The first option has been described earlier as the 'virtuous circle', with increased agricultural output associated with patterns of consumption for non-agriculture involving labour-intensive technologies in both urban and rural areas, thus leading to a mutually reinforcing growth in employment, incomes and consumption in both sectors. By contrast, industrialisation involving early expansion of capital-intensive production of capital goods and elite consumption goods may occur with little interaction with the agricultural sector and little regional dispersion of industry.

There are some natural links between the trade options and the internal options. The secondary import substitution strategy involves reduced links between industry and agriculture. It tends, in the long run, to lead to problems, both internally and externally. Internally, it is generally associated with continued – usually enhanced – discrimination against food producing agriculture, notably via terms of trade distortions. It leads to the perpetuation of enclaves, concentrating the benefits of development rather narrowly and causing problems of unemployment and maldistribution of income. Externally, it tends to require heavy borrowing with the subsequent emergence of debt problems. A balanced growth strategy is designed to avoid the internal 'enclave' phenomenon by spreading participation in development more widely geographically and across classes. Balanced growth is liable to generate a more self-reliant form of development, with internal sources of savings and markets. However, to maximise its benefits, the strategy also emphatically requires openness to the rest of the world to make efficient use of all available opportunities. The exportation of labour-intensive commodities and that of processed primary products represent natural adjuncts to a balanced growth strategy since the linkages involved reinforce the domestic linkages.

In short, our past overemphasis on foreign trade as a leading sector or as at least a formidable handmaiden of development has tended to lead us to neglect some essential internal dimensions of development. Here we have identified how a strategy of balanced growth, in the context of an open economy, can permit a broader participation in the growth process, while making efficient use of the international trading system and avoiding the external problems that have brought so many transition growth efforts to a halt. It remains for us to explore further the spatial dimensions of a domestic balanced growth process.

3 SPATIAL DIMENSIONS OF TRANSITION GROWTH

The issue of agricultural/non-agricultural linkages has an intrinsic spatial aspect because, by its nature, the agricultural sector is geographically dispersed. This section focuses on this spatial dimension, indicating the mutually positive effects that the agricultural and non-agricultural sectors may have on each other where there is close physical proximity between the two activities.

Most less-developed countries inherited a colonial system (political and/or economic) which involved certain spatial aspects. A colonial economic system includes two distinct types of economic regions (see Figure 2.1a), with an enclave region and a hinterland. The enclave region is formed by the linking of a hierarchy of urban centres (represented as squares) by rail, roads, and/or rivers. As a rule these enclaves represent those regions of the system which were initially most affluent because of their well-developed irrigation and transport networks. Typically, a major harbour, linking the system with that of the rest of the world, constitutes the urban centre of the highest hierarchy. Two aspects of the colonial economic system need to be emphasised, namely, the external sensitivity of the enclave and the internal compartmentalisation of growth. Both are relevant to the prospects for successful transition.

'Economic colonialism' describes a particular type of international economic relations, including international trade and international capital movements. A colonial economy is typically based on the export of a particular primary product produced in the enclave and exported through the major harbours to world markets. In return, the imports from the industrially advanced countries, consisting of manufactured consumer goods, and producer goods, enter through the same harbours, and are distributed to the country's primary producers. At later stages of colonial development, foreign capital inflows may support the establishment of foreign-owned factories and service establishments.

The colonial economic system is an open economy which is extremely sensitive to any changes in the external terms of trade of the primary product. Throughout the colonial period, the fluctuation between 'prosperity' and 'depression' in the enclave was very much governed by the secular movement of prices in world markets. When the price trend was favourable, capital inflows occurred to further the expansion and export of the primary product. Conversely, when price trends were unfavourable, there were long periods of 'colonial stagnation' accompanied by the cessation of net capital inflows or even the repatriation of capital and profits.

The major weakness of colonialism as an economic system can be traced to the fact that the economy is typically compartmentalised, that is, divided into two spatially unintegrated parts creating a dichotomy between what we have called the enclave and the hinterland. The enclave represents the relatively modern part in many senses: first of all, modern service and processing activities characterised by economies of scale, capital intensity, and the incorporation of modern science are located in the large urban centres. In contrast, small-scale industries and specialised handicrafts are located in the small urban centres of the hinterland, characterised by traditional technologies in terms of labour intensity and product characteristics. There thus exists a rather sharp contrast between the enclave and the traditional hinterland from a technological perspective. The relatively modern enclave offers a sharp contrast to the traditional hinterland as well from an organisational perspective, that is, the relatively greater community orientation of the latter contrasts sharply with the relatively greater market orientation of the former. Such contrasts can be more easily maintained given the lack of substantial interaction between the two.

When a country with such a heritage begins to make the effort to reach modern growth government action usually concentrates overwhelmingly on the enclave. It is here that colonial-type profits continue to be made. This situation also customarily leads to an overwhelming concern with stabilisation of the prices of primary products as a direct response to the problem of the external sensitivity of the colonial economic system. In more recent years the literature on the development of the open economy, encompassing issues like imports, exports, foreign aid and commercial capital inflows, has again centred on the more modern enclave portion of the economy, while issues related to the development of the traditional hinterland that may contain a very large fraction of the total population continue to be largely neglected – just as they were in the 'compartmentalised' days of the colonial era. In other words, while in many cases the enclave is gradually changing its character, from largely raw materials-oriented to largely industry-oriented, the relative situation of the hinterland has not been profoundly affected.

The notion of a linkages approach to modernisation takes on a special spatial connotation in this context, that is to say, the way to mobilise the mainly food producing agricultural sector and involve it in development is to break this residual compartmentalisation inherited from colonialism, through fuller economic interaction with the relatively advanced enclave. The spatial spread of the forces of modernisation, from both the technological and organisational standpoints, in fact amounts to such an integration between the two regions through which modern inputs, attitudes and organisational methods can be gradually transmitted from the 'modern' sector of the enclave to the traditional sector.

It should be noted that a third major contributing factor to understanding agricultural stagnation is traceable to the spatially relatively more dispersed pattern of location of the rural population (see Figure 2.1b), which makes it more difficult for its members to have contact with each other and/or with the urban population. The transformation of attitude and the acquisition of new knowledge become more difficult when both contacts and communication with other people are infrequent. Agricultural modernisation is especially difficult, not only because the farmers are alienated by distance from the modernisation core, but also because of their less frequent contacts with each other.

The locational disadvantages of the typical family farmer cannot be easily overcome because of other pervasive economic forces that determine the spatially dispersed pattern of his location in the first place. For one thing, agricultural production is characterised by joint inputs between population and land which forces a certain spatial spread. For another, in order to minimise their total daily cost of transport, as producers and households, farmers usually live in villages or, if separately, close to the fields they cultivate. Finally, since agricultural production is usually characterised by constant returns to scale, there exists no strong economic reason from the agricultural production side for higher population densities. This contrasts very sharply with non-agricultural production which is likely to be characterised by the existence of (i) economies of scale and (ii) conspicuous external economies, both tending to a spatially more centralised pattern of non-agricultural production at the urban centres.

The fact that the rural population is spatially dispersed also makes it more difficult to modernise agricultural production via a 'centrally co-ordinated command system' as experimented with in socialist societies. It is basically more difficult to gather 1000 farmers in one place for a combination of political indoctrination and economic instruction than to gather 5000 urban industrial workers. It is also more difficult to monitor peasants and to determine individual contributions to productive effort according to which an incentive system could be centrally enforced. This is one of the basic reasons why collectivist organisational systems have encountered problems in the performance of their agricultural sectors and have frequently been forced to experiment with different forms of incentives and organisations.

In the analysis which follows, a *dual standard market* is used to define such a rural community. In Figure 2.1c, the urban and rural populations of Figure 2.1b are partitioned into a number of localised 'market areas' Ω^1, Ω^2,...Ω^n each of which contains a single urban centre (with its urban population) and its share of the rural population.

Figure 2.1d presents a microscopic view of a typical standard market area. At the centre of Ω^i we find the urban centre with its spatially concentrated pattern of urban population and its share of the spatially dispersed rural population. The urban population engages in non-agricultural production (for example, rural handicrafts, food processing, retail trade), while this urban core also serves as the centre of educational and spiritual life (schools, recreation, religion) as well as of political administration (justice, police, tax collection, and government services). The urban centre is the focal point for contact among all the economic agents living within the standard market area, including the more dispersed farmers. Given the relatively primitive means of transport and communication, the only way farmers can communicate with members other than their own immediate family and neighbours is by their temporary physical presence in these urban centres. For personal contacts, it is necessary for the farmers to make occasional visits to the centre while engaging in both economic and non-economic activities.

We are now in a position to add a spatial dimension to our earlier account of intersectoral linkages. While agricultural production is carried out by spatially dispersed farmers, non-agricultural activities are partly carried out in the household and partly in urban centres at different levels of the hierarchy. Dualistic exchange, that is, the exchange of agricultural for non-agricultural goods, takes place; farmers carry their produce for sale to the market place at the urban centres and buy most of their non-agricultural requirements in the same centres. While carrying out these economic functions the farmers, however, also have other contacts which permit them to acquire modern products and ideas: they learn about incentive goods such as bicycles, sewing machines, and factory printed cloth, as well as about modern producer goods such as chemical fertilisers, agricultural machinery and new seeds. While formal education may

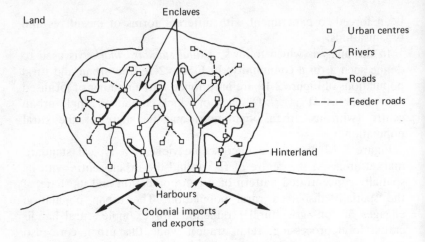

Figure 2.1a Spatial perspective of economic colonialism

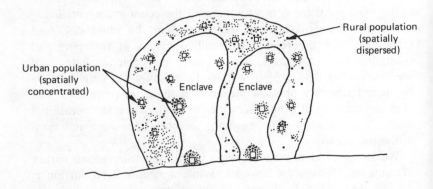

Figure 2.1b Location of population in a dualistic economy

help, it is more through these informal contacts that farmers learn about the world of the enclave and beyond, that is to say, mainly by contact with the urban population within the local marketing centres.[1]

The existence of these standard markets arises from the need to minimise transport time and costs. Where means of transport and communications are still linked the main way people communicate with each other is through personal contact. This sets a limit on the size of the standard market in an agrarian community. The maximum

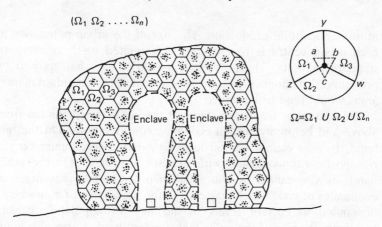

Figure 2.1c Standard market areas

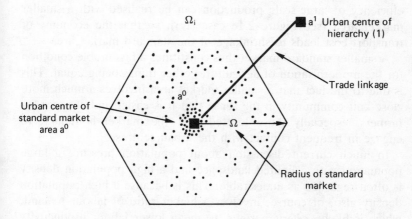

Figure 2.1d Standard market of a dualistic community

value of the radius of the standard market is such that it allows the least advantageously located farmer to make a round trip in a reasonable period of time (say, less than half a day) leaving some time for him to carry out the dualistic exchange in the urban centres.

A given region may thus be partitioned either into a large number of small market areas or a small number of large market areas (see Figure 2.1e, cases (i) and (ii)). In addition to transport cost, two other factors help determine the optimal size of the typical standard market, namely, population density and the extent of scale economies in non-agricultural production. The size of the urban population at each urban centre is roughly inversely related to the number of standard markets. Thus, if urban industries are characterised by pronounced economies of scale and externalities the standard market areas would tend to be larger.

The optimum size of the standard market is thus bounded from above and below by certain economic considerations. On the one hand, its size cannot be too large in order to economise on the transport costs associated with dualistic exchange. On the other hand, its size cannot be too small in order to take advantage of economies of scale which may exist in the production of goods being demanded at current levels of income. As population density increases, the size of the individual standard market area also tends to shrink, *ceteris paribus*, and the number of markets to increase. This is due to the fact that, with increasing population density, the efficiency of large-scale production can be realised with a smaller market area (see Figure 2.1e case (iv)), so that the economy of transport cost leads to shrinkage of the standard market area.

A smaller standard market thus constitutes a favourable condition for the modernisation of agriculture, other things being equal. This is due to the fact that a smaller market area involves a much more close-knit community in the sense that it is easier and cheaper for farmers, especially those located near the market boundary, to engage in frequent contact with the urban centres.

In much current discussion about population pressure a large population with a limited landspace and a high population density is often regarded as undesirable. This is because a high population density also, of course, involves a higher ratio of labour to land, which is likely, *ceteris paribus*, to mean lower labour productivity but higher land productivity. But, from the viewpoint of the modernisation of spatially dispersed farmers, we have come to the unorthodox conclusion that a larger population may, *ceteris paribus*, be helpful. For example, if we imagine the case of a very thinly populated region (for example, one or two persons per square mile) as in Tibet, the size of the standard market would have to be reckoned in terms of hundreds of square miles with farmers having to travel a month before they could reach an 'urban centre'. In that case, the thinness of the population is a barrier to human communication and thus to the adoption of new science-based inputs and techniques.[2]

A high population density is, by itself, of course not sufficient for

55

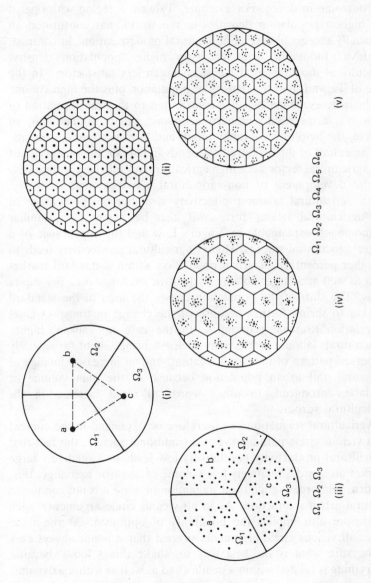

Figure 2.1e Size of the standard market

the modernisation of agriculture. Static diminishing returns may be seen as likely to be in conflict with dynamic linkage effects, with the outcome in doubt. For example, Taiwan, a region with one of the highest population densities in the world, has constituted an unusually successful case of agricultural modernisation. In contrast, in Java, Indonesia, with an even higher population density, agricultural modernisation has been much less satisfactory. In the case of Taiwan, it is the density of population plus the high volume of dualistic exchange that has contributed to the transformation of Taiwan's farmers into modern economic agents, along with, of course, the help of favourable 'input' and 'organisational' elements.

The extent of dualistic trade depends in part on the prosperity of the agricultural sector since high agricultural productivity is conducive to the development of non-agricultural activities, that is to say, when agricultural labour productivity is higher the percentage of non-agricultural labour force will also be higher – a familiar phenomenon explainable by Engel's Law and the appearance of a larger agricultural surplus. Higher agricultural productivity leads to a higher percentage of urban population within a standard market area as well as a larger volume of dualistic exchange on a per capita basis. The shift of the population causes the area of the standard market to shrink further because of the change in transport costs in relation to scale economies. In the case of Taiwan, higher agricultural labour productivity helped bring about a spatially dispersed pattern of industrial location, and an increased linkage of the rural and urban population because of the high volume of tradables produced, in other words, a rapid increase in the agricultural surplus.

Agricultural stagnation can therefore be explained in the context of a vicious circle paradigm. For a traditional society, the fact that agricultural productivity is relatively low leads to a relatively large market area and a relatively low volume of dualistic exchange; this, in turn, reinforces agricultural stagnation because it is not conducive to rural-urban interaction. As in all vicious circle arguments, such pessimism also implies the possibility of optimism. At the same time, all vicious circle arguments suggest that it is not always easy to be sure what is the best way to 'shake things loose' because everything is related within a deadlocked as well as within a dynamic system.

While we have portrayed the standard market as a locally self-sufficient economic unit as a first approximation, this is, of course, not a true representation. The higher the level of agricultural productivity (that is, the more affluent the rural community), the more likely that it will lose its autarkic status. The urban centre of the standard market area is, in turn, linked to towns of higher hierarchy. Thus the dispersed farmers in each standard market, while trading directly via their own urban centres, also trade with other urban centres for products that enjoy more conspicuous economies of scale and external economies. The urban centres of higher hierarchy thus serve a much larger market area encompassing several standard market areas.

The notion of a hierarchy of market centres can, of course, be carried further, with industrial activities subject to even more pronounced scale economies and serving an ever larger number of standard market areas. The fact that local farmers can trade with larger urban centres located far away is due to the fact that the economies of scale are sufficient to compensate for the higher transport costs.

Linkage between the agricultural and non-agricultural sectors thus has an important spatial dimension traceable to scale economies of non-agricultural production and transport costs. The gradual conversion of traditional farmers into modern economic agents, aware of the potential of new agricultural technology, experiencing wider consumption horizons, and aspiring to accumulate assets, can be accomplished only through the strengthening of linkages with the urban centres. Similarly, the small-scale rural industrial entrepreneur will become increasingly aware of his opportunities via linkages to urban industry, on the one hand, and cultivating farmers, on the other. A small-town industrial producer or a peasant in the hinterland may only be aware of the possibility of exchange within the local towns of a low hierarchy; but a modern farmer or a modern industrial entrepreneur is likely to become increasingly aware of the possibilities of carrying out all kinds of exchanges with far-away places – even including world markets.

4 SOME CONCLUDING COMMENTS

Our spatial perspective indicates that the compartmentalisation inherited from colonialism tends to restrict modernisation to the export-oriented enclave which usually encompasses only a small portion of the population. When the country is small, the task of transition to modern economic growth is easier because a small country really has the option of attempting development mainly through foreign trade; given a negligible hinterland, farmers can rely on exchange with far-away urban centres. Indeed, the early success of agricultural modernisation on Taiwan is partly a story of this type with her enhanced external orientation (after 1962) initially concentrated in the export of asparagus, mushrooms, and pineapples, in other words, farmers learning to take full advantage of international trade. In that sense, Taiwan's farmers were no less 'entrepreneurial' than the industrial exporters of Hong Kong. But, of course, this was not the whole story. In contrast to Hong Kong, Taiwan also experienced a substantial volume of strictly domestic balanced growth exchanges during the crucial decades of the 1960s and 1970s.

In the case of a large country, a large agricultural sector development achieved mainly through international trade is undoubtedly not a practical option. Here it is most necessary to form linkages between spatially dispersed farmers and urban centres, mostly within the domestic economy. The recent experience of India and mainland China has shown that it is indeed this linkage through dualistic exchange between agricultural and non-agricultural activities which is crucial to a system's chances of escaping from agrarian stagnation.

Our analysis suggests the importance of *proximity* between farmers and urban centres for agricultural and industrial modernisation. This concept of *proximity* has two dimensions: it is a function, first, of the average *distance* between the individual farmer and the relevant urban industrial centre; second, of the available means and costs of transport. The degree of such proximity has a number of effects on farmers' and rural industrialists' activities:

(i)   by increased contact with modern activities and consumer goods it may change their attitudes towards a more capitalist orientation;

(ii) the more immediate proximity of the various services (for example, technical advice, credit, fertiliser, seed supply, raw materials) may lead to greater use of modern inputs;

(iii) greater opportunities arise for farm family members to participate in non-agricultural activities for part of the year;

(iv) markets for both agricultural and non-agricultural products will be widened;

(v)   the price of all consumer goods (allowing for transport costs) is likely to be reduced *ceteris paribus* and their availability increased, that is, the farmer's terms of trade improved;

(vi) it enhances the visibility of incentive goods and investment opportunities.

These effects are likely to vary according to the stage of development and the size of the relevant urban centre. For example, at the early stages of development the effect on farmer attitudes through contact may be of paramount importance. However, in many countries it seems that most farmers already have a capitalist orientation to incomes and accumulation similar to that of dispersed non-agriculturalists; here proximity may be more important in terms of its effects on supplies and markets. Similarly, these proximity effects would tend to be larger the larger the size of the urban centre. Urban centres of higher hierarchies offer a wider range of services and consumer goods with greater contact with the enclave and the rest of the world.

What is required next is the resumption of empirical investigation attempting to explain differential intersectoral LDC performance by including the various specific proximity dimensions of linkage, along with the more traditional input and organisational variables, in the analysis. Such work is currently under way for one or two specific country cases. Assuming proximity does indeed contribute to balanced growth in the ways enumerated above, certain policy conclusions follow: actions which increase the degree of proximity contribute to the raising of agricultural and non-agricultural productivity. Such actions would include reducing intervention with the terms of trade as a result of macroeconomic policy choice. Moreover, sectoral policies relating to the improvement of transport and other infrastructural links between the agricultural and non-agricultural populations at various levels of urban hierarchy would serve to remove bottlenecks blocking the needed dynamic mutual interaction between agricultural and non-agricultural activities.

Notes

* This paper draws heavily on joint work with John Fei and Frances Stewart. I also wish to thank FAO and UNIDO for their support in closely related research activities.
1. The fact that an agrarian dualistic economy may be partitioned into a system of parallel localised standard market areas is basically due to the need to economise on transport costs. The principle of the delineation of the boundaries of the standard market area is demonstrated in the

insert of Figure 2.1c. Suppose there are three urban centres (indicated by '*a*', '*b*' and '*c*'). Let the triangle *abc* be constructed. The straight lines *ab*, *bc* and *ac* of the triangle may be interpreted as the roads linking the three urban centres. Let the straight lines *xy*, *xw* and *xz* be the perpendicular bisectors of the sides of the triangle *abc* that meet at a common point *x*. The lines *xy*, *xw* and *xz* then constitute the boundary of the three standard market areas Ω_1, Ω_2, Ω_3 (each containing its own urban centre '*a*', '*b*' or '*c*'). If all spatially dispersed farmers are to minimise their transportation time and cost in carrying out their dualistic exchanges, they will necessarily trade and affiliate with the urban centre of the area to which they belong.

2. This argument is reminiscent of E. Boserup's but not equivalent since she emphasises scale economies more than contact with non-agricultural activities.

References

Bell, C., Hazell, P. and Slade, R. (1982) *Project Evaluation in a Regional Perspective* (Baltimore: Johns Hopkins Press).

Boserup, E. (1965) *The Condition of Agricultural Growth* (Chicago: Aldine Publishing Company).

Johnston, B. and Kilby, P. (1972) '(Agricultural Strategy and Manufacturing, Stanford Food Research Institute Studies.

Mellor, John and Lele, Uma (1973) 'Growth Linkages of the New Food Grain Technologies', *Indian Journal of Agricultural Economics*, January.

Nicholls, W. (1969) 'Industrial–Urban Development as a Dynamic Force in Transforming Brazilian Agriculture, 1940–50' in Thorbecke, E. (ed.) *The Role of Agriculture in Economic Development* (New York: NBER).

Tang, A. (1958) *Economic Development in the Southern Piedmont* (Chapel Hill: University of North Carolina Press).

3 The Politics of Food Prices

Paul Streeten
WORLD DEVELOPMENT INSTITUTE,
BOSTON UNIVERSITY

The politics of food pricing is concerned with two sets of questions: first, what interests and pressures lie behind current policies of market intervention and the generation of political resources, particularly those that do not appear sensible from an economic point of view; second, what changes in political pressures can lead to reform?

1 INTERESTS AND PRESSURE GROUPS

Many governments have both a direct and an indirect interest in keeping food prices low for urban, industrial workers, government officials, members of the armed forces and students, and generating and transferring resources to them from the rural sector. As major employers of these groups, the direct interest is that the way to keep their real incomes up while resisting demands for higher money wages and salaries and to raise profits or reduce losses is to keep food prices down. Private industrialists are also their allies. The indirect interest is that these groups can cause a good deal of trouble by rioting and even overthrowing the government when food prices rise. But since governments also have an interest in raising agricultural production, they subsidise inputs into agriculture (fertiliser, machinery, seeds, credit, land), often benefiting mainly large and powerful farmers whose political support they thereby recruit. In countries where such large farmers figure prominently, such as the Ivory Coast and Kenya, agricultural policy takes on a different form.

Governments also have an interest in keeping the exchange rate overvalued (one of the principal tools of depressing the incomes of small farmers) because the resulting need for rationing and allocating foreign exchange gives politically established groups extra money and power. The power of these groups is one of the strongest sources of resistance to changing exchange rates in many countries. Rents caused by economically inefficient interventions present political resources which can be used to organise political support. 'Farming interests are opposed by urban workers who want low-priced food; urban industrialists, who want low wages and low prices for raw materials; bureaucrats and white collar workers who want higher salaries and lower food prices; and politicians who run governments which need taxes and which are major employers and industrialists in their own right' (see Bates, 1981; and also Bates, 1983 and Lipton, 1977).

Mancur Olson's approach is also illuminating. Agriculture and the rural sector is exploited in low-income countries because the large and dispersed members of this sector can neither organise themselves adequately nor exercise sufficient pressure on the government to act on their behalf. Any one member knows that the benefits from collective action go to everyone, whether or not he has borne the costs of the lobbying or the joint action. Everyone tries to be a 'free rider' and lacks the incentive to organise or pressurise. In advanced, industrial countries this large and dispersed sector is the urban, industrial interests, which are exploited for the benefit of more readily organised, smaller agriculture. Mancur Olson suggests that a more detailed investigation of sub-sectors, such as particular industrial or agricultural interests would throw additional light on this issue (Olson, 1965, 1982, 1985).

The analysis of political interest groupings is useful to explain policies with respect to food prices, the prices of inputs and the foreign exchange rate, but it can be overdone if narrow, competitive self-interest is regarded as the only motivating force. Coalitions to improve the efficient allocation of resources promise gains to all groups if compensation to losers can be incorporated, and should therefore not be excluded. Without going as far as Coase's theorem (Coase, 1960) according to which, in the absence of transaction costs and with optimising behaviour, it will always pay either an injurer to compensate his injured victims for accepting the injury, or the injured victims to compensate the injurer for forgoing it, it should not be assumed that the outcomes are necessarily of the prisoner's dilemma type, in which the unco-ordinated pursuit of self-interest impoverishes everybody. Real world outcomes will tend to be in between these two extremes.[1] Neither will self-interested, politically competitive behaviour inevitably lead to inefficient outcomes and mutual impoverishment, nor will free negotiations and enforcement of contracts always lead to the most efficient allocation of resources. On the assumptions of Robert Bates, disinterested government would be impossible. On the assumptions of Coase, government would be unnecessary.[2] But we know that, while there are elements of truth in both views, government in the public interest is possible and does occur.

2 THE ROLE OF THE STATE

Governments do, sometimes, transcend their individual and group interests and act in the common interest or in the interest of the poor and weak. The picture of the state painted by Robert Bates as an instrument for ruthlessly amassing wealth and power by those in office, and those on whose support they depend, without regard to either efficiency or the public interest, is surely limited. The principle of mutual impoverishment by competitive, short-term, self-interested political action of interest and pressure groups that attempt to frustrate the working of the invisible hand by rent-seeking and directly unproductive profit-seeking activities has been aptly called the 'invisible foot' by Stephen Magee (1984). It refers to the organised activities of individuals or groups to protect themselves against the working of market forces. The policy problem consists of finding ways to prevent the invisible foot trampling on and destroying the benefits bestowed by the invisible hand.

It is odd that, just at a time when writers such as Albert Hirschman, Amartya Sen, Thomas Schelling, Tibor Scitovsky and Harvey Leibenstein deepen our understanding of human choice beyond the simple preference ordering of economic man, some public choice theorists are applying a rather narrow interpretation of selfish economic man to transactions in the political arena. Just as we are getting rid of 'rational fools' in economics, they reappear in political science. And it is also odd that writers in the liberal conservative tradition (in the Manchester sense) take a view of the state that equates it to a pure instrument of inefficient exploitation, whereas writers in the Marxian tradition interpret it in much broader terms.[3]

According to one theory of the state, an idealistic and well informed government, like Platonic guardians, reigns above the interest conflicts and promotes the common good. In this theory the government can do no wrong. The opposite theory, represented by some Chicago economists, and members of the public choice school, holds that the government can do no right. Any intervention by this predatory state in the magic of the market place is bound to make matters worse. Government intervention is not the solution, it is the problem. A third theory, propounded by Anthony Downs (1957), holds that politicians maximise their own welfare by selling policies for votes. The social contract theories say that citizens surrender some of their rights in return for protection and other services from the state. Marxist theory says that the government is the executive committee of the ruling class and always serves the economic interests of that class. But this is open to different interpretations. Some regard the state as acting in the interest of international capital, extracting surplus from the periphery for the benefit of the centre. Others regard it as acting in the interest of an indigenous capitalist class, sometimes against the interest of the capitalists at the centre. According to both these views the state acts on behalf of the interest of a ruling class. A more sophisticated version of this theory holds that it is the function of the state to reconcile differences of interest within the ruling class so as to maintain its power and the capitalist mode of production. According to this version it is possible to impose price controls on food to keep workers quiet, in spite of the loss of short-term profits that this involves: the system is saved from revolt.

It has been argued in this chapter that governments are neither monolithic nor impervious to outside pressures, and that the obstacle to 'correct' policy making is neither stupidity nor cupidity, neither solely ignorance nor solely political constraints. At the same time, there are large areas in which a better analysis and a clearer sense of direction would help, just as there are areas where it is fairly clear what should be done, but vested interests prevent it from happening.

Yet it is futile (or tautological) to say, in such situations, that the political will is lacking. One does not have to be a behaviourist to believe that behaviour is the manifestation of the will. If the will to action is lacking, there is no point in asking for the will to have the will to action. It only leads to an infinite regress. It is a case of *ignotum per ignotius*. Political will itself can be subjected to analysis, to pressures, and to mobilisation, and it is more fruitful to think in terms of the construction of a political base for reform. Let us assume, for the purpose of this section, that the correct policies are known and that it is only a question of implementation. Compared with the large and growing literature on rent-seeking and directly unproductive profit-seeking activities, relatively little research has been done by political scientists into the question of how to build constituencies for reform or how to shape reformist coalitions or alliances between groups whose interests can be harnessed to the cause of reform. An exploration along these lines would draw attention to the desirability and feasibility of compensating losing groups, or to mobilisation of the power of dispersed, weak or inarticulate groups, or to participatory forms of organisation, or to the use of splits within the ruling groups for the benefit of the poor. It would analyse ways in which the work of the invisible foot can be co-ordinated to that of the invisible hand, how constituencies can be mobilised for the efficient and equitable allocation of resources.

3 PURSUIT OF SELF-INTEREST

People are, on the whole, quite good at discovering and pursuing their self-interest, and not much research is needed to steer them along this path. Yet there are many situations in which the individual is helpless and where procedures, rules or institutions are needed to give expression to his interests (Schelling, 1971). The rural and the urban poor are weak and powerless, particularly if not organised among themselves. It has been argued in a different context above that in societies in which power and wealth are very unequally distributed, both low producer prices and higher producer prices can reinforce the strength of powerful and rich groups. The interests behind low prices are the urban middle class, including the bureaucracy, the military, the police and politically active students, who have access to fair-price shops and to the imported food aid, and enjoy the benefits of low food prices. The rich and powerful farmers are often protected by subsidies and special allocations of scarce inputs. If this regime is changed to one of higher food prices, again the rich farmers may benefit, while the urban middle class may be protected by special measures under the pretext of protecting poor food consumers.

This does not mean that the interests of urban industrialists always prevail. The location of firms in politically important regions, even if less efficient, or the overmanning of factories to reduce urban unemployment, show that governments often sacrifice industrial profits for the benefit of other interest groups. But the poor rural producers' interests are neglected.

The fact that policies reflect power distributions is evident from the policies of rich countries which tend to tax the relatively poorer urban consumer for the benefit of the frequently better off farmer, while the opposite is true for most poor countries.[4]

The urban bias and discrimination against the rural sector that we observe so widely in the developing countries today were also practised by England and other European countries in the eighteenth and nineteenth centuries, long before current theories of industrialisation had been formulated. Adam Smith noted it in his *The Wealth of Nations*.[5]

It is possible to mobilise some powerful interests for the improvement of the fate of the poor, and to give the poor themselves more power. Thus in nineteenth-century England, before workers had organised themselves into powerful trade unions, or had the vote, the urban industrialists had an interest in low food prices in order to keep wages low, and agitated for the repeal of the Corn Laws, against the pressures of the Tory landlords who claimed that this would ruin British agriculture. It did not. The Tory landlords, on the other hand, under the leadership of the 7th Earl of Shaftesbury, opposed to the urban industrialists, agitated successfully for factory reforms, limiting the working day, getting children and women out of the mines, regulating and humanising conditions in factories, introducing safety legislation and so on, which the industrialists claimed would ruin British industry.[6] It did not. It was therefore the interest conflict between Tories and Liberals that benefited the poor, without destroying either industry or agriculture. Two main lessons can be learned from this experience. First, differences within the ruling group (in addition or as an alternative to the mobilisation of the poor) can be used to benefit the poor. Secondly, there is often scope for unperceived positive-sum games, in which feared losses from improvements in policies do not materialise and almost everybody benefits, even without compensation.

4 POLITICS AND FOOD POLICIES

We should like to know more about the links between politics and food policies. It would be interesting to relate, for instance, the removal of food subsidies to riots, disturbances or falls of governments. It would be useful to trace the groups that have an interest, direct or indirect, in higher food prices. It would be rewarding to trace the interests that can be mobilised for the measures needed in the period of transition.

In many developing countries the problem is how to mobilise interest groups for more remunerative prices to producers without harming poor food consumers. In some countries large and rich farmers are aligned with urban interests and against small and poor farmers. In others they make common cause with all agricultural interests. What are the conditions for this to occur?[7] But, not only in the advanced industrialised countries, high prices and other forms of protection for food producers have reached a point where political forces have to be mobilised for the reversal of these policies. South Korea, for example, has kept its high producer prices, which in the past fulfilled a useful function, for too long, and has created vested interests in their perpetuation. In such cases political coalitions for their reduction are needed. Subsidies to farmers tend to get capitalised into higher land values. The purchaser of the land with the inflated value would suffer unfairly if subsidies were reduced, and this adds to the difficulty in reducing or eliminating subsidies.

Making politics an endogenous variable is very attractive from the point of view of a relevant and realistic approach, but it raises a profound methodological difficulty. As long as we assume political forces to be exogenous variables, we can use them as levers to control the system: to preserve it, reform it or change it radically. But then they also lend themselves to the construction of Utopias, without practical constraints. However, once political factors are endogenous, they are determined within the system and advocacy of change becomes impossible. What appear to be obstacles in an analysis confined to economic variables become necessities when political variables are incorporated. If we accept determinism we have no choice. In order to get an Archimedean point from which to lift the system, we need some degrees of freedom within which ranges of policies can be regarded as independently determined.

There are some ways out of this dilemma. Max Corden (1984) suggests three. First, persons or groups concerned with the national or social interest, rather than with sectional interests, can, from a variety of motives, form part of the process of political pressure groups, and economic analysis can be used by them as the basis for their campaign. International agencies such as the World Bank may constitute such pressure groups, and the conditions attached to loans, aiming at the best interest of the receiving country, amounts to pressures that counteract the self-interested actions of the urban elites. It is then the external ever-juicier carrots, and even bigger sticks that provide the Archimedean point to lever the system out of its position. Second, normative economic analysis can show that the lobbies may not be efficient in pursuing their own interests, since they could all be better off if they followed efficient lines and compensated the losers. But this line of reasoning presents the difficulty that differences over the desirability and acceptability of the division of joint gains can prevent their achievement. Once gains are generally accepted, differences over their distribution are just as divisive as conflicts over the distribution without net gains. Compensation may be regarded as either undesirable, because the losers deserve to lose, or as not feasible, or, if feasible, excessively costly. Third, normative analysis may show the inefficiency of the competitive political lobbying process and suggest changes in institutions to produce better outcomes. In other words, the lobbying process need not be accepted as given but is itself subject to change. Of course this change can itself have costs and may produce non-optimal results. To this we might add a fourth possibility, viz. that the rulers do have the common interest at heart, at least partly, and resist the competitive self-interested pressures. (See Corden, 1984, p. 141.)

In this section the attempt has been made to incorporate political variables into the analysis of the response mechanism of food prices. Such an incorporation can provide a sounder basis for analysing responses to food prices than a narrow focus on producers' supply response and consumers' demand response, the way in which economic analysis is conventionally conducted. In principle, all relevant variables should be incorporated in a full analysis. In earlier sections we have paid some attention to the institutional arrangements which have an influence on responses. If, for example, marketing boards absorb a large proportion of higher prices, the supply response will be different from what it would be if the whole of extra profits were to accrue to the farmer. If women do the growing of food but men receive the money from its sale and make the decisions about expenditure, again supply responses will be different from what they would be if women themselves made the decisions. Or again the system of land ownership, such as share-cropping, and of tenurial arrangements will determine supply responses. Any analysis that claims to be useful to policy makers must not confine itself to the textbook variables of demand and supply and markets, but must investigate the institutional and political channels through which demand and supply are expressed.

Notes

1. For a brilliant discussion of the relation between prisoner's dilemma and Coase's theorem in a different context see Lipton (1985).
2. See Lipton (1985).
3. As Manfred Bienefeld (1986) points out at the end of his book *Markets and States in Tropical Africa*, Bates says, 'Alternatively, in response to the erosion of advantages engendered by shortfalls in production, the dominant interests may be persuaded to forsake the pursuit of unilateral short-run advantage, and instead to employ strategies that evoke co-operation by sharing joint gains.' But once this possibility is envisaged, the simplicity and neatness of Bates's argument is removed and choices become more complex and uncertain.
4. It might be thought that if high income countries with a small proportion of farmers protect them at the expense of the large urban population, while poor countries with a large agricultural population and a small urban population protect the urban minority at the expense of the rural majority, there must be some income level and distribution of population in between that is just right and where no discrimination, protection and exploitation takes place. The situation is reminiscent of the man who complained to a mathematician friend that, when he was young, he always liked much older women and when he was old, he always liked young girls. The mathematician friend said, 'But as you grew older and your tastes changed, there must have come a moment when they were the same age as you,' to which the man replied, 'Ah, but what is a moment!' Such a 'moment' must have occurred in South Korea, when it switched from discriminating against agriculture to discriminating in its favour. In England the 'moment' must have occurred in the late eighteenth or early nineteenth century.
5. 'The government of towns corporate was altogether in the hands of traders and artificers; and it was in the manifest interest of every particular class of them to prevent the market from being overstocked, as they commonly express it, with their own particular species of industry, which is in reality to keep it always understocked . . . In their dealings with the country they were all great gainers . . . Whatever regulations . . . tend to increase those wages and profits beyond what they would

otherwise be, tend to enable the town to purchase, with a smaller quantity of its labour, the produce of a greater quantity of the labour of the country. They give the traders and artificers of the town an advantage over the landlords, farmers and labourers in the country, and break down the natural equality which would otherwise take place in the commerce which is carried on between them . . . The industry that is carried on in towns is . . . more advantageous than that which is carried on in the country . . . In every country of Europe we find at least a hundred people who have acquired great fortunes . . . for every one who has done so by . . . raising of rude produce by the improvement and cultivation of land' Adam Smith (1776). I owe the quotation to the paper by Mancur Olson.

6. Gary Anderson and Robert Tollison (1984) argue that the Factory Acts were not the result of humanitarian impulses but 'actually represented the mechanism by which skilled male operatives attempted to limit competition from alternative labour supplies'. If this view is accepted, it reinforces the argument in the text that interest differences within powerful groups can be used for the benefit of the oppressed.

7. See Bienefeld (1986).

References

Anderson, G. and Tollison, R. (1984) 'A Rent-seeking Explanation of the British Factory Acts', Chapter 13 in Colander, David C. (ed.) *Neoclassical Political Economy: The Analysis of Rent Seeking and DUP Activities* (Cambridge, Mass.: Ballinger).

Bates, R.H. (1981) *Markets and States in Tropical Africa: The Political Basis of Agricultural Policies* (Berkeley: University of California Press).

Bates, R.H. (1983) *Essays on the Political Economy of Rural Africa* (Cambridge University Press).

Bienefeld, M. (1986) 'Analysing the Politics of African State Policy: Some Thoughts on Robert Bates's Work' *IDS Bulletin* vol. 17 no. 1.

Coase, R.H. (1960) 'The Problem of Social Cost', *Journal of Law and Economics* vol. 3 no. 3, October, pp. 1–44.

Corden, M. (1984) 'The Normative Theory of International Trade' in Jones, Ronald W. and Kenen, Peter B. (eds) *Handbook of International Economics* (Amsterdam: North Holland).

Downs, A. (1957) *An Economic Theory of Democracy* (New York: Harper and Row).

Lipton, M. (1977) *Why Poor People Stay Poor: Urban Bias in World Development* (Cambridge, Mass.: Harvard University Press).

Lipton, M. (1985) 'Prisoner's Dilemma and Coase's Theorem: A Case for Democracy in Less Developed Countries' in Matthews, R.C.O. (ed.) *Economy and Democracy* (London: Macmillan).

Magee, S. (1984) 'Endogenous Tariff Theory: A Survey' in Colander, David C. (ed.) *Neoclassical Political Economy: The Analysis of Rent Seeking and DUP Activities* (Cambridge, Mass.: Ballinger).

Olson, M. (1965) *The Logic of Collective Action* (Cambridge, Mass.: Harvard University Press).

Olson, M. (1982) *The Rise and Decline of Nations* (New Haven, Conn.: Yale University Press).

Olson, M. (1985) 'The Exploitation and Subsidization of Agriculture in Developing and Developed Countries' (mimeo).

Schelling, T. (1971) 'On the Ecology of Micro-Motives', *The Public Interest*, no 25, Fall and reproduced in Norton, W.W. (1978) *Micromotives and Macrobehavior*.

Smith, A. (1776) *The Wealth of Nations* Book 1, Chapter X Part II.

4 Contemporary Trends in Pricing of Industrial and Farm Products in the USSR and their Impact on Effectiveness of Production

V.I. Kiselev
USSR ACADEMY OF SCIENCES, MOSCOW

1 INTRODUCTION

The pricing policy for industrial and farm products in the USSR has exercised a substantial influence on rates of development and proportions of sectors of the agro-industrial complex (AIC) though its role is much less than in market economies. It is well known that in the USSR the basic proportions and directions of development are determined by the Plan and that prices act as the most important element of the mechanism for its fulfilment, determining to a considerable extent the level of production. Indeed the role of prices is now somewhat more important, and with the current development in markets the control functions of prices will become even more important. Nevertheless pricing problems need to be examined within the context of the whole mechanism of the centralised management of the economy, taking into account that prices determine the choice of economic decisions in combination with planning and accounting levers. To achieve a true understanding of the role and place of price-ratio problems in the economics of the AIC it is necessary to examine the basic conditions determining the character of the AIC development and its specific problems.

These problems became more acute especially in the second half of the 1970s and the beginning of the 1980s. In that period a growth

73

recession of the AIC economy emerged, which became more serious because of several successive years of poor harvests. Average rates of growth of farm output diminished by five-year periods (as compared to the preceding five-year period): 1966–70 by 21 per cent, 1971–5 by 16 per cent, 1976–80 by 13 per cent, 1981–5 by 7 per cent (*Narodnoye Khozyaistvo*, 1985, p. 228). In arable production the rate of growth as compared to the preceding period was only 4 per cent. The causes of this slump have been analysed in detail in Soviet economic and political publications and concrete actions were suggested. A plenary session of the CPSU Central Committee (May 1982) was devoted to the development problems of the agro-industrial complex, where the causes of adverse trends were analysed in detail and the principal means for their elimination determined. These were expressed in the food production programme and the decisions taken for its fulfilment (*Prodovolstvennaya programma SSSR*, 1983). That was the beginning of a radical reorganisation of the economic mechanism in the AIC carried out in the light of reforms of the economic and management system of the whole national economy. The main directions of these reforms were outlined by the XXVIIth Communist Party Congress (1986) and are now in the process of realisation.

2 CAUSES OF ADVERSE TRENDS

Let us examine briefly the main causes of the adverse trends in the agro-industrial complex that determined the substance of current reform.

1. Because of the multisectoral nature of agro-industrial sectors, the separate stages of final production based on agricultural raw materials were planned, financed and evaluated by different authorities using different approaches and criteria. As a consequence, the whole technological process disintegrated into a number of isolated elements. Economic separation of such important stages of the agro-industrial production process, including proper agriculture, its technical support and maintenance, fodder production, stocking and storage and processing of agricultural raw materials, led to unco-ordinated capacities of various stages of production and consequently to imbalance in the agro-industrial complex; to a divergence of economic interests;

to a natural drive to maximise sectoral gains with the neglect of the actual usefulness of these gains for the subsequent stages of production; and to the emergence of bottlenecks and losses at the interface of various stages of production.

2. There was a lessening in material incentives which expressed itself in weak relationships between wages and economic conditions in production units and ultimate results. It became the practice to support deficient production units at the expense of efficient ones by means of additional budget financing for the inefficient, providing them with financial privileges and so on. At the same time the valuations of work tasks were often reduced in the case of high economic achievers in order to curtail costs of farm products: pay differentials were less than the difference in economic results, which considerably undermined the stimuli to strive for high performance. The growth and improvement of production were prompted not by internal incentives but by orders and the Plan target sent out from above which exceeded, as a rule, the previous level and was sometimes unrelated to production capacity, social capabilities and material resources.

3. The weakening of economic control levers was of necessity compensated for by a strengthening of administrative methods of management. As a result continuous economic self-regulation, both in determining production plans and in current performance, was substantially lessened. Responsibility for results was reduced and the capacity of the production process continually to adapt to changes in conditions became rather limited.

4. The worsening of economic conditions in production units, caused by falling rates of return, thus led to deficiencies in the development of the agro-industrial complex. By 1980 more than half of all production units fell into great indebtedness and only an insignificant number of them possessed the means for their own development. The rate of return (the ratio of profit to capital assets and material circulating assets) was 10.2 per cent in 1970, then it fell to 2 per cent in 1975 and even became negative, at −0.3 per cent, in 1980. That is to say, agriculture as a whole had adverse balances of returns and costs (*Pribavochnyi product v APK*, 1983, p. 46).

3 THE PECULIARITIES OF THE PRICE SYSTEM

The obvious cause of the fall in the rate of return was the rapidly rising cost of agricultural production. In its turn that rise of costs was the consequence of several tendencies in the development of the agro-industrial complex and the national economy as a whole. First there was a rise in the volume of material and technical inputs, especially after 1965, when important decisions were taken concerning the rate of industrialisation of agriculture and the strengthening of its resource and technical base, resulting in a rapid build-up of capital investment in agricultural development. In 1961–5 the state invested 48.6 billion roubles in agriculture, but by 1966–70 the figure was 81.6 billion roubles, or 1.7 times more, and in the subsequent five-year period it was 130.5 billion roubles. As a result the per capita assets rose by 1980 to almost four times that of 1965. However, because of weak incentives and the other deficiencies mentioned above, those investments brought a rate of return much less than expected, which inevitably resulted in rising costs of agricultural output.

Second, an important part was played by the rise in prices of inputs for agriculture as well as of services provided by units of agroservice. One may regard the rise in the price of an industrial product as justified when it is followed by the proportional rise in its utility for the customer. But, as a number of case studies revealed, the prices of many products supplied to agriculture rose more rapidly than their efficient utilisation in agriculture. For example, the price of machines for ploughing rose by 3.1 times in 1970–80 when their productivity grew only by 1.9 times; for sowing, the growth was by 3.3 and 2.1 times respectively. The cost of shelter per head of cattle rose by 4 times between 1964 and 1980 (*Pribavochnyi product v APK* pp. 45–6). By the author's estimates, almost 60 per cent of the rise in agricultural production costs was due to excessive price rises for agricultural inputs.

What was behind such a price rise in the means of production? On the one hand there were increasing costs of raw materials, fuels and energy. On the other hand the deficiencies in the method of pricing also played their part. Prices of machines and equipment are set by the central authorities only for new models and types. Prices of modified models containing only minor changes in their design are set by collectives and ministries with reference to the basic price. Such a practice permits modifications to models to take account more rapidly of a new level of costs and reflect it in their prices, but at the same time it introduces the possibility of price increases under the guise of technical innovations which often have doubtful benefit for agriculture. These peculiarities of pricing have led to incessant price rises in the technical base of agriculture and hence increasing costs of crops.

The purchase prices of agricultural products are set only by the central bodies. They do not depend on the quality of crops produced or planned and are seldom reviewed to bring them into line with the actual costs of production, even if the latter have grown appreciably throughout the country as a whole.

The purchase prices of agricultural products appear to vary less than the prices of means of production for agriculture. To a certain degree this is connected with the social aspect of pricing policy. The Soviet prices for foodstuffs are fixed at a comparatively low level in order to ensure their availability for all strata of the population, having regard to the level of minimum wages. For these reasons certain foodstuffs are supplied to the population at prices which are below the costs of production. For example, the retail price of meat is about half its production cost. The state bears the large additional expense to cover the difference between the retail and purchases prices. In order to curtail such costs, purchase prices are maintained if possible below the retail price level.

Over time the situation is even more complex. First prices of production for agricultural inputs rose, which together with the increasing volume of material and technical resources used led to continuous rises in costs of farm products. At the same time purchase prices for particular products in certain regions were stable. When the rate of return fell and farm incomes dropped to an unbearable level, purchase prices were increased, the rate of return was restored for some time, then costs rose and all was repeated once again. The conditions of farm performance were thus dissimilar over time and this affected the rate of growth.

The complicated theoretical and practical problem is how to stabilise the costs of farm products over time, or at least to stabilise the economic conditions of production for collective and state farms. One possibility is to increase state subsidies to collective and state farms for the purchase of the means of production. Thus in the USSR some types of agricultural machinery, fuels, electrical power and fertilisers, are currently sold to farms at less than their wholesale prices. For example, the selling price of the first 100 grain harvesters of the 'Don' type was a quarter of their wholesale price (Borozdin, 1986) though such a large subsidy is exceptional. This is an effective way to stabilise external conditions for agriculture, but its extended use is limited by the level of financial resources of the state. On the other hand the increase in raw material and energy costs is a general phenomenon and there is no reason to make an exception for agriculture. If the rise in price of an input is reflected in the efficiency of its utilisation in agriculture, then it appears to be justified. The important thing is to prevent an unjustified rise in prices – see Section 5.

The second possibility consists of continuous synchronisation of purchase and wholesale prices. In this area new opportunities are now being created. From 1987, the Union Republics Councils of Ministers are permitted to alter, if necessary, purchase prices of selected farm products, within certain bounds. On a nationwide scale it is envisaged that purchase prices will be reviewed every five years, depending on the actual correlation between purchase prices of farm products and wholesale prices of industrial produce sold to farms. These measures in the aggregate create the necessary economic conditions for maintaining the rate of return of agricultural production in the bulk of farms and facilitate necessary savings for enlarged production.

4 THE REFORM OF AIC

These measures are directed not so much at reducing production costs but rather at eliminating the impact of price on industrial products used in agriculture. The bulk of the measures envisaged by the current reform is directed towards the reduction of production costs in agriculture by way of growth of crops, productivity of livestock and labour productivity. Their features are on the whole explained by those deficiencies of the economic mechanism mentioned in Sections 2 and 3. The most important elements of the reform in the agro-industrial complex are as follows.

First, the management systems at various levels of the economic hierarchy must be integrated by means of the formation of unified management bodies for agro-industrial production both in the centre (the USSR Gosagroprom) and in the provinces. The CPSU XXVIIth Congress set the task to plan, finance and manage the agro-industrial complex on all levels as a single whole. This means that local management systems, for example, district agro-industrial agencies, will be given plans only for the production and sale of farm products to state agencies without intermediate plans or targets, which were formerly generated in great numbers due to the departmental character of planning. Factories of the State Committee of Farm Machinery, for example, were given the plan for machinery repair works without consideration of the real need for repairs, and this to some extent adversely affected the quality of machinery repair. Budget financing will be allocated to local management agencies without detailed allocations, thus expanding their capacity to identify bottle-necks and to outline effective measures for their removal depending on the current situation. Thereby the real managing capacity of local management agencies, which directly carry out the production and possess the most complete information about the degree of balance between various elements of production, are expanded.

Second, a strict dependence of pay of labour on the results of economic activity has been introduced. In particular, from 1987 the wage fund in state farms and other state agricultural enterprises will be formed by the farms themselves on the basis of stable norms for 100 roubles of products sold, set for five years. Simultaneously the collective contract is introduced generally in agriculture, according to which labour is paid strictly in accord with volume and quality of output produced. (Before, labour was usually paid according to volume and quality of agrotechnical operations but not of output produced.) Together with a collective contract, it is recommended that the use of family contracts be developed, according to which output of cattle, machinery, fertilisers and so on, is sold by families to collective and state farms at prices stipulated in advance and under known conditions of use of socially owned lands. In order to strengthen the incentives to the economic use of plots of land attached to households, which in recent years have tended to decrease, livestock and poultry bred in households are purchased by agricultural co-operative organisations and collective and state farms at co-operative trade prices, so that purchased products are included in the fulfilment of the plan of sales to the state. The reform also envisages measures to stimulate the employment of management personnel as well as specialists to improve production and rates of return and to reduce costs. The size of bonuses will be set depending on these indicators.

Third, essential changes have been introduced in the financing of agro-industrial production. Specifically, state farms and other state agricultural enterprises are granted the right to distribute profits at their discretion and to use financial resources at their disposal for financing planned measures irrespective of their source. Granting of credits to collective and state farms will be carried out with consideration of rational employment of their own resources and the timely reimbursement of credits received. In their turn, credits will be granted without prescribed allotment to concrete purposes.

Fourth, measures have been taken to promote an interest in the growth and intensification of farm production. With this end in view, special funds are created to pay for output produced above the plan levels at substantially increased prices. This will facilitate the compensation of increased costs connected with a high level of intensification, as well as increasing profits due to a reduction in the level of costs. The increased prices take two forms: first, extra prices are introduced for farm products sold above the average level of the preceding five-year period. In particular, an extra price of 100 per cent is introduced for grains of all kinds (on condition of fulfilment of grain sales to the state plan) and a 50 per cent extra price for other farm products. Second, collective and state farms are permitted to sell the output produced above the plan as well as 30 per cent of the planned volume of fruit and vegetables to consumer co-operative organisations and on kolkhoz markets at contractual prices. It is noteworthy that prices in co-operative trade or at kolkhoz markets for these crops are, as a rule, several times higher than state purchase prices. Thus the range of prices at which collective and state farms can sell their output is expanded.

Only the most important directions of the reform designed to stimulate economic activity in the agro-industrial complex are selected here. The future will show what measures need to be developed further and what additional improvements will be needed. The analytical and constructive management style of the present administration guarantees that necessary measures will be taken without delay.

5 REQUIREMENTS OF THE PRICE SYSTEM

The very important socio-economic requirement to be satisfied is the provision of a favourable environment for rapid economic development. The necessary requirement of such an environment is to counter the trends of rising costs and to maintain a sound rate of return which depends to a large extent on pricing policy. A set of rather complicated problems needs to be solved for both purchase prices of farm products and the wholesale prices of industrial products supplied to agriculture.

First of all it is necessary that purchase prices fulfil their four main functions more effectively: *stimulating* – to ensure a sufficient return for enlarged production and labour remuneration; *planning* – to orientate economic units to the choice of optimal structures of output; *distributing* – to distribute the surplus product among various participants of production as well as among producers and the state; *equalising* – to ensure equal economic conditions for collective and state farms located in different conditions of soil and climate. At present all these functions are fulfilled only by purchase prices differentiated by regions with reference to land productivity. During the last decade it has become accepted that the three last functions are better fulfilled by the economic valuation of land. According to this idea, purchase prices of farm products must be fixed at the level of marginal costs (the charge for land being at its cadastral valuation). Surplus product, emerging in the best conditions of soil and climate, should be taken away with the help of differential rent corresponding to the economic valuation of land. Such an approach has several advantages:

1. In various long-range plans the economic effectiveness of different land uses is revealed quite obviously. Specifically influencing choices of crop are structure, variants of hydrotechnical and irrigation construction, land allotments for non-farm uses, and so on.
2. The specialisation of regions in most profitable outputs is carried out more consistently (provided that economic units are allowed to determine the crop area structure themselves).

   Indeed, the rate of differential rent is fixed by the economic valuation of land and does not depend on the actual volume of output. Output may be sold with high gains corresponding to low marginal costs but, within the plan limits, an economic unit would get normal profits, since surplus product is taken away in the form of rent in favour of the state. Surplus product emerging in the production of output in excess of the plan is fully retained in the economic unit. The better the natural conditions for the crop in the locality, the bigger the difference between the price and costs, the more profitable is the production of this crop in excess of plan. The system induces, on the one hand, intensification of profitable crop production and, on the other hand, the enlargement of area of this crop and thereby more specialisation of economic units.

3. Conditions of production are sometimes rather different, even within the same economic unit. Cadastral valuation can be differentiated in great detail, but at the same time purchase prices, fixed centrally, cannot be so differentiated.

4. When the use of land is paid for, then the problem of regulation of incomes from personal subsidiary plots is treated more rationally from the economic viewpoint, and opportunities to organise family contracts are increased.

The main objections to the transition to prices fixed at the level of marginal costs are as follows:

(a) For an economic unit the calculation will be complicated; first it will be paid a large sum of money and then a substantial part of it will be withdrawn as a differential rent. However, if the recalculation is carried out directly by purchasing agencies, then for economic units there would be no apparent difference.

(b) There would be an inevitable rise in purchase prices with transition to unified cadastral pricing and a consequent rise in prices of farm products. The effects of purchase price excess over retail prices are not clear.

(c) It would necessitate radical changes in the total price system as well as in the financial–credit system.

(d) Specialisation of regions can also be achieved with a differentiated price system since profitability of crops is different. The main obstacle to more intense specialisation is not, however, an absence of pay for land use, but the planned targets. The enlarged opportunities for economic units to choose the structure of crop areas will facilitate more specialisation. It is noteworthy that in the case of uniform prices the economic effectiveness of specialisation will be higher for economic units the higher are the marginal costs. Thus, if the actual cost (including sufficient profit for reinvestment) is 100 roubles per tonne and the planned cost is 500 roubles per tonne (such a differential in production cost is realistic in Soviet conditions), any above-plan output will yield additional profits of 400 roubles per tonne, thereby ensuring that the incentives for enlargement of output will be extremely strong. As already noted, at present the growth of output over the level previously achieved is also encouraged by a mark-up to a purchase price, but to a lesser degree. The question arises whether it is reasonable to create such a stimulatory mark-up. After all, it may lead to a strong preference of current interests over long-term ones, and as a consequence to a transition to a mono-crop economy in the most favourable regions.

Thus, the transition to uniform prices on the basis of marginal costs, demanding serious transformation of the financial calculation system, will have some advantages, but neither so great nor so certain that this concept can be used without further elaboration and precision.

It is logical to conclude that differential rent is the economic tool more appropriate to a management system using economic levers when the plan is not specifically applied to that system. In this case the state assures a guaranteed income for itself in the form of rent regardless of results of production. Economic units receive profit strictly as the difference between revenue and cost with an unlimited possibility to determine the output composition at their own discretion, being orientated by the system of prices and land valuations.

In the planned system, uniform prices are important only for the estimation of the effectiveness of different lines of development, including land use. Generally speaking, it is possible to use economic valuations of land in the projected elaborations without introducing actual pay for land use.

At the same time a justified view is that if prices and land valuations would not affect actual economic interests, then the incentives for their improvement disappear. With this viewpoint in mind, it appears reasonable to seek transitional forms according to which uniform prices are introduced by geographic–climatic zones and within them the conditions of economic activity are equalised with the aid of differential rent.

It is worth stressing that intensification and specialisation of production are likely to increase with the independence of economic units and payment in proportion to final results, but not with the introduction of economic valuation of land. The last functions only as a tool, equalising conditions of economic activity.

The prevention of a rise in unit costs in agriculture can be brought about by a number of means: lowering costs of industrial products, increasing their quality, accelerating growth of their productivity, prolongation of their service life, lowering collective and state farm outlays for maintaining machinery in working condition. Most of these problems are beyond the capacity of the agro-industrial complex and will be solved in the course of reform of the whole national economy. At present separate elements of such a reform are in the process of elaboration and gradual realisation. One of the elements of this reform is a set of measures designed to improve incentives to raise the technical level and the quality of farm machinery. In particular, prices to stimulate the production of farm machinery will be introduced over a two-year period, the increments being justified by the effect for the economy as a whole derived from improved reliability in use and reduced need for spare parts.

In a planned economy, the mechanism restraining unjustified rises in prices, that is, the price for a unit of consumer welfare gain, has its special features. If in market economies some restriction of a rise in prices is imposed by competition, then in planned economies such restrictions may be formed by consumers in the process of planned elaboration of economic normatives.

Improvement in prices of productive assets for agriculture has to be directed first of all to the complete and precise calculation of consumer welfare arising from this machinery. Here difficulties are not of a theoretical but of an organisational nature. At present such gains are calculated not by a consumer but by the producer of, for example, farm equipment. Naturally in such calculations this gain is overestimated. Agricultural bodies now participate in fixing prices of industrial products for farm use. They participate especially in the adoption of new models; they inform industries about preferred technical requirements of machines; they calculate the marginal price that indicates the limit within which the productive machine can be used by farms with profit. But often all these data are established at the discretion of the manufacturer, which undermines the authority of the customer and gives additional arguments for discouraging his participation in the adoption of new equipment. His very participation in the process is not considered necessary.

At present there remains only one decisive step to be taken in order to transform hypothetical opportunities envisaged by pricing regulations into reality (Borozdin, 1986; Biriukov, 1980). This step has two parts: first, to proceed strictly and consistently from consumer gain for the estimation of which it is necessary to organise interdepartmental commissions of experts; second, to fix prices centrally only for the products which define the structure of the AIC, and to fix prices for other products on the basis of contracts between a producer and a consumer, the latter having a decisive voice on whether to buy or not.

References

Biriukov, U.V. (1980) *Problemy sovershenstvovaniva tsen na sredstva proizvodstva dlia selskogo khoziaistva* (Problems of Improvement of Prices of the Means of Production for Agriculture) (Moscow: Politizdat).

Borozdin, U.V. (1986) 'Tseny i effectivnost' (Prices and Efficiency), *Ekonomicheskaya gazeta* 21.

Narodnoye khozyaistvo SSSR v 1984g. (1985) (Annual Statistics) (Moscow: Finansy i statistika).

XXVIIth Communist Party Congress, *Osnovnye napravlenia ekonomicheskogo i sotsialnogo razvitiya SSSR na 1986–90 gody i na period do 2000 goda* (1986) (Guidelines for Economic and Social Development in the USSR for the period 1986–90 and up to 2000) (Moscow: Politizdat).

Pribavochnyi product v APK (1986) (Surplus Product in AIC) (Moscow: Nauka 1983).

Prodovolstvennaya programma SSSR na period do 1990 goda i mery po eyo realizatsii (1983) (Food Programme of the USSR and Measures for its Realisation) (Moscow: Politizdat).

Discussion on Part I

PAPER BY ROMEO M. BAUTISTA

'Domestic Terms of Trade and Agricultural Growth in Developing Countries'

The lead discussant, Dr Hans Binswanger, saw the paper as addressing three important questions: (1) What has actually happened to agricultural terms of trade in low- and middle-income economies? (2) What determines terms of trade; are they determined independently of agricultural output and final demand? (3) What is the long-run aggregate supply elasticity of agricultural output?

He noted particularly that terms of trade had deteriorated in only a few developing countries, that instabilities were no larger in developing countries than in developed countries, and that supply elasticities appeared to be quite low.

The finding of low aggregate supply elasticities is consistent with the existing literature and work recently carried out by Binswanger, Mundlak, *et al.* Low elasticities in the short run arise because farmers need inelastically supplied inputs to expand aggregate agricultural output, and, unlike for individual crops, where supply elasticities are high, cannot obtain these inputs simply from other crops. Furthermore, expansion of aggregate output depends on investment in 'shifter variables' such as education and public infrastructure, which can be expanded only in the long run in response to price increases.

Binswanger liked Bautista's idea of trying to estimate supply responses by basing the regression analysis on aggregate data covering a long time span (1960–84) rather than annual changes. He felt that follow-up analysis could usefully examine the simultaneous interrelationships in more detail. Also, the possibility of building up

87

estimates of supply responses via an econometric approach that incorporated such variables as investment and migration responses could be worth exploring.

Professor Bautista acknowledged these problems, particularly the matter of data reliability and consistency over time and among countries. One discussant called special attention to inadequacies of national agricultural price statistics and how they were often vague averages, without anyone being clear about their locational or seasonal orientation, or the extent to which they reflected price controls and subsidies. Still, Bautista believed that his had been a useful exercise of trying to see what could be learned from the data at hand. He felt that need for such analysis was especially great for Africa, where little has been known about the prices facing farmers and their responses to these prices.

As pointed out by Binswanger, a major inference of Bautista's study was that, while some of the 41 countries had encountered periods of considerable deterioration and/or instability since 1960, there was no clear trend for agricultural terms of trade to decline or to become less stable. Regarding production trends, as measured by agricultural value added, growth rates for the African countries had been lower than for the others.

Ms Mukherji called attention to the new patterns of economic slowdowns and instabilities following the 1970s oil crisis, and urged closer examination of the exact mechanisms through which such changes are translated into terms of trade instabilities.

Krishan Rao expressed scepticism about focusing on price mechanisms when non-price factors including the predominance of public enterprises and administered prices have been playing important roles. Moreover price data used not only might be highly aggregative averages of unclear composition, but also obscured true relationships because of structural changes taking place. The selection of base period had significant bearing on results.

Bautista argued that the use of a 25-year time span, instead of impairing the analysis, filtered out some year-to-year irregularities. He said that regression analysis of the 1960–72 and 1972–84 periods separately had not brought out significant differences in coefficients.

Tyagi questioned whether the method of analysis could capture the technological changes that had affected agricultural output. Investment and farmers' incomes perhaps could have more influence on growth than do terms of trade.

B. Vaidyanathan raised the issue as to whether *gross value* of agricultural output would have been better than the agricultural *value added* indicator used in the analysis. Bautista stated that use of gross output had not occurred to him because of the problem of double-counting intermediate inputs.

Ms Mukherji found the net import function inadequate because food aid, which can have varying importance and effects, had not been made an explicit variable.

T.W. Schultz called attention to the need to think about *economic meaning* when selecting indicators and methodologies for such analysis. He illustrated by asking: what if the real cost of producing wheat were to be reduced by half? Would use of terms of trade (agricultural/non-agricultural price ratios) as an indicator adequately signal the implications for farmer response and equilibrium adjustments? This stimulated some discussion, centering on the fact that terms of trade reflect costs in very indirect manner only.

PAPER BY GUSTAV RANIS

'Macro Policies, the Terms of Trade and the Spatial Dimension of Balanced Growth'

The paper by Professor Gustav Ranis brought into sharper focus the spatial dimension of dualistic economies – the need for domestic terms of trade to encourage agricultural and industrial integration at local levels, building upon a honeycomb network of small urban centres and surrounding rural areas.

The lead discussant, Professor Lance Taylor, felt that Professor Ranis had offered astute observations about micro-level agricultural–industrial sectoral linkages, but how these all added up to form a cohesive model to guide analyses and policies had not been made clear.

He felt also that the Ranis analysis saw agriculture too much as a 'milch cow' – that it assumed there was a large economic surplus in the rural hinterland. In particular, (1) food and other rural outputs were often non-traded goods with their own unique set of opportunity costs, (2) price distortions often tended to resolve themselves, and (3) the key issue was how to help increase local productivity.

In his response, Ranis emphasised that his intended focus had not been on rural taxation (that is, not on 'where the milk goes') but, instead, on unexplored opportunities to increase both agricultural and non-agricultural productivity in rural areas. He felt that these opportunities lay beyond agricultural production technology *per se*; that the gains were to be found in fostering agriculture–industry interlinkages, through ties between urban centres and surrounding rural areas which facilitates urban–rural output and trade. The local market is a focal point for making the most of transport cost reductions and scale economies. In this context high population densities in certain localities could be beneficial. Ranis viewed governments as having important roles in improving transportation and avoiding discrimination against locally appropriate technologies and goods. His framework of analysis was particularly relevant to large countries, such as China and India and a number of the low-income countries of Africa.

Karl Wohlmuth raised the question as to what specific measures could strengthen the degree of rural–urban proximity. In large spread-out countries, integrated, efficient transport systems and port facilities are particularly important. Formation of market networks was a matter not only of physical marketing and distribution facilities but also communication and financial arrangements to enable people to make full use of these facilities.

Questions were also asked about the effect that the decentralised rural–urban network of Ranis would have upon the land values and the system of taxation and subsidy.

PAPER BY PAUL STREETEN

'The Politics of Food Prices'

Professor Irma Adelman, in introducing Professor Streeten's paper, stressed how she had come to appreciate the roles of prices – in particular food prices and industrial/agricultural terms of trade – which have important impacts on distribution as well as growth and which are closely interlinked with domestic politics. She noted that almost no country allows food prices to be completely free. For these reasons she welcomed Streeten's 'subtle analysis' of divergent interest groups and pressures impinging on policies relating to food prices – urban middle classes, industrial workers, government officials, the military, students, industrialists, land owners and large farmers, among others.

Adelman said that Streeten's paper viewed most policy balances as coming somewhere between two extremes: (1) Coase's positive-sum game situation which affords the possibility of arriving at policy agreements through spontaneous winner–loser compensation, based on well-defined property rights, and (2) prisoner's dilemma situations, in which unco-ordinated pursuits of individual interests lead to turmoil, confrontation, inefficient solutions, everyone ending up worse off, and need for strong government interventions. This applies not only to food price policies but also to policies bearing on input subsidies, agricultural research, and rural development.

Adelman noted also Streeten's attention to historical antecedents in England, where major industrial, finance, and wage-structure changes in the eighteenth and nineteenth centuries led to new alliances and pressures among the powerful interest groups that carried indirect benefits to the rural and urban poor. To her, an important point here was that policies related to agricultural institutions and prices must be able to change dynamically; they ought not to be regarded as just a static arrangement. That is, one must be prepared to shift out of a system such as food subsidies at some point in time.

In clarifying his paper further, Paul Streeten stressed four points:

1. He was attempting to examine why it is that countries do not often 'get prices right'. Agricultural and industrial terms of trade are seldom at their equilibrium points. One must examine the rural–urban relationships and pressures that lead to price levels and policies as they actually come about.

2. Concerning the government as the vehicle for correcting prices, in earlier times it was thought that the state could do no wrong; now, the state is often viewed as being able to do no right.

   The question raised in the paper is: if everything is determined within the political system, how can policies be changed for the better? Few economists have addressed this. One possible answer is to encourage formation of pressure groups to advocate the common good; to counterbalance pressures from various rural and urban special-interest groups. Another approach is to try to introduce institutional and compensatory changes which make everyone better off.

3. Do not swallow the *whole* public-choice story, according to which

a narrow interpretation of selfish man is transferred to politics. Some economists are correct in moving away from the single-goal economic man notion towards a perception that policies reflect multiple sets of preferences. But the public-choice school builds the motivation of selfish interest heavily into its model of political action. In contrast, he had come to think that there is need to build a political–economic theory which allows for self-critical and altruistic behaviour and other departures from maximum individual gain. Nor are interest groups monolithic.

4. Surprising results can occur in the political–economic arena. This was brought out in his example of England in the nineteenth century, where industry flourished after imposition of the labour laws, despite expectations of factory owners that they would be made worse off, and agriculture flourished after the repeal of the Corn Laws which was thought to ruin it. This showed (a) that the ruling class is divided and (b) that losses are not inevitable.

P.C. Sarker queried whether Streeten's paper had not concentrated too much on a particular role of prices. He felt that prices grow out of traditions that reflect several dimensions and that changes in pricing conditions could be viewed as a way to realise a set of public objectives.

Krishna Bharadwaj observed that an obsession with looking at the functioning of the economy in terms of pressure groups alone, as though they are autonomous formations, might lead to losing sight of the economic system. She noted that economists tend to go from one extreme to another – first emphasising technology, labour productivity, and profit maximisation and then, at the other extreme, talking in terms of human motivations and pressure groups without much objective analysis. She felt that some of both is needed, in which political and rent-seeking activities are cast within a framework of objective laws, such as Adam Smith had contributed in his day. She wondered what kind of objective system for viewing pressure-group activity Streeten had in mind.

L.S. Singh believed that price policies had often been too much against the rural sector. Also he felt that Streeten, when describing eighteenth- and nineteenth-century England, should have mentioned the social cost of British agricultural development and how it would be hard for many developing countries to emulate that.

H.M. Desarada expressed the view that Streeten's paper had not gone far enough – that it had not fully grappled with the economic problems underlying political pressures. Also he believed that to talk only in terms of rural–urban distinctions is too broad and that one must examine more closely the pressures within rural areas to maintain class balances. In his view, since 60 per cent of the rural masses are net buyers, relative prices matter very much.

R. Pradhan observed that economic models tend to take a narrow view of human behaviour. He was pleased that Streeten had taken a broader view. But he wondered what kind of model Streeten's line of thought could lead to. One that is oriented towards maximum utility? One that focuses on lines of political interaction? Or what?

Picking up a similar point, another speaker called attention to the last sentence of Streeten's paper, which says that, rather than being confined to supply and demand variables *per se*, useful analysis must examine the institutional and political channels through which these variables are expressed. An example in India that was mentioned was the way in which US production surpluses had led to the Public Law 480 programme, huge amounts of food aid and, in turn, significant price declines in India. It was felt that Streeten's analysis should come to grips with this type of political wave-effect.

P.N. John noted that needs and pressures for the government to keep food prices low in towns and cities still existed in India. He wonder how this fitted into Streeten's theory.

R.P. Singh said it was important to go beyond attention to *pressure* groups to examine the specific wants of the *interest* groups underlying these pressures. For example, small farmers have keen interest in increasing production, marketability of their output, and stability of prices and income.

D.D. Guru pointed to the need to look beyond state and national price policies to the forces affecting *international* price levels, which can have significant effects on domestic prices. However, he noted that, even when international and domestic prices have gone high, farm production in India has not responded quickly. Other elements seem to be involved.

Mahesh Bhatt asked whether one can really speak of the politics of *food prices* independently of the politics of *product mix*.

In concluding the discussion, Professor Streeten noted that much of the political–economics literature is about how policy decisions actually *do* get made. He would want to add a normative approach and focus on how food policy decisions *should* be made, and how a reformist coalition can be forged. He felt that vague terms like 'political will' should be banned from discussion and replaced by 'political base'. He noted with satisfaction some tendency for the normative diagnostics to receive more attention, but believed that a richer theory of the state was still needed.

Streeten attached considerable significance to the question of creating a 'political base' to defend the interests of the vulnerable classes and to use divisions within the ruling class for the benefit of the poor. He agreed with the view that it is not very meaningful to use only rural–urban distinctions when identifying important interest groups. (Is a large, rich and often absentee land-owner rural or urban? Is a villager embraced by a growing city rural or urban?) Instead he preferred rich–poor distinctions for analytical purposes.

PAPER BY V.I. KISELEV

'Contemporary Trends in Pricing of Industrial and Farm Products in the USSR and their Impact on Effectiveness of Production[1]

Professor Béla Csikós–Nagy, the lead discussant, helped to place Professor Kiselev's paper in the perspective of similar transitions and policy issues taking place in some other Eastern European countries. The collectivised economies like the Soviet Union face special challenges when establishing norms and information bases related to agricutural terms of trade, especially when central- and market-pricing approaches are being combined. The paper analyses the system which is now emerging and its effects on production incentives. It considers some specific methods for determining prices of agricultural products, labour, and inputs where state enterprises interface with collective contracting and supplementary household production.

The collective production system is still the mainstay. Private household production of certain crops and lifestock products is seen as only a *supplement* to state activities, in the interest of making fuller use of the available labour of women and children.

Professor Kiselev stressed that, in expanding the use of team contracts and to some extent family contracts, the main aim was to connect wages more strongly with the results of agricultural production.

The arrangement for contract labour and household production were still evolving and subject to further refinement. For example, subsidised energy and feed from state enterprises continued to bring windfall benefits to other production units and this needed re-examination.

The pricing of basic food staples and major farming inputs such as machinery is still mainly a state decision. Certain other items are free to move up or down in price only within certain bounds.

Part II

Influence of World Trade on the Balance Between Agriculture and Industry

Introduction to Part II

I.M.D. Little
NUFFIELD COLLEGE, OXFORD

The chapters in this part concentrate either on LDCs in general or Africa and Latin America. Indian problems are not to the fore, but since the setting was a *World* Congress there is no need to apologise. The papers also concentrate on trade in agricultural products. This was a deliberate choice, as I thought that trade in manufacturing was more likely to be covered extensively in other sessions.

The paper by MacBean in Chapter 5 examines the causes of decline in the share of developing countries in world exports. He finds explanation in the specialisation of certain tropical products where demand grows slowly and where the competition from synthetics is serious, in protection by developed countries and in policies in the developing countries themselves which have been detrimental, amongst other things hampering exports.

Then in Chapter 6, Lord looks at commodity exports from Latin America. He examines the situation of exporters *vis-à-vis* price changes and also against the new theory of trade dealing with product differentiation and monopolistic competition. He looks too at the demand side for the commodities. The findings confirm expectations that policies aimed at promoting the supply of exports would have favourable results in these countries, though because of variations in the response of export supply to price changes, the effectiveness of policies would vary from country to country.

Lastly the paper by Oyejide and Tran in Chapter 7 reports on empirical work that examines the structure and growth of food and agricultural imports into Africa, together with the causes of the high imports and elasticities of demand. They found very different factors underlying the demand for food imports according to the income of the countries concerned. The role of pricing policies in slowing down imports and their likely success is discussed.

It is possible to highlight some of the points from the papers presented. Clearly protection hinders agricultural exports from LDCs. But the LDC loss of shares in world trade in almost all agricultural products results from the fact that the growth of agriculture in most LDCs does not keep pace with rising demand, owing to population growth and higher living standards. LDCs became net food importers in the mid-1970s.

The growth of agriculture in LDCs has been inhibited by inappropriate policies – excessive industrial protection, overvalued exchange rates and taxation of agricultural exports. This is most especially true of Africa. There is a clear case for reform, though no need to strive for self-sufficiency. There is a wide consensus so far as this goes.

There were several contributions to the liberalisation debate. Clearly liberalisation by developed countries could result in an increase of agricultural exports from LDCs and hence an increase of output and rural employment. But LDCs' governments might thwart this tendency by preventing higher prices from reaching the farmers. There is some reason to fear this. Be that as it may, as against any benefits on the side of exports one has to set the fact that LDCs are now net importers of food, and that food prices would rise with reduced protection in the North. Calculation of the balance of cost and benefit is exceedingly difficult and tortuous, and involves many behavioural assumptions. The many calculators all seem to agree that whether plus or minus, the net benefit or loss would be small. I myself do not trust even this conclusion. I believe that econometricians always underestimate the long-run elasticities of response.

Much less doubt was expressed about the benefits that would accrue to LDCs if they liberalised themselves – that is, if their farmers could sell and buy at world market prices. However, one important aspect of this, the benefits that should accrue from increased agricultural trade among LDCs, was not explicitly examined.

Lastly, further consideration is merited by the idea in Lord's paper that agricultural products should be regarded as differentiated rather than homogeneous, and that there is therefore room for price-setting rather than simple price-taking, with potential competitive gains for LDCs, since for almost all products – the exceptions being tea, cocoa and coffee – LDCs would be competing with the industrialised countries as much as or more than with themselves.

5 Agricultural Exports of Developing Countries: Market Conditions and National Policies

Alasdair I. MacBean
UNIVERSITY OF LANCASTER AND WORLD
BANK, WASHINGTON

1 INTRODUCTION

The share of developing countries in world exports of agricultural products has declined sharply over the last 15 years. How far is this decline the result of factors beyond anyone's control or of policies in the industrial nations or of policies in the developing countries themselves? A rough assignment of causes is the modest objective of this paper.

Developing countries' main agricultural exports are tropical products: the beverages – cocoa, coffee and tea – cane sugar, vegetable oils, fibres (cotton, jute and hard fibres), rubber, timber, tobacco and rice – but also wheat, maize, meats, fruits and wine. The beverages have little direct competition from developed industrial countries, but most of the rest do meet direct, or fairly close indirect, competition from the agricultural sectors of the industrialised nations. This competition takes place both in the national markets of the industrial countries and in third markets. The policies of the industrial nations, by protecting domestic agricultural producers against foreign competition in their home markets, and by subsidising exports of agricultural surpluses, clearly damage developing countries' agricultural exports in both the short and long run. These policies not only restrict developing countries' exports, but also lower and destabilise their prices. Because they lower prices, they also provide benefits to food importing developing countries, at least in the short run. But the industrial countries'

101

system of agricultural economic policies is a wasteful means of trying to meet their political and social objectives.

The developing countries themselves have also reduced their agricultural exports by their own policies. Studies by the World Bank and academic scholars (See *World Bank, 1986*, pp. 162–8 for an extensive bibliography) have stressed the disincentive impact of overvalued exchange rates, low producer prices, export taxation, the effects of excessive industry protection and incentives for import substituting industries as major causes of poor agricultural performance and of retarded exports.

Finally, many analysts have pointed to the economic characteristics of agricultural products as a reason for developing countries to diversify out of them into manufactures. But this factor on its own, even accepting that the demand for agricultural products grows more slowly than the demand for manufactures, would not explain a falling share of world agricultural exports.

A possible explanation for a falling share could be that the particular commodity exports in which developing countries specialise grow more slowly than do the agricultural commodities exported by the rest of the world. This possibility is easily tested and a simple test for it is carried out in Section 3 of the paper.

2 THE GENERAL PICTURE ON AGRICULTURAL EXPORTS

Between 1961–3 and 1982–4 the share of developing countries' exports in total agricultural exports fell from 63 per cent to 48 per cent. The drop was particularly marked in food where their share fell from 45 to 34 per cent. In the mid-1970s developing countries' food trade balance went from positive to negative while the industrial countries' trade balance shifted from negative to a quite massive surplus (World Bank, 1986, p. 11).

Agricultural production did not, however, show the same relative performance. For agricultural production the LDCs trend rate of growth was faster than in the industrial countries (see Figure 5.1). Food production showed a similar performance (World Bank, 1986, p. 5).

Most of this growth in agricultural output was concentrated in cereals. China and India, the world's two most populous countries, increased cereal output, over 1971–84, at 3.2 per cent and 4.1 per cent a year, respectively. Over the same period several developing

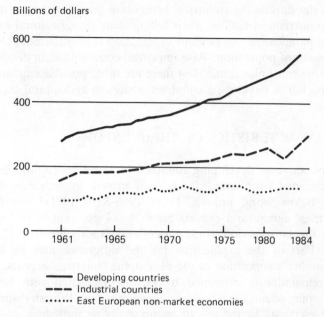

Note: Data are weighted by the 1978–82 world export unit prices. The decline in production in the industrial countries in 1983 was caused by a fall in US output due to the effects of the acreage reduction programme and a drought.

Source: World Bank, *World Development Report 1986*, p. 5, based on FAO data.

Figure 5.1 Trends in agricultural production, 1961–84

countries exceeded these rates quite comfortably: Indonesia, 5.1 per cent; Korea 5.0 per cent, Philippines 4.5 per cent and Pakistan 4.3 per cent (World Bank, 1986, p. 5). More people were fed, and fed better, than ever before in the combined population of the developing countries despite rapid population growth. A large proportion of these gains can be attributed to the new seeds, increased fertiliser and water supplies of the Green Revolution. But the effects were mainly limited to irrigated land. In many areas of the developing world, in particular Africa, food production benefited little from the new technology and lagged behind the growth of population. The stagnation of food production in Africa was a major factor in the recurrent crises of the 1980s. But the transmission mechanism may have been more through its effect on incomes (or 'entitlements' in A.K. Sen's terminology) than through supply effects (Sen, 1981, 1986).

As the developing countries' agriculture grew faster than that of the industrialised nations, their falling share of agricultural exports seems paradoxical. An obvious explanation is the difference in rates of growth of population. Also improved consumption in developing countries must play a role. But there are other possible explanations for the fall in developing countries' shares in agricultural exports.

3 CHARACTERISTICS OF THEIR EXPORTS

As the share of developing countries in world agricultural exports has declined over time, clearly their growth in such exports has been below world growth. From 1966–8 to 1981–3 developing countries' agricultural exports grew by 6.7 per cent in real terms. Over the same period world agricultural exports grew by 57.8 per cent. Part of the explanation for the difference may lie in the commodity composition of the developing countries' exports, while the remainder is explained by factors associated with being a developing country rather than a developed one. We can distinguish these elements by the use of 'components or shift-share analysis'. Treating the developing countries as a region of the world, the aim is to explain the difference between the actual growth of world exports and the growth of agricultural exports that developing countries would have experienced if their exports had grown by the same percentage as the world exports of each commodity.

Table 5.1 sets out the percentage change in exports for major commodities exported by developing countries from 1966–8 to 1981–3 in column (2) and for the world as a whole in column (4). Their shares in developing countries and in world exports are shown in columns (3) and (5) as 'weights'. The differences between growth for developing country exports and the world experience for the same products are shown in column (6). The total in the past column shows how much of the difference between developing country exports and world exports can be attributed to the commodity composition. (See footnotes to Table 5.1 for formula and definitions).

Although the results of component analysis are sensitive to the period chosen, averaging three years at the beginning and at the end helps to reduce the risk of bias from an exceptional year. The weights used are an average of the three year averages at the beginning and end of the period. We can at least conclude from the component analysis that the loss of market share by the developing countries is not due only to specialising in slow-growing exports.

Although this does 'explain' some 38 per cent of the difference between developing countries and the world's growth in agricultural exports, it leaves over 60 per cent to 'regional factors'. The following questions remain: why have the particular exports of developing countries grown more slowly than those of the industrial countries and what is it about the developing countries or the markets for their exports which would make their earnings from agricultural exports grow more slowly, even if they had the same composition as those of the industrial nations? Even when their growth for an identical export is much below the world growth, one cannot assume that the fault lies solely with the developing countries, as we shall see from the example of sugar.

4 PRODUCT CHARACTERISTICS

There is an extensive literature which maintains that there is an inherent tendency for the terms of trade to shift against primary products in favour of manufactures. Though not directly relevant to the explanation of developing countries' loss of share in agricultural export markets, the causal factors which that literature highlights – market structures, price and income elasticities, changes in taste and the direction of technological progress – are all highly relevant.

Coffee, at about 13.8 per cent, is the largest single agricultural export of the developing countries. Apart from a tiny amount produced in the industrial nations, all coffee is grown in developing countries, but about two-thirds is consumed elsewhere. Both price and income elasticities of demand are low (-0.23 and 0.50 respectively) [World Bank estimates] and there is a tendency for consumption to level off at about 3 kg a head. The United States and Europe account for about 75 per cent of world imports and in both areas the growth of consumption has been zero or even negative. In the United States, the biggest single consuming nation, consumption over the last 12 years has been declining at the rate of 1.6 per cent a year. Only in Japan and the United Kingdom, where coffee has been substituting for some tea consumption, and Spain, where incomes are much lower, has coffee consumption been growing fast. The other area of more rapid growth has been some centrally-planned economies (CPEs) and developing countries. Both of these groups have been receiving imports of non-quota coffee, that is, outside the International Coffee Agreement (ICA) quotas, at discounts of over 50 per cent on the ICA's official price. The

Table 5.1 Commodity composition and regional factors (1966-8 to 1981-3)

(1)	(2)	(3)	(4)	(5)	(6)	(7)
	Developing countries		World		DC-World difference (%)	
Commodities	change^a (%)	weight^b	change (%)	weight		CMC^c
Live animals	3.86	1.35	79.50	2.69	-75.64	-1.06
Fruit and vegetables	35.96	15.37	53.13	13.79	-17.18	0.84
Hides and skins	-75.09	1.34	12.69	2.76	-87.78	-0.18
Oil seeds	-40.79	3.18	81.62	5.16	-122.41	-1.62
Rubber	9.28	7.0	32.07	4.47	-22.79	1.04
Wood and lumber	38.34	7.02	56.53	8.00	18.19	0.55
Animal oils	-52.58	0.20	35.33	0.90	-87.92	0.25
Vegetable oils	124.15	5.62	134.48	3.38	-10.33	3.01
Meat fresh	30.09	3.81	117.93	7.72	87.83	-4.61
Meat dried	-68.39	0.6	-5.17	0.81	-63.22	0.04
Milk/cream	216.11	0.15	134.89	2.41	81.22	-3.05
Butter	58.05	0.58	134.89	2.41	81.22	-3.05
Cheese	89.67	0.10	125.87	2.00	-36.21	-2.39
Fish	282.60	4.36	185.07	4.62	97.53	-0.48
Wheat	69.55	1.91	80.59	9.04	-11.04	-5.75
Rice	9.74	3.52	34.87	2.48	-25.13	0.36

Barley	262.53	0.30	127.44	1.49	136.08	-1.52
Maize	15.29	3.45	119.29	5.09	-104.00	-1.96
Sugar and honey	-20.44	8.46	32.70	4.97	-53.14	1.14
Coffee	-11.38	13.78	-1.57	5.75	-9.81	-0.13
Cocoa	-0.95	3.79	17.54	1.84	-18.49	0.34
Tea	-41.38	2.81	-32.42	1.23	-8.96	-0.51
Spices	11.57	1.13	24.78	0.51	-13.21	0.15
Tobacco	15.20	3.08	7.72	2.60	7.48	0.04
Cotton	-55.61	6.79	-29.47	4.29	-26.14	-0.74
Jute	-78.93	0.72	-78.37	0.33	-0.55	-0.31
Total	6.77	100.58	57.75	100.04	-50.98	-19.42

Export values in constant 1980 dollars.

Notes: CMC is the commodity mix component. DC is the developing countries.

[a]Per cent change from 1966–8 to 1981–3.

[b]Weights are calculated as a commodity's average share in total agricultural exports for 1966–8 and 1981–3. The weights used here are an average of these two calculations.

[c]CMC has been calculated as the sum of $(W_{ij} - W_i)G_i$ for commodities one to N, where W_i is the world weight for the ith commodity, where W_{ij} is the developing country weight for the ith commodity and where G_i is the percentage change in the world's export value.

Source: Export commodity values from World Bank, Economic analysis and Projections Department.

actual growth rate of total developing country exports of coffee in volume terms 1961–84 was 1.6 per cent a year.

The other tropical beverages have much smaller shares; cocoa, 3.8 per cent, and tea 2.8 per cent. Exports from developing countries have been growing, in terms of volume, at 0.2 per cent a year for cocoa and 2.3 per cent a year for tea. In all three beverage crops the value of developing country exports in constant 1980 dollars declined over the 15-year period up to 1981–3. It is reasonable to argue that here they are faced by objective market conditions, plus some trade and tax barriers in Europe which limit their ability as a group to increase export earnings by raising productivity. Some countries can of course do so; for example, Ivory Coast and Brazil have greatly increased their share of the cocoa market at the expense of Ghana and Nigeria. East Africa has gained tea markets from India and Sri Lanka. For none of these commodities is the general outlook promising.

Sugar forms 8.5 per cent of the developing country exports. For developing countries sugar exports fell by 20 per cent while for the world they rose 33 per cent (Table 5.1). This might be held to demonstrate weaknesses in developing countries' sugar industries or export incentives, but that would be a false conclusion. The major cause here is the rapid growth of European Economic Community sugar production. From 1973 to 1983 the EEC changed from a major importer of sugar to the largest exporter to the world market. This drastic change was due to the protection and price incentives accorded by the Common Agricultural Policy (CAP) to beet sugar production and export, to improved yields and to the changes in the United Kingdom policy on accession to the EEC. The British up to 1973 had limited beet production and imported cane sugar from former colonies. After accession and adoption of the CAP, British beet production rose by 50 per cent while United Kingdom sugar consumption fell. While the EEC sugar protocol pays higher prices to some developing countries, the sugar which it dumps on world markets at subsidised prices inflicts great costs on most developing country exporters of sugar (Overseas Development Institute, 1986).

Further inspection of the weights in Table 5.1 reveals that for the products in which the developing countries are relatively specialised, for example, beverages, industrial fibres and natural rubber the growth has been poor, for reasons which are well known. For many of the others, such as sugar, vegetable oils, fruit and vegetables, meat, dairy products and grains they run into trade barriers in industrial country markets and/or subsidised exports in world markets. Although their exports of vegetable oils did well (for Brazil particularly so) they would presumably have done even better had the EEC not supported its butter production so heavily. These issues are discussed further in the next section.

5 PROTECTION IN INDUSTRIAL COUNTRIES

Industrial countries protect agriculture to achieve a mixture of objectives which include strategic, income distributional, environmental and political. The strategic objective can involve both the desire to be self-sufficient in key foodstuffs in case of wars which could threaten supplies and a desire to avoid the insecurity of having to pay scarcity prices at times of world shortage of 'essential' foods or raw materials. In many countries this objective is extended to one of maintaining relatively stable prices for producers and consumers. There is also a desire to maintain and stabilise farmers' incomes, and to reduce migration from the rural sectors to the cities. Some also argue that an active farming community is necessary for the preservation of an attractive and cared-for natural environment. The fact that protection has been shown to be a costly and relatively ineffective way of attaining these objectives lends support to the view that the real reason for continued agricultural protection is the power of the agricultural lobbies – including the agro-industries, which depend heavily on intensive farming for their markets and materials (see Body, 1982; Howarth, 1985; Johnson, 1973).

5.1 Methods of Protection

Countries have adopted a wide range of measures to assist farmers against foreign competition which can be broadly categorised as border measures and domestic interventions. Border measures include tariffs, quotas and variable import levies; but quality standards and surveillance are also used to inhibit imports. The policies of protection and other farmer income support measures often give rise to surpluses. To dispose of these, farmers are given subsidies to aid exports. In the EEC these usually take the form of export restitutions. The EEC farm budget meets the difference between the high domestic price and the much lower price for exports. Such policies for sugar, dairy products and wheat have dumped EEC surpluses on world markets and depressed and destabilised international prices.

Table 5.2 summarises data on non-tariff border measures against agricultural imports from developing and from developed countries for the EEC, Japan, USA and all the industrial market economies. This table shows that non-tariff barriers (NTBs) to trade in agriculture are widespread. They may be more frequent on products exported mainly by industrialised countries, but they also bear upon exports from developing countries. These are, of course, only listings of the frequency of the NTBs. We cannot deduce from them their protective effect. But we know that quotas and variable import levies are powerful instruments of protection. They bear particularly on meat, dairy products, sugar and cereals.

In addition to the NTBs, many agricultural products are subject to tariffs. Although various preferential arrangements such as the General System of Preferences and the Lomé Convention exist between the industrial and the developing countries they by no means exempt all agricultural exports from developing countries. For example, despite the Lomé Convention, over 50 per cent of developing countries' exports to the EEC of dutiable agricultural items pay the full MFN tariff rates (Overseas Development Institute, 1986).

In addition to border measures, countries often subsidise farm inputs, buy for stock and subsequent non-commercial disposal, and provide special assistance for marketing farm products.

It requires very detailed research to estimate the total protective effect of all these measures. One rough first step is to calculate nominal protection coefficients (NPCs). These are simply measures of the extent to which domestic agricultural prices are raised above the border price for a similar product. Estimates of NPCs using producers' prices and border prices for several products for major industrial countries and groups are shown in Table 5.3.

These are the best estimates of the protective effect of measures which raise domestic prices but even these estimates have to be taken with a pinch of salt. Agricultural prices in world markets are highly unstable, so the NPCs vary substantially from year to year, but the figures in Table 5.3 are averages for 1980–2, which reduces that problem. Products vary in quality and type, so border price and domestic price may not be for an exactly equivalent product.

Table 5.2 Extent of industrial countries' NTBs on agricultural products on imports from (a) developing and (b) industrial countries by type of measure, 1983 – number of instances

		Quantitative import restriction (1)	Voluntary export restraints (2)	Decreed prices (3)	Tariff-type (4)	Monitoring measures (5)	All NTBs: union of (1) to (5) (6)
EEC	a	12.7	0.0	12.9	7.5	3.6	27.2
	b	13.4	0.0	18.8	7.9	3.5	32.6
Japan	a	38.5	0.0	0.0	1.2	0.0	39.4
	b	30.1	0.0	1.2	1.9	0.0	32.5
USA	a	2.7	0.0	0.7	2.6	0.4	5.7
	b	4.9	0.0	0.3	2.5	0.7	7.2
Industrial countries	a	14.5	0.1	8.7	5.7	3.3	25.6
(except CPEs)	b	17.5	0.1	12.5	5.7	4.2	31.9

Notes: The table omits subsidies which are another important factor in reducing imports to OECD countries and in lowering world prices for agricultural exports, especially sugar, dairy products and wheat.
Note that column (6) is the 'union' of (1) to (5) *not* the sum. The reason is that many products are subject to more than one type of restriction.
Source: J. Nogues, A. Olechowski and A. Winters, 'The Extent of Non-Tariff Barriers to Imports of Industrial Countries, World Bank. Staff Working Paper No. 789 (1986) Table 5F.

Table 5.3 Nominal protection coefficients for producer prices of selected commodities in industrial countries, 1980–2

Country or region	Wheat NPC	Coarse grains NPC	Rice NPC	Beef and lamb NPC	Pork and poultry NPC	Dairy products NPC	Sugar NPC	Weighted average[a] NPC
Australia	1.04	1.00	1.15	1.00	1.00	1.30	1.00	1.04
Canada	1.15	1.00	1.00	1.00	1.10	1.95	1.30	1.17
EC[b]	1.25	1.40	1.40	1.90	1.25	1.75	1.50	1.54
Other Europe[c]	1.70	1.45	1.00	2.10	1.35	2.40	1.80	1.84
Japan	3.80	4.30	3.30	4.00	1.50	2.90	3.00	2.44
New Zealand	1.00	1.00	1.00	1.00	1.00	1.00	1.00	1.00
United States	1.15	1.00	1.30	1.00	1.00	2.00	1.40	1.16
Weighted average	1.19	1.11	2.49	1.47	1.17	1.88	1.49	1.40

[a] Averages are weighted by the values of production at border prices.
[b] Excludes Greece, Portugal, and Spain.
[c] Austria, Finland, Norway, Sweden, Switzerland.
Source: World Bank, 1986, pp. 112–13.

The policies adopted to protect domestic markets and, of course, any export subsidies, will depress world free market prices so the NPCs may over-estimate the protective effect and certainly cannot tell us what would happen if free trade were adopted. If domestic input subsidies, deficiency payments and acreage controls are in use their protective effects are not captured by NPCs.

Despite such weaknesses, these NPC estimates allow some broad conclusions. Agricultural protection in Japan is extremely high. Dairy products, sugar and rice are highly protected in most areas. As the NPCs vary greatly within countries, incentives in the agricultural sector are powerfully distorted.

6 COSTS OF AGRICULTURAL PROTECTION TO INDUSTRIAL COUNTRIES

The main costs of agricultural protection fall upon the protecting countries themselves. There have been many attempts to calculate the domestic real national income losses to individual countries or group of countries. They range widely from $100 to $400 million for Canada, $1.9 to $24.1 billion for Europe, $2.9 to $27.4 billion for Japan and $0.3 billion to $5.5 billion for USA. All of these are expressed in 1980 dollars (World Bank, 1986, p. 121). The wide differences are due to several factors. Fluctuations in both world prices and domestic outputs produce large year-to-year variations in the costs of protection. The product coverage varies in many of the studies. In a world of flexible exchange rates, where capital movements play a large part in their changes, it is only by chance that the exchange rate is in long-run equilibrium in the year that the costs are calculated. As the years for the estimates range from 1976 to 1985 these instabilities were common and are reflected in the variability of estimates. There is also a practical problem of locating a 'world price' for many commodities. There may be no world market, or only one that involves so few buyers and sellers that the prices there are a poor guide to competitive equilibrium prices. But a still more serious problem is that the prices in international markets are themselves the result of protection and subsidies.

Nevertheless even the direct efficiency costs due to resources being diverted from manufactures or services to agriculture, or within agriculture from one product to another, that is, from uses where they would be more productive to ones where they produce less value, are likely to be quite high. But there are other costs. In the longer run there is the effect of investment and research diverted from other activities to agriculture. The higher prices that consumers pay for food and the budgetary costs of supporting agriculture may make it more difficult to control inflation. In the EEC, price supports cost $23.5 billion in 1984, or about 70 per cent of the Community budget. This compares with $5.6 billion in 1974. Only about 10 per cent of the cost was met in 1984 from customs duties and levies on agricultural imports, so the burden on general taxes was quite high. Spending in USA ($11.9 billion) and Japan ($14.7 billion) tell the same story of high and rising budgetary costs of agricultural policies (World Bank, 1986, p. 122).

What success have the policies had in achieving the objectives? One main direct objective has been to provide income transfers to agricultural producers. But in each country or region the costs to consumers and taxpayers greatly exceed the 'benefits' to producers (World Bank, 1986, p. 121). The benefits are in any case questionable. Economic theory suggests that if labour and capital are mobile and only land is in fixed supply the effect of protecting agriculture will be largely absorbed in increased prices of land. Land-owners gain from increased rents and windfall gains from increased prices for agricultural land. Tenant farmers and farm workers gain little, if at all. If anything, correlation analysis between the level of protection and Gross Domestic Product (GDP) a head of work force in agriculture as a proportion of GDP a head in the whole economy, shows a negative relationship. Other studies reveal little or no support for the policy of protection as a means of improving the standard of living in agriculture over the long term (Howarth, 1985; World Bank 1986, Box 6.6 p. 122).

Self-sufficiency can certainly be achieved through protection, but is it a sensible objective? In a world where food products are easily obtained through trade, and normal trading stocks are relatively high, it is unnecessary. If all countries pursued self-sufficiency, trade in food would cease, trade stocks would be small and food insecurity would be increased. In a world with little or no trade in food a harvest failure in one region would be a disaster. Food security comes cheaper in an open world economy. Domestic food price stability does not require self-sufficiency. Adjusting variable levies and food subsidies could achieve the same objective at lower cost.

Strategic food security is hardly relevant to a nuclear war. Perhaps one can envisage a limited conflict which interrupted food trade. But this would interrupt supplies of the inputs of oil, fertilisers and pesticides, on which the highly intensive agriculture of the industrial nations depends.

The environment a nation wishes to preserve is largely a matter of taste. But, at least in Europe and the USA, there is increasing criticism of modern agriculture's effect upon the environment. The risks of damage from the powerful chemicals used are high. The objective of a healthy and attractive environment is more likely to be damaged than preserved by the intensive agriculture promoted by protection.

7 EFFECTS ON DEVELOPING COUNTRIES

The costs, particularly the budgetary costs, of industrial countries' policies are more likely to lead to reform than any consideration of their effects on developing countries. That is our justification for taking a little space to re-emphasise these costs. But our main interest is in the effect of developed countries' protection on the agricultural trade of the developing countries. There is another justification: feedback effects upon developed countries' supplies of manufactures.

Industrial countries' protection restricts markets, lowers world export prices and destabilises them. The effects upon developing countries depend on (a) the composition of their exports and imports and (b) their elasticities of supply of exports and import substitutes. Attempts to estimate the effects produce a variety of results. Differences in approach and assumptions make these difficult to interpret and compare. There are three basic approaches; market shares, partial equilibrium and general equilibrium analyses. The first compares the market shares of exporters to the protected area, such as the EEC before, and some time after, its formation, comparing their subsequent share with an assumption of constant shares, or shares predicted by trends or economic models. The effects of increased protection are assumed to be the difference between the predicted and the actual market shares. Problems are that this difference may be due to more than protection. Income and independent price changes would have affected supply and demand for agricultural exports. In the case of the EEC, pre-existing national systems of protection complicate the issue so that this approach cannot show the effects of liberalisation. The approach takes no account of exports from the EEC or of the repercussions in food importing countries. Finally, various studies use different definitions of market shares. The conclusions vary from significantly damaging effects to negligible effects on developing countries resulting from the CAP (Matthews, 1985, p. 104; UNCTAD, 1983, pp. 64–75).

Partial equilibrium approaches model each commodity and use supply and demand elasticities to estimate the changes which would result from complete or partial reduction of protection. Some do not allow for substitution among commodities resulting from the price changes while others allow for this. If the estimates are made for one commodity at a time assuming *ceteris paribus* and then summed, the effects of liberalisation will be exaggerated because of the possibilities of substitution in both production and consumption. To capture all the possibilities, including income effects, of the changes requires complex general equilibrium models. The results in terms of magnitude and distribution of the gains and losses to countries are sensitive to the sizes of the elasticities of supply and demand for each country, to the time allowed for adjustment and to whether countries pass on the price changes to producers and consumers.

One influential study which has used this approach is Valdés and Zietz (1980). It covered agricultural exports for 56 developing countries and estimated that a 50 per cent cut in OECD nations' tariff and non-tariff barriers would raise their value by $3 billion a year (in 1977 prices). The UNCTAD secretariat consider this an underestimate because the study excluded a major sugar exporter, Cuba, excluded some products, such as fish, and concentrated on short-run responses in developing countries' production (UNCTAD, 1983, pp. 66–7). But for Alan Matthews, Valdés and Zietz overestimate the gains because they included some exports of processed foods while they excluded dairy products which are a significant import for many developing countries. They appear also to have neglected special preferences for developing countries, for example, under the Lomé Treaty. Moreover, the current situation differs from the period they studied in that developing countries are now much larger importers of temperate agricultural products and have greater benefits under the general system of preferences (GSP) (Matthews, 1985, pp. 107–8).

Valdés and Zietz themselves actually arrive at a net income gain for developing countries of only $400 million after allowing for costs of producing the exports and increased costs of food imports. Some developing countries would be large gainers while others would lose. However, there would also be income distribution and employment effects which should be considered in arriving at some estimate of the welfare effects.

Four-fifths of the export value gains would go to middle-income developing countries. Brazil, Argentina, India, Philippines, Thailand and Colombia share the largest increases. If the increased earnings were passed on to farmers, incomes of relatively poorer sections in developing countries would probably be raised, and certainly increased output would create more jobs in rural areas and reduce income differences between rural and urban dwellers.

Matthews has carried out a similar partial equilibrium study to that of Valdés and Zietz, using more up-to-date information and testing the sensitivity of the results to different assumptions on elasticities and other factors. As his interest is purely in the effects of the CAP and developing countries he confines his analysis to EEC trade with developing countries. He concludes that there is a net loss to developing countries from total liberalisation of the CAP of between $0.3 and $1.0 billion (Matthews, 1985, p. 229). The gainers would be mainly in Latin America and the losers mainly in Africa and Asia, including oil exporters. The losses stem from the increased cost to developing countries of food imports and the loss of preferences for their exports in EEC markets when trade becomes free. The study is carefully done and the author properly cautions his readers on the underlying assumptions and judgements which lead to this result (pp. 228–31). As he notes, the results from CAP liberalisation would be more favourable for developing countries if their agriculture were to become more productive as a result of policy changes or in response to higher world prices. He considers this to be unlikely because domestic policies seem to him to be unlikely to change in the short run, international prices are not generally passed on to the developing countries' farmers or consumers and that in developing countries farmers' aggregate response to prices is in any case rather low, especially in the short run. Moreover, even if energetic policies were undertaken to promote agriculture in developing countries this might still lead to increased food imports because it would raise the incomes of the rural citizens whose income elasticity of demand for food tends to be quite high.

Matthews' arguments are persuasive. But there are one or two counter-arguments to be made. One is that the opportunity cost of resources which would be drawn into both exports and domestic food production in developing countries as a result of liberalising agricultural trade is relatively low. This would be true if there were underutilised labour or land in many countries. Reduced resource costs would raise the benefit to cost ratio from liberalisation – and there could be social gains if more jobs in rural areas slowed migration to the towns, which is an increasing and costly characteristic of most developing countries.

A further gain arises from the general equilibrium effects of reduced protection. In the EEC and Japan resources would be released from agriculture and the need to pay for more food imports would force the EEC and Japan to export more manufactures at lower prices. This should benefit the majority of developing countries who are net importers of manufactures. A recent study by Burniaux and Waelbroeck (1985) suggests that cheaper manufactures from Europe would improve developing countries' terms of trade and raise their income by 2.9 per cent. But their estimates are on the basis of projections to 1995 and assume that very high levels of protection for European agriculture prevail then. That probably biases their results upwards. A number of other general equilibrium models produce varying results. The conclusion which emerges from surveying them is that they are all subject to various objections but that 'Regardless of sign, the impact on developing countries is generally shown to be small' (Matthews, 1985, p. 110).

Tyers and Anderson (1986), reported in the World Bank (1986), present a more elaborate study of the effects of trade liberalisation on seven commodity groups: wheat, coarse grains, rice, beef and lamb, pork and poultry, dairy products and sugar. It is based on a set of supply and demand equations for the 'world' agriculture economy (thirty countries or groups of countries). Its results are necessarily limited by omissions and fairly restrictive assumptions. The gains and losses which would have occurred with liberalisation in 1985 on a 1980–2 base are summarised in Table 5.4.

As the study omits tropical products, the net effects on developing countries from industrial market economy trade liberalisation are more negative than in other studies (Valdés and Zietz, 1980). But they show considerable gains from simultaneous liberalisation in both developing countries and the industrial economies for both groups: $18.3 and $45.9 billion respectively.

For the world as a whole the gains from reduced agricultural

119

Table 5.4 Efficiency gains caused by liberalisation of selected commodities by country group, 1985
(billions of 1980 dollars)

Country group	Industrial-country liberalisation	Developing-country liberalisation	Industrial- and developing-country liberalisation
Developing countries	−11.8	28.2	18.3
Industrial market economies	48.5	−10.2	45.9
East European non-market economies	−11.1	−13.1	−23.1
World-wide	25.6	4.9	41.1

Note: Data are based on the removal of the rates of protection in effect in 1980–82.
Source: World Bank, 1986, p. 131.

protection would significantly outweigh the losses. In the protected countries of Western Europe and Japan lower food prices would directly benefit consumers. These benefits would be proportionately greater for lower-income groups as they spend a larger proportion of their income on food. The price of agricultural land would be lowered, making it easier for the sons of farmers and others to enter the industry, and some land would be released from food production to other uses: housing (particularly important in Japan), forestry, nature reserves. As protection was progressively reduced, falling food prices would ease the inflationary pressures which continue to plague some industrial nations despite the highest unemployment levels since the 1930s. In turn, any reduction in Western governments' fears of inflation should allow them to increase demand and operate their economies at higher activity rates, increasing growth and lowering unemployment. As resources were shifted from their inefficient marginal agricultural activities into the manufacturing and service sectors of their economies in which their comparative advantage lies, the nations' outputs would increase. They would demand more of all kinds of imports. Some of these increased demands would be met by developing countries which are food importers but exporters of anything from oil to manufactures. Such effects, though small, would probably be enough to outweigh the net losses to developing countries which the calculations of Matthews and others show to be, in any case, very small. If reduction in trade barriers included the reduction of tariff escalation on processed raw material and food products this would increase the probability of net gains to developing countries. If that were so then reduction of trade barriers in the field of agricultural products would save the centrally-planned economies of Eastern Europe which show little signs of ending their food deficits.

8 POLICIES IN THE DEVELOPING COUNTRIES

The intentions of most governments in developing countries, to judge from development plans and declarations, have been to increase agricultural production, achieve food self-sufficiency and raise rural employment and incomes. In many countries there have been large investments in irrigation and flood control, in research and extension services and in rural education and health programmes. In Asia these efforts have borne fruit. Investment in irrigation and spread of the new varieties of wheat and rice have been a major factor in raising food output in several Asian countries (see Table 5.5). But the average index for food production per capita in 1982–4, taking 1974–6 as 100, for low-income countries excluding China and India is only 102, and for Africa south of the Sahara, 92.

Table 5.5 Increases in food production

Country	Average index of food production per capita 1982–4 (1974–6 = 100)
China	128
India	110
Pakistan	104
Indonesia	120
Sri Lanka	125
Thailand	115

Source: World Bank, *World Development Report* (1986), Table 6, p. 190.

The problem is that even when governments have pursued policies to promote production in the agricultural sector their general economy-wide policies have militated against agricultural production and particularly against agricultural exports. This has been a major cause of sluggish performance in agriculture in many countries and even more so of declining exports, particularly in most of Africa. In addition, policies within agriculture, especially with respect to producer prices have often dampened incentives to produce cash crops.

8.1 General Economic Policies

Throughout most of the 1960s and 1970s the main policy goal of most developing countries was to establish and promote industry. Invariably the method adopted was to protect industry with relatively high trade barriers. These policies have been sufficiently documented in numerous studies to need no repetition here. But the trade, exchange rate, fiscal and macroeconomic policies which stemmed

Influence of World Trade

from these import substituting industrialisation policies had very detrimental effects on agricultural exports.

Certainly, protection of industry was high and this lowered value added in agriculture relative to industry (see Table 5.6). It increased the relative profitability of manufacture and drew resources from agriculture. If these were surplus resources, as many believed, this effect on agricultural production would have been small. But in some countries the loss of labour probably raised real wages in agriculture and lowered profitability. In most it meant that farming did not attract private investment.

Table 5.6 Protection of agriculture compared with manufacturing in selected developing countries

Country and period	Year	Relative Protection ratio[a]
In the 1960s		
Mexico	1960	0.79
Chile	1961	0.40
Malaysia	1965	0.98
Philippines	1965	0.66
Brazil	1966	0.46
Korea	1968	1.18
Argentina	1969	0.46
Colombia	1969	0.40
In the 1970s and 1980s		
Philippines	1974	0.76
Colombia	1978	0.49
Brazil[b]	1980	0.65
Mexico	1980	0.88
Nigeria	1980	0.35
Egypt	1981	0.57
Peru[b]	1981	0.68
Turkey	1981	0.77
Korea[b]	1982	1.36
Ecuador	1983	0.65

[a]Calculated at $(1+EPR_a)/(1+EPR_m)$, where EPR_a and EPR_m are the effective rates of protection for agriculture and the manufacturing sector, respectively. A ratio of 1.00 indicates that effective protection is equal in both sectors; a ratio greater than 1.00 means that protection is in favour of agriculture.
[b]Refers to primary sector.
Source: World Bank, *World Development Report* (1986) p. 62.

The deliberate policy of fostering import substituting industries by tariffs and quotas was reinforced by its effect on the exchange rate. Because foreign exchange was rationed the official exchange rate overvalued the local currency and undervalued foreign exchange. This lowered the real value in local currency of exports, most of which were agricultural.

The extent of overvaluation was often increased when governments resisted lowering exchange rates to adjust for relatively high domestic inflation. Instead they resorted to more stringent import controls and licensing of use of foreign exchange. This in turn shifted the terms of trade still further against exports and agriculture generally. Even when some of the agriculture was import substituting, for example, competing with food imports, it was seldom allowed to benefit from protection. Rather, food imports were often used to keep urban food prices down to protect living standards of urban workers.

8.2 Sectoral Policies

Export crops were often a major target for government revenue taxes. This was partly a matter of convenience in countries where income taxes have a tiny base, partly a hangover from the experience of the windfall gains from export taxes in the early 1950s, and partly a belief that the low price elasticities of demand for major exports like coffee, cocoa and tea would allow monopoly rents to be gained from consumers. A further motive, in some cases, for taxing a raw material export was to discriminate in favour of a local processing industry. Less commonly, taxes on export crops have been used to discourage their protection in favour of food crops. The effects of these policies have generally been damaging. Exports have been handicapped without there being corresponding gains elsewhere.

In many countries, particularly in Africa, a substantial part of the taxation of export crops has been collected by marketing boards. These were originally intended to stabilise producer prices and collect some revenue to finance their operations and services intended to help producers in improving productivity and the quality of their crops. Soon after independence they became major sources of government revenue. The combined impact of over-valued exchange rates and heavy taxation of producers is evident in several African countries' loss of market share in cocoa and palm oil to South-East Asian and Latin American producers. Table 5.7 shows the change in market shares of major producers of cocoa and palm oil between 1961–3 and 1982–4. Ivory Coast, which is a clear exception to this trend, maintained much more incentives to producers than did Ghana and Nigeria. The Ghanaian cocoa price relative to the Togo price fell from 96 per cent in 1965 to 23 per cent in 1980 and from 97 per cent of the Ivory Coast producer price in 1965 to 30 per cent in 1982 (18 per cent in 1980) (World Bank, 1986, p. 76).

In Tanzania a combination of sectoral and macroeconomic policies discriminated powerfully against agriculture and especially against export crops. By 1984 the weighted average of official prices to farmers was 46 per cent below its 1970 level in real terms. For export crops the price was halved. Increases in export taxes and marketing board costs cut the farmers' share of the export price from 70 per cent in 1970 to 41 per cent in 1980. The bias against exports was even stronger than this shows because producers of food crops could sell them on the parallel markets for higher prices. Export commodities marketed by Tanzania fell from about 400 000 tons 1970–3 to about 270 000 tons 1982–4 (World Bank, 1986, pp. 74–5).

8.3 Elasticities of Supply

The implication of the foregoing is that supply elasticities both for individual crops and for agriculture as a whole are positive; that farmers really do respond to price incentives. Fortunately, despite widespread belief that farmers in developing countries are not very responsive to price incentives, a good deal of evidence, accumulated over the years, suggests that they are. The range of estimates for most of the important crops shows that they are all positive and some exceed unity. An extensive review of the literature on the aggregate agricultural supply by Yair Mundlak (1985) concludes, 'Indeed, agricultural output does respond to prices, and therefore to policies which affect prices' (Mundlak, 1985, p. 68).

9 CONCLUSIONS

Developing countries' loss of market share can be explained by: (1) specialisation in products such as tropical beverages, cotton, jute and hard fibres for which demand grows slowly and where inroads

Table 5.7 Growth in output and exports, and the export market shares of cocoa and palm oil in selected developing countries, 1961–84

Commodity and country	Average annual percentage change in output, 1961–84	Average annual percentage change in exports, 1961–84	Export market shares	
			1961–3	1982–4
Cocoa				
Africa	0.1	−0.6	80.0	64.1
Cameroon	1.5	0.5	6.8	6.9
Côte d'Ivoire	7.3	6.0	9.3	26.3
Ghana	−3.7	−4.2	40.1	14.4
Nigeria	−2.0	−1.9	18.0	11.2
Latin America	3.2	0.9	16.7	18.5
Brazil	4.5	2.7	7.3	10.9
Ecuador	2.5	2.2	3.2	2.6
Palm oil				
Africa	1.8	−6.4	55.8	1.9
Nigeria	1.4	−23.6	23.3	0.2
Zaire	−1.8	−15.5	25.1	0.1
Asia	15.0	14.8	41.8	95.0
Indonesia	9.7	6.2	18.4	8.2
Malaysia	19.0	18.0	17.9	70.6

Source: World Bank, *World Development Report* (1986) p. 73.

from synthetics continue to threaten their markets; (2) policies in the industrial nations which, by protecting their agricultural sectors and subsidising exported surpluses, restrict and depress markets in which developing and developed countries compete with similar products, for example, temperate zone agriculture and tropical substitutes such as oil seeds which compete with butter and oils for margarine; (3) policies in some, probably most, developing countries which have significantly handicapped their agricultural production and discriminated, even more, against their exports. But this has probably led more to switches in market shares among developing countries in the tropical products whose share of total world agricultural exports was, in any case, declining. *

The inability of African countries to feed their rapidly growing populations, together with the increased demands for food, and higher quality foods, from oil exporters and other more dynamic economies has been a factor in the growth of industrial nations' exports of grains, meat, dairy products, sugar and vegetable oils. This has been reinforced by the tendency of industrial nations' policies to produce surpluses in agriculture and then to dispose of these at heavily subsidised prices. That the budgetary costs and trade distortions produced by these policies are becoming increasingly intolerable is evidenced by recent disputes within the EEC and between the EEC and the United States.

Note

* My thanks go to Mr Anandarup Ray, principal author of the 1986 World Development Report for his amiable co-operation when I was a consultant on that report, and for allowing me to read a draft of his paper 'Agricultural Policies in Developing Countries: National and International Aspects', to Josephine Bassinette for research assistance, to Ron Duncan for recent information on prospects for commodities, to Tin Nguyen for suggestions on the components analysis, to Patricia Hillebrandt for editorial suggestions, to Professor Bela Balassa for helpful comments given as discussant at the IEA meetings and to Banjonglak Duangrat for painstaking typing.

I am indebted to the Oxford University Press for permission to quote from the World Development Reports.

References

Body, R. (1982) *Agriculture: The Triumph and the Shame* (London: Temple Smith).

Burniaux, J.M. and Waelbroeck, J. (1985) 'The Impact of the CAP in Developing Countries: A General Equilibrium Analysis' in Stevens C. and van Themeat J. (eds) *Pressure Groups, Politics and Development: EEC and the Third World, A Survey*, (London: Hodder and Stoughton) Chapter 6.

Howarth, R.W. (1985) *Farming for Farmers?* (London: The Institute of Economic Affairs; Hobart Paperback 20).

Johnson, D.G. (1973) *World Agriculture in Disarray* (London: Macmillan).

Matthews, A. (1985) *The Common Agricultural Policy and the Less Developed Countries* (Trocaire, Gill & MacMillan).

Mundlak, Y. (1985) 'The Aggregate Agricultural Supply', World Development Report Background Paper, September 1985.

Overseas Development Institute (1986) 'The Cap and Its Impact on the Third World', briefing paper, June 1.

Sen, A. (1981) *Poverty and Famines: An Essay on Entitlement and Deprivation* (Oxford: Clarendon Press).

Sen, A. (1986) *Food, Economics, and Entitlements* (Helsinki: World Institute for Development Economics Research, United Nations University).

Tyers, R. and Anderson, K. (1986) 'Distortions in World Food Markets: A Quantitative Assessment', World Development Report, background paper. United Nations Conference on Trade and Development (1983) *Protectionism and Structural Adjustment in Agriculture* TD/B/939, March.

United Nations Conference on Trade and Development (1983) *Protectionism and Structural Adjustment in Agriculture* TD/B/939, March.

Valdés, A. and Zietz, J. (1980) *Agricultural Protection in OECD Countries: Its cost to Less Developed Countries* Research Report 21 (Washington, DC: International Food Policy Research Institute).

World Bank (1986) *World Development Report* (Oxford University Press).

Zietz, J. and Valdés, A. (1986) *The Costs of Protectionism to Developing Countries: An Analysis for Selected Agricultural Products* World Bank Staff Working Paper 769, Washington, DC.

6 Primary Commodities as an Engine for Export Growth of Latin America

Montague J. Lord
INTER-AMERICAN DEVELOPMENT BANK

1 INTRODUCTION

There are three important features of the overall long-term growth of commodity exports from Latin America: (a) the growth rate of commodity exports from this region has been substantially higher than that of other developing regions; (b) commodity exports from the industrialised countries have increased at a substantially higher rate than exports of the same type of goods from Latin America; and (c) exports of manufactured goods from the industrialised countries have expanded at a much faster rate than have commodity exports from Latin America. The objective of this study is to examine the potential for Latin America to reduce or eliminate the disparity between its export growth rate and that of the industrialised countries. The approach is applicable to other developing regions or countries outside Latin America. The possibility of lowering the disparity in growth rates for these regions or countries would also depend upon the particular characteristics confronting the supply and demand for these exports.

In the past measures to increase export growth of the developing countries have focused on export supply. The recently elaborated trade theory dealing with product differentiation and monopolistic competition offers another means of expanding export growth through policies aimed at influencing export demand. Both approaches will be examined in this study. However, emphasis will be placed on measures to expand the demand for exports of the Latin American countries since there has been far less work undertaken in this area.

Table 6.1 shows the pattern of trade in primary commodities and manufactured exports during the last 25 years. World trade in

129

manufactured goods has expanded 1.6 times faster than trade in primary commodities. In commodity trade, exports by the industrialised countries have expanded 1.6 times faster than exports by the developing countries. As a result, the export market share of the developing countries in world trade of primary commodities gradually fell from 35 per cent in the first half of the 1960s to 29 per cent in the first half of the 1980s; the industrialised countries increased their market share of traded commodities from 55 to 63 per cent during the same period. This pattern continues to prevail. According to the International Monetary Fund (1986a) and the Organisation for Economic Co-operation and Development (1986),

Table 6.1 Trade in primary commodities and manufactured goods, 1960–84 (average annual growth rates and percentage shares of real values)

	Growth rate 1960–84	*Market shares 1960–4*	*Market shares 1980–4*
World			
Total Merchandise Trade	6.1		
of which:			
Primary commodities[a]	4.6		
Manufactured goods[b]	7.3	100.0[c]	100.0[c]
Developing countries			
Primary Commodity Exports[a]	3.5	34.7	28.6
of which:			
Latin America	4.7	12.4	12.5
Other developing regions	2.9	22.3	16.2
Industrialised countries			
Total Merchandise Exports	6.8		
of which:			
Primary commodity exports[a]	5.5	54.8	63.3
Manufactured exports[b]	7.1		

[a]Primary commodities are covered by the SITC, Rev. 2, categories 0+1+2+4.
[b]Manufactured goods are covered by the SITC, Rev. 2, categories 5+6+7+8.
[c]The difference between total world trade of primary commodities and commodity exports of the developing and industrialised countries is equal to exports of the centrally-planned economies.
Source: Derived from trade value data and unit value data in United Nations (1986) and International Monetary Fund (1986b).

exports of manufactured goods from the industrialised countries have grown at an average annual rate of 6.3 per cent in 1984–6, while the comparable growth rate of primary commodity exports from the developing countries has been 4.5 per cent.

Latin American commodity exports have, in general, fared considerably better over the long run than have those of other developing countries. Total export growth of primary commodities in this region averaged 4.7 per cent a year during 1960–84, compared to an average of only 2.9 per cent a year in other developing regions. Yet the rate of growth of commodity exports in Latin America was only 0.85 times that of commodity exports in the industrialised countries. Consequently, the region has been unable to capture a greater share of the market for primary commodities.

An expansion in the growth rate of commodity exports of the Latin American countries need not be at the expense of lower rates of export growth in countries from other developing regions. It has long been recognised that the industrialised countries compete in many of the same commodities (see, for example, Kravis, 1970; and Little, Scitovsky, and Scott, 1970, ch. 7). Figure 6.1 shows the distribution of market shares between the industrialised and developing countries in the major non-fuel commodity exports of Latin America.[1] While Latin America and other developing countries supply almost all of the world exports of coffee, cocoa, and bananas, the chief competitors in world trade of beef, maize, and soybeans are the industrialised countries; these countries are also important competitors in the markets for sugar, cotton, copper and iron ore.

As mentioned above, policies to improve the commodity export performance of the developing countries have traditionally relied upon the responsiveness of exporters to price changes. The new theory of trade dealing with product differentiation and monopolistic competition suggests that, if importers differentiate among suppliers of commodities, countries may alter their relative prices in the market in order to affect the quantity demanded for their goods. The characterisation of commodity trade in this framework is described in Section 2. In Section 3 a model is used to examine the traditional issue of the responsiveness of exporters to real price improvements and to measure the magnitude of the export supply response of commodity exports from the Latin American countries. Section 4 then turns to the demand side. It discusses issues dealing with overall demand for commodity exports and the more recent concern about the ability of countries to affect the demand for their

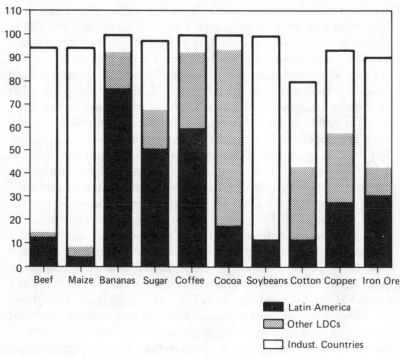

Figure 6.1 Market shares in Latin America's major commodity exports*, 1980–85

* The remaining shares belong to the centrally-planned economies.

exports. This ability is quantitatively assessed in Section 5, where simulations of the model provide empirical evidence of the capacity of the Latin American countries to influence the demand for their exports through relative price changes. The final section summarises the findings and discusses their major implications.

2 A MODEL OF MONOPOLISTIC COMPETITION IN COMMODITY TRADE

When an importer differentiates among supplying countries of the same type of commodity, even though the commodity is physically homogeneous, exporters can exert some control over the price at which they sell their products. Product differentiation thus gives rise to imperfect competition in international commodity trade, usually in the form of Chamberlinian monopolistic competition. This situation has been extensively used to explain intra-industry trade among the industrialised countries. Grubel and Lloyd (1975) calculated that intra-industry trade represented one-half of the total amount of goods traded by the industrialised countries and, of this trade, intra-industry trade in primary commodities was equal to 30 per cent.

One explanation of commodity differentiation, associated with the work of Lancaster (1979), is that the characteristics of a good differ among suppliers. The fact that goods enter international trade under a variety of conditions allows a product exported by one country to be considered as being imperfectly substitutable for the same product exported by another country. These conditions relate to quality (size, condition, grade, uniformity, colour, variety), marketing conditions (delivery time, credit terms, reliability of supplies), and cultural, historical, or political ties between trading partners.

In so far as importers differentiate among suppliers of Latin America's major commodity exports, countries in the region can alter their relative prices in order to influence the demand for their exports.[2] At the same time, the large number of exporting countries and the existence of free entry tend to drive pure profits to zero in the long run and to prevent pure monopoly or oligopoly in these commodity markets. Despite the existence of large producers in several of the markets, actions taken by exporting countries have not had a perceptible influence on long-run profits. There were unsuccessful attempts by major producers to raise market prices in copper during 1974–5 and in coffee during 1974 and 1980. In the banana market, Ecuador has entered the market whenever pure profits have arisen as a result of cutbacks in exports by the Central American countries. A similar situation exists in the coffee market when production shortfalls occur in Brazil, although the four- to seven-year delay between the time when coffee trees are planted and when mature yields are obtained can give rise to pure profits in the short run. As a consequence, product differentiation in Latin America's major commodity exports can give rise to a negatively sloped demand curve, but the large number of suppliers and free entry into these markets drive pure profits to zero, a situation characterised by monopolistic competition.

However, the conditions for monopolistic competition in these markets are violated when international commodity agreements or preferential trade arrangements establish prices that are significantly higher than what they would otherwise be. Latin American exporters take the prices offered under these arrangements as given and thus have a perfectly price-elastic demand schedule. The only international commodity agreement for Latin America's major exports that has significantly regulated prices has been the 1983 International Coffee Agreement, which effectively maintained prices above what they would otherwise have been during 1983–5. Latin American exports of sugar to the United States market and to the European Economic Community (EEC) market by African, Caribbean and Pacific (ACP) member countries under the Lomé Convention have had a more pervasive influence. The effects of these preferential trade arrangements on Latin American sugar exports are well illustrated in the empirical results presented in Sections 4 and 5 below.

The characterisation of product differentiation in international commodity trade in this study is based on the models developed by Dixit and Stiglitz (1977) and by Krugman (1981), where the characteristics approach is used to explain how product differentiation can arise in internationally traded goods. The preference ordering of an importer of a differentiated commodity is described by the utility tree. At the first level of decision, the importer decides how much to consume of commodity M and all other goods, whose composite forms the numeraire N_o, based on total expenditures and prices of the goods. In order to derive a system of equations that lends itself to empirical application, it is assumed that both intersectoral substitution between M and N_o and intrasectoral substitution among alternative export products $X_1, \ldots, X_n$ take place in the constant elasticity form. The utility maximisation problem for the first level of decision by geographic market j, given a commodity import price P and a level of nominal dollar income Y^η, yields as its solution the overall demand schedule for commodity imports M by importing country j:

$$M_j^d = k_1 \left[\frac{P_j}{D_j} \right]^\alpha Y_j \tag{1}$$

where D is the deflator and Y is constant dollar income.

The supply of imports, M^s, depends on circumstances in both foreign supplying countries and the import market itself. When the importer has little or no influence on the market price of a commodity then the import price can be derived from the inverse of the import supply schedule:

$$P_j = k_2 P \tag{2}$$

where P is the world market price of the commodity. The constant term k_2 accounts for the difference between the two prices which arises from transportation costs, distinctions between methods of valuation, tariffs, and purchase agreements under long-term contracts.

Once the importer has determined the total amount of the commodity to be purchased from foreign supply sources, he then determines how much to purchase from alternative suppliers $i = 1,\ldots,n$. The utility maximisation problem for the second-level decision yields the export demand schedule:

$$X_{ij}^d = k_3 \left[\frac{P_{ii}}{P_j}\right]^\beta M_j \tag{3}$$

where β is the price elasticity of export demand.

The export supply schedule is derived from the objective of the exporter to maximise profits with a cost-minimising combination of factor inputs. Again, so as to derive a system of equations that lends itself to empirical application, it is assumed that the production schedule of the exporter takes on the constant elasticity of substitution (CES) form. Then the first-order condition yields as a solution the export supply schedule:

$$X_{ij}^s = k_4 \left[\frac{P_{ij}}{D}\right]^\gamma t^{\Phi_1} w^{\Phi_2} \tag{4}$$

The variable w represents a shift variable that measures major disturbances in export supply, and the variable t measures technological changes in the production and export processes which bring about a long-term, or secular, shift in the export supply schedule.

The dynamics of the system of equations in (1)–(4) above have been represented by the introduction of a lag structure that suitably characterises the underlying nature of the response to price changes (for details, see Lord, 1985, vol. 1, ch. 3). The model was estimated in its structural form with 1960–79 data, and it was validated with 1980–4 data[3]. The sample size consisted of over 200 trade flows. In all commodities, the principal markets of the Latin American countries are industrialised countries.

3 PRICE RESPONSIVENESS OF EXPORT SUPPLY

It has generally been recognised that the developing countries have the capacity greatly to expand their exports. Given the opportunity, producers can respond to market improvements in the form of higher prices for their products. What often impedes them in reacting to higher prices is government policies that prevent market prices from being transmitted to producer prices. Little, Scitovsky and Scott (1970), for example, found that unfavourable policies, including inefficient government intervention programmes and controls, had the effect of lowering exports from Argentina and Brazil. On the other hand, they found that effective government policies that permitted a favourable price structure stimulated fishmeal exports of Peru and cotton exports of the Central American countries.

More recently, Krueger (1983) has shown that the results of the National Bureau of Economic Research Project on Alternative Trade Strategies and Employment indicate that trade regimes in developing countries often severely discriminate against exports. The effective rate of protection in these countries is often much higher than that in the industrialised countries and import substitution occurs at the expense of export competitiveness. Hence it is argued that the use of the price mechanism would be a more effective way to promote exports than government intervention and controls.

The export supply relationship has been estimated for commodity exports of each Latin American country and the trade-weighted averages of the price elasticities are reported in Table 6.2. The results support the view that the supply of commodity exports from the Latin American countries is, in general, strongly responsive to price changes. In terms of magnitude, the long-run price elasticities of export supply average 2.1, which is two-thirds of the average price elasticity of export supply of the industrialised countries estimated in other studies (see the survey by Goldstein and Khan, 1985).

In the short run, however, the price elasticity of export supply tends to be low. This is explained by the fairly long time lags involved in the adjustment of export supply to price changes. For example, some perennial crops take as long as five years to complete their response to price changes. On the other hand, tree crops and minerals, which are usually characterised by long lags in their production response, have been found to have short-term adjustments in their export supply. These short-term adjustments are associated with the ability of exporters to vary their supplies through changes in stocks, yields, and levels of capacity utilisation. The shape of all lags has been found to have a 'tailing off' distribution, and the speed of adjustment is closely associated with the length of the lag.

As would be expected, considerable variation exists in the responsiveness of export supply. There are large commodity-to-commodity variations, with elasticities ranging from less than unity to more than six. Equally important is the large difference in export supply elasticities that exists across countries exporting the same type of commodity. These findings suggest that the effectiveness of export promotion policies would vary significantly from country to country.

There are a number of mechanisms through which the quantity of exports supplied by the Latin American countries could be

Table 6.2 Latin America: average price elasticities of export supply[1]

Commodity	Short Run	Long Run	Commodity	Short Run	Long Run
Beef	0.41	2.20	Cocoa	0.23	1.34
Maize	0.47	1.35	Soybeans	0.79	3.84
Bananas	0.90	3.26	Cotton	0.50	3.11
Sugar	0.32	0.70	Iron ore	0.43	5.89
Coffee	0.11	1.24	Copper	0.46	2.32

[1]Calculations based on estimates of the export supply of each Latin American country to each of its principal export markets.
Source: Derived from the results of estimates for equation (4) reported in Lord (1985, vol. 2).

increased. At the macroeconomic level, exchange rate policies could take the form of adjustments, not only in real exchange rates, but also in their stabilisation. At the sector or industry level, lower taxes or improvements in market information systems could be adopted. However, Diaz–Alejandro (1975, p. 121) has argued that often the costs of such export promotion policies are more visible to policy makers than are the costs of import-substitution policies, and they may therefore be more difficult to implement. Certainly, one policy that would have a low cost of implementation is the removal of producer price systems regulated by government agencies that do not permit producers and exporters to respond to changes in market conditions. Such systems are used extensively in the Latin American countries for traditional exports and tend to be inefficient. The removal of administered pricing mechanisms would allow producers to respond to long-term market improvements in the form of higher prices for their products.

4 THE DEMAND FOR COMMODITY EXPORTS

Production differentiation has been mainly associated with trade in manufactured goods. Since primary commodities are often homogenous in quality, it is usually assumed that the demand for these types of goods are perfectly elastic with respect to relative price changes (see, for example, Stern and Zupnick, 1962, pp. 585–6; and Isard, 1977, p. 942). However, goods that differ in quality refer to vertically differentiated commodities (for an analysis of this type of differentiation, see Shaked and Sutton, 1983; and Sutton, 1986). The more widely studied type, following Lancaster (1979), is that of 'horizontal differentiation', where the proportion of characteristics of a good exported from alternative sources differs but the total amount of characteristics is the same. What distinguishes a commodity exported from one country from the same type of commodity exported from another one is that importers have different preferences for the characteristics that make up a commodity export. It is this type of product differentiation that is applicable to primary commodity trade and that underlies the model used in this study to represent commodity trade.

The extent to which relative price changes have affected the demand for the major commodity exports of the Latin American countries is summarised in Table 6.3. The elasticities are trade-weighted averages, adjusted by so-called 'distribution elasticities' (Barker, 1969), of separate estimates of demand functions for countries in the region to each of their major export markets.

The results show that relative price movements are, in general, important in determining demand for primary commodity exports. On average, the price elasticity of export demand for the combined major commodity exports of the region is equal to −0.6 in the short run and −1.5 in the long run. By way of comparison, the average estimated price elasticity of demand for exports of the industrialised countries estimated by others is around −1.2 in the short run, and it is −2.0 in the long run (Goldstein and Khan, 1985, Table 4.2).

These findings suggest that pricing policies might be used by the Latin American countries to expand their export market shares. However, pricing policies could only increase foreign exchange earnings of the Latin American countries if the demand for their exports were elastic in the long run. The commodities that have price elasticities of export demand that are greater than unity are beef, coffee, copper, bananas and iron ore. Regional exports whose demand is inelastic with respect to prices are cotton, maize, soybeans, cocoa and sugar. Considerable variations also exist in the sensitivity of export demand to price changes among exporters of the same type of commodity, and among geographic markets of the same exporter. Nevertheless, the results point to the important role of relative prices in the demand for commodity exports of the Latin American countries.

Table 6.3 Latin America: average price elasticity of export demand[1]

Commodity	Short Run	Long Run	Commodity	Short Run	Long Run
Beef	−1.40	−2.53	Cocoa	−0.13	−0.19
Maize	−0.47	−0.56	Soybeans	−0.32	−0.42
Bananas	−1.19	−1.68	Cotton	−0.57	−0.74
Sugar	−0.17	−0.06	Iron ore	−0.33	−1.47
Coffee	−0.45	−2.19	Copper	−0.84	−2.12

[1]Calculations based on estimates of the export demand of each Latin American country by each of its principal export markets.
Source: Derived from the results of estimates for equation (3) reported in Lord (1985, vol. 2).

5 THE POTENTIAL FOR EXPORT GROWTH THROUGH COMPETITION

The above results suggest that the Latin American countries could substantially increase their major commodity exports by engaging in a greater amount of competition in the markets for these products. The structure of the market that in the past provided a strong impetus for the industrialised countries to expand their exports could offer the developing countries the means to stimulate their traditional exports in the future. This section quantitatively assesses the extent to which changes in relative export prices of countries in Latin America could be used to accelerate the rate of growth of exports.

It is reasonable to assume that the basic structures of commodity markets will remain fairly similar to those that existed in the past. Commodity markets that have been dominated by bilateral agreements (for example, sugar) are unlikely to be altered, while commodities whose markets have remained fairly unencumbered by non-tariff barriers to trade will probably not confront increased trade restrictions in the future (copper, cocoa, bananas, and cotton). This assumption allows the parameters of the model estimated from historical data to be used to simulate future outcomes of pricing policies.

In order to illustrate the potential growth in exports resulting from a change in relative prices, suppose that the Latin American countries decided to increase the average growth of their export volume to a rate that would equal that which has been anticipated for manufactured exports from the industrial countries, viz. 3.6 per cent a year during 1987–92. From the results obtained in the previous section, it can be shown that this objective could be achieved by lowering the relative price of their exports by 1.25 per cent each year during this six-year period.

The outcome of such a pricing policy has been compared to the outcome of a policy that would maintain the competitive position of the Latin American countries in the world markets. If the competitive position of the countries of the region remained the same, then an increase in overall demand for primary commodities would lead to a proportional increase in the demand for their exports. The rate of increase in overall world trade and exports of Latin America is based on assumptions about future movements in the predetermined variables of the model in Section 2, obtained from recent simulations of proprietary models. In general, they predict cyclical upswings in world-wide economic activity during 1988 and 1991 and cyclical downswings during 1990 and 1992.

Dynamic simulations of the model with the competitive positions of the Latin American countries held constant show that total world demand for exports of the major non-fuel commodities of the region would grow at an average annual rate of 2.4 per cent during the next six years. With relative prices held constant, demand for exports of Latin America would grow at the same rate as demand in the world commodity markets. By way of comparison, the rate of growth of manufactured exports of the industrialised countries projected by major proprietary models averages 3.6 per cent a year during the same period.

The results of a reduction initiated in 1987 of the relative prices of Latin America's major non-fuel exports are shown in Figure 6.2. In the short run, a reduction in relative export prices by 1.25 per cent would increase the quantity of exports demanded from the region by 0.7 per cent. By 1992, the 1.25 per cent reduction in relative export prices would cause the quantity of exports demanded to expand by 1.9 per cent. This expansion incorporates the short-term effect of the relative price change initiated in 1992, as well as the lagged effects of the reductions in relative price initiated in 1987. The resulting effect of the greater competitiveness of the region would be to increase the export market share of Latin America from 27.7 per cent in 1986 to 29.2 per cent in 1992.

These aggregate results naturally obscure the diversity of responses that would occur among different commodity exports, as well as among different exporting countries. As discussed in the previous section, there are considerable variations in the sensitivity of export demand to relative price changes among exporters. For example, a reduction in the relative price of sugar exports from Latin American has a minimal impact on demand for exports since, as noted earlier, most shipments are directed to the United States where the price is administered. Consequently, the price elasticity of demand for exports of Latin American countries in the United States sugar market is infinite with respect to price. This lack of price responsiveness of demand for sugar significantly lowered the results of the simulations reported above for the combined exports of commodities from Latin America. If sugar exports were excluded from the analysis, exports of the region would have augmented by

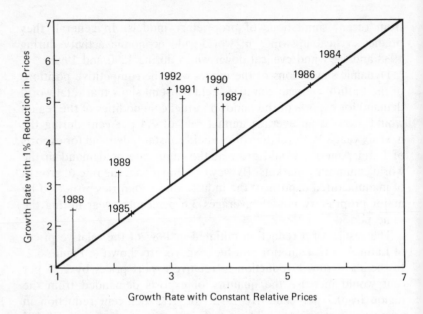

Source: Simulations of relationships that comprise the model in Section 2
estimated with export data from national statistical offices and with
import data from United Nations Statistical Office, Trade Tapes
(for details of parameter estimates of the model, see Lord, 1985 and
1986).

Figure 6.2 Comparison of real growth in Latin America's major commodity
exports with and without relative price changes 1987–92
(Average annual percentage change of real values)

an average of 1.4 per cent a year. However, it is beyond the scope
of this paper to examine detailed differences in the responsiveness
of particular exports to relative price variations.

A policy to expand the quantity of exports demanded by
lowering relative export prices could not be continued indefinitely.
Nonetheless, it could be used to bring in more foreign exchange
earnings over a medium-term period, as is currently required by the
Latin American countries to service their external debt and sustain
economic growth. Moreover, it could serve to offset the temporary
downturn in their exports of manufactured goods that occurred
when the debt crisis forced their outlets, principally intra-regional
markets, to restrict imports of these goods.

6 SUMMARY AND CONCLUSION

This study has examined how the Latin American countries could expand the rate of growth of their major primary commodity exports. Although commodity exports of the region have generally grown faster than commodity exports of other developing regions, the rate of growth has been substantially below that of exports from the industrialised countries for the same type of goods and much lower than that of manufactured goods exported by the industrialised countries. The analysis of measures to reduce or eliminate the disparity in these growth rates has been based on the recently elaborated theory of monopolistic competition dealing with product differentiation. This approach expands the range of export promotion measures since both export supply and demand can be affected by the Latin American countries.

The empirical results support the 'export optimism' view that emerged after the early 1960s about the supply of commodity exports from the developing countries. Once the full adjustment to a price change has occurred, the price elasticity of export supply for the Latin American countries is significantly greater than unity for most commodities, with the important exception of sugar. These findings confirm expectations that policies aimed at promoting the supply of exports would have favourable results in these countries. However, there is considerable variation in the response of export supply to price changes, which indicates that the effectiveness of such policies would vary from country to country.

On the demand side, a model similar to the ones developed by Dixit and Stiglitz (1977) and Krugman (1981) was used to represent international commodity trade. However, it adopted the characteristics approach associated with the work of Lancaster (1979) to explain commodity differentiation, that is to say, by the variety of conditions under which goods are traded, which give rise to imperfect substitutability of the same type of good exported by different countries.

The results of the estimates for the export demand relationship in the model suggest that the market structure for most commodities affords an opportunity for the Latin American countries to influence the growth in their exports through relative price changes. Simulations of the effect of variations in relative export prices demonstrated that it would be possible for these countries to expand their commodity exports by the same rate as that of manufactured goods exported by the industrialised countries. With few exceptions, increased price competition by countries in the Latin American region would not cause their exports to expand at the expense of other developing regions since the industrialised countries compete in many of the same commodity markets.

Notes

* The views expressed are the sole responsibility of the author and do not necessarily reflect the views of the institution with which the author is affiliated. I am grateful to Dr I.M.D. Little for useful comments on an earlier version of this paper and to Ms. Greta Boye for undertaking the calculations described herein.
1. Major non-fuel commodity exports of Latin America have been defined as those products that in the recent past have represented at least one per cent of the total regional value of merchandise exports. The degree of importance was measured over a relatively long time span, the 1970s, so as to avoid transient influences on the choice of commodities. Ten commodities met this criterion: coffee, soybeans, copper, iron ore, sugar, beef, bananas, maize, cocoa and cotton.
2. It bears noting at this point that differences in prices of exports of the same type of a good do not reflect product differentiation. Price differences among exports can arise for a variety of reasons that are unrelated to product differentiation. For example, they may occur because of differences between prices in a relatively free world market and price supports in markets where there are preferential trade arrangements. It is the impact of changes in relative prices over time on the demand for exports that reflects commodity differentiation.
3. The data were obtained from questionnaires sent to national statistical offices and are published in Lord (1985, vol. 3).

References

Barker, T.S. (1969) 'Aggregation Error and Estimation of the U.K. Import Demand Function' in Hilton, K. and Heathfield, D.E. (eds) *The Econometric Study of the United Kingdom* (London: Macmillan).

Diaz-Alejandro, C. (1975) 'Trade Policies and Economic Development' in Kenen, P.B. (ed) *International Trade and Finance* (Cambridge University Press).

Dixit, A.K. and Stiglitz, J.E. (1977) 'Monopolistic Competition and Optimum Product Diversity', *American Economic Review*, vol. 67, no. 3, pp. 297–308.

Goldstein, M. and Khan, M.S. (1985) 'Income and Price Effects in Foreign Trade' in Jones, R.W. and Kenen, P.B. (eds) *Handbook of International Economics*, vol. 2 (Amsterdam: North-Holland Publishing Company).

Grubel, H.G. and Lloyd, P.J. (1975) *Intra-Industry Trade: The Theory and Measurement of International Trade in Differentiated Products* (New York: John Wiley).

International Monetary Fund (1986a) *World Economic Outlook* (Washington, DC).

International Monetary Fund (1986b) *International Financial Statistics: Yearbook* (Washington, DC).

Isard, P. (1977) 'How Far Can We Push the 'Law of One Price'?', *American Economic Review,* vol. 67, no. 5, pp. 942–8.

Kravis, I.B. (1970) 'Trade as the Handmaiden of Growth: Similarities between the Nineteenth and Twentieth Centuries', *Economic Journal,* vol. 80, pp. 850–72.

Krueger, A.O. (1983) *Alternative Trade Strategies and Employment,* vol. 3 (Chicago: Chicago University Press for the National Bureau of Economic Research).

Krugman, P.R. (1981) 'Intraindustry Specialization and the Gains from Trade', *Journal of Political Economy,* vol. 89, no. 5, pp. 959–73.

Lancaster, K.J. (1979) *Variety, Equity, and Efficiency* (Oxford: Basil Blackwell).

Little, I.M.D., Scitovsky, T. and Scott, M. (1970) *Industry and Trade in Some Developing Countries: A Comparative Study* (London: Oxford University Press).

Lord, M.J. (1985) *The Econometric Analysis of Latin America's Commodity Exports* (Discussion Paper 85/1, in three volumes) Department of Economic and Social Development, Inter-American Development Bank.

Lord, M.J. (1986) *Market Price Models for Latin America's Major Commodity Exports* (Working Paper 86/1) Department of Economic and Social Development, Inter-American Development Bank.

Organisation for Economic Co-operation and Development (1986) *Economic Outlook,* vol. 39.

Shaked, A. and Sutton, J. (1983) 'Natural Oligopolies', *Econometrica,* vol.. 51, no. 5, pp. 1469–83.

Stern, R.M., and E. Zupnick (1962) 'The Theory and Measurement of Elasticity of Substitution in International Trade', *Kyklos,* vol. 15, no. 3, pp. 580–93.

Sutton, J. (1986) 'Vertical Product Differentiation: Some Basic Themes', *American Economic Review. Papers and Proceedings,* vol. 76, no. 2, pp. 393–8.

United Nations (1986) *Monthly Bulletin of Statistics,* vol. no. 5.

7 Food and Agricultural Imports of Sub-Saharan Africa

T. Ademola Oyejide*
UNIVERSITY OF IBADAN

Lien H. Tran*
WORLD BANK

1 INTRODUCTION

Although agriculture dominates the economies of most of the countries of Sub-Saharan Africa the rapidly rising rate of import of food and agricultural products over the last two decades has given considerable cause for concern (World Bank, 1981; Paulino and Mellor, 1984; FAO 1985). As food self-sufficiency in these countries declined, incremental demand for food has been met increasingly by imports; but the poor performance of exports has been threatening the ability of many Sub-Saharan African countries to finance increased imports of food and agricultural products, in addition to other critical import requirements (Valdés and Huddleston 1977). Hence, a food problem exists, and is reflected both in the volume and the structure of imports. Food aid and other emergency relief arrangements play a role in addressing aspects of this problem (Huddleston, 1984). But longer-term policy initiatives would have to be based on a careful and comprehensive analysis of the determinants of Sub-Saharan Africa's imports of food and agricultural products.

This paper offers a contribution along this line. Its primary objectives are: (a) to examine the structure and growth of food and agricultural imports, (b) to identify the main factors influencing the demand for food and agricultural imports, and (c) to estimate import demand functions showing the relationships between these factors and selected components of food and agricultural imports. This

147

analysis is based on the experience of some 37 countries in Sub-Saharan Africa over the 1962–84 period. These countries do not constitute a homogeneous group, of course. It is established, however, that low-income countries do, in general, receive relatively more food aid (Huddleston, 1984), while the middle-income countries tend to rely more on commercial food and agricultural imports (Wagstaff, 1982; Morrison, 1984). In recognition of these and other differences, this paper has adopted the World Bank's classification of the 37 countries into the following three broad groups (World Bank, 1981): low-income countries[1] as Group I, middle-income oil-importing countries[2] as Group II, and middle-income oil-exporters[3] as Group III.

The rest of the paper is organised as follows: Section 2 examines the size, structure and growth of food and agricultural imports in relation to total imports as well as export earnings. The focus of section 3 is a discussion of the general determinants of food and agricultural imports, while Section 4 presents a model of the relationship between imports and the factors which influence it. Finally, Section 5 discusses the major empirical findings and Section 6 draws some general implications for policy based on these findings.

2 SIZE, STRUCTURE AND GROWTH

Sub-Saharan Africa's food and agricultural imports have grown rapidly in both volume and value, since the 1960s. Several indicators of the size of food and agricultural imports are given in Table 7.1. In the 24 low-income (Group I) countries, the value of food and agricultural imports averaged $16.5 million annually in the 1962–9 period; the average rose to $42.1 million in 1970–9 and reached an annual average of about $83.7 million in 1980–4. The ten middle-income oil-importing countries as a group (Group II) had higher average annual food and agricultural imports over each of the three periods; between 1962 and 1969, this group's annual imports averaged $27.4 million rising to $74.7 million in 1970–9 and $158.9 million in 1980–4. The three middle-income oil-exporting (Group III) countries recorded annual average food and agricultural imports worth $33 million in 1962–9; this annual average increased to $215.9 million in 1970–9 and further to $616.3 million during the 1980–4 period.

Table 7.1 Food and agricultural imports

Countries	1962–9	1970–9	1980–4
Group I: low-income countries			
Food and agricultural imports ($ mil)	16.5	42.1	83.7
As % of total imports	12.0	13.4	14.7
As % of export earnings	17.0	21.4	29.7
Per capita ($)	3.7	8.2	14.7
Group II: middle-income oil importers			
Food and agricultural imports ($ mil)	27.4	74.7	158.9
As % of total imports	17.4	15.6	14.1
As % of export earnings	19.5	19.4	19.1
Per capita ($)	14.0	31.7	58.9
Group III: middle-income oil exporters			
Food and agricultural imports ($ mil)	33.0	215.9	616.3
As % of total imports	7.8	7.1	7.1
As % of export earnings	9.7	8.3	7.8
Per capita ($)	6.8	26.0	57.2

Sources: FAO Trade Tape and IMF Data Base.

As a proportion of total imports, the share of food and agricultural imports rose, in low-income countries, from an average of 12 per cent in 1962–9 to 13 per cent in 1970–9 and 15 per cent in 1980–4. But the share declined, in middle-income oil-importing countries, from 17 per cent in 1962–9 to 14 per cent in 1980–4. Similarly, in oil-exporting countries the share fell from an annual average of about 8 per cent in 1962–9 to 7 per cent in 1980–4.

The low-income countries have had to devote an increasing proportion of their export earnings to pay for their food and agricultural imports; for these countries, food and agricultural imports accounted for an average of 17 per cent of their export earnings annually during 1962–9, the proportion increased to 21 per cent in 1970–9, rising further to 30 per cent annually in 1980–4. The middle-income oil-importing and oil-exporting countries devoted relatively less of their export earnings to paying for their food and agricultural imports. For the oil-importers in this group, the proportion fell marginally from 20 per cent in 1962–9 to 19 per cent in 1980–4 while for the oil-exporters food and agricultural imports as a proportion of export earnings declined from an annual average of about 10 per cent in 1962–9 to 8 per cent during the 1980–4 period.

Our three groups of countries differ markedly, of course, in population. Hence a comparison of average import in per capita terms may provide an additional insight. Per capita imports (see Table 7.1) exhibit the same general upward trend through 1980–4 noted previously. In the case of low-income countries, per capita imports of food and agricultural products increased from an annual average of $4 in 1962–9 to $15 in 1980–4. The annual average for the middle-income countries also rose rapidly. In the case of the oil-importers, the annual average per capita of food and agricultural imports rose from $14 to $59, while, for the oil-exporters, the average increased from $7 to $57 over the 1962–9 to 1980–1 period. Thus, although the oil-exporters have imported larger amounts of food and agricultural imports, their per capita import has been generally lower than that of the oil-importers.

Table 7.2 provides the basis for a more detailed examination of the food and agricultural imports trends by country group. This table shows that the sharp increase in food and agricultural imports occurred largely during 1970–9; the average growth rate which was less than 3 per cent in 1962–9 soared to between 18 and 25 per cent

Table 7.2   Average growth rates (%) of major components of food and agricultural imports by value

Countries	1962–9	1970–9	1980–4
Group I: low-income countries			
Food and agricultural imports	0.31	21.23	12.04
Non-cereal	−0.47	17.54	8.78
Cereal	14.73	56.14	37.87
Group II: middle-income oil importers			
Food and agricultural imports	−0.49	17.94	11.55
Non-cereal	1.96	17.89	6.89
Cereal	5.76	26.05	38.41
Group III: middle-income oil exporters			
Food and agricultural imports	2.10	24.61	3.35
Non-cereal	5.98	23.50	6.05
Cereal	3.01	32.11	3.82

Source: FAO Trade Tape

in 1970–9 before falling back in the 1980–4 period, although for low-income and middle-income oil-importers, the average growth rate over this last period remained around 12 per cent.

Cereals and cereal preparations have become important components of Sub-Saharan Africa's food and agricultural imports. As Table 7.3 indicates, in the low-income countries, the share of cereal and cereal preparations in food and agricultural imports increased from an average of 33 per cent in 1962–9 to 43 per cent in 1970–9 and further to 60 per cent in 1980–4. In the middle-income oil-importing countries, the share rose from 40 per cent in 1962–9 to 50 per cent in 1980–4; and, in the oil-exporting countries, the average share of cereals and cereal preparations increased from 28 per cent in 1962–9 to 41 per cent in 1980–4. Table 7.3 also shows that wheat and rice constituted the most important components of cereal imports of Sub-Saharan Africa. Of the two rice was the more important in the low-income and middle-income oil-importing countries; in the former, the share of rice in cereal imports was between 41 and 61 per cent over the 1962–84 period, while in the latter, the share was 41 to 48 per cent. But, in the case of the oil-

Table 7.3 Structure of imports

Countries	1960–9	1970–9	1980–4
Group I			
Cereals as % of food and agricultural imports	32.8	43.1	60.3
Wheat as % of cereal imports	24.3	42.3	35.1
Rice as % of cereal imports	60.6	40.7	43.4
Group II			
Cereals as % of food and agricultural imports	39.8	40.9	50.3
Wheat as % of cereal imports	40.1	48.7	33.6
Rice as % of cereal imports	48.0	41.3	41.3
Group III			
Cereals as % of food and agricultural imports	27.9	40.2	40.8
Wheat as % of cereal imports	72.3	79.1	69.4
Rice as % of cereal imports	26.7	18.4	26.6

Source: FAO Trade Tape.

exporting countries, wheat imports were more important and accounted for 69 to 79 per cent of total cereal imports over the same period.

Our analysis of the trends and structure of food and agricultural imports of Sub-Saharan Africa reveals some general patterns. These imports increased significantly between 1962 and 1984, about five- or six-fold in low-income and middle-income oil-importing countries. In the oil-exporting countries, the upsurge in food and agricultural imports was particularly substantial both in absolute value and per capita terms. However, the burden of food and agricultural imports remained relatively low in the oil-exporting countries where these imports constituted less than 10 per cent of both total imports and export earnings. In the low-income countries, the share of food and agricultural imports as a proportion of total imports increased while it declined in the case of middle-income oil-importing countries. Similarly, an increasing share (from 17 to 30 per cent) of exporting earnings was needed to finance food and agricultural imports whereas this share was more or less constant (at 20 per cent) in middle-income oil-importing countries. It is clear also that while the 1970–9 period marked the era of especially sharp increases in food and agricultural imports for the three country groups, the rate of growth of imports decelerated noticeably during the 1980–4 period. Finally the importance of cereals, especially wheat and rice, as the dominant components of food and agricultural imports emerges quite clearly. This appears consistent with the changes in food consumption patterns documented in Delgado and Miller (1985), but may also have been influenced by other factors as the analysis in the remaining part of this paper indicates.

3 IMPORT DETERMINANTS

According to the empirical literature, food imports of developing countries are influenced by several factors. Some of these are internal or relate to domestic policies. Others are external factors reflecting developments in international markets.

Taking the internal factors first, note that the traditional model relates imports to the level of income. Import growth, in this scheme, arises from an accelerated rate of economic development which is accompanied by increasing domestic income and expenditures. Wagstaff (1982, p. 62) finds that food import reliance is greater among middle-income countries because import growth is partly related to the growth of income. Similarly, noting that estimates of income elasticities for these imports are generally positive, Morrison (1984, p. 18) argues that countries with higher per capita income tend to have greater per capita food imports. Thus the literature speculates that the level of development, reflected by GDP or income per capita, may be expected to be positively related to food imports.

Another major internal factor which contributes to changes in the volume of food and agricultural imports demanded is domestic production of food and agricultural products. Increases in food imports are associated with relative stagnation of domestic agriculture to the extent that domestic food production does not keep up with increasing consumption and imports must make up the difference. The interaction between increasing income and urbanisation poses a special problem which cannot easily be solved through increased domestic food production for the following reasons. As development occurs and income grows, urbanisation also increases. These processes are associated with changes in tastes and consumption patterns. The demand for cereal-intensive foods increases as consumption preferences shift into wheat and rice. As this occurs in countries where domestic production of such foods is made difficult or impossible by ecological constraints (Morrison, 1984; Delgado and Miller, 1985), food imports tend to increase even if domestic agriculture is not stagnating. Thus, the extent to which an increased rate of food imports is a reflection of the performance of domestic agriculture remains unclear.

Traditional theory suggests that food imports can be expected to be responsive to change in domestic and import prices. Delgado and Miller (1985, p. 55) find that policy-distorted relative prices have been an important factor, encouraging the shift from West Africa's domestic foods into 'superior' cereals. Drought and other factors which inhibit domestic production may alter domestic/import relative prices sufficiently to make imported foods cheaper and therefore more attractive.

The major external factors which are expected to influence the demand for imports of food and agricultural products by developing countries include foreign exchange earnings and reserves, food aid and the trade policies of industrially advanced countries which influence the supply and world prices of cereals. Hemphill (1974) proposed an import demand model in which a country's imports are determined by the foreign exchange generated by its exports and its foreign reserves assets; with such a balance of payments adjustment approach, other relevant factors such as relative prices and income growth are regarded as secondary. For countries that are able to borrow, the stock of debt is also important since borrowing enables a country to spend more on imports than its accumulated foreign exchange earnings can accommodate. However, for low-income countries without access to external debt and trade credit, increased food imports can constitute a serious drain on foreign exchange. In other words, unless external borrowing is made available, low export earnings combined with a weak foreign reserves position can be major constraints on food and agricultural imports of developing countries. Food aid may relax this constraint to some extent and thus permit recipient countries to import more food than they could otherwise. But food aid is alleged to have some negative effects; it may hasten the shift in consumption patterns in favour of imported cereals and create disincentives for domestic production by depressing prices.

4 REGRESSION ANALYSIS OF IMPORT DEMAND FUNCTIONS: A FRAMEWORK

Studies of aggregate import demand functions have been formulated in terms of price and income effects (Houthakker and Magee, 1969). Other studies have considered explicitly the effect of the price of domestic substitutes and exchange rate policies on import demand (Bautista, 1978). In applying his model to the study of food imports in the Philippines, Bautista explicitly examined the interaction between the market for imported foods and the market for domestic substitutes and the effect of this interaction on food imports demand response to its own price change. In such a framework, the role of exchange rate policies is recognised by formulating the import policy equation as a function of import price in local currency – using the policy-determined exchange rate to convert the border price in foreign currency into local currency. Interaction between the markets for domestic substitutes and for imported foods is considered by including the effect of the domestic food price index on food imports.

Such a formulation of the import policy equation requires domestic food prices and production indices for food import substitutes which are not available for each country in our sample. Instead, in our analytical framework, we consider the direct effects of import prices on cereal imports together with the effects of per capita income, export earnings, foreign exchange reserves, food production index, and shift in taste through urbanisation. Urban population as percentage of total population represents a surrogate for urban tastes.

The import demand equation for each country is of the following form:

$$M_{it} = f(y_t, p_{it}, p_{jt}, F_t, E_t, FEX_{t-1}, UPOP)$$

with t denoting time, i denoting the cereals group.

The variables are described in the following:

M_{it}	= per capita demand for rice, or wheat, or maize, or total cereals, in metric tons (Source: FAO Trade Tape);
y_t	= GNP per capita in 1980 US\$ (Source: World Bank National Accounts Data Base);
p_{it}	= own import price defined as import unit value in 1980 US\$ per metric ton (Source: FAO Trade Tape);
p_{jt}, p_{kt}	= price of other cereal imports defined as import unit value in 1980 US\$ per metric ton (Source: FAO Trade Tape);
F_t	= food production index per capita (World Bank National Accounts Data Base);
E_t	= export earnings per capita per US\$, deflated by the import price index (Source: World Bank Data Base);
FEX_{t-1}	= lagged foreign exchange reserves per capita in US\$, deflated by the import price index (Source: International Monetary Fund Data Base);
$UPOP$	= urban population as a percentage of the total population. (Source: World Bank Social Indicators Data Base).
$\dfrac{\partial M_{it}}{\partial y_t}$	response of imports with respect to income per capita, is expected to be positive for all country groups, although it may vary across groups.

$\dfrac{\partial M_{it}}{\partial p_{it}}$ response of imports with respect to own price, is expected to be negative and significantly different across country groups.

$\dfrac{\partial M_{it}}{\partial p_{jt}} > 0$ indicates the degree of substitution between cereals group i and cereals group j.

$\dfrac{\partial M_{it}}{\partial F_t} < 0$ indicates the extent to which cereals are imported to close the gap between domestic consumption and domestic food production.

$\dfrac{\partial M_{it}}{\partial E_t}$ is expected to be positive if in the long run imports are to be financed by export earnings without reliance on some form of balance of payments support, or other external sources of financing.

$\dfrac{\partial M_{it}}{\partial FEX_{t-1}}$ is expected to be positive as payments for imports are limited by the level of the stock of foreign exchange reserves at the end of the previous period.

$\dfrac{\partial M_{it}}{\partial UPOP}$ is expected to be positive where the urban bias is particularly pronounced, as in the case of middle- to high-income countries.

Demand equations for each country group are estimated, using pooled time series over the period 1962–84 and cross-country data for the 37 Sub-Sahara countries described above. To the extent that country grouping reflects the income range and the degree of openness with regard to oil trade, it offers a more appropriate way of controlling for the level of development and trade characteristics than using the income level alone, as suggested by Morrison (1984).

5 EMPIRICAL RESULTS

We estimated various functional forms for the above system of demand equations. Out of all specifications, the log-log form gave the best fit. We also estimated the system employing Zellner's seemingly unrelated regression (SUR) method (Zellner, 1962) with which more efficient estimates for the regression coefficients could be obtained. If the above system of demand equations can be thought of as the aggregate utility maximising decisions of the households subject to their budget constraints with the error terms representing the left-out factors in such decision making, then simultaneous optimisation across import demands for different cereals would imply that at the individual level as well as at the aggregate level the cross equations error terms might be correlated. However, the SUR results do not differ significantly from the ordinary least squares (OLS) results. Therefore, we present below in Tables 7.4–7.6 the OLS results for the log-log specification only.

Table 7.4 Demand for cereals imports: Group I

			Cereals groups	
Determinants	*Rice*	*Maize*	*Wheat*	*All Cereals*
GNP per capita	1.42**	1.30**	0.90**	0.82**
Food production per capita	0.40	−0.68**	−0.55**	0.27**
Rice price	−2.11**	0.11	1.18**	—
Maize price	−0.71**	−2.10**	−0.80**	—
Wheat price	1.48**	0.93	−1.23**	—
Price of all cereals	—	—	—	−0.41**
Price of other cereals (incl. millet and sorghum)	0.34	0.04	−0.10	—
Foreign exchange reserves, lagged	−0.05	−0.20	0.01	−0.002
Export earnings	−0.75**	−0.002	−0.17	−0.21*
Percentage of urban population	−0.02	−0.01	0.01	−0.01
R^2	0.54	0.42	0.24	0.32

**Significant at 5% level.
*Significant at 10% level.

Table 7.5 Demand for cereals imports: Group II

Determinants	Rice	Maize	Wheat	All Cereals
			Cereals groups	
GNP per capita	1.39*	1.40	0.33	0.51
Food production per capita	0.30	1.02**	−1.29**	0.87**
Rice price	−2.54**	0.58	1.65**	—
Maize price	−0.26	−3.29**	−0.54	—
Wheat price	2.73**	1.40	−1.42*	—
Price of all cereals	—	—	—	−0.78**
Price of other cereals (incl. millet and sorghum)	−0.12	−1.12**	−0.23	—
Foreign exchange reserves, lagged	−0.32**	0.09	−0.21	−0.23**
Export earnings	−0.63	−0.90	−1.87**	0.03
Percentage of urban population	0.04**	0.01	0.02	0.02**
R^2	0.76	0.62	0.74	0.42

**Significant at 5% level.
*Significant at 10% level.

5.1 Income Elasticities

We took GNP and GDP alternatively as measures of income. Since the results were not sensitive to the above definitions of income, we adopt the GNP definition of income, which we believe is more appropriate in our context.

While the income elasticities for each cereal are significantly positive for the Group I countries, the income elasticities are insignificant but positive for the other two groups, with the exception that the income elasticity for rice import is significantly positive for Group II. Moreover, these elasticities are lower, the higher the

Table 7.6 Demand for cereals imports: Group III

	Cereals groups			
Determinants	Rice	Maize	Wheat	All Cereals
GNP per capita	−0.41	0.10	0.15	0.50
Food production per capita	−0.11	−1.15**	−1.10	0.03
Rice price	−0.77	0.50	0.36*	—
Maize price	0.30	−1.36**	0.05	—
Wheat price	−2.32**	−2.06*	−1.24**	—
Price of all cereals	—	—	—	−1.04**
Price of other cereals (incl. millet and sorghum)	−0.86**	0.41	0.18**	—
Foreign exchange reserves, lagged	0.54*	−0.08	−0.07	0.01
Export earnings	2.20**	0.93	0.43**	0.56**
Percentage of urban population	0.01	−0.03	−0.003	0.006
R^2	0.85	0.88	0.78	0.78

**Significant at 5% level.
*Significant at 10% level.

countries are in the income groupings. Note for instance that the elasticities for total cereals are 0.82 for Group I, 0.51 for Group II, and 0.50 for Group III. However, these coefficients are significant only for the low-income countries, that is, Group I. For middle-income oil importing countries, the income elasticities are not significant at all.

Therefore evidence is not strong for the hypothesis that cereal imports accelerate with the level of economic development. Nevertheless, for low-income countries, income remains a significant factor for each type of cereal and total cereals as well. Elasticity for rice is the highest, at 1.42, followed by that for maize, 1.30, and that for wheat, 0.90.

5.2 Price Elasticities

We will first examine the own price elasticities for each cereal, and then for cereals altogether. Discussion of cross-price elasticities will follow.

Observe that our price elasticity of rice is highest for Group II and Group I (-2.54 and -2.11) and lowest for Group III (-0.77). The own price elasticity of maize is highest for Group II and Group I (-3.29 and -2.10) and lowest for Group III (-1.35). The own price elasticity of wheat is highest for Group II (-1.42) and about the same for Groups I and III (-1.24 and -1.23). There might be two sources of bias in the estimation of these elasticities. First, note that the import prices may depend on the volume of imports, and thus may cause a downward endogeneity bias in our estimation procedure (see Orcutt, 1950). However, this is unlikely since the demand from each African country is small relative to world demand and one can assume that the world supply facing each country to be highly elastic. Secondly, failure to consider explicitly the interaction between the market for the import commodity and that for the competing home good may result in overestimation of the total elasticity of imports with respect to the import price (see Bautista, 1978). The elasticity of the demand for imports would be lower if the effect of import price change on the market for domestic substitutes is allowed for. Moreover, the closer substitutes the home good and the imported good are, the lower the demand elasticity for the imported good would be with respect to import price change.

For all cereals together, the own price elasticity tends to be lower than for each cereal. It is the highest for Group III (-1.04), the next highest for Group II (-0.77), and the lowest for Group I (-0.41).

For the regression coefficients to represent the cross-price elasticities, they should satisfy certain cross-equation restrictions. However, we have not incorporated these cross-equation restrictions in our estimation procedure and hence, strictly speaking, the regression coefficients are not the cross-elasticities. Even so, if they are loosely interpreted as cross-elasticities, then certain patterns emerge from our results. Wheat and rice appear to be substitutes. The rice equations respectively indicate own price and cross-price elasticities with respect to wheat of -2.11 and 1.48 for Group I, -2.54 and 2.73 for Group II. The wheat equations respectively indicate own price and cross-price elasticities with respect to rice of

−1.23 and 1.18 for Group I, −1.42 and 1.65 for Group II, −1.24 and 0.36 for Group III.

5.3 Food Production Index

Our results do indicate some correspondence between the patterns of imports and food production shortfalls. The coefficients for food production index per capita are found negative and significant for the maize and wheat equations for Group I. For Group II, major rice importers, rice imports are significantly related with the relative size of the urban population. For the same group, wheat imports are negatively related to food production. For Group III, only maize imports are negatively related with food production. However, for this group which are major wheat importers (see Table 7.3), the acceleration of wheat imports is not significantly associated with food production shortfalls.

5.4 Capacity to Import

We measure capacity to import in the short run by lagged foreign exchange reserves, and in the long run by export earnings. While it affects the low- and middle-income countries negatively, its effects on the high-income groups are positive. This suggests that low- and middle-income countries must have financed their cereal imports from a source that is negatively related with foreign exchange earnings or lagged foreign exchange reserves. Food aid may be such a source of external assistance relied upon by countries in need of such assistance because of their weak foreign exchange position. For Group I, the coefficients of export earnings are −0.75 for rice and −0.21 for all cereals together. For Group II, for instance, the coefficients of lagged foreign exchange reserves are −0.32 for rice and −0.23 for all cereals together; the effect of export earnings on wheat is also significant (−1.87) for this country group. For Group III, on the other hand, the coefficients of export earnings for rice and wheat imports are respectively 2.20 and 0.43. Moreover, for these two import demand equations, export earnings seem to be the major driving factor. This is not surprising since for this country group, the effect of oil exports could be so strong as to weaken the effects of the other variables in the import demand equations, per capita income being one such variable.

5.5 Urban Population

Only for middle-income oil-importing countries (Group II) the urban population as a percentage of total population significantly affects the imports of rice and all cereals together. This implies that when income level and income groupings are controlled for, the effects of urban population is not as strong. However, this result could be due to the ways certain variables are defined in our data set. For instance, each type of cereal is defined as unmilled cereal, and the commodity group 'all cereals' include wheat flour, but not wheat-based products. Had all cereal-based products been included in our import variables, the effect of urban population would probably have been more pronounced.

6 CONCLUSIONS

Although food and agricultural imports for Sub-Saharan countries as a whole continue to grow, factors underlying the demand for those imports vary across country groups. For low-income countries, income growth, food production shortfalls and import prices are the most significant determinants. For middle-income oil-importing countries, import prices and relative size of the urban population are the most significant determinants. For middle-income oil-exporting countries, import prices and export earnings are the main factors driving cereal imports. Import prices emerge clearly as significant determinants for each country group. Although our price elasticities of cereals imports may have been somewhat overestimated, they provide some evidence that import demand elasticities may not be as low as the empirical literature suggests (Abbott, 1979; Jabara, 1982).

To the extent that cereals import demand is price elastic for all country groups, there may be scope in these countries for price policy to slow down cereal imports through appropriate trade and exchange rate policies, especially when these are aimed at realigning the price of cereals imports relative to that of domestic substitutes. Policies aimed at increasing food production also have a role in slowing down imports, particularly in low-income countries, where poor agricultural performance significantly contributes to high food imports.

Of course how large a role such policies would play depends on the food supply elasticity. If the food supply is entirely inelastic, then such price policies would have little effect on food and agricultural imports. In such a case, food and agricultural products would have to be imported to meet increasing consumption needs against an inelastic domestic suppply. The literature findings on this are certainly mixed, but there is some evidence that the agricultural supply in African countries is not entirely inelastic, especially when it is associated with increased capital availability, population density and so on (Binswanger *et al.*, 1985; Bond, 1983).

Notes

* We are grateful to Dr I.M.D. Little, L.K. Raut and C. Else for many helpful comments and valuable suggestions on an earlier version of the paper. The views expressed herein are our own and not necessarily those of the institutions with which we are affiliated.
1. Low-income countries are Chad, Somalia, Mali, Burkina Faso, Gambia, Niger, Mauritania, Ethiopia, Guinea-Bissau, Burundi, Malawi, Rwanda, Benin, Mozambique, Sierra Leone, Tanzania, Zaire, Guinea, Central African Republic, Madagascar, Uganda, Lesotho, Togo, and Sudan.
2. Middle-income oil-importing countries are Kenya, Ghana, Senegal, Zimbabwe, Liberia, Zambia, Cameroon, Botswana, Mauritius, and Ivory Coast.
3. Oil-exporting middle-income countries included are Congo, Nigeria, and Gabon.

References

Abbott, P.C. (1979) 'Modeling International Grain Trade with Government Controlled Markets', *American Journal of Agricultural Economics,* vol. 61, pp. 22–31.

Bautista, R.M. (1978) 'Import Demand in a Small Country with Trade Restrictions', *Oxford Economic Papers*, vol. 30, July 1978, pp. 199–216.

Binswanger, H., Mundlak, Y., Yang, M.C. and Bowers, A. (1985) *Estimation of Aggregate Agricultural Supply Response from Time Series of Cross-country Data*, ARU Report 48, October (Washington DC: World Bank).

Bond, M.E. (1983) 'Agricultural Responses to Prices in Sub-Saharan African Countries', *IMF Staff Papers*, vol. 30, pp. 703–26.

Delgado, C.D. and Miller, C.P.J. (1985) 'Changing Food Patterns in West Africa: Implications for Policy Research', *Food Policy*, February, pp. 55–62.

Food and Agricultural Organization (1985) *Food Situation in African Countries Affected by Emergencies: Special Report*, October.

Hemphill, W.L. (1974) 'The Effects of Foreign Exchange Receipts on Imports of Less Developed Countries', *IMF Staff Papers*, vol. 21, pp. 637–76.

Houthakker, H.S. and Magee, S.P. (1969) 'Income and Price Elasticities in World Trade', *Review of Economics and Statistics*, vol LI, May, pp. 111–25.

Huddleston, B. (1984) *Closing the Cereals Gap with Trade and Food Aid*, Research Report 43, January (Washington DC: International Food Policy Research Institute).

Jabara, C.L. (1982) 'Cross-sectional Analysis of Wheat Import Demand among Middle-Income Developing Countries', *Agricultural Economics Research*, vol. 34, pp. 34–7..

Morrison, T.K. (1984) 'Cereal Imports by Developing Countries', *Food Policy*, February, pp. 13–26.

Orcutt, G.H. (1950) 'Measurement of Price Elasticities in International Trade', *Review of Economics and Statistics*, vol. XXXII, May, pp. 117–32.

Paulino, L.A. and Mellor, J.W. (1984), 'The Food Situation in Developing countries', *Food Policy*, November 1984, pp. 291–303.

Valdés, A. and Huddleston, B. (1977) *The Potential of Agricultural Exports to Finance Increased Food Imports in Selected Developing Countries*, Occasional Paper 2 (Washington DC: International Food Policy Research Institute).

Wagstaff, H. (1982) 'Food Imports of Developing Countries', *Food Policy*, February, pp. 57–68.

World Bank (1981) *Accelerated Development in Sub-Saharan Africa: an Agenda for Action* (Washington DC, IBRD).

Zellner, A. (1962) 'An Efficient Method of Estimating Seemingly Unrelated Regressions and Tests for Aggregation bias', *Journal of the American Statistical Association*, vol. 57, pp. 348–68.

Discussion on Part II

PAPER BY ALASDAIR I. MACBEAN

'Agricultural Exports of Developing Countries: Market Conditions and National Policies'

In his lead-off discussion, Professor Bela Balassa highlighted the point that, while inelastic demand growth and industrialised country subsidies and protections did enter the picture for some commodities, the main problem of expanding exports of developing countries pertained to their own adverse incentive structures. He noted that agricultural exports of developing countries tended to expand more rapidly during the period 1973–84 than during 1967–73. This was possible because of more realistic pricing, export taxation and exchange rate policies. He saw MacBean's data on loss of market shares – Ghana's cocoa and Nigeria's palm oil – as striking examples of what can happen when attention is not paid to incentives. He noted also the tendency for many developing countries to give more protection and incentives to their manufacturing sector than to agriculture. Professor Balassa agreed that industrialised country import barriers for certain commodities, such as sugar and dairy products, did have an important bearing on developing countries. However, too much importance should not be attached to developed-country trade barriers as a sole explanation of their agricultural export difficulties. When evaluating import restrictions imposed by EEC and other developed countries, Balassa preferred the use of nominal protection coefficients to non-tariff barrier indicators. A related question concerning LDC exports was the prospect of expansion of intra-LDC trade.

In his response Professor Alasdair MacBean stressed that one should not underestimate the impact of developed-country protections and subsidies, such as those placed by the EEC on dairy products and the subtle non-tariff barriers operating for fruits and vegetables. Developing countries are very dependent on developed countries to avert further declines in export shares. Developing-country protection is weak and ineffective relative to that of developed countries. Moroeover, the industrialised countries themselves have much to gain from trade liberalisation. He considered the liberalisation of developed-country trade policies as a major target.

Montague Lord felt that the responsiveness of producers to price incentives should not be overstated. The estimated supply elasticities tend to be low. Moreover, one should distinguish between price elasticities of *export supply* (which may be high) and price elasticities of *production* (which may be considerably lower). Lord called attention also to the relevance of price and income elasticities of export demand when analysing the effects of incentives on the expansion of trade among developing countries.

MacBean agreed with the points about supply and demand elasticities. In connection with the latter, he noted the examples of high income demand elasticities for some foods and beverages associated with rising income in Latin America and also rising consumption of tea in India.

Nurul Islam raised the question of primary producers having greatly to expand their exports in order to pay for their debts and thus facing declines in export prices and/or declines in terms of trade in view of over-supply in the world market for many primary commodities in the face of weak or inelastic demand. He also noted that trade among developing countries in many primary commodities has been expanding rapidly in recent years.

Usha Dar questioned whether protectionism in underdeveloped countries necessarily leads to inefficiency. It may in fact allow them breathing space to restructure and improve the efficiency of domestic industries to make them internationally competitive.

MacBean observed that, while the infant-industry argument has some validity, many developing countries become excessively devoted to this. The Session Chairman, I.M.D. Little concluded that the short answer to this question is: do not pursue protectionism too far.

T. Gupta noted the point made in MacBean's paper about agricultural protection being capitalised into land values and rents, benefiting landowners, but not helping most tenants and farm workers. But he did not feel that this would be a universal argument against protecting agriculture, as not all situations were dominated by the kind of landowner–tenant/worker situation that MacBean had depicted. He mentioned the Punjab as an example of how overall farmer wealth had increased with help of some protection. MacBean agreed that owner–farmers could benefit to some degree from such capital gains. Gupta observed also that possibilities of exporting processed forest products had not received adequate study. He felt that, whereas developing countries were now exporting mostly raw forest products, they could be doing much of the processing themselves. Also he thought there were possibilities of more inter-LDC trade in forest products. MacBean agreed that there was a promising market for timber products.

John Mellor pointed to the World Bank forecast of further declines in world cereal prices of perhaps 30 per cent, the high domestic-resource cost of rice production in the Philippines, and the likelihood that certain countries like the Philippines may no longer have comparative advantages in rice production. Many developing countries could quickly find themselves with domestic price arrangements that are completely out of line.

MacBean observed that the Bank projections may have reflected optimistic assumptions about new technology and efficiency gains. But it was true that real prices of grain had declined during the previous 30 years and were continuing to fall as well as to fluctuate from year to year. To him this made it important for developing countries to have good forecasts, especially as a basis for deciding to plant coffee and other long-lived crops.

Islam pointed out that, in the face of dumping and falling prices on the world markets, developing countries are likely to consider shutting off agricultural imports to protect their farmers. This led MacBean to reiterate the need to reduce developed countries' subsidies and protection. He thought that there would be some natural erosion of the protection that now exist.

Mellor thought it was more complicated than this. If the world moves towards lower food prices, it will have important implications for the incomes of farmers and others. By and large, developing countries will continue to be dependent on agriculture and their comparative advantages in food production. These countries have very large potentials for reducing food production costs, so that their prices can come into line with international prices. This can be done through public investment in transport and other ways to bring down costs of agricultural inputs. But many developing countries have problems seeing this.

MacBean interjected that, when making decisions about how to feed itself, a developing country should not think in terms of absolutes. Instead, it is a matter of making investment decisions that take into account what future world prices are likely to be, the marginal costs of producing more of one's own food, and the opportunity costs of committing resources to this purpose.

D.D. Guru raised the point that, if downward price trends continued, the developing countries would only exacerbate their balance of payments deficits. He wondered what was the way to reverse such balance-of-payments declines. He further observed that, if industrial commodities are to be protected, then agricultural protection is needed too. However, MacBean felt that, as developing countries were net importers of foodgrains, they would *benefit* from declines in foodgrain prices; rising food prices would hurt them. MacBean said also that, while he was worried about *industrial* protection in developing countries, it was true that LDC industrial exports were rising much faster than developed-country industrial exports.

Referring to MacBean's comment about taking opportunity costs into account when considering desirability of food self-sufficiency, Aasha Kapur said she had observed that most decisions are made on *political* grounds. MacBean replied that this is true but that many politicians seem to understand and use opportunity-cost logic. They are very concerned about excessive costs.

Gerald Meier, endeavouring to set things in perspective, felt that a dominating concern should be the tremendous growth of imports by developing countries. These are absorbing more and more export earnings, much of them being equipment for industrial development. They are financed mainly through credits from foreign banks.

He observed further that this problem of international finance has been compounded in the early 1980s by close interrelationships with two other problems: (1) international trade difficulties and (2) internal problems within the developing countries themselves.

Referring to African countries, MacBean felt there was a need to distinguish between a country like Nigeria, whose expanded imports reflect oil earnings, and African Sahel countries, whose imports are mainly foodgrains financed via food aid. He observed that in many African countries harsh climate, errors in aid, and inappropriate domestic policies (low producer prices for food or cash crops, overgrazing and desertification and so on) contributed to these economic difficulties.

S. Mukerjee raised the question as to whether, with inflation, the domestic markets in some developing countries had become more attractive relative to export markets. Exchange rates did not always reflect this. Her own feeling was that one could not group all developing countries together in this respect; that those with marked patterns of rising consumption were quite different from least developed countries. MacBean agreed that government-controlled exchange rates often had not reflected changes in domestic prices and real exchange rates. He agreed also that developing countries really embraced a spectrum of contrasting characteristics.

In concluding discussion of his paper, MacBean emphasised that, while LDC policies often have been self-damaging, there is still the reality that elasticities of demand for manufactured items are, overall, much higher than elasticities for agricultural products. He saw no gain from simultaneous expansion of such exports as tea, coffee and cocoa. When one developing country gains, another loses. Referring to Balassa's suggestion that cartels be formed, MacBean observed that (a) this would be hard to do, (b) it would be impossible to restrict entry, and (c) synthetic substitutes were now appearing. He concluded that, if developing countries overemphasise traditional export crops, they will only hurt themselves.

PAPER BY MONTAGUE J. LORD

'Primary Commodities as an Engine for Export Growth of Latin America'

Dr Lord gave a summary of his own paper. He highlighted the orientation of his analysis to recent trade theory by Lancaster and others. This places importers in a monopolistic competition framework, and emphasises *horizontal* differentiation (blending from various sources) as distinct from *vertical* differentiation (quality differences). He saw this as a help to Latin American exporters in envisioning how importers are likely to decide what total amounts to import, from which country or countries, and at what prices.

On the supply side, except for sugar (which has a preferential quota system), Lord had calculated that export price elasticities of the ten commodities were quite high. The average long-run coefficient was 2.1. This reinforced the hypotheses of others that Latin American producers are quite price-responsive and that export-promotion policies might work for these countries.

In order to examine how price competition might be used to

accelerate growth of Latin American exports of primary commodities, Lord had performed two types of simulations: (1) a historical analysis embracing the 1961–85 period and (2) simulation of what could be sold at successively lower prices. Also, he had inverted the latter model to see by how much Latin America would have to reduce prices in order to achieve a specified rate of growth by selling to large developed countries.

The historical analysis had shown ambiguous results. There was no consistent pattern of Latin American market shares increasing during periods when relative prices were low. Lord's discussions with Latin American traders had led him to believe they tended to act as price takers, without realising that they might increase their market shares by lowering their *relative* prices.

The other analytical approach, which is reported in the paper, suggested that relatively small price reductions could yield quite large export gains for Latin America. Overall, it was estimated that an annual cut in relative export prices of 1.3 per cent would bring about a 3.6 per cent expansion of exports over a five-year period. This rate is the same as that anticipated for manufactured exports of the industrialised countries.

In opening the discussion, Ernesto S. Liboreiro commented on several points:

1. The model is highly interesting because it allows one to think that there is one way out for developing countries to compete with developed countries. However, the policy of reducing prices to compete with developed countries is very risky because:

   (a) Coffee, sugar, cotton, copper, bananas and cocoa are produced mainly by developing countries, and trying to increase each country's share of world trade would lead to losses for all the developing countries involved.

   (b) Beef exports are being subsidised by the EEC to an extent that production costs of Argentinean beef are greatly undercut.

   (c) Maize and soybeans are produced by the USA, and Argentina would be subject to reprisals by means of GATT Section 301 provisions, which enable US traders to sell below US market prices when 'unfair' trade practices are being encountered. Argentina has already been confronted with this type of US procedure on at least three occasions.

2. The smaller shares of trade of *some* commodities (beef, maize and other grains) in the international markets can be explained by the protectionist policies of the USA and the EEC.

Mahender Reddy enquired whether there could be any substitution between price and non-price factors, that is, instead of reducing prices, could an aggressive export marketing strategy help achieve the same objective? Also he questioned whether reduced prices could increase Latin American exports as much as Dr Lord's co-efficients suggest. There would be effects on developing countries elsewhere in the world that produce similar primary commodities.

Along the same line of thought, Reddy suggested that it might be useful to have a simulation exercise like Lord's which focuses on *low-cost manufactures*, which may not have as strong interactions with other developing countries as primary commodities.

Raghunath Pradhan argued that, given the Dixit–Stiglitz, Krugman, and Lancaster–Hotelling models of international trade, increasing returns to scale may not apply to primary exports. He questioned the policy recommendation of reducing prices, given the inherent tendency for terms of trade of developing countries to deteriorate. In view of the Emmanuel unequal-exchange hypothesis, would Lord recommend further depressing the relative prices of exports in order to increase Latin America's exports?

Eva Rabinowicz pointed out that agricultural policies of developed countries, and the political pressures associated with them, can impede exports of developing countries. She cited the example of the EEC and pressures on Thailand to reduce 'voluntarily' cassava exports.

Bhashyam said that imperfections and oligopolistic markets exist, whereas monopolistic competition is assumed in the paper. Furthermore price elasticities of demand are not specified for imports. The competitive model suggested by Dr Lord leads to a decline in prices. Given inelastic demand for primary commodities, agricultural export earnings may fall. He saw Lord's prescription as dangerous from the developing-country point of view.

Christa Luft raised the question of trade with socialist countries. She enquired as to how over time better relationships with developing countries could be established that meshed the complementary and substitutional nature of trade. She also asked whether there was a place in Lord's model for regional integration processes.

B. Sahu remarked that the analysis would have been more pertinent if it had examined whether the share of developing countries in world agricultural exports had declined partly as a result of their shift to non-agricultural exports. He noted furthermore that the falling shares could also reflect the fact that agricultural productivity is greater in developed countries.

Lynden Moore was concerned that some of the commodities included in Lord's analysis – that is, coffee and iron ore – had been traded under long-term agreements, and also that beef and bananas had been affected by preferential policies of the EEC. She asked how this factor entered the analysis.

McCall saw Lord's approach as interesting. But he wondered whether developed countries like the USA, Canada and Australia could be assumed to sit idly by while Latin America undercut their prices. Would they not be likely to reduce their prices in retaliation?

Little was somewhat puzzled by the model with regard to the way the decision-making process would actually work. In what way would Colombia, for example, decide to lower its price? Would the quota for coffee be established first? If so, from where – which country? In what way is Colombia considered especially competitive in coffee? How would the coffee markets actually function? Even if one could assume coffee quality to be all the same (which would not be true), the reliability of exports may be greater for one country than for another. In such circumstances, how can price reduction alone lead to greater competitiveness of that country's exports?

Lord closed the discussion with a few remarks. First addressing Little's query, he agreed that quality differentiation could be used as a strategy along with, or as a substitute for, relative price variations. Colombian coffee offers a very good example of how consumers perceive differentiation by origin.

Lord suggested that one could think in terms of a two-stage decision process, *à la* Dixit and Stiglitz and some others, and convexity of indifference curves (which implies differentiated products) in order to characterise the data-generating process of international commodity trade. That is why he drew heavily on Lancaster's work, as well as that of Armington.

Concerning his market structure assumption, Lord indicated that Chamberlin's monopolistic competition formulation did not depend on competition. His formulation could incorporate quota agreements that include both efficient and inefficient sugar producers, long-term contracts for iron ore sales, and other realities.

Lord emphasised the importance of knowing income elasticities of demand for the kind of policy analysis he has been doing. These elasticities vary significantly from country to country. His model demonstrates that it is important to direct one's exports at markets having high price elasticities of export demand. Also, Lord stressed that these elasticities cannot be treated as time invariant.

PAPER BY T. ADEMOLA OYEJIDE AND LIEN H. TRAN

'*Food and Agricultural Imports of Sub-Saharan Africa*'

Dr John Mellor, leading the discussion, noted that the paper was mainly a report of empirical work that examined (1) the structure and growth of food and agricultural imports in Africa, (2) factors leading to the high food import propensities, and (3) estimates of elasticities of import demand.

Mellor observed that, while these results showed that food import growth was not particularly greater than in some other places in the world, one characteristic unique to Africa has been the inelastic demand for root crops and maize. He noted that, since much of the food in Africa is produced by women and the opportunity costs of their labour are rising, the need to find ways to reduce labour requirements in crop production has become important.

He noted that wheat and rice imports have tended to be very elastic. Another point was that urbanisation *per se* appeared to have little effect on food imports; growth of such imports was more a reflection of changes in incomes.

Mellor expressed the view that price policies which increase incentives to produce food will have the effect of attracting many Africans back to rural areas from the towns and cities. However, resulting gains in food production are likely to be less striking than in Asia because of the present lack of infrastructure and agricultural technology base. Alasdair MacBean asked whether it might not have been useful – rather than grouping African countries into low-income, middle-income oil-importing, and middle-income oil-exporting categories – to analyse separately those countries that have been major recipients of food aid. Mellor replied that this in essence had been done by the authors, as the low-income African countries are mostly food-aid importers. Nurul Islam thought that perhaps it would be useful analytically to separate food aid from commercial imports.

D.D. Guru, referring to the relatively high-income elasticities of demand for cereals in Africa, said that in India increased food production had led to sharply falling prices and, in turn, lower incomes to farmers. Mellor responded that the Indian experience was in contrast to Africa in that growth in demand for food was very slow. This had been a factor in the decline of barter terms of trade in Indian agriculture back to the levels where they had been in the 1960s.

Part III

Protection of Agricultural and Industrial Products

Introduction to Part III

Bela Balassa
JOHNS HOPKINS UNIVERSITY, BALTIMORE
AND WORLD BANK

Four of the papers discussed at the session on Protection of Agricultural and Industrial Products are included in this volume. The first deals with overall developed–developing country trade; and the fourth deals with policies of the developing countries themselves.

In 'The Old and New Export Pessimism: A Critical Survey' Gerald M. Meier examines the arguments put forward by export pessimists in the 1950s and the 1960s as well as in recent years. In the earlier period, it was suggested that world income and price elasticities of demand for developing-country exports were low, and hence these countries would do well to follow an import substitution-oriented development strategy. Meier notes that the pessimists failed to consider the possibilities for developing countries to export manufactured goods, which have spearheaded the rapid expansion of exports that has occurred since. Export expansion, in turn, had led to rapid economic growth in countries oriented towards exports while countries pursuing import substitution-oriented industrialisation (ISI) experienced a slow-down of economic growth.

While recognising these results, the new export pessimists claim that (1) export-oriented countries benefited from favourable initial conditions specific to them; (2) future demand by developed countries would not support growth by additional developing countries; and (3) in any case, exports do not really act as an 'engine of growth'. Meier finds, however, that in successful exporting countries 'strong development performance is not attributable to favourable initial conditions but rather to [the] undertaking of appropriate policy measures.' He further adds that, as the NICs proceeded to higher stages of comparative advantage, their place was taken by less developed countries, thereby providing possibilities for their export growth. Finally he cites available evidence indicating the favourable effects of exports on economic growth. Thus he concludes that 'the lesson is one of policy reform to promote exports. Even if growth overseas is low and the protection threat is not reduced, it would be a mistake for the developing country to try and adjust by reducing imports through ISI'.

This is not to deny the gains that developing countries would derive from trade liberalisation by the developed countries. In 'Protection in Agriculture and Manufacturing: Meeting the Objectives of the Uruguay Round', Gary P. Sampson provides information on the tariff and non-tariff measures applied by the developed countries to the exports originating from the developing countries. He then proceeds to estimate the effects of trade liberalisation by the developed countries for the exports of developing countries.

Apart from its trade-creating effects, the elimination of tariffs by the developed countries would cause trade diversion in the case of developing countries whose exports are subject to lower duties under the General Scheme of Preferences. Nevertheless, except for some sectors in some of the developed countries, trade creation would substantially exceed trade diversion. This conclusion is strengthened if consideration is given to the abolition of non-tariff barriers, in which case diversion would not occur.

The author notes that benefits to the developing countries would be greater if the developed countries eliminated their tariffs on a preferential rather than on a most-favoured-nation basis – that is, if only developing country exports entered duty-free in developed country markets and existing tariffs on trade among the developed countries were retained. But gains to the developing countries from the abolition of non-tariff barriers by the developed countries would far exceed those derived from the preferential elimination of tariffs.

In 'Lowering Agricultural Protection: A Developing Country Perspective Towards the Uruguay Round', Alberto Valdés and Joachim Zietz concentrate on agricultural protection. This is of particular interest because, for the first time in the history of multilateral trade negotiations, prominence is given to measures affecting agricultural trade. The measures in question include tariff and non-tariff barriers and price support, as well as export subsidies. The authors suggest that the first step toward the liberalisation of agriculture should be to bind existing protection levels on a commodity-by-commodity basis. This would take the form of an agreement that levels of nominal protection, including production and export subsidies, could not again be raised. It would be followed by reductions in protection and the use of tariffs in place of other measures.

According to Valdés and Zietz, 'it would probably be unrealistic to believe that industrialised countries are willing to open their agricultural markets any further to developing countries without expecting reciprocity or some kind of compensation, at least for the more advanced LDCs'.

In 'Economic Incentives and Agricultural Exports in Developing Countries,' Bela Balassa suggests that such market opening is in the interests of the developing countries themselves. He provides evidence, for the period preceding the quadrupling of oil prices as well as for subsequent periods, that countries following outward-oriented policies in general did considerably better in increasing both agricultural and merchandise exports than did inward-oriented countries.

Outward orientation has been defined as a strategy that provides similar incentives, on the average, to exports and import substitution; in turn, import substitution is favoured at the expense of exports under inward orientation. Outward-oriented countries have also maintained realistic exchange rates. This has not generally been the case under inward orientation. At the same time, an econometric analysis of 53 developing countries has shown the responsiveness of exports to the real exchange rate.

In addition to the four papers in this volume that have just been reviewed, papers dealing specifically with India, the Philippines and South Korea were presented and discussed at the session. It is not possible to include them here, but the following are their main contentions.

In 'Taxes, Tariffs, and Trade in an Industrialising Low Income Country: Simulating Policy Choices in India, 1973–4 to 1983–4', Henrik Dahl and Pradeep K. Mitra discussed a general-equilibrium model to examine the economic effects of a 50 per cent unilateral tariff reduction. They concluded that such a change would bring little welfare gain to India, if the resulting revenue loss to the government budget was compensated by increases in other taxes.

They added, however, that the gains would have to be revised upwards if account is taken of improvements in technical and X-efficiency in response to reductions in tariff protection. Further gains would be obtained through the liberalisation of quantitative import restrictions which, rather than tariffs, represent the principal barriers to trade in India.

In 'The Relative Welfare Cost of Industrial and Agricultural Policy

Distortions: A Philippines Illustration', Professors Ramon L. Clarete and James A. Roumasset also reported that removing tariffs alone would not bring welfare gains to the Philippines. But gains would be obtained through the elimination of quantitative import restrictions. Moreover, removing all industrial protection would increase welfare, measured as the Hicksian equivalent of variation of benchmark income, by 4.9 per cent.

In considering additional policy alternatives in the general equilibrium model they utilised, the authors found also that removing all industrial and agricultural policy distortions would increase incomes in the Philippines by 7.9 per cent. However, if only agricultural distortions were removed while industrial protection was maintained, the welfare gain would be small and eliminating export taxes would even give rise to a welfare loss.

Finally, Kym Anderson and Peter C. Warr examined 'Distributional Effects of Agricultural Price Distortions: A General Equilibrium Analysis for Korea'. Their paper commanded particular interest since, in contradistinction with India and the Philippines, agriculture is heavily protected in South Korea. The authors found that agricultural protection benefits the land-owners and unskilled labour at the expense of skilled labour. The resulting decline in the skill differential, in turn, has adverse effects on economic growth by discouraging investment in human capital. This loss, then, adds to the decline in national income associated with protection that encourages agriculture over manufacturing and services in which South Korea has comparative advantages.

8 Economic Incentives and Agricultural Exports in Developing Countries

Bela Balassa
JOHNS HOPKINS UNIVERSITY, BALTIMORE
AND WORLD BANK

This paper examines the effects of economic incentives on exports in general, and on agricultural exports in particular, in the developing countries. Section 1 introduces a simple econometric model to estimate the effects of price incentives on exports. In Section 2, the model is applied to the exports of goods and non-factor services and to merchandise exports. In Section 3, the same model is used to indicate the effects of price incentives on agricultural exports. Finally, Sections 4, 5, and 6 present information on the responsiveness of merchandise and agricultural exports to incentives in the 1960–73, 1973–8, and 1978–81 periods respectively, by making use of intercountry comparisons.

1 MODELLING THE RESPONSE OF EXPORTS TO PRICE INCENTIVES

In this section, a simple model consisting of (foreign) export demand and (domestic) export supply equations is put forward for estimating the effects of price incentives, and of other relevant variables, on exports. Foreign demand for a country's exports (X^F) will be affected by changes in its international competitiveness. This may be indicated by changes in the index of the real exchange rate, derived as the nominal exchange rate (R) adjusted for changes in the prices of traded goods (defined in terms of wholesale prices)[1] in foreign countries (P_T^F) and in the domestic economy (P_T^D).[2] Introducing foreign incomes (Y^F) as an additional variable affecting exports, we obtain equation (1).

$$X^F = f(R.P_T^F/P_T^D; Y^F) \tag{1}$$

In turn, the supply of a country's exports (X^D) will be affected by changes in relative incentives to traded versus non-traded goods. This may be indicated by an index of relative prices in the domestic economy, derived as the ratio of domestic price indices for traded goods (P_T^D) and for non-traded goods (P_N^D).[3] Introducing a domestic capacity variable (C^D), we obtain equation (2). Finally, (3) represents the equilibrium condition.

$$X^D = g(P_T^D/P_N^D; C^D) \tag{2}$$

$$X^D = X^F \tag{3}$$

The reduced-form equilibrium equation, derived from this system of equations, has been estimated by utilising time-series data for 53 developing countries for the periods 1965–73 and 1974–82 as well as for the two periods combined. The first of the two periods was characterised by rapid growth in the world economy while the second included the two oil shocks and the ensuing recessions.[4] The choice of the countries has been dictated by data availabilities, including trade and national income statistics and domestic price indices.[5]

In view of the existence of an intercorrelation between exports and domestic capacity, the export–output ratio has been used as the dependent variable in the estimation. Separate estimates have been made for the exports of goods and non-factor services as well as for merchandise exports, with the gross domestic product used as the output variable in both cases. In turn, the combined gross domestic product of the developed countries, the principal markets for the exports of developing countries, has been used as the foreign income variable.

Estimation has been carried out by expressing all variables in terms of rates of change between successive years and combining time-series observations for individual countries. Experimentation with lag structures has not been successful; hence the reported estimates utilise data in an unlagged form.

In the event, the real exchange rate variable, but not the relative price variable for traded and non-traded goods, proved to be statistically significant in the estimation. This is not surprising since changes in the real exchange rate may, practically instantaneously, result in the redirection of production from domestic to foreign markets while the effects of changes in the relative prices of traded and non-traded goods are slower in coming and may affect exports and output in similar ways.[6]

2 EFFECTS OF PRICE INCENTIVES ON EXPORTS

Table 8.1 reports the results of estimates for the exports of goods and non-factor services and for merchandise exports, obtained by the use of the model described in Section 1, for the 53 developing countries. The table shows the individual regression coefficients, their t-values, the number of observations, F-statistics, and the (adjusted) a coefficient of determination. The estimates pertain to the 1965–73 and the 1974–82 periods and to the two periods combined.

The real exchange rate variable has the expected sign and it is statistically significant at the 1 per cent level for the merchandise exports of the 53 developing countries in all the equations. The foreign income variable also has the expected sign and it attains the 1 per cent level of significance in the equations for the 1965–73 and the 1974–82 periods. However its significance level declines to 5 per cent in the equation for the exports of goods and non-factor services and to 10 per cent in the equation for merchandise exports in cases when the two periods are combined.

According to the estimates, a one per cent change in the real exchange rate is associated with a 0.77 per cent change in the ratio of merchandise exports to output over the entire 1965–82 period. The regression coefficient is slightly lower for the first period (0.71), and slightly higher for the second (0.78), but the difference is not significant statistically.

Larger differences have been obtained for the exports of goods and non-factor services; the regression coefficient for the real exchange rate variable rises from 0.25 in 1965–73 to 0.58 in 1974–82; it takes the value of 0.48 for the entire period. The difference between the regression coefficients for the 1965–73 and 1974–82 periods is statistically significant at the 1 per cent level, indicating a shift in the underlying function.

In view of the relative constancy of the regression coefficient of the real exchange rate variable in the case of merchandise exports, a shift appears to have occurred in regard to non-factor services.

Table 8.1 Regression equations for export output ratios in developing countries (t-values in parenthesis)

	Constant	Real exchange rate	Foreign income	N	F	R^{-2}
I 1965–73						
(a) exports of goods and non-factor services	-0.11 (-3.11)**	0.25 (3.19)**	2.69 (3.82)**	424	12.64	0.052
(b) merchandise exports	-0.16 (-4.42)**	0.71 (8.50)**	3.75 (5.07)**	424	49.90	0.188
II 1974–82						
(a) exports of goods and non-factor services	-0.02 (-1.97)*	0.58 (9.79)**	1.16 (3.11)**	424	54.92	0.203
(b) merchandise exports	-0.03 (-1.77)+	0.78 (9.93)**	1.49 (2.98)**	424	55.84	0.206
III 1965–82						
(a) exports of goods and non-factor services	0.00 (0.25)	0.48 (9.84)**	0.51 (2.00)*	901	53.08	0.104
(b) merchandise exports	0.00 (0.39)	0.77 (12.63)**	0.56 (1.76)+	901	84.59	0.157

Note: (a) The variables have been expressed in terms of rates of changes between successive years for individual countries combining time-series and cross-section observations.
(b) Levels of statistical significance: +10%; *5%; **1%.
Source: World Bank data base.

At the same time, the weaker response obtained in regard to services may be explained by reference to the fact that some service items, such as licence and management fees, are hardly responsive to exchange rate changes.

The regression coefficients of the foreign income variable declined between the two periods, irrespective of whether one considers the exports of goods and non-factor services or of goods alone. The coefficients are 2.69 for the exports of goods and non-factor services and 3.75 for merchandise exports in the first period and 1.16 and 1.49 respectively in the second, with estimated coefficients of 0.51 and 0.56 for the two periods combined. The differences are statistically significant at the 10 per cent and the 5 per cent level respectively. It would appear, then, that the income elasticity of demand in the developed countries for the exports of the developing countries decreased in the period of external shocks.

These considerations may explain the fact that the decline in the foreign income elasticity is larger for merchandise exports than for the exports of goods and non-factor services. Nevertheless the elasticity continues to be lower for goods and non-factor services than for goods alone, indicating that some service items, such as dividends and interest, are not responsive to income changes in the developed countries.

Note finally that the coefficient of determination of the regression equations is low. This is not surprising, given that the variables are expressed in terms of rates of change; in particular, taking the rate of change of the export–output ratio tends to magnify the errors in the export and output data. Nevertheless, the F-statistics are uniformly high, indicating the existence of a significant and systematic relationship of the underlying economic variables.

3 EFFECTS OF PRICE INCENTIVES ON AGRICULTURAL EXPORTS

The above equations have also been estimated for agriculture, with data on agricultural exports and production used in calculating the export–output ratio. In the case of agriculture, estimates have further been made for the ratio of net exports (exports less imports) to output. The estimates pertain to 52 developing countries (51 countries in the case of the net export equations), with the omissions being due to the lack of data on agricultural output and/or exports.

The results again show the responsiveness of exports to changes in the real exchange rate. In the equations for the developing country group, the estimated regression coefficients for agricultural exports are 0.55 for the 1960–73, 0.79 for the 1974–82, and 0.68 for the 1965–82 period. All the coefficients are statistically significant at the 1 per cent level (see Table 9.2). As in the case of merchandise exports, then, the regression coefficients estimated for the two periods combined lies between that for the first and for the second period, with coefficient values rising between the two.

A comparison of the results reported in Tables 8.1 and 8.2 indicates that the regression coefficients for agricultural exports exceed the coefficients estimated for the exports of goods and services by a considerable margin. At the same time, apart from the 1974–82 period, the coefficients are slightly lower than those for merchandise exports. The following comparisons will be limited to merchandise exports.

The regression coefficient for foreign incomes is shown to decline between the two periods in the case of agricultural exports, but the differences are not significant statistically and the decline is much smaller than for merchandise exports, which include fuels where developing country exports decreased over time. Finally, the regression coefficient of the foreign income variable for the combined period is substantially lower than for the two periods taken individually, although the level of significance of the estimates is low.

The coefficient of determination is lower for agricultural exports than for merchandise exports. The differences in the results may be explained by non-price factors, such as the weather, which affect agricultural production. Nevertheless, apart from the 1965–73 period, the F-statistics are high, in particular in the developing country equations.

The adjusted R^2s and the F-statistics are substantially lower in the equations utilising the net export ratio as the dependent variable. This result may be explained in part by the fact that errors in the export and the import data are amplified when one takes the difference between the two and in part by the effects on imports of changes in foreign exchange receipts and in the availability of food aid. The above considerations may also explain the fact that the statistical significance of the real exchange rate variable is lower in the net export equations than in the export equations. Nevertheless the variable is statistically significant at the 5 per cent level for the

Table 8.2 Regression equations for agricultural exports in developing
countries

		Constant	Real exchange rate	Foreign income	N	F	R^{-2}
		A *Export–output ratio*					
I	1965–73	−0.05 (−0.81)	0.55 (3.54)**	1.69 (1.22)	416	7.10	0.029
II	1974–82	−0.03 (−1.57)	0.79 (7.44)**	1.54 (2.28)*	416	31.52	0.128
III	1965–82	−0.00 (−0.21)	0.68 (7.47)**	0.73 (1.56)	884	30.73	0.063
		B *Net export–output ratio*					
I	1965–73	0.17 (0.19)	0.42 (0.21)	−7.58 (−0.42)	408	0.11	−0.004
II	1974–82	−1.30 (−2.14)*	7.89 (2.45)*	46.58 (2.25)*	408	5.93	0.024
III	1965–82	−0.65 (−1.53)	4.96 (2.38)*	14.00 (1.30)	867	4.02	0.007

Notes: See Table 8.1.

1974–82 and 1965–82 periods, although it is not significant for the 1965–73 period.

In the former two cases, the values of the regression coefficients are high: 7.9 and 5.0 respectively. In interpreting this result, it should be recognised that net export–output ratios tend to be small, and hence even a relatively small absolute change can lead to large changes in percentage terms. Finally, the coefficients of the foreign income variable are high, but their level of statistical significance is low.

4 INCENTIVES AND EXPORT PERFORMANCE: COUNTRY EXPERIENCES IN THE 1960–73 PERIOD[7]

A comparison of the experience of eleven semi-industrial countries provides additional evidence on the effects of incentives on agricultural exports in the 1960–73 period of rapid world economic growth. These countries were classified into four groups on the basis of the system of incentives applied during the period.

The countries of the first group, Korea, Singapore and Taiwan, adopted outward-oriented policies in the early 1960s. These countries provided essentially a free-trade regime to exports, further granting some export subsidies that ensured similar treatment to exports and to import substitution in the industry sector. Nor was there discrimination against agricultural exports as agriculture and industry received similar incentives.

The second group, Argentina, Brazil, Colombia and Mexico, adopted inward-oriented policies, entailing discrimination against exports as well as against agriculture in the postwar period. In the mid-1960s, Brazil and Colombia and, to a lesser extent, Argentina and Mexico reduced – but did not eliminate – the bias of the system of incentives against manufactured exports. The extent of discrimination remained especially pronounced against traditional agricultural exports while non-traditional exports received similar treatment as manufactured exports in Brazil and Colombia but not in Argentina and Mexico.

The third group, Israel and Yugoslavia, limited the bias of the incentive system against exports during the 1950s, but increased this bias afterwards. Finally, inward-oriented policies continued to be applied in Chile and India, which are classified in the fourth group. Chile made some attempts to promote exports in the early 1960s but subsequently resumed its inward-oriented stance, from which India hardly deviated during the period under consideration.

Korea, Singapore and Taiwan increased their manufactured exports several times faster than the developing country average during the 1960–73 period. The system of incentives applied also permitted them to raise agricultural exports at a rapid rate, averaging 28 per cent in Korea, 16 per cent in Taiwan, and 11 per cent in Singapore which hardly has any agricultural base. Correspondingly, the total merchandise exports of the three countries rose at average annual rates of 42, 29, and 30 per cent between 1960 and 1973[8] (see Table 8.3).

At the other extreme, total exports as well as agricultural exports increased at average annual rates of less than 7 per cent in India. And while export growth accelerated in Chile between 1960 and 1966 in response to the incentives provided, agricultural and manufactured exports changed little afterwards as the bias against exports greatly intensified.

Table 8.3 Export growth rates, 1960–73

	Merchandise exports			Agricultural exports		
	1960–66	*1966–73*	*1960–73*	*1960–66*	*1966–73*	*1960–73*
Korea	40.0	44.0	42.1	25.2	29.5	27.5
Singapore	28.5	28.5	28.5	2.9	19.2	11.4
Taiwan	23.5	35.5	29.8	15.6	16.3	16.0
Argentina	6.7	10.8	8.9	6.2	7.9	7.1
Brazil	5.4	19.9	13.0	4.5	16.7	10.9
Colombia	1.5	12.7	7.4	1.0	11.1	6.3
Mexico	7.8	8.1	8.0	7.7	5.7	6.6
Israel	15.3	17.0	16.2	9.5	11.7	10.7
Yugoslavia	13.6	13.8	13.7	6.7	9.8	8.4
Chile	10.1	5.3	7.5	22.5	2.7	11.4
India	5.5	7.0	6.3	3.7	9.5	6.8

Source: Bela Balassa and Associates, 1982, Table 3.1.

Israel and Yugoslavia occupied an intermediate position in regard to export incentives as well as export performance. Between 1960 and 1973, their merchandise exports rose at average annual rates of 16 and 14 per cent, respectively, while agricultural exports increased 11 and 8 per cent a year.

Finally, in the second group, Brazil and Colombia experienced a considerable acceleration of the growth of both agricultural and manufactured exports after 1966 in response to increased incentives while smaller changes occurred in Argentina and in Mexico where the reform of the incentive system was less far-reaching. In the first two countries, the acceleration was particularly rapid in agricultural exports, with annual average increases of 17 and 11 per cent respectively between 1966 and 1973. The corresponding figures were 8 per cent for Argentina and 6 per cent for Mexico. In all four cases, the rates of growth of manufactured exports, and hence of total merchandise exports, were higher, but this occurred from a low base. Thus, the share of manufactured exports in industrial output did not surpass 4 per cent in 1973 in Argentina and Brazil while it exceeded 40 per cent in the countries of the first group.

5 INCENTIVES AND EXPORT PERFORMANCE: COUNTRY EXPERIENCES IN THE 1973–8 PERIOD[9]

The 1973–8 period was characterised by external shocks in the form of the quadrupling of oil prices in 1973–4 and the world recession of 1974–5. At the same time, policy responses to external shocks differed to a considerable extent among newly-industrialising countries, defined as having per capita incomes between $1100 and $3000 in 1978 and a manufacturing share in GDP of 20 per cent or higher in 1977, as well as among less developed countries that occupy the range between the newly-industrialising and the least developed countries.

Within the first group, Korea, Singapore, and Taiwan continued with their outward-oriented policies and were joined by Chile and Uruguay. In turn, after lesser or greater efforts made to reduce the bias of the incentive system against exports in the earlier period, Argentina, Brazil, Israel, Mexico, Portugal, Turkey and Yugoslavia reaffirmed their inward-oriented policy stance.

Among less developed countries, Kenya, Mauritius, Thailand and Tunisia applied relatively outward-oriented policies during the period under consideration. Conversely, inward orientation predominated in Egypt, India, Jamaica, Morocco, Peru, the Philippines, Tanzania and Zambia.

The choice between outward and inward orientation was associated with differences in macroeconomic policies in both newly-industrialising and less developed economies. While outward-oriented countries adopted realistic exchange rates and limited reliance on foreign borrowing, most inward-oriented countries let their exchange rate appreciate, supported by foreign borrowing. At the same time, the borrowed funds were not generally used to promote efficient activities oriented towards exportation.

The policies applied greatly affected export performance in the countries under consideration. This is evidenced by changes in export market shares for each country's merchandise exports as well as for its agricultural exports. In each case the results reported in Table 8.4 to 8.6 show the ratio of average export market shares in the 1974–8 period to the average for the 1971–3 base period.

All the outward-oriented NICs increased their export market shares in the period under consideration, with gains ranging from 3 to 53 per cent. In turn, inward-oriented NICs experienced losses in market shares, the only exception being Brazil where the continuation of export subsidies led to moderate gains (Table 8.4). The losses

Table 8.4   Changes in export market shares: the newly industrialising countries

Country	Merchandise exports		Traditional agricultural exports	
	1974–8	*1979–81*	*1974–8*	*1979–81*
Korea	153.4	167.4	—	—
Singapore	103.0	135.1	—	—
Taiwan	102.5	116.0	—	—
Chile	136.2	160.3	—	—
Uruguay	122.4	128.5	106.6	100.9
Argentina	99.3	93.7	96.8	92.0
Brazil	108.4	126.6	96.0	96.3
Israel	86.9	85.2	96.0	88.5
Mexico	79.1	92.2	78.3	68.9
Portugal	60.7	54.4	82.6	56.9
Turkey	91.6	103.8	78.1	73.7
Yugoslavia	91.1	87.2	67.1	39.6

Note: The results show the ratio of a country's export market share in the period under consideration to its share in the base period. For 1974–8, the base period is 1971–3; for 1979–81, it is 1976–8.

The average ratio for merchandise exports has been derived as the weighted average of the ratios calculated for traditional primary exports, defined as accounting for more than 1.5 per cent in total exports in 1971–3, for non-traditional primary exports, for fuel exports, and for manufactured exports. For traditional agricultural exports, the average pertains to agricultural products within the traditional primary export group.
Source: World Bank data tapes.

were the largest in Portugal (39 per cent), where the April 1974 Revolution also affected the results.

A similar picture emerges in the case of less developed countries. All outward-oriented LDCs gained export market shares, ranging from 8 to 21 per cent. In turn, inward-oriented LDCs experienced losses of market shares, ranging from 9 to 29 per cent, except that the Philippines had a small gain in response to incentives provided to manufactured exports (Table 8.5).

The effects of the policies applied on export performance are also apparent in the averages calculated for the various groups Thus the outward-oriented newly-industrialising countries experienced an average gain of 18 per cent in export market shares, compared with

Table 8.5   Changes in export market shares: less developed countries

Country	Merchandise exports		Traditional agricultural exports	
	1974–8	*1979–81*	*1974–8*	*1979–81*
Kenya	109.0	101.2	123.8	118.7
Mauritius	108.1	117.9	89.1	87.3
Thailand	121.0	145.6	116.5	123.7
Tunisia	114.3	142.3	100.0	80.3
India	91.0	62.6	100.7	90.4
Egypt	76.0	53.2	59.3	44.8
Jamaica	83.9	59.6	73.7	51.3
Morocco	85.2	86.7	77.6	61.3
Philippines	104.8	136.1	72.7	47.9
Peru	90.3	121.1	84.9	60.5
Tanzania	71.4	59.8	99.4	81.1
Zambia	87.4	77.9	—	—

Note: See Table 8.4.
Source: See Table 8.4.

a loss of 8 per cent for the inward-oriented NICs. In turn, the outward-oriented and the inward-oriented less developed countries had gains of 18 per cent and losses of 10 per cent respectively.

Tables 8.4 to 8.6 further provide information on the performance of individual countries and country groups in regard to traditional agricultural exports, defined as accounting for at least 1.5 per cent of export value in 1971–73.[10] The results confirm the findings relating to total merchandise exports.

Among outward-oriented newly-industrialising countries, only one country, Uruguay, had traditional agricultural exports in the 1971–3 period, and it experienced increases in export market shares during the 1974–8 period. In turn, all inward-oriented NICs lost market shares in their traditional agricultural exports, ranging from 3 per cent in Argentina to 33 per cent in Yugoslavia.

The less developed countries show a broadly similar pattern. Among outward-oriented LDCs, Kenya and Thailand made gains of 24 and 17 per cent respectively, Tunisia experienced no change, and only Mauritius had losses in traditional agriculture exports (11 per cent). By contrast, apart from India's unchanged position, all inward-oriented LDCs lost market shares, reaching 41 per cent in

Table 8.6 Changes in export market shares: country groupings

Country Group	Merchandise exports		Traditional primary exports	
	1974–8	1979–81	1974–8	1979–81
Outward-oriented NICs	118.3	137.2	124.4	129.0
Outward-oriented LDCs	117.5	137.3	114.1	118.0
Outward-oriented NICs and LDCs	118.2	137.2	119.6	123.5
Inward-oriented NICs	91.9	96.1	90.5	88.0
Inward-oriented LDCs	89.8	80.8	86.3	78.6
Inward-oriented NICs and LDCs	91.2	91.3	88.7	84.2

Note: See Table 8.4.
Source: See Table 8.4.

the case of Egypt, where the appreciation of the real exchange rate was especially large.

For groups of countries, data are available for all traditional primary exports that include non-agricultural products as well. As shown in Table 8.6, outward-oriented NICs had average gains of 24 per cent, compared with losses of 10 per cent for inward-oriented LDCs. Also, outward-oriented LDCs had gains of 14 per cent while inward-oriented LDCs had losses of an equal magnitude.

6 INCENTIVES AND EXPORT PERFORMANCE: COUNTRY EXPERIENCES IN THE 1978–81 PERIOD[11]

In the 1978–81 period, developing countries suffered the effects of the two-and-a-half fold increase in oil prices, the ensuing recession in the developed countries, and the rapid rise in world interest rates. At the same time, as shown in Tables 8.4 to 8.6, the export performance of these countries again reflected the policies applied.[12]

All outward-oriented newly-industrialising countries gained market shares in total merchandise exports, ranging from 16 to 67 per cent. In turn, apart from Brazil, which provided substantial export incentives, and Turkey, where important policy changes occurred in 1980, all inward-oriented NICs lost market shares, with Portugal showing the largest losses (46 per cent).

The situation was similar in the case of the less developed countries. While outward-oriented LDCs gained export market shares, ranging from 1 to 45 per cent, inward-oriented LDCs experienced losses of 13 to 47 per cent, the exceptions being the Philippines and Peru. However, in the case of Peru, the discovery of oil reserves pushed the results into the plus column.

As far as country groups are concerned, the outward-oriented NICs and LDCs both increased their average market shares in merchandise exports by 37 per cent. Conversely, inward-oriented NICs and LDCs experienced losses of 4 and 19 per cent respectively, although the results were improved by petroleum discoveries in Mexico in the first case and in Peru in the second.

All inward-oriented NICs lost market shares in traditional agricultural exports, ranging from 4 per cent in Brazil to 40 per cent in Yugoslavia. In turn, Uruguay, the only outward-oriented newly-industrialising country with traditional agricultural exports, had a small gain.

Also all inward-oriented LDCs lost market shares in their

traditional agricultural exports, with Egypt (55 per cent), the Philippines (52 per cent), and Jamaica (49 per cent) incurring the largest losses. As in the previous period, Kenya (19 per cent), and Thailand (24 per cent) made gains among outward-oriented LDCs while Mauritius (13 per cent) and Tunisia (20 per cent) experienced losses.

Finally, gains in market shares in traditional primary exports averaged 29 per cent in outward-oriented NICs and 18 per cent in outward-oriented LDCs. Conversely, average losses were 12 per cent in inward-oriented NICs and 21 per cent in inward-oriented LDCs.

CONCLUSIONS

The findings of this paper indicate that exports in general, and agricultural exports in particular, strongly respond to price incentives. This conclusion has been established by an econometric analysis of data as well as by comparisons of the experience of countries at different levels of development and following different policies.

The econometric analysis shows the responsiveness of the exports of goods and non-factor services, merchandise exports, and agricultural exports to changes in the real exchange. At the same time, the econometric estimates are subject to a downward bias, due in part to the use of ordinary least squares (OLS) estimation techniques and in part to the absence of a lag structure in the estimates. Evidence on the downward-bias of OLS is provided in estimates for export demand and export supply functions for Greece and Korea.[13]

The country analyses further indicate that outward-oriented countries had a far better export performance in regard to merchandise exports as well as traditional agricultural exports than inward-oriented economies. This conclusion applies to all the periods under consideration as well as to countries at different levels of development. The findings obtained by different methods of investigation thus complement and reinforce each other. At the same time, they disprove the oft-voiced views that agricultural exports and exports from countries at low levels of development would not respond to incentives.

Notes

1. Wholesale price indices are superior to consumer price indices that include the prices of non-traded goods and are affected by price controls

applied in a number of developing countries. The former, but not the latter, objection also applies to the use of GDP deflator in the calculations.

2. On alternative concepts of the real exchange rate, see Balassa (1987).
3. Ideally, one would need to consider the price of value added (the effective rate of protection) rather than product prices.
4. Also, fixed exchange rates among major currencies prevailed in the first period while flexible exchange rates dominated in the second period. This will have relevance, however, primarily for those developing countries that fixed their currency values in terms of a single foreign currency.
5. Needless to say, the data are subject to considerable error. Nevertheless there is no reason to assume that these errors would introduce a bias in the results.
6. Because of its lack of statistical significance, the relative price variable for traded and non-traded goods has been dropped from the estimating equations reported in the paper.
7. The discussion draws on Balassa and Associates (1982, ch. 3).
8. In the absence of appropriate deflators, the data refer to the dollar value of exports.
9. The discussion draws on the material presented in Balassa, 1984a and 1984b. The latter paper also describes the scheme of classification utilised in this paper.
10. This represents a subgroup of the traditional primary exports referred to earlier. In turn, it was not possible to separate non-traditional agricultural exports from other primary exports in the data.
11. The discussion draws on the material presented in Balassa, 1984b.
12. The data relate to the ratio of average export market shares in the 1979–81 period to average shares in the 1976–78 period.
13. Balassa, Voloudakis, Fylaktos, and Suh, 1985.

References

Balassa, B. (1984a) 'Adjustment to External Shocks in Developing Countries', in Csikós-Nagy, B., Hague, D. and Hill, G. (eds) *The Economics of Relative Prices* (London: Macmillan), pp. 352–84.

Balassa, B. (1984b) 'Adjustment Policies in Developing Countries: A Reassessment', *World Development* vol. 12, no. 9, pp. 955–72.

Balassa, B. (1987) 'Effects of Exchange Rate Changes in Developing Countries', *Indian Journal of Economics*, forthcoming.

Balassa, B. and Associates (1982) *Development Strategies in Semi-Industrial Economies* (Baltimore, Md: The Johns Hopkins University Press).

Balassa, B., Voloudakis, E., Fylaktos, P. and Suh, S.T. (1985) 'Export Incentives and Export Growth in Developing Countries: An Econometric Investigation', World Bank Development Research Department Discussion Paper No. 159 (Washington, DC) October.

9 The Old and New Export Pessimism: A Critical Survey

Gerald M. Meier
STANFORD UNIVERSITY

The very success of the East Asian NICs (newly industrialising countries) has, ironically, evoked a new export pessimism. This paper sorts out the arguments underlying this pessimism and evaluates their credibility.[1] The discussion moves from a summary of the old export pessimism and the results of import substitution (Section 1), to the case for export promotion (Section 2), and to an evaluation of the new export pessimism (Section 3).

1 THE OLD EXPORT PESSIMISM

In the 1950s and 1960s many newly developing countries embraced a strategy of import-substituting industrialisation (ISI). In large part, the ISI strategy was based on a pessimistic view regarding primary product exports – stemming from the dismal interwar experience and the allegations of low price elasticity, low income elasticity, fluctuation in export receipts, and deterioration in the commodity and double factoral terms of trade.

In this early period there were three different types of elasticity pessimists; Nurkse's inward-looking balanced growth; Rosenstein–Rodan's argument for co-ordinated investments in a balanced growth pattern; and Mahalanobis's case for heavy sector import substitution industrialisation (Bhagwati, 1984, pp. 199–200).

Economists also formulated some logical protectionist arguments for an import-substituting strategy. A case could be made for protection based on dynamic external economies, the learning effects in an infant industry, and factor market disequilibrium. In reality, however, ISI became the preferred trade strategy not because of the rational arguments of economists but rather because of expeditious policy actions to meet balance of payments crises and because of social and political forces acting on policy makers. Interest groups were catered for in the political market. In their promotion of a sheltered home market, a common interest was found on the part of the bureaucratic–authoritarian state, urban manufacturing entrepreneurs, and multinationals supplying technology and capital. Protection also met the State's objectives of pursuing revenue (and expenditure) maximising activities through maximum revenue tariffs and export taxes.[2]

The adverse results of ISI have been chronicled in detail for numerous countries (Little, Scitovsky, and Scott, 1970; Bhagwati, 1978; Krueger, 1978; Balassa, 1982). Given the government's use of 'nth best' policy instruments, such as overvalued exchange rates combined with direct quantitative controls and high effective rates of protection, it is not surprising that ISI was not targeted according to systematic economic criteria but was pursued in a chaotic, inefficient manner and for too long a time. The ISI syndrome imposed dynamic losses on the entire economy that were far greater than simply the loss of neoclassical static allocative efficiency.

2 EXPORT-ORIENTED INDUSTRIALISATION

While many countries continued to pursue ISI, a few departed from import substitution after the first stage in the late 1950s and early 1960s and adopted an export orientation programme. In part, the policy change was influenced by the resurgence of neoclassical economics.[3] More generally, policy makers had to react against the adverse effects of ISI and seek measures that would accelerate growth, promote employment, and relax the foreign exchange constraint. In addition, there was a desire for greater autonomy – a desire not to depend on foreign aid or borrowing that had to be resorted to when there was the eventual shortage of foreign exchange under ISI (Findlay, 1986, p. 21). And it was clear that international trade was growing at an historically record rate. As Sir Arthur Lewis said in the 1960s of Jamaica, 'If Jamaica could capture just a fraction of one per cent of something (world trade in manufactures) that is growing by 10 per cent a year, its development problems would be solved.' Jamaica did not succeed in doing so, but the East Asian NICs did.

To support the export sector, the government reduced protectionist policies that discriminated against exports and also introduced positive measures that discriminated in favour of exports. On the one side, the government liberalised the foreign trade regime and made exports competitive through a high real effective exchange rate (real depreciation). On the other side, positive export incentives were provided, as in Korea, through a drawback system, indirect domestic tax exemptions, direct tax reductions on income earned from exports, preferential public utility rates, generous wastage allowances on imported raw materials, indirect domestic tax exemptions on intermediate inputs used for the production of exports, and accelerated depreciation allowances.

Except in Hong Kong, exports were promoted not through *laissez-faire* but through an active role of the State in directing the economy towards reliance on world market forces. Although there was actually considerable intervention by the government, it was for the purpose of fostering a market-oriented economy that provided trading opportunities and changed incentives of market participants who made economic decisions. In essence, the highly interactive relationship between government and the private sector was effective in removing the bias against exports and correcting macroeconomic and microeconomic price signals. The export orientation required that the country be competitive on world markets through control of inflation, a fall in the real effective exchange rate, attraction of foreign capital, and use of multinationals for technology and marketing. Not only was national economic management efficient and honest, but in addition political stability and the government's lasting policy commitment to export-led industrialisation stimulated investment in the export sector.[4]

The dramatic results of export-oriented industrialisation programmes are now well known (Tyler, 1981; Balassa, 1982; Lal *et al.* 1987; Solis and Montemayor, 1986; Kravis, 1970). Table 9.1 summarises the rise in manufactured exports from the NICs. Among these countries the super exporters became the super performers in development achievement. Table 9.2 portrays achievements in the East Asian NICs. As their exports rose, and as both export and import growth exceeded the rate of growth of GNP, so too did the NICs experience high rates of overall growth, increasing employment, and a greater degree of industrialisation.

Not only was the rise in the quantum index of exports remarkable (for instance, in Taiwan from less than 5 in 1950 (1976 = 100) to

Table 9.1 Manufactured exports[a] of newly industrialising countries (NICs), 1965–82

Countries	Value in mill US $			Share in total exports %		Annual real rates of growth %	
	1965	1973	1982	1965	1982	1965–73	1973–82
First Generation NICs	2 645	16 797	77 735	33	58	19	10
Argentina	84	735	1 846	6	24	24	2
Brazil	124	1 217	7 721	8	38	26	14
Hong Kong[c]	820	3 650	13 161	93	96	14	7
India	813	1 561	5 000[d]	48	56[d]	3	5[e]
Israel	276	1 109	4 243	64	80	13	7
Mexico	166	1 130	2 013	14	10	21	–1
Singapore[c]	72	1 004	5 034	52	37	32	11
South Korea	104	2 717	19 121[d]	59	90[d]	43	16[e]
Taiwan	187	3 674	19 595	42	89	38	11
Second Generation NICs	230	1 500	10 325	1	21	21	15
Chile	15	45	780[d]	2	21[d]	9	30[e]
Colombia	34	307	746	6	24	25	2
Indonesia	—	61	808	—	4	—	23
Malaysia	64	347	2 735	6	23	17	16
Morocco	23	130	706	5	34	24	12
Peru	4	29	377	1	14	21	23
Philippines	66	220	1 146	8	23	10	11
Thailand	12	255	1 872	2	22	39	15
Tunisia	12	84	834[d]	10	33[d]	21	21[e]
Uruguay	—	24	323	—	32	—	23
Total	2 876	18 297	88 061	7	44	20	10

in p.c. of developing countries' exports	68	79	79	—	—	17	10
in p.c. of world exports	3	5	9	—	—	11	5
Manufactured exports of developing countries	4 212	23 148	111 519	—	—		
world	102 137	346 851	1 042 052	—	—		

[a] SITC 5+6+7+8–68.
[b] Export values deflated by unit value indices for manufactured exports of industrialised countries.
[c] Excluding re-exports.
[d] 1981.
[e] 1973–1981

Sources: UN, Yearbook of International Trade Statistics, Department of International Economic and Social Affairs, New York, various issues. – UN, Commodity Trade Statistics, Department of International Economic and Social Affairs, Statistical Papers, New York, various issues. – UN, Monthly Bulletin of Statistics, Department of International Economic and Social Affairs, Statistical Office, New York, various issues. – UNCTAD, Handbook of International Trade and Development Statistics, New York 1983; Supplement 1984. – Estadísticas de Exportación hasta 1969, Banco Industrial del Peru, Division de Commercio Exterior, Lima 1971. – Analisis Estadistico, Importacion – Exportacion, Centro de Estadisticas Nacionales y Comercio Internacional Edicion no. 17, Montevideo 1973. – Economic Survey of Singapore 1979/80, Chief Statistician Department of Statistics, Singapore. – The Trade of China (Taiwan District) 1982, Compiled and published by the Statistical Department Inspectorate General of Customs, Taipei, Taiwan, The Republic of China, Chinese Maritime Customs, Statistical Series No. 1, 1983. – Economic Survey 1982–83, Government of India, printed by the Manager, Govt. of India Press, New Delhi 1984.

Adapted from Juergen B. Donges and Ulrich Hiemenz, 'Export Liberalization and the Outward-Oriented Trade Regime,' Kiel Working Papers, No. 241, September, 1986, p. 29.

Table 9.2 Comparative structure and growth

	Hong Kong	South Korea	Singapore	All middle-income countries
1 Per Capita GNP				
1965	2019	626	1743	700
1984	6330	2110	7260	1250
2 Population 1984 (million)	5.4	40.1	2.5	1187.6
3 Per cent of GDP in				
a Agriculture				
1965	2	38	3	21
1984	1	14	1	14
b Manufacturing				
1965	24	18	15	20
1984	n.a.	28	25	22
c Investment				
1965	36	15	22	21
1984	24	29	47	21
4 Average annual growth rate, per cent				
a Per capita Real GNP				
1965–84	6.2	6.6	7.8	3.1
b Real GDP				
1965–73	7.9	10.0	13.0	7.4
1973–84	9.1	7.2	8.2	4.4
c Real manufacturing output				
1965–73	n.a.	21.1	19.5	9.2
1973–84	n.a.	11.5	7.6	5.5
d Exports				
1965–73	11.7	31.7	11.0	6.3
1973–84	12.9	15.1	7.1	0.8
e Imports				
1965–73	10.6	22.4	9.8	8.4
1973–84	9.3	9.7	7.1	4.4
5 Structure of trade				
a Percentage manufactured exports				
1965	86	59	34	16
1983	91	91	57	46
b Exports of goods and services as per cent of GDP				
1965	71	9	123	18
1984	107	37	n.a.	25

n.a. = Not available
Source: World Bank, *World Development Report 1986*, Various Tables.

more than 138 in 1980), but there was also a rapid transformation from one export commodity to another – a steady progression in the Asian NICs to higher value added exports that are skill- and technology-intensive.

It is true that the countries that pursued outward-looking policies were more vulnerable to the external shocks of the 1970s and early 1980s – oil price increases, rising real interest rates, deterioration in the terms of trade, and international recession. But at the same time these countries proved the most capable in adjusting to the external shocks by expanding their exports instead of being forced to make drastic cuts in their imports or to rely more heavily on foreign capital as other countries did (Balassa, 1981; Solis and Montemayor, 1986).

3 THE NEW EXPORT PESSIMISM

In recent years, a number of arguments have been advanced that constitute a new form of export pessimism. Now there is scepticism regarding the potential for exports of manufactures from additional NICs. Cline (1982) has asked whether the East Asian model of development can be generalised. Lewis (1980) has expressed concern about the slowing down in the growth of world trade. Streeten (1982) has taken a cool look at outward-looking strategies for development. Considering the various sceptical views, we can classify them into three categories: (1) the belief that the countries that have been able to follow export-led industrialisation have done so because of favourable initial conditions not to be replicated elsewhere; (2) the assertion that future demand will not support exports from additional developing countries: and (3) the argument that, in any case, exports do not really act as an 'engine of growth'.

Consider first the contention that the success stories of the NICs are special cases based on initial conditions that cannot be repeated elsewhere. It has been claimed that the initial conditions for the East Asian NICs were peculiarly favourable – their colonial legacy of infrastructure and human resources, Chinese cultural heritage, geographic and cultural homogeneity, postwar land reforms, inflow of foreign aid, and proximity to Japan as a growth pole. But on the other side, there were also especially adverse initial conditions. Korea and Taiwan suffered severely from the Second World War and Korea was left a devastated half-economy after the Korean

War. Both countries had very unfavourable natural resource endowments and extremely high labour-land ratios. From the analytical histories of development of these countries the weight of evidence is that their strong development performance is not attributable to favourable initial conditions but rather to their adopting appropriate policy measures.

If their successes were to be attributed to unusually favourable initial conditions, both domestically and externally, rather than to good policies, then we too would have to be pessimistic about future development through trade. But the lesson of the NICs is that effective demand management and efficient supply-oriented policies have been the strategic policy variables accounting for successful development performance. As Ranis (1978, p. 398) notes, we must differentiate between those elements of 'non-transferability' that relate to obstacles 'in nature' versus those relating to obstacles 'in man'. The latter can be overcome by institutional choices and the political process. Appropriate policy measures need not be confined to any one country. The lessons of the NICs can be transferred to other countries by the creation and extension of social, economic and political institutions and mechanisms that promote the mobilisation of resources, their efficient allocation and increase in total factor productivity.

Another set of arguments underlying the new export pessimism focuses on the constraint of external demand. The fallacy of composition is invoked to maintain that it is impossible to generalise the experience of the Asian NICs. If many other developing countries reach the same high ratio of exports to GDP as have the NICs, would not the market be saturated (Cline, 1982)? And would not their terms of trade deteriorate (Streeten, 1982, p. 165)?

It is, however, unreasonable to expect that other countries will attain the same very high ratios of export to GDP as have the NICs. Moreover one should not view the future problem of trade as simply a division of a fixed bill of exports: the range of exports is ever-changing. It is characteristic of the export of manufactures that they become ever more diversified. Empirical studies have shown that intra-industry trade through horizontal specialisation has increased and that the extent of intra-industry trade in industrialised countries has grown much more rapidly with the developing countries than with other industrialised countries (Balassa, 1983). There appears to be wide scope for horizontal specialisation or intra-industry specialisation.

The outward-looking strategy has been successful because the NICs have been able to capitalise on dynamic forces that produce stages in comparative advantage and that allow a 'multiple catch-up' process. The ever-changing structure of comparative costs allows a given country to proceed up the ladder of comparative advantage from specialisation in resource-intensive exports to unskilled labour-intensive exports, to skilled labour-intensive exports, to capital-intensive exports, to knowledge-intensive exports. And as a given country moves up the ladder, another country in the queue is able to climb another rung on the ladder. Thus, as Japan has risen on the ladder, the East Asian NICs have become major suppliers of Japan's former exports. As Hong Kong, Singapore, Taiwan, and South Korea proceed to the higher stages of comparative advantage, their former positions are being taken by Thailand, Malaysia, Indonesia, and the Philippines. As the East Asian exporters increase their real wages and accumulate capital, they should in turn become markets for other countries that acquire comparative advantage in the labour-intensive products that have been abandoned by countries that are advancing up the ladder of comparative advantage.

The fear that the terms of trade will worsen must depend on a belief that, as exports increase, the growth in the more developed countries will be so low and protectionist policies so severe that export prices must fall relatively to import prices. But it may be noted that even if demand were so constrained, it would still be possible for the governments of the exporting countries to restrict the volume of manufactured exports through a system of mutually-agreed export duties, with the rates of duties probably varying as between different broad commodity groups (Henderson, 1982, pp. 295–6).

The period 1945–73 was indeed a unique period of growth in world real GNP and an even higher rate of growth in world exports. Against this exceptional period and the subsequent recession in the early 1980s, it is not surprising that much of the new export pessimism stems from the fear that the external demand for exports from the developing countries will be insufficient because of slower income growth in the more developed countries and the spread of protectionism against imports from developing countries. High demand for imports is especially important in the American, Japanese and European markets. If external demand slackens, or if LDCs are denied market access, then it will of course be more difficult to maintain an export-led growth strategy.

But this fear can be exaggerated. Contradicting the commonly held belief that LDC export growth depends on income growth in the more developed countries, a study by Riedel emphasises supply conditions in the developing countries rather than external demand factors as the principal determinants of a developing country's export performance in manufactures (Riedel, 1984). Unlike exports of primary products, the exports of manufactures are not so dependent on growth in the more developed countries because they can substitute for the production of competitive manufactured goods in the more developed countries. Several country studies also show that domestic policy is much more important than overseas market constraints in explaining export performance (see Wolf, 1982). Superior export performance has come not from passive acceptance of external demand but rather from what Kravis measured as the 'competitiveness factor' and the 'diversification factor', especially the former (Kravis, 1970, pp. 867–9).

The declining share of India's and Sub-Saharan Africa's exports during the 1970s while other developing countries increased their shares is attributable to their not being competitive on world markets rather than to the constraint of external demand.

It should also be realised that the share of imports from developing countries in the consumption of manufactured goods in industrial countries was only 4.35 per cent in 1980, varying from a low of 1.75 per cent in Canada to a high of 6.8 per cent in the Netherlands (Anjaria *et al.*, 1982, Table 4, p. 85). Given the low import penetration ratios, there is clearly considerable potential for a substantial growth in manufactured exports from developing countries. If they can be competitive on the side of export supply, their share of the import demand in the developed countries can increase even if consumption in industrial countries does not grow as rapidly as it did in the 1945–73 period.

Moreover there is potential for more trade among the developing countries themselves – not as a substitute for, but as a complement to North-South trade in manufactures. For example, although intra-Asian trade has been expanding, the Asian NICs now export only about 12 per cent of their total exports to ASEAN countries, and some 3 per cent to South Asia, while ASEAN countries export only some 4 per cent to other ASEAN countries and 20 per cent to the Asian NICs. The application of the stages approach to comparative advantage indicates considerable potential for the extension of trade among countries at similar or at lower levels of development. This expansion might be realised if an outward-oriented development strategy were accepted by all the developing countries so that the developing countries did not try to produce similar, or even identical, commodities. And, of course, the higher the rate of growth achieved by the developing countries, the greater can be the amount of South–South trade, and the less must the developing countries depend on the growth of the United States, Japan, and the EEC.

Lewis (1980) has emphasised this potential for South–South trade. Taken as a group the LDCs could quickly end their dependence on the more developed countries for fertilisers, cement and steel, and gradually throw off their dependence for machinery. The new theories of international trade that incorporate economies of scale and intra-industry specialisation in intermediate products and in differentiated final products also indicate an increasing scope for South–South trade (Stewart, 1984, p. 105).

The emphasis on protection can also be overdone. During a period of rising protectionism, the share of developing countries in the world export of manufactures increased from 5 per cent in 1970 to 9 per cent in 1980 and was 13 per cent in 1984. Some 62 per cent of the developing countries' total manufactured exports were consigned to developed market-economy countries.

In a study of the period of the 1970s when protection increased, Hughes and Krueger (1984) presented the following empirical findings:

(i) Despite the widespread efforts to increase protection in the industrial countries, the penetration of manufactured goods imports from all sources into the industrial countries increased from 11.6 per cent of the absorption of the manufactured goods in 1970 to 17.6 per cent in 1980. At the same time the share of developing countries in the absorption of manufactured goods in the industrial countries increased from 1.7 per cent to 3.4 per cent. About half of the developing countries' gain would have accrued had the developing countries merely maintained their share in the general expansion of imports in domestic markets, but the other half may be regarded as growth at the expense of imports from developed country suppliers.

(ii) The gains from the exports of the developing countries were widely dispersed among the countries in general, although the Asian developing countries fared best.

(iii) The commodity composition of developing country manufactured exports to industrial countries shifted towards the more sophisticated products, with largest increases in shares for fabricated metal products, machinery and equipment, manufactured chemicals, petroleum, coal and rubber products.

Hughes and Krueger (1984, p. 413) concluded that 'the overwhelming impression is that despite all the public discussion of protection and the political pressures for it, the effects on imports of manufactures from developing countries of protectionist measures were relatively small. The rate of increase of LDC market shares was sufficiently great that it is difficult to imagine that rates would have been significantly higher in the absence of any protectionist measures. . .'

An OECD study also concluded that the most important effect of protectionist policies has been to accelerate the geographical diversification of LDC exports of manufactures. During the late 1970s the five top export earning NICs most exposed to protectionist measures by industrial nations diverted a large share of their exports to non-OECD countries. Another change helping to maintain export growth has been the deliberate shifting of certain production activities out of the East Asian NICs into less restricted low labour cost countries. Further, in the 1970s middle-income countries with substantial manufacturing sectors that turned toward export-oriented growth were able to capture market shares from the more inward-looking LDCs (OECD, 1985, pp. 177–80).

The question that is now relevant is what might be the future demand for protection. In considering this question, Michaely (1985) examined the specific attributes of the industrial exports of the NICS which distinguished them from exports of developed countries, and would make them particularly likely to be considered as a threat. The fact that some of the exports from the NICs provoked particular attention in the developed economies, leading to strong negative reactions and specific protectionist measures, would indicate that these exports possess attributes that enhance some impacts beyond what would be expected from their relatively small share of aggregate imports of manufactures in the developed countries. Michaely found that the following elements contributed to the demand for protection in recent years: (1) the factor content of the NICs' exports – specifically, their relative intensity in unskilled and semi-skilled labour; (ii) the nature of the exported goods, which consist largely of final consumer goods rather than of machinery and equipment;

(iii) the NICs' lack of retaliatory power, and (iv) the context of a relatively stagnant world economy suffering from high unemployment.

In so far as the future demand for protection depends on these elements, there are reasons to believe that the demand may diminish. As the NICs keep developing, their relative factor scarcities must gradually approach those of the more developed countries. Already there has been a tendency for the abundance of unskilled and semi-skilled labour to be reduced and for the factor content of goods exported by the NICs to become more similar to that of the developed countries, with less impact of this trade on factor displacement and income distribution. As the share of capital goods in manufactured exports of the NICs increases, this too should mean that the difference in composition of the exports of manufactures will become less significant as a source of discriminatory treatment of the exports of NICs.

Michaely also points to the fact that contraction in the importing countries of activities competing with exports of the NICs has been taking place and seems most likely to proceed gradually in future years. Hence the smaller the size of the potentially protected sector, the lower should be the demand for protection.

A study by Havrylyshyn and Civan (1983) also relates the degree of protection to the amount of intra-industry trade and indicates that there is a high level of intra-industry trade for the NICs. It is submitted that adjustment will be made easier the more the nature of trade becomes intra-industry as opposed to inter-industry. As development proceeds, the evolution of international trade patterns will tend towards more intra-industry trade and hence less demand for protection as the industries that compete against imports from developing countries become the same ones that export to developing countries.

To the extent that the more developed countries experience higher rates of growth in the future, there should also be less protection. And if in the Uruguay Round countries can be brought back to the principles of GATT with a reformed market safeguard clause for domestic injury (Article XIX), there may also be less resort to Orderly Market Agreements and Voluntary Export Restraints. Even under quantitative restrictions, however, there is scope for product improvement because the various restraint agreements tend to specify a maximum growth rate in quantity, but not in value. The exporting countries may then shift toward higher value-added manufactures.

A final set of arguments question the power of exports to act as an 'engine of growth'. Even if exports do increase, is not the scope for export-led development limited? Is not the carry-over to the domestic economy weak? Strong critics of the export-led strategy are represented by the school of dependency. In milder form, some sceptics refer to 'export enclaves' and to 'branch plant societies' with footloose industries that yield only shallow, short-lived development.

In considering the different effects of exports, we should recognise that with the use of different combinations of inputs to produce different types of export commodities there will be different rates of learning and different linkage effects. We would normally expect the stimulating forces to be stronger under the following conditions: the higher the growth rate of the export sector, the greater the direct impact of the export sector on employment and personal income; the more the expansion of exports has a 'learning effect' in terms of increasing productivity and instilling new skills, the more the export sector is supplied through domestic inputs instead of imports; the more the distribution of export income favours those with a propensity to consume domestic goods instead of imports, the more productive is the investment resulting from any saving of export income; the more extensive are the externalities and linkages connected with the export sector, and the more stable are the export receipts that are retained at home.

After analysing the character of a country's export base for an indication of the strength of the stimulus to development provided by its export commodities, we must go on to examine the strength of the response of the diffusion mechanism within the domestic economy for evidence of how receptive the domestic economy is to the stimulus from exports. The strength of the response mechanism to the export stimulus will depend on the extent of market imperfections in the domestic economy and also on non-economic barriers in the general environment. The response is stronger under the following conditions: the more developed the infrastructure of the economy, the more market institutions are developed; the more extensive is the development of human resources, the fewer are the pricing distortions that affect resource allocation; and the greater is the capacity to bear risks.

What has been outstanding in the experience of countries that have pursued export-oriented industrialisation is that their development performances have been much more impressive after departing from ISI, and that their superior performances have been based not only on the static gains from trade but even more importantly on the dynamic gains that improve a country's development foundations.

Bhagwati (1978) has shown that for countries that liberalise their foreign trade regimes, the average ratio of effective exchange rate of exports to effective exchange rate of imports (EERx/EERm) is much closer to unity than under restrictive type regimes. In retreating from ISI, there is a reduction in allocative inefficiency. The incentives for export promotion are also less chaotic and more 'neutral' under the liberalised trade regimes. This is because the incentives for exports are first used to offset the previous bias against exports. Subsequently, an oversubsidisation of exports is avoided because measures that give incentives to exports incur self-evident costs that fall directly on the budget and invoke a quicker and stronger policy reversal, whereas inefficient ISI based on quantitative restrictions had no such bounds. By reducing import quotas, the export promotion strategy also eliminates the practice of rent seeking, and a removal of tariffs reduces the activity of revenue seeking (Bhagwati and Srinivasan, 1980).

As exports rise, there is greater growth in the economy than can be accounted for simply by the removal of trade distortions and the realisation of the direct gains of trade. The indirect or dynamic gains are even more important – extending far beyond the gains from the neo-classical trade model. Allowing for increasing returns to scale in production and departing from the assumption of perfectly competitive markets, we can readily realise that there will be gains from reducing the monopolistic practices that arose under ISI and gains from realising economies of scale in the export sector. In an inward-looking economy, import-competing industries tend to be concentrated because the narrow domestic market cannot absorb the output of even a few plants of optimal scale. If scale economies are important in several industries, some of which have export markets, a restrictive trade policy is likely to result in a non-optimal industrial structure. Trade liberalisation then brings about a reduction of monopolistic practices in the concentrated import-competing industries and allows exploitation of scale economies in exporting industries (Srinivasan, 1986).

Production for world markets allows not only the establishment of more efficient size of plants that overcome indivisibilities, utilise capital more fully, and realise economies of scale. It also confers benefits from the exposure to more competition – improvement in product quality, x-efficiency, reduction of production costs, and an enlargement of technological capability by facilitating technology transfer. Export production also has had a more favourable impact on employment creation than has production for import replacement. Export promotion has mitigated the problem of labour surplus through higher rates of growth in outputs and through greater use of labour per unit of capital and per unit of output (Krueger, 1983).

The increase in exports, in turn, makes the economy all the more open. The foreign exchange constraint is relaxed, and this allows less restrictive control over imports. The country becomes more credit-worthy on international capital markets. Direct foreign investment may also be attracted to take advantage of the developing country's factor endowment.

The openness of the economy extends not only to the foreign trade sector and to international capital flows but also to a whole range of domestic policies. It is the integrative combination of improvement in the domestic economic organisation and the increase in exports that together yield such large dynamic gains. These gains can best be understood by following Myint's emphasis on the 'organisational dualism' in a developing economy and the indirect induced effects of trade on growth. Myint submits that, even if one could remove all the policy induced distortions, a sub-stratum of 'natural' dualism would still remain, reflecting the incomplete state of development of the domestic organisation framework of the underdeveloped countries. A natural dualism exists in factor markets, goods markets, and in the administration and fiscal system because of institutional conditions and the costs of transactions, transportation, information and administration.[5] In Myint's 'dualism' model, the underdeveloped country will not be on its production possibility curve: even in the absence of any distortion, it will be on a lower curve – its production feasibility curve, which is only feasible with the incomplete state of development of its domestic organisational framework. Further, the gap between the production possibility curve and the production feasibility curve will be skewed against the increase in output of the traditional sector as frictional costs will be higher within the unorganised traditional sector and in the transactions between the traditional and modern sectors and will be lower within the modern sector and in the transactions between the modern sector and outside world.

In this model one may look upon the incompletely developed organisational framework of an underdeveloped country as being in a state of formation which can be improved or repressed by appropriate or inappropriate trade policies. The production feasibility curve is shiftable through the induced effects of trade policy whereas ISI policies tend to aggravate the organisational dualism of the domestic economic framework. The expansion of exports in accordance with the country's potential comparative advantage will improve the longer-run effectiveness of the domestic economic framework in promoting development. The gains from trade are then realised by a movement towards the production frontier and not simply by a movement along the production frontier as in neoclassical trade theory (Myint, 1985, 1987).

Not only is there a direct gain from more efficient resource allocation, but also gains from an increase in the supply of investable resources and an increase in the productivity of resources in the more general sense. There is an improvement in the organisation of production, more effective incentives, and more market information. All this improves the domestic economic organisation to take advantage of available external opportunities in the form of international trade, foreign capital, technology and ideas.

4 CONCLUSIONS

The dismal science has always had a pessimistic bias towards the long-run future. Export pessimism is part of that bias. But history abounds with a sequence of NICs – from Britain to Germany to Sweden to Japan to Spain and Yugoslavia, to East Asian countries. Can other countries follow in the future? Is not export pessimism now justified?

It cannot be denied that the external forces of growth in the more developed countries and protection do affect demand for exports from the developing countries. But we have contended that a successful export performance is more a function of appropriate policies in the developing country than of external demand. A competitive export supply is what matters most. In the successful cases, this has been a matter of appropriate macro and micro policies – not any exceptional set of favourable initial conditions.

The lesson is one of policy reform to promote exports. Even if growth overseas is low and the protection threat is not reduced, it would be a mistake for the developing country to try and adjust by reducing imports through ISI. The old export pessimism criticised the dictates of neoclassical trade theory. That theory, however, focused only on the direct static gains from trade and the effect of a given autonomous pattern of economic growth on trade. Because of these limitations in its perfect competition model of the domestic economy, the neoclassical trade theory did not give proper emphasis to the indirect gains or losses from trade and the longer-run effects that a given pattern of trade had on growth. Only later – with the experience of the NICs as evidence – has it been realised that the major explanation of the superior development performance of countries that follow export-oriented industrialisation is to be found in the indirect dynamic benefits from trade that extend far beyond simply the direct static gains from a removal of distortions (Myint, 1987). Whereas proponents of the old export pessimism could criticise neoclassical trade theory and assert that the dynamic gains from ISI would outweigh the possible static costs of protection, it is now realised that the dynamic gains are far superior for export promotion. The case for development through trade can be expressed in stronger terms than in its neoclassical version.

The present call for policy reform, however, may go unheeded – and that is the real basis for the new export pessimism. The undertaking of a trade liberalisation programme may have to be underwritten with external finance. Unless this can be done, a country may be unwilling to incur the threat of balance of payments problems during the transition period before the liberalised regime becomes effective in reallocating resources and increasing exports. And, in the first place, economists must be listened to. They may advocate policies of the new orthodoxy but, as the new political economy shows, they may none the less be ignored. Instead of viewing the policy-maker as exogenous, and the State as a Platonic guardian concerned with movement toward a Pareto optimum, the new political economy views the policy-maker as endogenous and examines why the government behaves as it does (Colander, 1984). The rationale of the political market is not that of the economic market. In such a clash, the economist's policy recommendations may well be ignored.

Much of our discussion has been informal and rather impressionistic. If further research were to be done on this subject, it would be desirable to have an econometric study of the relative influences on exports of demand and supply factors. Quantification of the 'competitiveness factor' and of an 'index of transformation' to new exports would be especially informative. There is also a need to quantify the effects of protection on exports from various developing countries. And if appropriate policies to maintain competitive export supply are so important, additional research in the new political economy must be undertaken to determine the obstacles to policy reform and how these obstacles can be removed so that policy reform may be instituted.

Notes

1. Some sections appeared in a preliminary version in Meier, (1985) Ch. 2.
2. For a political economy explanation of ISI see Hirschman (1968), Evans (1979), Magee (1984) ch. 3, Findlay and Wellisz (1982).
3. The influence of policy advice by economists is difficult to document, but Professors T.C. Liu and S.C. Tsiang were influential in Taiwan in 1958 in achieving a devaluation coupled with trade liberalisation. See Tsiang (1985) pp. 36–7. Also influential in Korea in 1965 was a report on financial reforms by Professors Edward Shaw, John Gurley and Hugh Patrick.
4. For details of measures undertaken to promote exports in the NICs see Jones and Sakong (1980), Westphal and Kim (1977), Corbo *et al.* (1985), Galenson (1985).
5. See also the related analysis by Matthews (1986).

References

Anjaria, S. *et al.* (1982) 'Developments in Trade Policy', International Monetary Fund Occasional Paper no. 16.

Balassa, B. (1981) 'The Newly Industrializing Developing Countries after the Oil Crisis', *Weltwirtschaftliches Archiv*, Band 117, Heft 1, pp. 124–42.

Balassa, B. (1982) *Development Strategies in Semi-industrial Economies* (Baltimore, Md: Johns Hopkins University Press).

Balassa, B. (1983) 'Comments' in Cline, W.R. (ed.) *Trade Policy in the 1980s* (Cambridge, Mass.: MIT Press) pp. 713–14.

Bhagwati, J.N. (1978) *The Anatomy and Consequences of Exchange Control Regimes* (Cambridge, Mass.: Ballinger).

Bhagwati, J.N. (1984) 'Comment' in Meier, Gerald M. and Seers, Dudley (eds) *Pioneers in Development* (Oxford University Press).

Bhagwati, J., N. and Srinivasan, T.N. (1980) 'Revenue Seeking: A Generalization of the Theory of Tariffs', *Journal of Political Economy*, vol. 88, no. 6, December, pp. 1069–87.

Bradford, C.I., Jr. (1986) 'East Asian Models: Myths and Lessons' in Lewis, J.P. and Kallab, V. (eds) *Development Strategies Reconsidered* (Washington DC: Overseas Development Council) pp. 115–28.

Cline, W.R. (1982) 'Can the East Asian Model of Development be Generalized?', *World Development*, vol. 10, no. 2, February, pp. 81–90.

Colander, D.C. (ed.) (1984) *Neo-classical Political Economy* (Cambridge Mass.: Ballinger).

Corbo, V., Krueger, A. and Ossa, F. (eds) (1985) *Export-Oriented Development Strategies* (Boulder and London: Westview Press).

Evans, P. (1979) *Dependent Development* (Princeton University Press).

Findlay, R. (1986) 'Trade, Development, and the State', Economic Growth Center, Yale University, processed.

Findlay, R. and Wellisz, S. (1982) 'Endogenous Tariffs, the Political Economy of Trade Restrictions and Welfare' in Bhagwati, J.N. (ed.) *Import Competition and Response* (University of Chicago Press).

Galenson, W. (ed.) (1985) *Foreign Trade and Investment* (Madison: University of Wisconsin Press).

Havrylyshyn, O. and Civan, E. (1983) 'Intra-industry Trade and the Stage of Development: A Regression Analysis of Industrial and Developing Countries' in Tharakan, P.K.M. (ed.) *Intra-Industry Trade: Empirical and Methodological Aspects* (Amsterdam: North Holland) pp. 111–40.

Henderson, P.D. (1982) 'Trade Policies and Strategies – Case for a Liberal Approach', *The World Economy*, vol. 5, no. 3, November, pp. 291–302.

Hirschman, A.O. (1968) 'The Political Economy of Import-Substituting Industrialization in Latin America', *Quarterly Journal of Economics*, vol. 82, no. 1, February, pp. 3–32.

Hughes, H. and Krueger, A.O. (1984) 'Effects of Protection in Developed Countries on Developing Countries' Exports of Manufactures' in Baldwin, R.E. and Krueger, A.O. (eds) *The Structure and Evolution of US Trade Policy* (University of Chicago Press) chapter 11.

Jones, P. and Sakong, I. (1980) *Government, Business, and Entrepreneurship in Economic Development: The Korean Case* (Cambridge Mass.: Harvard University Press).

Kravis, I.B. (1970) 'Trade as a Handmaiden of Growth: Similarities between the Nineteenth and Twentieth Centuries', Economic Journal, vol. 80, no. 320, December, pp. 850–72.

Krueger, A.O. (1978) *Liberalization Attempts and Consequences* (New York: National Bureau of Economic Research).

Krueger, A.O. (1983) *Trade and Employment in Developing Countries*, Col. 3: Synthesis and Conclusions (University of Chicago Press).

Lal, D., and Rajapatiraha, S. (1987) 'Foreign Trade Regimes and Economic Growth in Developing Countries', *World Bank Research Observer*, vol. 2, no. 2, July.

Lewis, W.A. (1980) 'The Slowing Down of the Engine of Growth', *American Economic Review*. vol. 70, no. 2, September, pp. 555–64.

Little, I., Scitovsky, T. and Scott, M. (1970) *Industry and Trade in Some Developing Countries* (London: Oxford University Press)..

Magee, S.P. (1984) 'Endogenous Tariff Theory: A Survey' in Colander, D.C. (ed.) *Neoclassical Political Economy* (Cambridge, Mass.: Ballinger).

Matthews, R.C.O. (1986) 'The Economics of Institutions and the Source of Growth', *Economic Journal*, vol. 96, no. 384, December, pp. 903–18.

Meier, G.M. (1985) 'The New Export Pessimism' in Shishido, T. and Sato,

R. (eds) *Economic Policy and Development: New Perspectives* (Dover, Mass.: Auburn House Publishing Co.).

Michaely, M. (1985) 'The Demand for Protection against Exports of Newly Industrializing Countries', *Journal of Policy Modeling*, vol. 7, no. 1, pp. 123–32.

Myint, H. (1985) 'Organizational Dualism and Economic Development', *Asian Development Review*, vol. 3, no. 1, pp. 24–42.

Myint, H. (1987) 'The Neoclassical Resurgence in Development Economics: Its Strength and Limitations' in Meier, G.M. (ed.) *Pioneers in Development, Second Series* (New York: Oxford University Press).

OECD (1985) *Costs and Benefits of Protection* (Paris: OECD).

Ranis, G. (1978) 'Equity with Growth in Taiwan: How "Special" is the Special Case?', *World Development*, vol. 6, no. 1, January, pp. 397–409.

Riedel, J. (1984) 'Trade as an Engine of Growth in Developing Countries, Revisited', *Economic Journal*, vol. 94, no. 373, March, pp. 56–73.

Solis, L. and Montemayor, A. (1986) 'A Mexican View of the Choice between Outward and Inward Orientation' in Lewis, J.P. and Kallab, V. (eds) *Development Strategies Reconsidered* (Washington DC: Overseas Development Council) pp. 105–14.

Srinivasan, T.N. (1986) 'International Trade and Factor Movements in Development Theory, Policy and Experience', Twenty-fifth Anniversary Symposium on the State of Development Economics, 11–13 April 1986, Yale University, New Haven, Conn.

Stewart, F. (1984) 'Recent Theories of International Trade: Some Implications for the South' in Kierzkowski, Henry K. (ed.) *Monopolistic Competition and International Trade* (Oxford: Clarendon Press) pp. 84–107.

Streeten, Paul (1982) 'A Cool Look at "Outward-Looking' Strategies for Development', *The World Economy*, vol. 5, no. 2, September, pp. 159–69.

Tsiang, S.C. (1985) 'Foreign Trade and Investment as Boosters for Takeoff: The Experience of Taiwan' in Corbo *et al.* (eds) *Export-Oriented Development Strategies* (Boulder and London: Westview Press).

Tyler, W.J. (1981) 'Growth and Export Expansion in Developing Countries: Some Empirical Evidence', *Journal of Development Economics*, vol. 9, no. 1, August, pp. 121–48.

Westphal, L. and Kim, K.S. (1977) 'Industrial Policy and Development in Korea', World Bank Staff Working Paper no. 263 (Washington DC: World Bank).

Wolf, M. (1982) *India's Exports* (London: Oxford University Press).

10 Protection in Agriculture and Manufacturing: Meeting the Objectives of the Uruguay Round

Gary P. Sampson[1]
UNCTAD

1 INTRODUCTION

Among the objectives of the Bretton Woods system was a freer international exchange of goods, coupled with non-discriminatory trade relations, with national goals being pursued within the constraints of a multilateral framework. Recent actions, however, indicate that governments are moving outside the agreed framework; national priorities increasingly take precedence over multilateral commitments. Concern over these developments culminated in the meeting in September 1986 in Punta del Este, Uruguay, of ministers from the 91 contracting parties of the General Agreement on Tariffs and Trade (GATT). As a result of this meeting, a declaration was made announcing the start of a new round of multilateral trade negotiations. The list of topics to be discussed is long; the negotiations that are about to commence may have important implications for the trading system for the rest of the century and beyond.

The Ministerial Declaration states as a primary objective the desire to 'bring about further liberalisation and expansion of world trade to the benefit of . . . especially less developed contracting parties' and the 'improvement of access to markets by the reduction . . . of tariffs . . . and other non-tariff measures'.[2] This paper quantitatively examines some of the key matters of relevance for the attainment of this objective. The following section estimates the extent of tariff and non-tariff protection in the major developed countries. While quantitative evidence is crucial for a successful round of negotiations, it is argued that the information base is far from complete. However, from the information presented, it is clear that there is very considerable scope for trade liberalisation in both tariff and non-tariff barriers. It is argued that for developing countries, it is particularly important to be aware of the potential effects of the liberalisation. Therefore, Section 3 of the paper presents the results of a partial equilibrium model which has been used to estimate the impact on developing country exports of trade liberalisation in developed countries of both tariff and non-tariff barriers. A crucial question before developing countries in the next round will be the degree of importance they assign to the provisions relating to special and differential treatment. Estimates are therefore made of the implications for developing countries of both most-favoured-nation and preferential reductions in tariff and non-tariff barriers.

Trade liberalisation will not come easily. Estimates of trade creation and diversion of disaggregated product groupings indicate that the areas of greatest potential benefit to developing countries are precisely those where resistance to liberalisation will be strongest. Much of the regulation impeding trade is inextricably linked to *domestic* policies in developed countries; while this has long been the case for much of agricultural trade, trade policy which *accommodates* national policies designed to achieve specific national objectives is increasingly evident in the manufacturing (and services) sector. This greatly complicates (as it always has for agriculture) the exchange of concessions in trade-liberalising negotiations as national 'plans' are threatened. Indeed, for future trade liberalisation to be successful, relative prices will change, resources will be reallocated, markets will be disturbed and trade liberalisation will be resisted. As developing countries have on occasions born the brunt of protection against 'market disruption' (for example, the Multifibre Arrangement), the fourth section of the paper looks at the recent performance of developing countries exporting manufactured goods. It is found that while trade is highly concentrated in terms of products and markets, there is considerable scope for greater market penetration if the necessary structural adjustment is forthcoming.[3] Increased imports have frequently been coupled with 'market disruption' as international competitiveness changes more rapidly than countries can, or are willing to, change their structure of production. While history makes clear that structural change is the *sine qua non* of economic growth and development, this change entails private and social costs which are apparent and not easily dissipated. The debate on industrial restructuring in the Uruguay Round should crystallise in attempts to rewrite the GATT 'safeguard provision' (where producers of import-competing goods can be protected from trade induced 'serious injury'). It is the author's opinion that a successful negotiation of a new safeguard code built on simple economic principles holds the key to the success of the Uruguay Round.

2 RESTRICTIONS ON TRADE

2.1 Tariff Protection

There are well known problems associated with using tariff averages as a summary of the extent of tariff protection or the tariff profile of countries. In particular, concern is expressed over the shortcomings of both trade weighted and arithmetic tariff averages.[4] Most estimates of tariffs, however, are estimates of MFN (most favoured nation) rates. A point that is neglected in these calculations is that there are special arrangements between countries that result in the application of different tariff rates for the same product depending on the origin of the import.[5]

Table 10.1 shows the post-Tokyo Round tariff rates and the value of imports into the United States, EEC and Japan. Weighted and non-weighted MFN rates have been calculated along with the *actual* rate. This rate is the average of the tariff applied to different products after taking into account the source of the imported good, and whether the import has entered under most favoured nation conditions, the generalised system of preferences, special preferential trading arrangements or some other tariff rate. The tariffs are weighted by tariff line trade flows.[6]

As can be seen from the table, the weighted and non-weighted actual rates are generally speaking lower than the MFN rates. What is interesting is that the extent to which the average MFN rate is higher than the actual rate differs markedly between countries. In the EEC, for example, the trade weighted MFN rate facing imports from developed countries, is 4.9 per cent (that is, a margin of 2.1 per cent as the corresponding actual tariff rate is 2.8 per cent). This is not the experience of the United States where the actual and MFN trade weighted rates are the same for imports from developed countries (viz. 3.4 per cent). As far as the US imports from

Table 10.1   Value of trade, weighted and unweighted tariffs in USA, EEC and Japan

Country	Imports US$ mill 1985	wmfn per cent	nwmfn per cent	wactual per cent	nwactual per cent
USA					
World	358 704	3.9	6.2	3.4	6.4
Developed		3.4	6.1	3.4	7.5
Developing		4.7	6.4	3.6	4.6
EEC					
World	621 832	4.2	7.3	2.5	4.9
Developed		4.9	7.2	2.8	4.7
Developing		3.2	7.3	2.1	5.3
Japan					
World	127 512	3.6	7.2	3.1	6.1
Developed		4.3	7.1	4.1	6.9
Developing		3.1	7.2	2.4	4.5

Note: The tariff rates are averaged using 1981 tariff line trade flows; wmfn = weighted MFN tariff rates, nwmfn = non-weighted MFN rates, wactual = weighted actual rates, nwactual = non-weighted actual rates.
Source: Computerised Tariff Tapes of GATT, Series D Trade Tapes of the United Nations Statistical Office, Data Base on Trade Measures.

developing countries are concerned, the preferential margin is clear, as the actual trade weighted rate of 3.6 per cent, reflecting the preferential treatment for developing countries, is 1.1 per cent below the weighted MFN rate.

The difficulties in using these summary measures is made apparent by noting that the unweighted actual tariff applied by the United States is higher than the unweighted MFN rate on imports from developed countries and the world as a whole. This, however, reflects the fact that for the United States, the MFN rate is a preferential rate and not all trading partners receive MFN treatment. As the value of such trade is relatively unimportant, this difference is not reflected in the trade-weighted averages.

Comparing across countries it is apparent that the lowest actual tariff rates were applied by the EEC. The trade-weighted actual rate for EEC imports from developed countries is 2.8 per cent. For the United States, the corresponding figure is 3.4 per cent, and for Japan 4.1 per cent. Imports from developing countries face an actual rate of 2.1 per cent in the EEC, 3.6 per cent in the United States, and 2.4 per cent in Japan.

While these results lend quantitative support to the fact that average tariffs are low, a number of very important qualifications to this general statement presumably go some way to explaining why tariff liberalisation remains an objective in the Punta del Este Declaration. First, the above figures are heavily influenced by the low tariffs on imports of raw mineral products, in particular, imports of petroleum. The actual rates were recalculated for non-fuel imports into the EEC, the United States and Japan from developing countries exclusive of raw mineral products. These rates were found to be considerably higher at 4.3 per cent, 5.2 per cent and 4.7 per cent respectively.

Second, average tariffs hide the fact that for a wide variety of products, tariff rates remain high, even after taking into account the preferential arrangements under which they may be imported. In Japan, for example, tariffs facing agricultural imports are high; the trade-weighted tariff averages facing developing-country sugar, beverages, dairy products and miscellaneous food preparations imports are 80.6, 42.2, 28.1 and 16.6 per cent respectively. In the United States, the weighted actual tariff rate on imported clothing is 17.8 per cent and the weighted MFN rate is 21.1 per cent. For footwear, the corresponding rates are 9.4 and 12.4 per cent. In the EEC, the highest tariffs are found in the agriculture sector; weighted actual rates are 22.4 per cent on beverages imported from developing countries and 11.5 per cent on fish and fish preparations.[7]

A third reason for the concern over tariffs relates to the fact that labour-intensive manufactured exports from developing countries may confront higher tariff rates in some importing markets than other, less labour-intensive, products. Actual tariff rates were calculated for products classified according to their degree of processing; the first category contains raw materials and semi-finished goods, the second are labour-intensive goods and the third are other final products. It has been estimated that in both the United States and the EEC, the actual tariff facing imported labour-intensive goods from the world as a whole is higher than the average for all imported products. In the United States, the average rate facing imported labour-intensive goods is 17.2 per cent, while for total imports it is 3.4 per cent. In the case of the EEC, the corresponding figures are 5.0 per cent and 2.5 per cent (see UNCTAD, 1982, Chapter 2).

Finally, these facts taken together indicate that, while tariffs may be considered low on average, for some countries they remain a priority issue. For the United States, the trade-weighted tariff averages facing Chinese, Korean and Hong Kong imports for example, are 11.5 per cent, 10.7 per cent and 10.9 per cent respectively, even after taking into account preferential trading arrangements. For a variety of other countries (for example, Brazil, Argentina, Malaysia), the actual trade-weighted average tariff is substantially higher than the average for imports of the United States from the world. Similarly, labour-intensive imports from the Republic of Korea and India into the EEC face tariff rates of 14.9 per cent and 11.4 per cent respectively – rates that are considerably higher than the world average for the EEC in the case of both total trade and trade in labour-intensive products (UNCTAD, 1982, Chapter 2).

2.2 Non-Tariff Measures

An objective of the Uruguay Round (as indeed it was in the Tokyo Round) is to liberalise non-tariff barriers to trade; in this respect, there are two very important practical considerations. First, an official (that is, government-endorsed) listing of all non-tariff barriers applied by the contracting parties to GATT simply does not exist. It is difficult to imagine how multilateral trade liberalising negotiations can seriously address non-tariff barriers in the absence of this information.[8] In particular, it is difficult to imagine how trade can be liberalised in the traditional GATT sense through an 'exchange of concessions' between trading partners if the profile of non-tariff barriers is not known. It is equally difficult to imagine how the numerous commitments to a 'standstill and rollback' of protective measures that have emerged from intergovernmental meetings in recent years – and most recently in the Punta del Este Declaration – can be monitored in the absence of this information. A further problem arises as much of the recent protection has been what some international trade lawyers describe as 'contingent protection' or 'made to measure protection'; protection which is 'legitimate' providing certain legal conditions are met.[9] The idea of 'made to measure' protection, however, (a term coined by Max Corden almost twenty years ago with respect to the tariff) is certainly not new. The difference between made to measure tariff protection and contingent administered protection is that the latter opens the door to a high degree of bureaucratic discretion in its application. Thus, in many instances there is not agreement on the trade intentions of governments imposing 'administered' measures, and therefore the list of non-tariff measures to be included on the agenda for liberalisation. Further complications arise when, even if intentions are clear, there is disagreement on what actions governments can legitimately take. As far as the EEC is concerned, for example, its traditional position *vis à vis* the Common Agricultural Policy and the subsidisation of EEC farmers is that the CAP has as its objective the meeting of the special requirements of the Community. Its 'principles and machinery cannot be called into question' and are 'not a matter for negotiation' (Commission, 1976).

These and other problems are thrown into sharp relief in attempting to establish an information system on non-tariff barriers to trade. Not only is it a formidable task to identify non-tariff barriers, it is also unclear as to what should and should not be considered a barrier. However, bearing these limitations in mind, an inventory of *governmental* non-tariff measures has been constructed to give some idea of the importance of non-tariff measures. A nomenclature was devised for recording non-tariff measures and the country composition includes all developed and over 50 developing countries. The system contains some two million entries stored in machine-retrievable form; all non-tariff measures are documented with their governmental sources.[10]

The information included in the data base could be considered conservative. Only official governmental measures which are registered in national legislation have been included; 'unofficial' government action (for example, unnecessarily demanding health and quarantine standards for imports) and restraints by private corporations (such as market-sharing arrangements) are not included. Also, there is a 'conservative bias' to the extent that it is simply not possible to identify all governmental measures that restrict trade. The information is less conservative in the sense that governmental actions relating to anti dumping and countervailing duty action have been included. A further point is that while some administrative procedures (for example, import licensing and surveillance) are trade barriers for some products (for example, footwear in some countries), these same measures are used by other countries for reasons unrelated to import control. In particular, most countries monitor the import of petroleum, even though the intention of some governments is not to restrict trade. These administrative measures have been included as it is not possible to ascertain the true intention of governments. To the extent that imported fuels is the major problem, results have been presented with and without fuel imports.

As with tariffs, non-tariff measures are recorded at the tariff line level of product aggregation. While this information has many uses (for example, identifying barriers to very specific export items), the volume of the information is unmanageable for analytical purposes as tariff schedules contain many thousands of tariff line items. As with tariffs, it is necessary to summarise the information. In doing this, one of two types of summary statistics is normally employed: (i) a frequency index of the use of the measures; and (ii) a trade coverage ratio. The *frequency index* indicates the total number of tariff items in any product group that are subject to non-tariff barriers expressed as a percentage of the total number of items in the product category. It has its counterpart in an arithmetic tariff average and as such has similar merits and shortcomings. An advantage is that if a particular measure prohibits trade, it is still recorded in the index. One of the shortcomings is that all tariff line items receive the same weight in the index. The *trade coverage ratio* is the value of imports in any product group subject to non-tariff barriers expressed as a percentage of the total value of imports of the same product group. It has its counterpart in a trade-weighted average tariff; while trade weights are assigned to import items, those goods for which the non-tariff measure severely restricts trade receive little or no weight.

Table 10.2 provides information on the frequency of incidence of the non-tariff measures along with the trade-weighted indices (denoted by 'trade index' in the table) and frequency of occurrence indices (denoted by 'freq index'). Both indices were calculated with a view to determining whether the same conclusions are drawn regardless of which measure is used. The countries covered are the USA, Japan, and the EEC.

As can be seen from the table, some product categories have particularly high coverage ratios. In the United States, for example, it was found that on a trade coverage basis, the highest ratios applied to clothing (82 per cent), iron and steel (85 per cent), textile yarn and fabrics (52 per cent) and food and live animals (36 per cent). In Japan, the most affected sectors are food and live animals (61 per cent), textiles (52 per cent) and chemicals (31 per cent).

Table 10.2 Import coverage ratios for the United States, Japan and the EEC of non-tariff measures applied to imports – 1986 (percentages)

SITC	Product coverage	United States		Japan		EEC	
		Trade index	Freq. index	Trade index	Freq. index	Trade index	Freq. index
0 + 1+ 22 + 4	All food items	29.7	9.8	54.5	42.7	45.0	51.6
0	Food and live animals	35.6	11.7	61.4	46.5	53.5	58.0
22	Oil seeds/nuts	77.1	25.5	4.3	16.7	6.9	1.7
4	Animal/vegetable oils	1.1	1.5	1.9	11.7	12.0	6.2
2 (less 22 + 27 + 28)	Agricultural raw materials	32.7	3.8	1.9	16.2	4.5	14.9
27 + 28 + 67 + 68	Ores and metals	47.6	23.1	9.2	7.4	18.3	16.3
67	Iron and steel	85.3	61.4	1.0	1.0	68.9	40.8
68	Non-ferrous metals	2.6	0.9	0.4	0.8	13.4	4.4
3	Fuels	0.0	0.3	9.8	14.7	25.3	21.4
5	Chemicals	4.6	0.7	30.7	11.9	6.4	5.0
6–8 (less 67 + 68)	Manufactures other than chemicals	23.3	8.7	11.2	6.7	25.1	19.1
61	Leather	0.0	0.3	10.2	15.5	14.5	13.2
65	Textile yarn and fabrics	51.9	30.7	51.8	39.7	47.9	43.9
84	Clothing	81.7	33.9	0.0	0.0	72.4	59.9
85	Footwear	0.1	1.3	6.9	29.2	99.8	97.7
0–9 less 3	All items, excluding fuels	25.7	8.5	22.1	12.2	24.4	20.8
0–9	All items	17.6	8.5	15.9	12.2	24.7	20.9

Notes: The ratios have been computed using 1981 import trade weights. Computations have been made at the tariff-line level and results aggregated to relevant product group levels. The frequency index and trade index are as defined in the text.
Source: Data Base on Trade Measures.

For the EEC, the most affected sectors are footwear (100 per cent), clothing (72 per cent), iron and steel (69 per cent) and food and live animals (54 per cent).

Perhaps the most important finding that emerges from the table is the extraordinary difference that exists between the frequency and trade-weighted indices. In the case of the United States, this is apparent even at the total level of aggregation where for total non-fuel trade, the trade index is almost treble the frequency index; for Japan the difference is substantial (22 per cent compared with 12 per cent). In individual product categories, however, the frequency index gives a totally different picture of the degree of non-tariff protection to the trade weighted index. In the United States, over 30 per cent of trade in agricultural raw materials was found to face a non-tariff measure, while only 4 per cent of the tariff line items included in this product category were subject to control. Similar pictures emerge for food items and ores and metals imported into the United States. In Japan, almost 30 per cent of footwear items face a non-tariff measure, but only 7 per cent of trade is covered.

3 TRADE LIBERALISATION

According to the Punta del Este Declaration, trade is to be liberalised and special account is to be taken of the interests of less developed countries. The purpose of this section is to estimate the benefits for developing countries of trade liberalisation; both generalised liberalisation on an MFN basis and liberalisation of a preferential nature. In carrying out this exercise, an *ex ante* partial equilibrium model, measuring the first-round effects of the simulated reduction in trade barriers has been employed.[11] It is similar to that used by Cline *et al.* at The Brookings Institution to analyse the effects of the Tokyo Round and by the International Monetary Fund to quantify the effects of trade liberalisation initiatives on developing country export earnings.[12] The model is applied to tariff line trade data and can be used for simulating the effects of reductions in both tariffs and the *ad valorem* equivalents of non-tariff barriers. As with most models, this model has its limitations.[13]

For present purposes, the most important estimates relate to the direct trade effects. Two distinct effects are calculated:

(i) The *trade creation* (or loss) effect following the changed level of domestic demand for imports from a particular trading partner resulting from the changed domestic price of the imported good after the tariff change. In this it is assumed that the tariff change would be fully reflected in the price change.

(ii) The *trade diversion* effect is also estimated, both for preference-receiving and non-preference-receiving countries. This effect results from the changes in the relative import prices of goods from the two different sources resulting from changes in the margins of preference. This could occur through, for example, eliminating preferences by moving preferential rates to the MFN rate, moving all rates to zero, or simply by varying the preference schemes.

The trade creation and trade diversion effects are summed to provide the net effect in each market for each partner country, whether or not preference-receiving. An important assumption needs to be mentioned: that any other limitations on the growth of imports, (such as non-tariff barriers or limits on GSP treatment) would be lifted to the extent necessary to permit the projected tariff-induced trade expansion to take place. If these limitations were maintained, then the trade volume would not rise to the extent predicted, and quota rents, for example, would increase.

Simulations have been carried out for a full MFN reduction in tariffs and for preferential reductions (to zero) of manufactured goods imported from developing countries. These preferential reductions could be considered to be a generalisation of GSP treatment to other products. Simulations have also been carried out using the *ad valorem* equivalents of non-tariff barriers where such information is available.

The first set of results shown in Table 10.3 are estimates of the expanded trade flows following a simultaneous reduction to zero of tariffs on all manufactured goods in the 20 major OECD countries. The effects on developing countries are shown, both under an MFN liberalisation and under a reduction to zero of rates currently facing them in each market. The estimated effect of an MFN liberalisation would be an initial increase in imports by the OECD countries from the developing countries of the order of US $12 million – an increase of 8.7 per cent over imports in 1983. Under a preferential liberalisation the increase in imports from the developing countries would be almost US $5 billion more than the increase under the MFN liberalisation, that is, some $16.9 billion – an increase of 12.3 per cent over imports in 1983.

230

Table 10.3 Gains to developing countries of trade liberalisation through a reduction to zero of tariffs in twenty developed market non-tariff barriers in EEC, Japan and the United States (millions of United States dollars)

ISIC	Industry	Twenty developed countries			EEC, Japan and United States				
		Imports 1983	MFN tariff reduction	Preferential tariff reduction	Imports 1983	MFN tariff reduction	MFN tariff + NTB reduction	Preferential tariff reduction	Preferential tariff + NTB reduction
311	Food products	20 236	900	1 272	18 538	835	4 087	1 177	5 122
312	Food products nec	399	16	26	266	16	40	24	58
313	Beverages	544	47	304	478	44	48	286	298
314	Tobacco	293	32	38	285	30	30	35	35
321	Textiles	7 921	1 190	2 007	6 502	826	3 194	1 191	5 162
322	Wearing apparel	9 779	4 728	5 076	9 146	4 506	11 785	4 688	12 461
323	Leather and products	1 322	228	304	1 123	167	261	208	303
324	Footwear	219	30	35	206	25	123	29	137
331	Wood products	2 521	116	201	2 296	102	102	166	166
341	Paper and products	701	10	42	589	7	12	34	43
342	Printing, publishing	319	2	12	261	2	3	10	13
351	Industrial chemicals	3 401	82	274	2 928	67	79	235	251

231

352	Other chemical prods.	1 350	11	51	1 102	13	33	47	161
353	Petroleum refineries	21 440	648	1 078	17 741	645	645	1 071	1 071
354	Petroleum, coal prods.	30 770	157	158	31 069	156	156	157	157
355	Rubber products	2 267	1 359	1 495	1 977	1 209	2 207	1 234	2 234
356	Plastic products, nec	542	148	229	440	85	85	143	183
361	Pottery, china, etc.	169	74	105	149	70	70	92	92
362	Glass and products	218	10	36	191	9	16	29	51
369	Non-metal prods, nec	327	11	36	333	9	9	28	30
371	Iron and steel	2 905	181	247	2 440	168	702	212	1 043
372	Non-ferrous metals	7 361	45	190	7 850	46	229	187	436
380	Fab. metal products	946	0	0	157	0	8	0	8
381	Metal products	1 486	154	355	1 264	79	296	199	529
382	Machinery nec	2 939	205	434	2 978	196	200	394	407
383	Electrical machinery	8 462	871	1 514	8 017	781	1 337	1 305	2 076
384	Transport equipment	2 727	177	382	2 003	146	274	283	450
385	Professional goods	3 086	194	425	2 492	100	100	272	272
390	Other industries	2 946	398	545	2 566	364	438	468	563
Total $ US bln		137.6	12.0	16.9	125.4	10.7	26.6	14.2	33.8

Source: Computed using trade creation and trade diversion model as described in text. The 20 DMECS are Australia, Austria, Canada, EEC (10 countries), Finland, Japan, New Zealand, Norway, Sweden, Switzerland and the United States.

However, in some sectors in some OECD countries the effects of liberalisation would be such that there would be a net loss for the developing countries under an MFN liberalisation. This follows from the fact that trade diversion from developing to OECD countries (from the erosion of preference margins) exceeds the trade creation effect. Thus, the effects of liberalisation are such that there would be gainers and losers in different markets and in different sectors.

It is possible to draw two conclusions from these results. First, residual tariffs facing developing countries in the OECD markets are still substantial and there would be considerable trade gains to the developing countries if these were reduced to zero. Second, there remains considerable scope for improving the position of the developing countries – perhaps through a full extension of GSP treatment.

The second set of results shown in Table 10.3 relate to the reduction to zero tariff barriers and the elimination of non-tariff barriers in the three major developed country markets: EEC, Japan and the United States.[14] Simulations were carried out for MFN liberalisation of tariffs and NTBs. In addition, simulations have been carried out for the elimination of non-tariff barriers facing developing countries and the preferential reduction to zero rates of tariffs. The projected increase in imports from developing countries of the three major OECD countries under MFN tariff liberalisation would be of the order of $10.7 billion, compared with $14.2 billion with a preferential reduction. However, if the tariff reduction was combined with an elimination of NTBs, then the increases are projected to be of the order of $26.6 billion and $33.8 billion respectively.

There are important differences as between sectors in the sizes of preferences granted by individual OECD countries relative to those granted by EEC, Japan or the United States. In some markets the negative trade diversion effect for the preference-receivers exceeds the trade-creation effect. For these products, the overall gain from liberalisation in all 20 OECD countries can be smaller than the gain from liberalisation in the three major markets (for instance, for ISIC industry 352 other chemical products, the gain of $13 million for developing countries in EEC, Japan and the United States exceeds the gain of $11 million in the 20 combined DMEC markets).

From Table 10.3 it can be seen that the industrial sectors in which liberalisation would be of greatest benefit to the developing countries are: crude petroleum, food products, textiles, wearing apparel, petroleum refineries, rubber products, iron and steel, and electrical machinery. Non-tariff distortions are relatively important in all these sectors, with the exception of crude petroleum and petroleum refinery industries. Indeed, in these latter sectors, the gain from tariff liberalisation is quite small in percentage terms.

The model has been used to identify a key list of items – within the above sectors – where liberalisation of tariff and non-tariff barriers would be of greatest benefit to the developing countries. Trade in these products would need to be included in any liberalisation effort designed to have a significant impact on the exports of developing countries. In the cases of EEC and Japan, the model identified the top 50 4-digit CCCN items (out of a total of some 1100 such items) where developing countries would benefit most from liberalisation. In the case of the United States, the top 80 5-digit TSUS items (out of several thousands) were identified. This short list of tariff items accounts for a total of US $30.1 billion out of the total of US $33.8 billion of increased imports by the three major developed countries following trade liberalisation on a preferential basis. It also accounts for $25.4 billion out of the $26.6 billion increase in imports from the developing countries under MFN liberalisation.

The important point is that this list represents an extraordinarily high concentration of a few products (overwhelmingly in very sensitive sectors such as apparel, textiles, agricultural goods) where liberalisation in favour of the developing countries, whether on an MFN or a preferential basis, would yield substantial benefits in terms of trade expansion. The question then naturally arises as to what extent liberalisation in agriculture, textiles, clothing and other sensitive sectors is a realistic possibility.

The success that the new round has with respect to liberalisation will depend to a large extent on the capacity (and willingness) of countries to adjust structurally (something to which priority is assigned in the Punta del Este Declaration) in the face of expanded import competition. The manner in which 'disturbed markets' are dealt with within the legal framework of GATT may well be the issue which will 'make or break' the next round of negotiations. It is in discussions of reform of the 'safeguard' provisions of GATT that the adjustment problems will be crystallised. Matters relevant to this occupy the rest of the paper.

4 DEVELOPING COUNTRIES AND DISRUPTION

Article XIX of the GATT sets out the conditions under which producers who are 'seriously injured' as a result of import competition can be 'safeguarded' against market disturbances; they are protected as their governments legal 'escape' from their GATT obligations to refrain from raising barriers to trade. The conditions under which governments can 'legally' (in GATT terms) protect their producers from 'market disruption' in the coming years is something of paramount importance to developing countries. This derives from a number of considerations.[15]

First, the success which a small number of developing countries have had in expanding their exports of manufactured goods has attracted a great deal of attention. This export expansion has also led to developing countries being considered as the source of market disturbances in some sectors. A major issue in the next round will be whether safeguard protection can be selectively applied to developing country exports, in the same manner as it has been selectively (and 'legally' in GATT terms) applied to their textile trade for the past two decades. Future market access for manufactured exports from developing countries is of crucial importance in their efforts to expand export revenues. The export of manufactured goods has been an area of substantial growth for developing countries, in fact to such an extent that *the value of manufactured exports of developing countries has now achieved such a level that it is greater than all non-energy commodity exports combined.*[16]

The extent to which increased competition from developing countries has harmed the import-competing industries of developed countries, and the extent to which disturbances are due to internal causes is difficult to determine. The answer to this question is not straightforward, for the two effects are intertwined – without the availability of imported substitutes, the advance of real labour costs beyond productivity that has characterised many activities in OECD countries in the past decade would be less critical, as would the effect of recession. Also, import competition may have been a stimulus to productivity growth. In practical terms, however, the manner in which market disturbances are dealt with in future years is a priority issue for the dozens of developing countries hoping to emulate the 'successful' exporters of manufactured goods.

This leads to a second important consideration, which is that the degree of concentration of 'success' and 'disturbance' is high. Thus, while the overall value of manufactured exports from developing countries to developed countries increased 14-fold in the period 1970–84, increasing five-fold between 1970 and 1977 (to US$43.1 billion) and almost three-fold between 1977 and 1984 (to US$121.1 billion), the degree of concentration of manufactured exports among export suppliers and import markets has been high. Indeed, as is evident from Table 10.4, *three developing countries, Taiwan, South Korea and Hong Kong, currently account for almost half of the manufactured exports of developing countries to developed market economy countries, and the United States is the destination for over half of these exports.*

Table 10.4 Concentration of developing country manufactured exports to developed market economy countries by market, product and share in total manufactured exports 1970–77 and 1984 (millions of US$ and percentage)

	1970	1977	1984
Total exports (in $ million)	8 562	43 090	121 100
By major suppliers, percentage			
1 Taiwan	10.0	14.5	19.0
2 Korea (South)	6.2	14.4	13.6
3 Hong Kong	21.3	15.4	13.2
4 Brazil	4.2	6.0	8.0
5 Mexico	5.6	5.6	6.3
6 China	3.2	3.2	5.2
7 Singapore	1.4	3.6	5.1
8 India	6.9	5.8	3.7
9 Malaysia	1.6	2.7	3.1
10 Yugoslavia	6.7	4.3	2.9
11 Argentina	2.9	1.7	0.9
12 Other devg.	30.0	22.8	19.0
By major markets, percentage			
US	38.8	40.1	55.1
EEC (12)	42.0	38.5	25.9
Japan	7.2	9.3	9.3
Other DMEC	12.0	12.1	9.7

Source: Calculated from Series D Tapes, UN Statistical Office.

A third consideration is that, while in the fifties and sixties the overall momentum in the developed countries was towards trade liberalisation (with exceptions such as the MFA), the late seventies saw the emergence of pressures challenging this momentum. There were expectations that continued export expansion would not characterise the 1980s. On the contrary, the 1980s have indeed seen a continuation of the growth in total manufactured exports from developing countries. This, however, is not an indication that the structural adjustment problems in OECD countries which received so much attention in the late seventies have diminished. Indeed, the Punta del Este Declaration emphasises this fact.

In this respect, the period since 1979 is particularly interesting. Although total developing country exports to developed countries declined over the period 1980 to 1984, their exports of manufactured goods expanded substantially; developing countries raised their market share in total manufactured imports into developed countries from 10 to 14.5 per cent between 1979 and 1984. This achievement was, however, heavily concentrated: *of the total increment of US$48 billion, two-thirds occurred in 1983 and 1984. In terms of markets, the United States accounted for nearly 80 per cent of the increase between 1979 and 1984, increasing its share of developing countries' manufactured exports to developed economies from just over 40 per ent in 1979 to almost 60 per cent today.*[17]

It could be argued that the growth of manufactured exports continued into the eighties because of exceptional circumstances; more specifically, largely because of expansion of the developing countries' share of manufactured exports destined for the US market. The US experience, compared to that of the EEC is illuminating. For developing countries and China as a group, the US was the destination for 39 per cent of their manufactured exports in 1970. This rose slightly to 40 per cent in 1977 and by 1984 the share had risen to 55 per cent. The experience of the EEC is quite different. In 1970 the EEC was the market for 42 per cent of developing country manufactured exports; this had fallen to 39 per cent in 1977 and stood at only 26 per cent in 1984. Also of interest is the fact that for these 11 developing country exporters of manufactured goods, the USA is the destination for over half of their exports in all but three of the cases (India, Yugoslavia and China).

Given the success of this limited number of exporters, what does the future hold for greater market access in the principal importing countries? In view of the considerations discussed above, this raises the important question as to the extent to which the importing markets are saturated by manufactured imports from developing countries. A measure which is sometimes used to address this question is the import penetration ratio; it measures the share of domestic consumption which is accounted for by imports.[18]

As can be seen from Table 10.5, there has been an increase in the import penetration in major importing developed countries. This is most marked in the European countries; the penetration ratio – referring to total manufactured imports – increased for Germany from 19.3 to 35.1 per cent, for the United Kingdom from 16.2 to 29.3 per cent and for France from 16.2 to 26.2 per cent. In all cases, the developed market economy countries are, of course, the principal suppliers.

In 1983, the share of manufactured imports from developing country exporters of manufactures was 2.1 per cent of total apparent consumption in the United States. In Japan, manufactured imports from the same group of countries comprised 0.9 per cent of domestic consumption; for Germany, United Kingdom and France, the corresponding figures were 1.9, 1.4 and 0.9 per cent respectively. By any standards these must be considered low. Perhaps more revealing, however, is that over the entire time period of 1970 to 1983, the largest increase in penetration in any of the markets was in the United States – just 1.6 percentage points. No other group of developing countries (that is, developing Africa, Asia or America) fared as well as the group of developing country exporters of manufactured goods.

It has often been argued that, while the aggregate figures indicate a limited degree of penetration, this masks the fact that the problems occur at the sectoral level where the penetration ratios are much higher. This can be checked, by way of example, for the penetration ratios for the clothing sector, where indeed, the overall ratios are higher than the average for all countries. As with the manufacturing average, the exporters of manufactured goods have the greatest share among the groups of developing countries; in 1984, their share was 12.8 per cent in US, 7.5 per cent in Japan, 20.0 per cent in Germany, 13.6 per cent in the United Kingdom and 2.4 per cent in France. However, except for the United States and Japan, these ratios remained well below those originating from exports of OECD countries. While penetration ratios are surely higher for some more disaggregated product categories, it is clear that the potential for an expansion in the share of developing countries in total consumption

Table 10.5 Import penetration ratios: developed market-economy countries 1970, 1975, 1980 and 1983 (per cent)

Origin of imports	United States				Japan				Germany				United Kingdom				France			
	1970	1975	1980	1983	1970	1975	1980	1983	1970	1975	1980	1983	1970	1975	1980	1983	1970	1975	1980	1983
All manufacturing																				
World	5.5	7.0	9.3	10.3	4.7	4.9	5.8	5.3	19.3	24.3	31.4	35.1	16.2	22.0	28.1	29.3	16.2	17.9	23.3	26.2
OECD	4.3	4.9	6.1	6.7	3.2	2.9	3.3	3.2	16.5	20.5	25.6	28.9	12.5	17.6	21.6	24.6	14.2	15.9	19.8	22.3
EEC	1.4	1.9	1.9	1.9	0.8	0.8	0.9	0.8	11.2	14.7	17.0	18.8	5.1	9.6	13.0	14.9	10.6	11.8	14.1	15.7
Developing countries																				
Africa	0.1	0.1	0.2	0.2	0.2	0.1	0.1	0.1	0.3	0.3	0.5	0.5	0.6	0.6	0.4	0.5	0.8	0.6	0.8	1.0
Asia	0.2	0.3	0.5	0.5	0.5	0.8	1.0	0.9	0.3	0.5	0.9	1.0	0.4	0.6	0.8	0.9	0.2	0.3	0.6	0.6
America	0.5	0.8	0.9	0.7	0.1	0.1	0.2	0.1	0.7	0.5	0.7	0.6	0.6	0.6	0.4	0.3	0.3	0.2	0.3	0.3
Exporters of manufactures[a]	0.5	0.9	1.5	2.1	0.3	0.7	0.9	0.9	0.6	1.2	1.7	1.9	0.5	0.8	1.2	1.4	0.2	0.3	0.7	0.9
Clothing (ISIC 322)																				
World	6.4	9.8	17.3	20.3	4.4	8.3	13.8	13.0	26.8	44.9	60.1	73.2	13.5	27.5	39.8	40.0	10.4	16.6	29.1	33.1
OECD	3.0	1.9	1.9	2.2	1.3	2.1	4.0	2.9	19.8	26.3	33.1	38.3	7.0	12.0	17.7	19.2	9.4	11.9	18.9	21.5
EEC	1.1	0.9	1.1	1.1	0.9	1.6	2.7	2.1	17.5	22.9	26.8	29.4	3.4	6.7	10.9	12.9	8.7	10.2	15.4	17.2
Developing countries																				
Asia	0.0	0.0	0.0	0.0	0.0	0.0	0.0	0.0	0.3	0.3	1.3	2.0	0.0	0.0	0.4	0.3	0.2	1.2	2.5	3.7
Africa	0.9	0.9	2.5	4.0	0.6	1.1	2.6	2.6	0.4	1.0	4.4	6.1	0.2	1.0	3.5	3.4	0.4	1.3	3.1	3.1
America	0.1	0.5	0.9	1.0	0.0	0.0	0.0	0.0	0.0	0.3	0.8	0.6	0.0	0.0	0.1	0.1	0.0	0.1	0.1	0.1
Exporters of manufactures[a]	3.0	6.3	11.8	12.8	2.5	5.1	7.1	7.5	5.0	13.1	15.1	20.0	15.6	12.7	15.9	13.6	0.1	0.8	2.5	2.4

Note: [a]Includes Brazil, Hong Kong, Mexico, Republic of Korea, Singapore, Taiwan, Province of China and Yugoslavia.

Source: Drawn from *Compatible Trade and Production Base*, Department of Economics and Statistics, DES/NI(84)19, OECD, Paris, 17 October 1984 and Haders Brodin and Derek Blades, *The OECD Compatible Trade and Production Data Base*, Department of Economics and Statistics, Working Paper No. 31, March 1986.

in developed countries exists, and the need for discussion and international co-operation in this respect is imperative.

5 CONCLUSION

The principal conclusions of this paper are as follows. Tariff barriers remain a problem for a number of countries and there are significant gains to be had through tariff liberalisation. For developing countries, MFN tariff liberalisation in developed countries is estimated to increase their exports by US$12 billion. A preferential tariff reduction would increase their exports by US$16.9 billion. For this expansion to take place, it must not be inhibited by non-tariff barriers. It is found that it is exceedingly difficult to estimate precisely the extent of non-tariff barriers, but their incidence in a number of sectors is high. Conventional measures of the incidence of non-tariff barriers (frequency of incidence and trade coverage) in many instances give very different indications of the importance of non-tariff barriers for different sectors.

To the extent that estimates of the *ad valorem* equivalents of non-tariff barriers are available, they are incorporated into the trade liberalisation scenarios. Here it is estimated that the gains to developing countries through an MFN reduction in tariff and non-tariff barriers would be an export expansion of US$26.6 billion. A preferential reduction would expand exports by US$33.8 billion. The products in which the greatest expansion would take place are found to be in those sectors where the resistance to import competition will be greatest. However, while there will be resistance, import penetration ratios remain low. These results lend quantitative support to the priority assigned to facilitate structural adjustment and rewriting the safeguard provisions of GATT in the Punta del Este Declaration.

Notes

1. A special debt is owed to Sam Laird for his substantial contribution to the modelling section and Rene Vossenaar for his work on non-tariff barriers. Helpful comments from Bela Balassa (the session organiser) and Paul Streeten (who presented the paper) are also gratefully acknowledged. The author's views are not necessarily those of the institution for which he works.

2. See *Ministerial Declaration on the Uruguay Round*, GATT/1396, Geneva, 25 September 1986.
3. What follows naturally from this is that the high priority of the contracting parties to GATT (according to the Punta del Este declaration) to 'increase the responsiveness of the GATT system . . . through facilitating the necessary structural adjustment' is something that developing countries should monitor carefully.
4. Simply put, arithmetic averages assign equal weight to all imported goods regardless of their importance, while trade weighted averages do not take account of the fact that the level of trade is influenced by the height of the tariff. In the extreme case, prohibitive tariffs receive no weight.
5. In the EEC countries, for example, special tariff preferences are given for imports from all EFTA countries, the Lomé Convention countries, Israel, Egypt, Algeria, Morocco, Tunisia, Jordan, Lebanon, the Syrian Arab Republic, Malta and Turkey. Furthermore, under the generalised system of preferences (GSP) EEC offers duty-free entry (up to a ceiling) for many exports of developing countries. In fact, since trade within the EEC is, in principle, duty-free, it is principally only in respect of imports from a limited number of developed market-economy countries and certain socialist countries of Eastern Europe that MFN rules apply. These countries are the United States, Japan, Canada, Australia, South Africa and New Zealand. Differential tariffs are also applied by the USA, Japan and other developed countries to imports from different sources.
6. The tariff line is the most disaggregate level at which trade flows are recorded. The trade weights are for 1983.
7. These rates, however, pale into insignificance when compared with the *ad valorem* equivalents of variable levies. See Sampson and Snape (1980).
8. For various reasons, the GATT inventory of non-tariff barriers to trade does not contain all non-tariff trade barriers. The UNCTAD inventory is more comprehensive but was not constructed with a view to negotiating non-tariff barriers.
9. In the Tokyo Round, in the absence of a comprehensive information base on non-tariff barriers, 'codes' of behaviour were negotiated. Some have argued that while the intention of the codes was to discipline the use of non-tariff measures, they have in fact served to define situations in which trade restriction can be legitimised in terms of GATT. Thus, rather than control the spread of non-tariff measures, the codes have given rise to increasing use of 'administered protection' (e.g. misused anti-dumping and countervailing duty provisions) that apparently meet the 'political' needs of government. See Finger, Hall and Nelson (1982) and Rodney de C. Grey (1986).
10. For a description of the non-tariff measures included along with other matters concerning the data base see UNCTAD (1985).
11. For a full description and a discussion of the shortcomings of models such as this see Laird and Yeats (1986).
12. Cline (1978) and IMF (1984). See also Sapir and Baldwin (1983). For

a non-technical discussion of the use of such models for evaluating the effects of various trade liberalisation proposals, see Robert Stern (1976).

13. It is partial in nature and it is necessary, for example, to invoke assumptions to permit the aggregation of the tariff line information to the more manageable product groupings. The limitations are fully described in Laird and Yeats (1986). For a discussion of the limitations and an alternative formulation of the same model, see Snape (1986).

14. The information on the *ad valorem* incidence of non-tariff barriers has been culled from a literature search. It is therefore incomplete. For this reason, and because the estimates relate to price disadvantages of the OECD countries *vis à vis* world suppliers (cf just developing countries) the estimated trade expansion in favour of developing countries from NTB elimination is believed to be conservative.

15. For a discussion of the sources and symptoms of market disturbances see Corden (1986). For a discussion with reference to the textiles sector, see Sampson (1986) in the same volume.

16. Manufactured exports accounted for 12.5 per cent of developing country non-energy exports to developed countries in 1963; this share had increased to 55.2 per cent by 1983.

17. The increase in imports of manufactured goods can be attributed to the joint phenomena of rapidly rising US demand coupled with supply side factors in developing countries. A calculation based on broad geographical markets suggests that growing total OECD demand explains only 60 per cent of the increment in OECD imports of manufactures over the period 1979–84. This leaves some 40 per cent of the contribution to the increased country shares unaccounted for; the OECD attributes this increment to flexibility-inducing supply factors. See OECD (1986).

18. The import-penetration ratio (IPR) is defined by $IPRj/(Pj + Mj − Xj)$. That is, a given reporting country's imports of the output of industry j from trade partner i, as a percentage of the reporting country's domestic consumption of j. For a discussion, see Brodin and Blades (1986) p. 6.

References

Brodin, H. and Blades, D. (1986) *The OECD Compatible Trade and Production Data Base,* Department of Economics and Statistics Working Papers no. 31, March (Paris: OECD).

Cline, W.R. (1978) *Trade Negotiations in the Tokyo Round – A Quantitative Assessment* (Washington DC: The Brookings Institution).

Commission of the European Communities (1976) Newsletter on the Common Agricultural Policy: Extract from the 1975 Report on the Agricultural Situation in the Community (Brussels and Luxembourg).

Corden, W.M. (1986) 'Policies towards Market Disturbances' in Snape, R.H. (ed.) *Issues in World Trade Policy: GATT at the Crossroads* (London: Macmillan).

Finger, J.M., Hall, H.K. and Nelson, D.R. (1982) 'The Political Economy of Administered Protection', *American Economic Review* vol. 73, no. 3, June.

GATT (1986) *Ministerial Declaration on the Uruguay Round* (Geneva: GATT) 25 September.

Grey, R. de C. (1986) 'The Decay of the Trade Relation System' in Snape, R.H. (ed.) *Issues in World Trade Policy: GATT at the Crossroads* (London: Macmillan).

International Monetary Fund (1984) *Effects of Increased Market Access on Selected Developing Country Export Earnings: An Illustrative Exercise* (Washington: IMF) DM/84/54, 24 August.

Laird, S. and Yeats, A.J. (1986) The UNCTAD Trade Policy Simulation Model: a Note of Methodology, Data and Uses', *UNCTAD Discussion Papers* no. 19.

OECD (1986) *Change and Continuity in OECD Trade in Manufactures with Developing Countries 1979–84* (Paris: OECD) DCD 86.6, 10 March.

Sampson, G.P. (1986) 'Market Disturbances and the MFA' in Snape, R.H. (ed.) *Issues in World Trade Policy: GATT at the Crossroads* (London: Macmillan).

Sampson, G.P. and Snape, R.H. (1980) 'Effects of the EEC's Variable Import Levies', *Journal of Political Economy*, vol. 88, no. 5.

Sapir, A. and Baldwin, R.E. (1983) 'India and the Tokyo Round', *World Development* vol. 11, no. 7.

Snape, R.H. (1986) *Should Australia seek a Trade Agreement with the United States?* (Economic Planning Advisory Council) Discussion Paper no. 86/01, June.

Stern, R. (1976) 'Evaluating Alternative Formulae for Reducing Industrial Tariffs', *Journal of World Trade Law*, vol. 10, Jan./Feb. pp. 50–64.

UNCTAD (1982) *Protectionism and Structural Adjustment in the World Economy* (Geneva: UNCTAD) TD/888/Rev.1. Chapter 2.

UNCTAD Secretariat (1985) *Introductory Note on Methodology and the Problems of Definition* (Geneva: UNCTAD) TD/B/AC/42/2, 4 September.

11 Lowering Agricultural Protection: A Developing Country Perspective Towards the Uruguay Round

Alberto Valdés
IFPRI, WASHINGTON
and
Joachim Zietz
KIEL INSTITUTE OF WORLD ECONOMICS

1 INTRODUCTION

A number of exceptions to the basic GATT principles of non-discrimination and protection by bound tariffs together with a rather loose enforcement of the existing trading rules have the effect of according agriculture a special status.[1] Reflecting this special status is the fact that today's trade in agricultural products is characterised more than most other trade by non-tariff barriers, trade disputes among industrialised countries, and protectionism *vis-à-vis* the developing world.

In recognising the problem case of agriculture a committee on trade in agriculture (CTA) was set up within the GATT in 1982. After a number of years of deliberation the CTA has recently made several suggestions on how to bring agriculture under the disciplines of GATT. In the remainder of this paper the recommendations of the CTA along with some alternative suggestions on how to bring agriculture under GATT disciplines will be examined in somewhat greater detail. To set the stage, the distinguishing features of the current GATT round and its chance of bringing about trade reform in agriculture will be discussed first.

2 DISTINGUISHING FEATURES OF THE CURRENT GATT ROUND

The initiative for the current round of negotiations under the aegis of the GATT has come from developed countries, mainly the USA and the EEC. In this respect the Uruguay Round is not different from the previous GATT rounds. What distinguishes the current negotiations, however, is the central role accorded to areas that were neglected in previous GATT rounds, among them non-tariff barriers to trade and agriculture. The prominence given to agriculture in this GATT round reflects two developments of growing concern to industrialised countries. First, the number of trade disputes among themselves over export markets has increased perceptively over the past years. Second, the budgetary problems of supporting the domestic farm sector have assumed alarming proportions, in particular for the USA and the EEC.

At the same time, a considerable number of research results have accumulated over the years to aid in the assessment of trade liberalisation in agriculture. This is also a novel feature of MTNs. Never before has so much empirical work been available before negotiations came actually under way. In particular, there is ample support for the notion that liberalisation of agricultural trade on the part of developed countries would mean a considerable boost to LDC exports.[2] LDCs should have a particular interest in tropical products as well as in processed agricultural products. Especially, in the latter category of goods, negotiations could lead to significant progress, since tariffs rather than non-tariff barriers are still prominent in this area. The likely foreign exchange gains of a thorough liberalisation of agricultural markets are substantial in absolute terms (see Table 11.1) and also relative to the amount of development aid currently flowing to LDCs.[3] Middle-income LDCs, in particular those of Latin America and Asia, have probably the most to gain from trade liberalisation. Incidentally, the countries with the largest foreign debt problems can be found among this group of countries.

One may hypothesise that the evidence summarised above has already played a role in getting a number of LDCs to prepare to take an active role in the present MTNs. To co-ordinate their efforts several of them have recently formed the group of 'non-subsidising agricultural exporters',[4] along with the most efficient developed-country agricultural exporters. The developing countries involved

Table 11.1 Changes in export revenue for selected commodities of developing countries caused by a 50 per cent decrease in OECD tariff rates, 1975–7

	Absolute increase		
	All developing countries	Low-income countries	Middle- and high-income countries
	millions of 1980 US dollars		
Sugar	2 108	394	1 714
Beverages and tobacco	686	191	495
Meats	655	33	620
Coffee	540	123	417
Vegetable oils	400	60	339
Cocoa	287	21	265
Temperate-zone fruits and vegetables	197	60	137
Oilseeds and oil nuts	109	19	90
Other commodities	883	96	788
Total increase of all exports	5 866	998	4 867

Source: Valdés and Zietz, 1980, pp. 31, 47.

are Argentina, Brazil, Chile, Colombia, Fiji, Indonesia, Malaysia, the Philippines, Thailand, and Uruguay. They are joined on the part of industrialised countries by Australia, Canada, Hungary and New Zealand. Since the members of the 'fair trading group' pledged continued consultation and co-operation during the course of the GATT talks, it seems certain that the GATT negotiations will not merely concentrate on settling the trade disputes between the USA and the EEC but also extend to those issues of particular interest to developing countries. Having joined forces with the major non-subsidising industrialised countries it appears that developing countries have a better chance than ever before to influence the outcome of the trade negotiations. This fact alone could be considered a third distinguishing feature of the forthcoming trade negotiations.

3 FACTORS INHIBITING AND FACTORS FAVOURING A SUCCESSFUL GATT ROUND

There is no doubt that domestic political pressures against reform of the current system are going to be strong in industrialised countries, in particular in the USA and the EEC, but possibly also in LDCs.

3.1 The Case of Industrialised Countries

Farm support programmes are well entrenched and the reasons why farm support is provided on the current scale have not lost any of their significance. They are summed up in the following three points (Johnson, 1986):

1. The relatively small size of the agricultural sector in most developed countries makes it relatively easy for farmers to organise their interests.
2. The decline in the relative importance of the farm sector has lessened the significance of and hence the opposition to agricultural protection. Its cost per non-farm household constitutes an ever-smaller proportion of the household's rising income.
3. The unfavourable treatment of rural areas in the allocation of public resources over a long time period has made rural adjustment more difficult than necessary. Farm support as currently observed is a form of compensation for these earlier policies of neglect of the rural sector in terms of the availability of education and training facilities, infrastructure, alternative employment opportunities and agricultural research and extension.

Also, if current policies were suddenly abandoned, a sizeable segment of the farm population would suffer adverse effects of considerable proportions (Johnson, 1986, p. 40). Politically, this could hardly be justified in the light of the fact that farmers have continually been promised help rather than adjustment. Finally, the large stocks of protected agricultural products that have accumulated over the years make any quick move towards market-oriented production unfeasible.

On the other hand at least a couple of reasons exist which can make one believe that, at a minimum, a beginning towards trade liberalisation could be effected during this GATT round. First, the budgetary problems caused by the currently followed support programmes, at least in the USA and the EEC, have assumed unknown proportions and are causing serious concern among governments.[5] Second, it is apparent that the likely opposition to policy reform and trade liberalisation can be resisted more easily by policy makers if reforms are initiated in as many countries as possible at the same time. This is simply because the world price of a particular commodity rises the most if all protecting countries liberalise jointly rather than just one country in isolation.[6] But the higher the world price rises, the lower will be the costs borne by the producers in the liberalising countries. The GATT offers one of the few forums where such kinds of joint action could be achieved.

3.2 The Case of Developing Countries

It would probably be unrealistic to believe that industrialised countries are willing to open their agricultural markets any further to developing countries without expecting reciprocity or some kind of compensation, at least from the more advanced LDCs. After all, GATT negotiations have always been conducted on a give-and-take basis. For LDCs this would probably imply opening up their markets for industrial goods and services in return for concessions in the area of agriculture. Wrapping export expansion in agriculture and import expansion in industrial goods in one package would require policy makers in LDCs to re-evaluate the relative importance of agriculture in domestic development. This may help to make the true costs of import protection through tariffs, quantitative restrictions, and overvalued exchange rates and their relation to the widespread debt problem more apparent than when sectoral policies are considered in isolation.

Domestic economic adjustment, however, cannot be achieved at zero cost. If one is familiar with the political and economic problems of structural adjustment in industrialised countries, it is not hard to imagine that adjustments in developing countries are at least equally difficult to accomplish, especially if they touch the heart of the economy. Since public choice arguments also apply to LDCs, it is unlikely that governments will embark lightly on far-reaching adjustment programmes in exchange for the hope of some as yet uncertain long-run economic benefit. It is more probable that countries for which this analysis applies would be willing only to accept the GATT principles and hence internal adjustment programmes if financial help were forthcoming from industrialised countries, either directly or via development organisations, to cover the time period of the worst hardships of adjustment.

But even for those LDCs for which domestic structural adjustment would not be a major problem, politically and/or socially, participation in the GATT process could be uninteresting. First, acceptance of the basic GATT principles of reciprocity and non-discrimination *vis-à-vis* the developed world is often perceived as disadvantageous in the sense that it would erode or, at worst, eliminate current trade preferences without making compensation through increased exports sufficiently likely. But even for sugar and beef, commodities for which the group of LDCs as a whole could expect very large increases in foreign exchange earnings in the case of trade liberalisation,[7] there are still countries that stand to lose. This applies, for example, to the group of African, Caribbean and Pacific (ACP) countries which currently have preferential access to the EEC market. Trade liberalisation would most likely entail a loss of their trade preferences or at a minimum a decrease in internal EEC prices and hence a reduction of their present monopoly rents.

Apart from the loss of preferences, the prospect of higher cereal or dairy prices on the world market is probably one of the main reasons why the majority of LDCs remains uninterested in the GATT negotiations and consequent trade liberalisation. A fair number of LDCs, especially among the least developed ones, are currently food importers. Since any liberalisation of agricultural imports or stricter interpretation of GATT rules on the part of developed countries is likely to increase the world price of the affected commodities, a number of countries would be faced with higher food bills or the option to reduce imports, at least in the short run. This is true in particular for cereals. Table 11.2 presents some figures for the case of wheat.

Temporarily rising food bills, reduced imports or monopoly rents, however, seem to be a questionable guide when it comes to deciding whether to take part in the GATT negotiations or not; this is so for at least two reasons. The first is that, for developed countries, the trade regime in cereals and dairy products is going to be of primary interest, regardless of LDC participation. But any move towards trade liberalisation in these areas is almost certain to lead to higher world prices. Hence, since mere absence from the negotiations would not permit LDCs to stop an increase in food

Table 11.2 Regional impact of trade liberalisation on developing
countries – wheat

	Change		Distribution of change in foreign exchange earnings	Change in foreign exchange earnings	Change in import bill
	Foreign exchange earnings	Net welfare			
	millions of 1980 US dollars		per cent	per cent	millions of 1980 US dollars
Sub-Saharan Africa	4	−71	0.3	n.a.	23
North Africa/ Middle East	345	−325	29.6	453	−89
Asia	611	−127	52.4	n.a.	−288
Latin America	208	−132	17.8	29	3
Total	1,167	−656	100.0	146	−351

Note: n.a. indicates that pre-liberalisation exports are zero or negligible.
The results refer to a complete removal of tariffs and non-tariff barriers
to trade.
Source: Zietz and Valdés, 1986a.

import costs, it seems to be in their interest to take an active stance
in the MTNs. At least this would make it more likely that their
short-run problems would receive adequate attention.

The second factor is that non-participation on the part of LDCs
would imply that the potential long-run benefits of a more liberalised
trade regime are considered less important than the short-run
problems of internal adjustment that such a trading regime may
require from a good number of developing countries. The long-run
benefits of more liberalised world markets in agricultural products
are manifold. First, liberalised markets decrease market instability.
That world market prices would be much less volatile is convincingly
shown by Schiff (1985) for the case of wheat and by Tyers and
Anderson (1986) for several other heavily traded agricultural
commodities. Second, monopoly rents as currently reaped by ACP
countries may actually be detrimental to the development process
in the long run in that they lead certain sectors to expand far beyond
the level sustainable under world market prices. In doing so they

pull resources away from other, potentially more profitable, uses and possibly result in unfavourable specialisation. Some evidence on this can be found in Dick *et al.* (1982). Third, similar to monopoly rents, cheap food imports may have a long-run negative impact on domestic production in those countries that have not managed to take advantage of this terms of trade gain without providing at the same time a disincentive to domestic production. There is ample evidence[8] that a number of developing countries are food importers only because of a domestic incentive structure biased against agriculture. On the other hand there are those countries that are going to continue to be food importers regardless of the type of internal incentive structure. Unless they belong to the group of resource-rich countries, external help may be necessary in these cases to avoid unnecessary hardship. But the point is that this help may be much more efficiently administered through direct income transfers than through distorting world agricultural markets.

4 STRATEGIES OF BRINGING AGRICULTURE UNDER GATT DISCIPLINES

4.1 Restrictions on the Use of Individual Policy Instruments

In view of the unsatisfactory situation of trade in agricultural products the CTA seems to prefer tighter restrictions on the existing GATT rules, in particular on those governing export subsidies. It also appears to favour new rules relating to minimum access guarantees for imports. Incidentally, this strategy is also supported by the group of 'non-subsidising exporters'.

As for export subsidies, there seems to be a preference in the CTA for disallowing them altogether except for some well-defined exceptions. This preference for totally outlawing export subsidies can be understood in the light of the experience with the 'strengthened' GATT rules on export subsidies negotiated during the Tokyo Round. Although the rules adopted at that time provided that export subsidies were not to be used to gain more than an equitable share of the world market or to cause serious prejudice to the interest of a contracting party, in most cases it has proven to be impossible to determine conclusively whether the conditions of the agreement had been violated.

Producer-financed export subsidies (PFES) is the one exception to a complete elimination of export subsidies apparently favoured by the CTA. It is, however, questionable to what extent this scheme could bring about a noticeable reduction in protectionism. There are at least two reasons which may cause some scepticism in this respect. First, many highly protective OECD countries would evade the GATT disciplines under this scheme because they simply do not export the commodity in question. This is, for example, the case for the USA and Japan with regard to sugar and beef. The products for which producer-financed export subsidies would have the most impact on the world market are likely to be the cereals and dairy products. But only a few developing countries are exporters of these commodities. Hence the benefits of PFES would be largely reaped by those developed countries that are exporting these commodities without the help of subsidies. Furthermore it is unclear whether PFES would reduce the downward pressure on prices in world markets. In fact, as suggested by Tangermann (1986), the need for subsidised exports could actually increase should the PFES be managed along the lines of the producer co-responsibility levies implemented in the EEC. Here the net price received by producers remained constant and the levy was simply added on to the consumer price, thus resulting in a tax on consumers rather than on producers. As a result, consumption contracted further and the pressure to export increased rather than diminished. A further consideration that weakens the case for PFES relates to the exact definition of these subsidies. As of now it remains an unresolved question what measures should be considered as export subsidies. Is it only the direct payments needed to export a given surplus at world market prices, including such things as export credits, or does it include also any domestic farm programme that affects production and hence, potentially, exports? Finally, one may want to pose the question of how likely it would be for countries to substitute input subsidies or some other protective mechanism for at least part of the direct export subsidies.

The potential problems associated with minimum access schemes of the type considered by the CTA are not any less troublesome. Similar to the PFES proposal, a minimum access scheme is unlikely to force the majority of import-restricting countries under GATT disciplines. For example, a minimum access requirement of 10 per cent of domestic consumption would not require any adjustments in the US sugar regime or of Japanese beef imports. In both cases imports are far in excess of the minimum level. Yet as mentioned before, protection levels are particularly high in both cases. Even increasing the minimum access level to 20 per cent of domestic production would not change the thrust of this result.

Apart from the problem that many highly protective countries would not be forced by the minimum access scheme to alter their trade regime, minimum access requirements have the unfortunate implication that, even for countries that would be obliged to adjust, there are various options available on exactly how to accomplish this. For example, countries could increase imports to the required minimum while at the same time maintaining their initial protection level, opting for a constant domestic support price,[9] a constant market surplus,[10] or settling for a domestic market clearing approach.[11] Of these various adjustment schemes only the 'constant absolute surplus' and the 'domestic market clearing' approach are likely to lead to a trade expansion and could thus be considered potentially beneficial for developing countries (Valdés and Zietz, 1987). Hence, unless the minimum access requirement also carries with it provisions for its implementation within the country, an unlikely occurrence given the apprehension of most countries to discuss their internal economic policies, their use seems to be rather limited.

4.2 Binding the Overall Level of Protection

The potential problems with PFES and minimum access guarantees suggest that a more general approach to containing or rolling back protectionism may be called for. A method that relies on an overall measure of the level of protection seems to be the best suited to avoidance of an evasion strategy on the part of protecting countries. Such an approach is not all that new. Incidentally, it was put on the negotiating table once before during multilateral trade negotiations. During the Kennedy Round the EEC made such a suggestion in the form of the now famous '*montant de soutien*' or margin of support strategy. This proposal implied the binding of domestic support levels. Given a set of international reference prices for basic farm commodities, the difference between the domestic price and the international price was supposed to be the basis for determining the level of import levies and export subsidies. The proposal was rejected by the USA at that time because it did not contain minimum access guarantees to the EEC market and endangered US market access to the EEC of products already covered by bound tariffs.

The main advantage of a margin of support-type approach at this stage is the apparent unwillingness of the EEC to link the trade talks with a discussion of a reform of its internal agricultural policy regime. Such an unwillingness may also be presumed for other parties of the negotiating round. But since export subsidies, variable levies or other trade distorting measures are an integral part of domestic policies of farm support, any negotiating strategy which focuses on the removal of these measures is unlikely to proceed very far.

Apart from the political advantages of an approach based on the binding of overall levels of protection, possibly along the lines of Josling's producer (PSE) and consumer subsidy equivalents (CSE),[12] there are definite economic advantages. One of the main attractions is that few protectionist devices escape its disciplines. The reason is that most protectionist measures affect the price differential between world market and domestic price. For those measures for which this is not the case,[13] the nominal protection coefficient (NPC) found through price comparisons could be amended appropriately. Total budgetary expenses on agriculture or certain well-defined categories of budgetary outlays could help in assessing the protective content of these measures. Once the problems of measurement are solved, the level of protection that is made part of a country's GATT concessions could be determined by reference to a particular year or average of past years. Alternatively, there could be some freely-negotiated level of protection. At any rate, once an overall protection level is agreed upon on a commodity-specific basis, it could be bound in exactly the same way as a tariff. Also, there would not be a strong need for a general prohibition of export subsidies, since the underlying cause of export subsidies, that is, excess supply of a particular commodity because of domestic market protection, would be figured into the overall protection level. Similarly, PFES could be expected to work under a bound overall protection level. A situation such as that experienced by the EEC in connection with the introduction of co-responsibility levies would not occur since raising consumer prices instead of lowering producer prices implies an increase in protection and thus an apparent violation of the bound protection level.[14]

Measuring the overall protection level with the nominal protection coefficient (NPC) is well suited for those cases where protection comes in the form of quotas, variable levies, tariffs and deficiency payments.[15] It is also useful for capturing the trade-impeding effects of non-tariff measures such as diversion payments, that is, payments to farmers for the purpose of limiting output, and denaturing premiums.[16] In fact, the commodity-specific NPC can serve as the default measure and only in a few cases would there be a need for supplementary calculations to arrive at an approximate tariff equivalent of the protection level.

One such case where establishing a bound overall protection level cannot prevent countermeasures by protecting countries is input subsidies. Similar cases are product-specific subsidies, price-support payments, and the effect of denaturing premiums on the market of the denatured product. Here it may be useful to investigate to what extent budgetary expenditures could be distributed over the quantity produced to raise the NPC measure accordingly to incorporate fully the trade-impeding effect of the above methods of farm support. How this could be done has been demonstrated by Josling in FAO (1975). A question that remains is how direct income transfers are to be treated. Assuming that the tax money used for these transfers would have been spent in a similar way as the transfers are, direct income transfers do not influence production and hence do not distort trade. Hence one may argue that direct income transfers could simply be left out of the calculations of the protection level.

What the binding of an overall protection level cannot avoid is the element of discrimination of trading partners by the protectionist country. A protective scheme for which this is particularly acute is voluntary export restrictions (VERs). But the same problem arises in the context of quotas or selective tariffs. How this element of trade discrimination could be handled in a world of bound rates of protection is an open question. The only way this could be effected may be through empowering the GATT or some other organisation with a stronger monitoring capability and possibly providing for the option to intervene once a case of trade discrimination becomes apparent.

It is clear that there are other unresolved problems of binding overall protection levels on a commodity-specific basis. An example is quality differences. Although space prevents a thorough discussion at this point, it is clear that this and other issues will require careful investigation before bound protection levels could be agreed upon at the negotiating table.

5 CONCLUSION

Fixing the overall protection level on a commodity-specific basis would seem to be a definite step forward in solving the problem of bringing agricultural trade under the disciplines of the GATT. Such a scheme, if properly implemented, is likely to prevent a surge in protectionist evasion strategies similar to those one could expect if particular trade policy instruments were merely made more inaccessible. In view of the experience of the EEC with producer co-responsibility levies, bound protection levels also appear to be essential if one favours, as the CTA does, producer-financed export subsidies as an exception to a general prohibition of export subsidies. Furthermore a price-based system of binding protection levels has all the advantages that are characteristic of a resource allocation scheme based on price indicators as opposed to one based on quantity indicators. Most importantly, adaptation to changes in comparative advantages are not prevented. Also countries protecting the domestic market could be caught, regardless of what instruments they are using: tariffs or non-tariff barriers. Yet they would be free to choose those measures which fit best into their politico-economic climate. It is not hard to imagine that under such an incentive structure there would be a tendency among countries to return to regular tariffs, at least in the long run, since compared to all other measures they cost the protecting country the least in economic terms. There is no loss of tariff revenue and no transfer of rents to foreign exporters.

Notes

1. See Hanrahan *et al.* (1984) for more details.
2. See, for example, Valdés and Zietz (1987) for a survey.
3. The figure of US$ 59 billion in Table 12.1 equals one quarter of the average development aid of OECD countries for the years 1979–81 or 50 per cent of all official aid commitments to agriculture.
4. The group of 14 non-subsidising countries was formed in Cairns, Australia, 25–27 August 1986. See *The Economist*, 30 August –5 September issue, p. 12.
5. See Bergmann (1986) for more detail.
6. See the *World Development Report 1986* for details on this.
7. Compare, for example, the study by Zietz and Valdés (1986b) on the potential benefits to LDCs of trade liberalisation by developed countries in these two commodities.

8. See, for example, the material collected in the *World Development Report 1986* of the World Bank.
9. Countries reduce their protection level in the face of a rising world price so as to keep the domestic price level constant in absolute terms.
10. The protection level is reduced so that the domestic surplus in the final equilibrium just equals the initial surplus before minimum access.
11. The protection level is reduced to a level that just brings domestic demand and supply into equilibrium.
12. See FAO (1975) and Josling (1980) for an application of these concepts.
13. Protective measures that fall into this group are voluntary export restraints, technical or health standards and product-specific subsidies.
14. This again depends on how NPCs are defined, whether in terms of consumer prices or producer prices.
15. The NPC measure suffices to assess the trade-impeding content of deficiency payments as long as the NPC is defined in terms of producer prices.
16. For the market of the denatured product these premiums lead to an increase in supply that is equivalent to a product-specific subsidy.

References

Bergmann, D.R. (1986) 'The Transition to an Overproducing Agricultural System in Europe: An Economic and Institutional Analysis', paper presented at the Nomisma International Conference on 'The Agro-Technological System Towards 2000: A European Perspective', Bologna, Italy, September 18–20.

Dick, H., Gerken, E. and Vincent, D.P. (1982) 'The Benefits of the CAP for Developing Countries. A Case Study of the Ivory Coast', *European Review of Agricultural Economics*, pp. 157–81.

FAO (1975) 'Agricultural Protection and Stabilization Policies: A Framework of Measurement in the Context of Agricultural Adjustment', C 75/Lim/2, October.

Hanrahan, C.E., Cate, P. and Vogt, D.U. (1984) 'Agriculture in the GATT: Toward the Next Round of Multilateral Trade Negotiations', Environment and Natural Resources Policy Division, Congressional Research Service, The Library of Congress, September 11.

Hayami, Y. (1986) 'The Roots of Agricultural Protectionism' in Anderson, Kym and Hayami, Yujiro, *The Political Economy of Agricultural Protection* (London: George Allen & Unwin).

Johnson, D. Gale (1986) 'Constraints to Price Adjustments: Structural, Institutional and Financial Rigidities', paper presented at the Nomisma International Conference on 'The Agro-Technological System Towards 2000: A European Perspective', Bologna, Italy, September 18–20.

Josling, T. (1980) 'Developed-Country Agricultural Policies and Developing-Country Supplies: The Case of Wheat', IFPRI Research Report No. 14, Washington, DC, March.

Schiff, M. (1985) 'An Econometric Analysis of the World Wheat Market and Simulation of Alternative Policies, 1960–80', US Department of Agriculture, Economic Research Service, October.

Tangermann, S. (1986) 'Putting Agriculture in the GATT', Agricultural Project of the American Enterprise Institute, Institute of Agricultural Economics, University of Göttingen, March.

Tyers, R. and Anderson, K. (1986) 'Distortions in World Food Markets: A Quantitative Assessment', background paper for the *World Development Report 1986* of the World Bank.

Valdés, A. and Zietz, J. (1980) 'Agricultural Protection in OECD Countries: Its Cost to Less Developed Countries', IFPRI, Research Report No. 21, Washington, DC.

Valdés, A. and Zietz, J. (1987) 'Export Subsidies and Minimum Access Guarantees in Agricultural Trade Negotiations: A Developing Country Perspective', *World Development*, forthcoming.

World Bank (1986) *World Development Report 1986*, International Bank for Reconstruction and Development, Washington, DC.

Zietz, J. and Valdés, A. (1986a) 'The Costs of Protectionism to Developing Countries. An Analysis for Selected Agricultural Products', World Bank Staff Working Papers No. 769, January.

Zietz, J. and Valdés, A. (1986b) 'The Potential Benefits to LDCs of Trade Liberalization in Beef and Sugar by Industrialized Countries', *Weltwirtschaftliches Archiv*, vol 122, no. 1, March, pp. 93–112.

Discussion on Part III

PAPER BY BELA BALASSA

'Economic Incentives and Agricultural Exports in Developing Countries'

In his introduction of Balassa's paper, Professor Gustav Ranis applauded Professor Balassa's effort to quantify effects of price incentives on exports. He agreed with the conclusion that there was no need for export pessimism on the part of developing countries. Then he made a few comments on Balassa's model.

First, in this model, lags did not work. This needed an explanation as prices, which played a major role in the model, tend to act with a lag. Perhaps the author could explore various lags before coming to a firm conclusion.

Second, the inclusion of the OPEC countries in the sample may adversely affect the importance of income as an explanatory variable. To gain a clearer picture, the OPEC countries should be either treated separately or taken out of the sample. This, in Professor Ranis's view, might improve the regression results.

Third, the main explanatory variable in the model turned out to be the real exchange rate. But the explanation for the behaviour of African countries appears *ad hoc*. This could stem from their highly overvalued nominal exchange rates in the initial period. In this context, Ranis felt it would be useful to examine the relationship between the official and equilibrium rates.

Fourth, the full regression equations were not stable. The R^2s were very low. To improve the results, one might have to try other specifications.

Fifth, the author divided the countries into several sub-groups, on the basis of the kinds of incentives used during the 1960–81 study period. Ranis observed that national incentive systems, rather than having 'black-and-white' differences, in fact have various shades of grey. In other words, it is not possible to classify most countries as clearly having import-substitution regimes or export-promotion regimes. Such an *ex ante* classification can lead to circularity in reasoning. He urged Balassa to follow a classification based on an independent set of criteria.

Finally, Ranis thought that Professor Balassa might have used protectionism by the developed countries as an explanatory variable, as this has become increasingly important in recent years. One should also try to compare the 'before' and 'after' effects of the new protectionism in developed countries in relation to the experience of newly-industrialising countries such as South Korea and other East Asian countries.

Balassa agreed with most of Ranis's comments, especially the last point dealing with protectionism of the developed countries. However he pointed out the difficulties in introducing these aspects in an econometric model, owing to numerous data problems. One example was his having to use nominal rather than effective exchange rates which would have been more appropriate had there been the necessary data. Balassa agreed that the lags did not work in his model but, at the same time, there was room for some experimentation.

Regarding the R^2s, Balassa argued that they were not low, as the variables of the model were specified in the form of rates of change and not in absolute terms. Under these circumstances it would be desirable to gauge the explanatory power of the equations by F values rather than R^2s.

He did not agree with Ranis that there was circularity of reasoning in his paper. However, even if this were true, there would be no practical way out as data to overcome this problem do not exist for most of these countries. Balassa also denied any bias against import-substitution regimes in his paper. At this point Professor Ranis intervened to say that, for proper analysis of the problem, one should go by sectors in individual countries instead of groups of countries.

Montague Lord pointed out that cross-section analysis of countries tended to impose uniform coefficients for all countries. It would be useful to test for the similarity of the coefficients among countries before presenting the results. He wanted to know the theory behind the equations presented.

Narain Sinha wanted the author to distinguish between developing countries' exports to the socialist countries and those to the developed capitalist countries. He regarded this distinction as important because factors affecting exports to socialist countries are very different from those affecting exports to developed capitalist countries.

With regard to the classification of countries, Siddarthan suggested that such variables as ratios of effective exchange rates of imports to exports, or differences between purchasing power parities and official exchange rates, may prove more useful.

In responding to these comments, Balassa argued that the theory behind the equations was the standard demand and supply framework. He advocated the use of dummy variables in regression analysis to capture individual country effects. With regard to the distinction between exports to socialist and to developed countries, Balassa said that the distinction would be important for India and perhaps for certain other countries like Greece. But for most of the developing countries, this distinction would not be relevant as they exported very little to socialist countries.

He regarded effective exchange rates as certainly being relevant to the analysis, but noted that these were difficult to calculate in the presence of quota restrictions. Hence they could not be introduced in the empirical work.

While protection by developed countries is important, in Balassa's view it has not prevented the East Asian countries like South Korea from penetrating developed countries' markets. In his opinion, the impacts of the protectionism of developed countries are usually exaggerated.

PAPER BY GERALD M. MEIER

'The Old and New Export Pessimism: A Critical Survey'

Dr I.M.D. Little started the discussion of this paper in a light vein saying that Professor Meier, unlike most others, is not a two-handed economist. He is very clear about what he thinks and advocates his viewpoint forcefully. There has been a lot of pessimism regarding export potentials of the developing countries. This export pessimism has damaged the interest of the developing countries, as it is not based on facts. It is in their interest to remain open and avoid the adverse effects of import substitution. The success of South Korea and other East Asian countries in their exports was not affected adversely by the low growth of the developed countries. Furthermore, many firms in the more developed countries may transfer production of goods that are based on labour-intensive technologies to the developing countries. Indications are that South Korea may already be shifting away from the most labour-intensive goods thus making way for other developing countries. It is important to note also that the export industries in these successful countries yielded high social gains. Hence, Little said, the developing countries should be less pessimistic and more enthusiastic about the GATT negotiations.

Reacting to Meier's and Little's comments, MacBean declared that, unlike the author, he was a two-handed economist. He did not agree with the view that countries like South Korea may give way to other developing countries when moving up the ladder. These countries enjoy quotas with the developed countries and they wish to continue to receive their quota rents rather than give way to other developing countries. Also, he did not agree with the view that the multinational corporations (MNCs) favour free trade. Since many of their branches produce mainly for the local domestic markets, they might also demand protection.

Agreeing with MacBean, Raffer stated that to cite the example of South Korea is misleading, as that country has demanded a free trade for exports only and not for imports. Furthermore, political considerations had led to few restrictions on Korean exports into the US. Hence it might not be possible for other developing countries to replicate the South Korean example. Also, the situation in the 1980s was very different from that of the 1970s, when the European countries were encouraged to set up their labour-intensive units in the developing countries and even to import labour from the latter. But the tables have turned now.

Neither was Paul Streeten in favour of a naive one-handed economist's approach, as the world is more complex and needs more hands. He believed it was not correct to group all countries that were successful in exports into one category. The commodity composition of these success cases varies widely. For example, countries like South Korea and Taiwan started by exporting labour-intensive commodities while Brazil exported more land-intensive commodities. Further, the timing of exports was also different. These countries succeeded under conditions of boom in world trade, conditions which are absent today. When one talks of the benefits of large exports, one should also look at the cost side. This is a point largely ignored by advocates of this strategy. Why not do a cost-benefit analysis of the possible alternatives and weigh the results?

There were also suggestions from the floor regarding the necessity to analyse the net benefits of trade-liberalisation and macroeconomic adjustments. If the costs of macroeconomic adjustments are very high, developing countries might not favour trade liberalisation. In this context Sunanda Sen stressed the importance of examining the relationship between liberalisation and foreign capital flows, as well as the indirect effects. Experience suggests that foreign capital interests begin to influence and change the state structure and government in the developing countries.

D.M. Nanjundappa wondered whether food surpluses in India are real or illusory. In his judgement, given the percentage of population below the poverty line, there are no real surpluses available for exports.

Lynden Moore felt that a disaggregated analysis by type of product would be desirable. She noted that one of the fastest growing exports of South Asian countries was of electronic products, where real prices were falling despite increase in the size of the market. In the long run, excessive specialisation in particular products could pose serious problems for export growth.

With regard to declines in exports resulting from demand factors or competition, several speakers from India, such as Usha Dar and Aasha Kapur from Delhi and Guru from Patna, felt the declining share of India in world exports was because of competitive losses more than declining real demand. To Usha Dar, mere export incentives might not help as the costs in India have been very high, mainly because of various domestic industrial policies.

Reacting to these comments, Professor Meier agreed that one should go beyond neoclassical theory. His main concern was with long-term and stable policies and not with short-term fluctuations. In response to Paul Streeten's suggestion, Meier said that it was very difficult to undertake a cost-benefit analysis of export promotion versus import substitution. However, in his judgement, it would be a mistake to revert back to import-substitution policies, the real costs of which are widely known. He agreed that trade liberalisation implies liberalisation in the whole set of domestic policies.

PAPER BY GARY P. SAMPSON

'Protection in Agriculture and Manufacturing: Meeting the Objectives of the Uruguay Round'

In his remarks, Professor Paul Streeten said that, as the arguments in favour of free trade and against controls and trade barriers are fairly well known, many of the points made in Sampson's paper are not new to economists. But he wondered why it is that economists' pleas for liberalisation are not listened to by Governments. Part of the answer could be that these recommendations do not coincide with national self-interest. Even the United States, an affluent society with a large domestic market, has to calculate the benefits of extra income through trade liberalisation against the costs of shifting workers from the declining industries to the growing industries. Here it should be remembered that, in a changing world, costs of occupational geographical shifts would have to be incurred continuously. Thus comparative advantage may become a policy for tramps.

As for the protectionism of the developed countries, Streeten observed that Western bankers who have made loans to developing countries should be a useful pressure group for the removal of import restrictions by the developed countries, since poor export prospects for the developing countries make loan repayment difficult or impossible. In his view the real issue was not one of import substitution versus export promotion but rather one of doing both efficiently and in the correct sequence.

Dr Sampson during his reply to remarks about the political economy of protection, stressed the need to evaluate claims for protection by considering the implications for the economy as a whole. By doing this through a process of public inquiry would mean that an economy wide cost-benefit analysis of protection could be used to put pressure on policy makers to pursue the right policy rather than respond to the demands of pressure groups pursuing their own interests.

PAPER BY ALBERTO VALDÉS AND JOACHIM ZIETZ

'Lowering Agricultural Protection: A Developing Country Perspective towards the Uruguay Round'

Examination of the Uruguay Round was continued by Dr Joachim Zietz who, in the absence of a lead discussant, summarised the paper by himself and Alberto Valdés.

Their basic idea was as follows:

Developing countries can only gain from an active participation in the Uruguay Round. Fixing the overall protection level on a commodity-specific basis would be a preferable approach in solving agricultural trade problems.

Most of the subsequent discussion from the floor concentrated on agricultural protection and export subsidies by the developed countries. To Zietz's suggestion that, at a minimum, nominal protection rates should be fixed at negotiated and agreed levels, it was pointed out that a country could use domestic subsidies as a substitute for export subsidies. This way, while the nominal protection coefficient is held fixed, protection can be afforded indirectly.

Raffer mentioned the Australian complaint about the US subsidies to agriculture. Developing countries also complain about the protections and subsidies granted by the USA and other developed countries. Many developed countries themselves are victims of EEC and Japanese protection and have been complaining about it.

A delegate from the Swedish University of Agricultural Sciences felt that too much emphasis on technical aspects of the problem, such as the behaviour of protection coefficients and subsidies, might not be very useful. With regard to the agricultural policies of the developed countries the real issue would go well beyond these technicalities. The developed countries must accept lower agricultural production and higher import levels, and this is very much a political decision.

Echoing this argument, a delegate from Argentina remarked that not only did the EEC and United States give export subsidies to boost their exports, but the USA has also had an export-enhancement programme. These countries get away with these programmes mainly because the developing countries cannot twist the arms of the European community, the USA and Japan.

Gary Sampson further developed the point of arm twisting. Since the developing countries are at serious disadvantage in this respect, the only option left to them is to relax some of their protectionist measures in industry in return for better access to agricultural markets of the developed countries.

For Sulekh Gupta the problem really lay with the OECD countries. Developed countries advocate agricultural and agro-based industries for the developing countries. This is based on comparative advantage theory. But at the same time they protect their domestic markets from the import of agricultural commodities from the third-world countries. In this context, South–South co-operation was not seen as a possible solution since many developing countries produce similar products.

Muchkund Dubey, on the basis of his long experience as a negotiator in GATT and other forums on behalf of the Government of India, saw no scope for the developing countries having any leverage in GATT negotiations. He asked if, as had been argued, trade liberalisation implied changing or even negotiating domestic economic policies of the developed, what then remained for the developing countries to do. It is the protectionism of the developed countries that has led to subsidisation of agriculture in the developing countries as a means of guarding their subsistence and food security.

Zietz, responding to these comments, agreed with most of the points made from the floor. He reiterated his advocacy of an active developing-country participation in the GATT negotiations. He said a positive sign is that some developing countries are trying to influence the course of GATT actions through the Cairns group which includes Australia and New Zealand.

DISCUSSION OF ANALYSES RELATED TO INDIA, THE PHILIPPINES AND SOUTH KOREA

Discussion of the three country-specific papers made available to session participants but not included in this volume brought out several additional points of relevance to future analysis of the effects of protectionism.

In discussing the World Bank-based model of India provided by Henrik Dahl and Pradeep Mitra, Professor Lance Taylor noted that computable general-equilibrium models could be either supply-driven or demand-driven. In this supply-driven model, various exercises had explored the impact of trade liberalisation on welfare gains. The results indicated that there is not much to gain from trade liberalisation from the point of view of welfare. And yet faith in liberalisation persists, mainly on the grounds of gains in efficiency. If there is an efficiency gain from liberalisation (Professor Taylor made it very clear that he does not believe in that assumption), one would need to ask: what would be the mechanism to realise it? To Professor Taylor the general-equilibrium model may not be the most appropriate method for dealing with welfare-gain issues. In his opinion, a political economy approach would be a far better approach.

Susmitha Rakshit felt that sector classifications used in such models often do not take into account such production conditions as increasing returns to scale. Liberalisation benefits would to a large extent depend on this.

Lynden Moore felt that estimates of the increase in efficiency in consumption and production may underestimate the benefit of liberalisation in a dynamic situation, in so far as the distorted system consistently leaves out the real return to capital.

Bela Balassa felt that such models tend to be too aggregative and delineate very few sectors. Many of the points the literature related to welfare implications, notably the writings of Harry Johnson, cannot be tested when there are only six sectors in a model. There is need also to take into account not only tariff rates but also restrictions on trade quantities, which are very important in the real world today.

Kirit Parikh turned attention to the Philippines analysis by Ramon Clarete and James Roumasset, as well as to the Korean analysis by Kym Anderson and Peter Warr. In the case of the Philippines paper he found it surprising that the estimates of welfare gains under all variants of the model were nearly the same (around five per cent) and that the results did not differ between rent-seeking and non-rent-seeking cases. He noted that, in the Korean model, as fixed capital did not feature, intermediate inputs were assumed to be used in rigid proportion, and there was no allowance for input substitutions. Nor was there allowance for capital accumulation or investment in land.

To Professor Parikh these assumptions were disturbing. They can result in domestic price increases in agriculture being shown to produce an overall welfare decline simply because wages of skilled labour are forced in the analysis to fall, while wages of unskilled labour and also rents are forced to rise. Welfare gains from agricultural trade liberalisation are likely to be shown in such models. Parikh added that IIASA models of this type show no more than two per cent welfare gains from trade liberalisation over a 20-year period. Also Parikh noted that both models used a comparative-static approach, whereas in reality the process of adjustment matters. He felt that the dynamic paths resulting from policy changes needed more attention in such studies.

Reacting to this, Dr Peter Warr stated that the main aim of the Korean analysis was to study the distributional effects of agricultural protection. He and Dr Anderson were not interested in the gains from trade liberalisation as such. They had assumed that capital goods were traded at fixed international prices. Hence their prices, but not their quantities, were considered fixed in their model. There was no assumption that inputs were used in rigid proportions and input substitutions were an important element in the functioning of the model. Professor Parikh had misinterpreted the model in this respect.

The final discussant, Gary Sampson, observed that general-equilibrium models were too aggregative to be useful for policy.

Part IV

Industrialisation in Primary Export Economies

Introduction to Part IV

Shigeru Ishikawa
AOYAMA GAKUIN UNIVERSITY, TOKYO

In contrast to other sessions which dealt with the subject of 'balance between industry and agriculture in economic development' in terms of functionally separated issues, this Session focussed a special category of countries characterised as 'primary export economies'. It examines the nature of the economic problems and difficulties which these countries are facing and investigates why and how they have chosen industrialisation as a long-term measure to solve such difficulties and achieve self-sustained economic growth.

1 'TYPOLOGY-BASED ECONOMIC DEVELOPMENT MODELS'

To begin with, it may be noted that the primary export economies are here regarded as economies which have the following character-istics: (1) population is sparse and land and natural resources are abundant; (2) the economies specialise in the production and export of a few primary products with a significantly high rate of natural rents; but (3) the formation of modern industry has not yet occurred or, if it has begun, is still not significant in either production or export. The primary export economies are as such clearly differentiated from other types of economies. Old established economies, with dense population and scarce land and natural resources, with a relatively developed handicraft sector and even a small segment of modern industry, still tend to export mainly primary products in large quantity, implying excessive exploitation of land and natural resources pertaining to each of them. However, to tackle the subject area effectively, such a broad and apparent distinction of the primary export economies is not enough. Remembering the fact that even within the same category, the primary export economies vary significantly in their initial conditions of economic development, the study should be conducted in at least three steps.

(a) Some attempt is made to classify various countries in which primary exports predominate according to the remaining differences in the initial conditions.
(b) With respect to each individual type of country thus identified, the commonly recognisable process of economic development, particularly the industrialisation component, is stylised and presented as an economic development model and
(c) All the different types of countries thus stylised and modelled are summarised to derive a generalised process of economic development, and in particular that of the primary export economies' industrialisation.

This approach is along the lines of what may be called a 'typology-based economic development models approach'. As may be seen, the arrangement of the papers seek to derive findings from step (b) for individual country groups chosen from the typology of step (a). However, the scope of the primary export economies is here extended to cover those economies which are presently more or less industrialised and even in which manufactured products occupy a significant proportion in export trade but which were in the past primary export economies according to the above definition. The aim of this extension is to obtain thereby richer observation of the processes of industrialisation of the primary export economies and hence to gain deeper insights into the issue. I do not wish to go into these papers' individual findings here. But with regard to some more or less generalised findings relating to step (c) three points may be made.

2 GENERALISED PROCESS OF ECONOMIC DEVELOPMENT

2.1 Linkages from Natural Resources

The most clear-cut finding is that the emergence and development of manufacturing exports in the primary export economies is often a continuum from the natural resource exports of the traditional types to the natural resource-based manufacturing exports on the one hand, and to the exports of non-durable consumer industry products on the other. Underlying this continuum is the spontaneous development of manufacturing both through the effect of the input–output linkages between agriculture and industry and through the income effect of natural resource development and export. The result is the creation of an urban servicing sector and an urban populace and hence the emergence of consumer demand on a substantial scale. Once these spontaneously developed industries become firmly established, their accumulated managerial and technological capabilities are likely to be large enough to enable new industries (even if they are artificially introduced by import-substitution) to become import-competing and even to transform them into export industries. Thus the above continuum would open up a new horizon. These possibilities are explicitly propounded by Teitel in the Latin American case and by Yamazawa in the cases of Japan and her Asian neighbours. They argue that the usual presentation of the issue – import substitution versus export promotion in industrialisation – is often erroneous at least for the primary export economies. Both are likely to be interconnected steps in a natural and efficient continuum. Lal's paper, however, indicates that in the state ruled by an ideological charismatic leader there is a tendency to seek import-substituting industrialisation beyond the range of the spontaneous development, this resulting not only in unsuccessful industrialisation, but also, in the extreme case, in fiscal, foreign exchange and domestic output crises such as occurred in Ghana after 1961 and in Tanzania in the 1970s and 1980s.

2.2 Mobilisation and Allocation of High 'Natural' Rents

In the primary export economies, the sources of funds required for initiating and proceeding with industrialisation exist in an easily identified form (that is, in high 'natural' rents of a few major primary exports) and are easily captured by government (for example, by the apparatus of marketing board or export taxes) if it so wishes. But, whether the funds thus mobilised do not involve significant leakages, and how they are allocated efficiently among the alternative uses are problems of another kind. Regardless of the result of the use of mobilised funds, the contrast with densely-populated low-income countries, poor in natural resources, is clear enough. There lump-sum funds for industrialisation are difficult to locate and, therefore, the direction and magnitude of net resource transfers between traditional agriculture and emerging industry are also subtle and complicated, defying a straightforward assessment.

Among our papers at least one by Wohlmuth deals fairly explicitly with this issue of financing industrialisation. This case of the Sudan, however, is one in which the financing mechanism characteristic of the primary export economies worked in an extremely negative direction, where monoculture exports, mainly cotton, accounted for most of the government receipts as well as the export proceeds. However, depression of the producers' price of cotton entailed a serious loss of production incentives for cotton farmers and hence a drastic decline in the share of cotton in Sudan's total export trade – from 75 per cent in 1950 to 20 per cent in 1981 and 1982. In addition, there was obvious inefficiency and carelessness in the use of the mobilised natural rents of the primary crops for building up the parastatals, in particular state mechanised farms and modern large-scale agro-industries, which resulted in what Wohlmuth calls a crisis of industrialisation.

2.3 The Role of Food Production

While the chances of it being taken up explicitly in the session were few, there is certainly a common issue of whether successful industrialisation requires parallel development of domestic food production. In the case of the Lewis-type closed, dualistic development model which fits the development of resource-poor, densely populated low-income economies, the supply of labour from the traditional agricultural sector to the dynamic industrial sector is 'unlimited', as the former sector holds sufficiently large 'surplus labour'. But the supplies of wage goods (mainly food products) to feed this inflow of labour are by no means easy, as labour productivity of the agricultural sector is very low and hence there is little surplus food. Thus, development of domestic food production is evidently a very important, necessary condition for successful industrialisation.

In the primary export economies, it appears that the extra amount of wage goods necessary for industrialisation can be imported using the proceeds from the export of primary products. And this is even efficient in terms of comparative advantage. In fact, in many primary export economies of the mining and plantation types, where considerable growth was or is achieved relying upon unskilled labour supplied from the foreign immigrant workers, the wage goods used to or do come, not from domestic food production but from imports. However, in cases where natural rents of the economies' main primary exports decrease as a result either of over-exploitation of natural resources and/or a declining international demand, imports of food are likely to be subject to a foreign exchange constraint. The policy of self-sufficiency of food is therefore liable to become popular. Moreover, when and where these mines and plantations depend upon internal migrants as the source of labour recruitment, the supply of such labour is likely to be constrained by the capacity to produce food in the farming communities from which the migrants come. This is because, as Uma Lele observes, in the labour allocation of the farm households in Africa high value is placed on producing food crops to ensure domestic food security. It is a common practice for the peasants to produce export cash crops side by side with the subsistence crops either as a supplementary occupation or as a complement to the cash crop, intercropping for example. Hence, although often unnoticed, the extent of cash crop production is constrained by the success of food production. There is a similar relation in the peasant exports of grains between the export surplus and the efficiency of food production. Thus, even in the primary export economies, the increase in output and productivity of food production is becoming a prerequisite to industrialisation, and this tendency is enhanced by the population explosion in these economies. Wohlmuth described post-independence Sudan's agriculture as a three-tier structure: (1) the irrigated farming sector traditionally producing export cotton; (2) the mechanised farming sector producing domestic food and export crops; and (3) the traditional rain-fed farming sector. Government attempted to put policy priority on the first two tiers. Though this attempt resulted in a failure, their intention should be evaluated in connection with the food problem the Sudanese were encountering.

3 POLITICAL ECONOMY APPROACH

With regard to Lal's 'new political economy' approach, its effectiveness in dealing with the subject of this session seems to have been amply demonstrated. And in providing geometrical rigour to the approach the paper is even path-breaking. As usual in the recent political economy exercises, the main motive of the study is an attempt to explain why the economic policies actually chosen in many developing countries diverge from those which are considered to be socially optimal and which would be chosen if the democratic majority rule, or otherwise the Platonic Guardian rule prevailed.

Specifically, Lal's problem is: whereas during the pre-war days and mostly under the colonial rule, the primary export economies selected in his paper were all successful in achieving significant growth, why did many of them aim to have an excessive degree of industrialisation, beyond 'natural' import-substitution industrialisation, and thus necessarily suffer poor results? Lal tries to explain this divergence in terms of the nature of the state and the citizens' interests which in turn are influenced by the resource potential of individual countries. Thus his approach goes far beyond usual political economy. It involves the task of typology of the countries under question; it even traces the outcome of a specific policy in terms of the 'story' of the ensuing development, which in turn differs according to the 'type' of the economy.

As is seen, his approach is in fact similar to our 'typology-based economic development models approach.' The only difference seems to be one of the emphasis on explanatory factors. While his is placed on the interrelationship between specific initial conditions and specific developmental policies, ours is placed on that between initial conditions and the structure of the economy.

4 FURTHER RESEARCH TASKS

On the basis of the above comments on the aim and discussion of the Session, some of the research tasks relating to the Session subject are clear.

First, regarding the linkages emanating from natural resources, the most important is to extend the scope of the empirical research so as to cover most regions in which the primary export economies are located and thereby to increase our knowledge on the nature of the spontaneous development of industries (including development by the accumulated learning effect) as well as on the boundary line separating these economies from artificial and unsuccessful industrialisation. For example, successful linkages are found, in addition to the ones indicated earlier, in the development of small-scale metal-working factories in Thailand, Indonesia and the Philippines. These were originally the repair and maintenance workshops of the machinery and equipment of the factories processing the export products, such as natural rubber, sugar cane and tin. Moreover, the strength of the linkage and learning effects seems to be significantly associated with the length of time which has elapsed since the beginning of natural resource exports, in particular natural resource-based manufacturing exports. It should be cautioned, however, that direct foreign investment could possibly play a role in supplementing the above learning effect.

Secondly as to the issue of financing industrialisation, we have also to extend the number of actually observed cases, including both successful and unsuccessful ones. Investigation of the factors responsible for these varying performances should cover not only policy factors, but also factors relating to objective conditions. For example, Côte d'Ivoire, an economy exporting primarily coffee and cocoa, is often referred to as a successful case in this connection. While mobilisation of 'natural' rents through export taxes and their use in rural and agricultural development were highly successful, it is also important to note that development of these export crops started quite recently: one-third of the existing cultivated land was opened up by peasants themselves over the past 20 years. Therefore the natural rent must be still quite high, easily subject to mobilisation. The opposite case seems to be Ghana, where, as indicated before, an excessive mobilisation of natural rent from cocoa beans and an inefficient use of it entailed degeneration of cocoa farming into subsistence production as well as negative growth of the economy. But this sorry tale is likely to have been caused partly by structural factors: extension of land under cocoa crop at a speed much higher than that with which family labour can cope and unbalanced growth of export crops and domestic food crops.

Thirdly, relating to further studies on the possible effect of food production capacity on industrialisation of the primary export economies, three points may be worthy of special attention. First, even among these countries (for example, Kenya, Tanzania, Zambia, Peru and Brazil) there is a tendency on the one hand for the producers' prices of food to be officially raised (and/or input prices subsidised), and on the other for the consumer prices of food to be stabilised on a low level by state subsidies. Two factors lie behind this tendency: (1) population explosion and the working of diminishing returns in the food producing sector and (2) expansion of political power of an increasing number of urban consumers. Secondly, there are the implications of the diffusion of the Green Revolution in three types of countries: non-food grain primary export economies, food grain primary export economies and non-primary export economies. Finally, whereas Taiwan was once a rice and sugar exporting colony, since the mid-1960s she has become a net grain-importing area: in the early 1980s, the proportion of domestically produced grains to total grain supply, both in terms of tons, fell to 40 per cent from more than 90 per cent in the mid-1960s. This indicates the complete shift of comparative advantage from agriculture to manufacturing. Taiwan's case may suggest a typical scenario of successful industrialisation of the primary export economies in terms of food supplies.

An additional task is the necessity to conduct more comprehensive studies of the primary export economies along step (c) of the 'typology-based economic development models approach.' The first thing to do is to develop typology. Although many classification criteria are conceivable, as an intermediate device several important countries in the categories of the primary export economies might be selected from the regions of the world represented in this session, and their characteristics compared in terms of the following criteria: (1) types and amounts of raw materials; (2) types of management units (family or capitalist enterprises, the size of operation) and labour force (family labour, domestic migrant labour or foreign immigrants); (3) the length of time which has passed since the first natural resource export; (4) the agricultural infrastructure and the economic environment of agriculture and (5) the political economy factors. A series of groupings for the four regions may be attempted on these criteria, at least as a first approximation. Next, in order to try to build up economic development models which fit the types of countries thus identified, it is desirable to make a careful inventory of the existing development models and then to make use of them as at least a building block for a new model. A Vent-for-Surplus model by Myint and a Staple Theory by Watkins, McCarty and others are particularly relevant. Related concepts, a 'Vent-for-Surplus Trap' and a 'Staple Trap' are also relevant. These denote the phase in which the operation of the original models ceases and the economy is caught in a growth trap. For example, the development of Brazil after the 1930s may be considered as a new phase of deliberate domestic industrialisation (the model of which is yet to be devised) succeeding the phase of a Staple Trap. Brazil's Staple Trap arrived as she could not discover the kind of staple which is comparable to the wheat of Canada and Australia. When, after successive switching of export staples those two countries discovered a new export staple, wheat, they moved to the sustained industrial growth process through the effects of significant forward, backward and final demand linkages which emanated from production and transportation of wheat. None of Brazil's sugar, cotton or coffee was that kind of staple.

12 The Political Economy of Industrialisation in Primary Product Exporting Economies: Some Cautionary Tales

Deepak Lal*
UNIVERSITY COLLEGE, LONDON AND
WORLD BANK

1 INTRODUCTION

Ever since the collapse of primary commodity prices during the Great Depression and the attendant balance of payments problems faced by most of the primary product export economies of the third world, industrialisation has been viewed as the major panacea for developing most of these economies. Much of the resulting industrialisation has been import substituting – some of it naturally induced as the relative profitability of domestic import substitutes rose with the terms of trade and accompanying real exchange rate changes which resulted from the inter-war collapse of primary commodity prices and the subsequent disruption of international trade during the Second World War. But in many countries both the inter-war difficulties with primary product export-led growth and the rise of economic nationalism – which has been a characteristic of most of the Third World since the Second World War – has led to the institution of protective systems which have pushed industrialisation beyond these 'natural' levels by tariff- and quota-induced 'hothouse' import-substituting industrialisation.

However, one of the best researched and well-established stylised facts about postwar economic development is the inefficiency and inequity associated with this hothouse industrialisation.[1] Some countries have recognised this and have established more 'neutral'

279

trade regimes, others have had cycles in their trade regimes – with partial trade liberalisation followed by a backsliding to controls and vice-versa – while some, despite the accumulating evidence of the dysfunctional nature of their protectionist trade and payment regimes, have tenaciously clung to them even though it is apparent that liberalisation would help to improve the rate as well as the quality of their economic growth.

These differences in public behaviour would seem to pose a problem for those who like Keynes believe that: 'Madmen in authority, who hear voices in the air, are distilling their frenzy from some academic scribbler of a few years back . . . soon or late, it is ideas not vested interests which are dangerous for good or ill' (Keynes, *General Theory*, p. 384). Memories may be long, but there are new hungry generations waiting to tread on those whose ideas were set in the thirties and forties. More seriously, while the influence of ideas on public policies is undeniable, a belief in their primacy over interests depends upon assuming a State which is moved entirely by the best arguments of the day (when its mind was formed), and with no autonomous ends of its own. This is a view of the *benevolent State* as a committee of ageing Platonic Guardians closeted in their studies reading and cogitating on the essays in persuasion written by their technocratic peers. It is a view which is becoming less and less persuasive.

By contrast the emerging 'new political economy' takes a more even-handed view of the motives of the State and its citizens, regarding them as being equally self-regarding. Ideas clearly play a role but the interests (possibly shifting) of those who comprise the State must be equally important. Moreover, as a result of the State's conversion of certain ideas into policies, particular interest groups may be created which make it impossible to reverse policies even when the ideas on which they are based are generally recognised to be hollow. The 'irrational' policies that are then followed can be said to be ideological, where ideology is used in its literal sense, viz. 'thinking or theorising of an idealistic abstract or impractical nature; fanciful speculation'.

In sorting out these more subtle interactions between ideas, ideology and interests it is useful to consider the determinants and outcomes of policies in countries where 'ecological' conditions could be expected to favour the emergence of interests more conducive towards those 'outward-oriented' development policies which past research has shown aid development. In this paper therefore I consider the long-run development policies and outcomes of five export economies with abundant land and natural resources relative to their past and current populations. Their comparative advantage has clearly been in primary product exports.[2] Two of these are in Latin America – Argentina and Peru; two in Africa – Ghana and Tanzania; and one in Asia – Thailand.[3]

All five countries have in the past been highly successful primary product export economies, but their contemporary fortunes have diverged sharply (see Table 12.1).[4] Three of these countries, Thailand, Ghana and Tanzania have traditionally been peasant economies. Their output of export crops grown by peasant households rose with the growth in export demand following their integration in the world economy in the last century. Argentina by contrast is a land-abundant country where the main primary commodities – wool, wheat and meat – are produced mainly by medium- and large-scale agricultural units with hired labour. Peru is the classic dual economy, with a largely untouched subsistence peasant sector in the Sierra, co-existing with wage based farms (in the coastal plain) and mining and fishing enterprises which have produced most of the primary product exports which have been the basis of Peruvian growth since about 1850.

One of our major theses is that these initial 'ecological' conditions provide a strong predisposition towards a particular path of development. In this paper therefore I will tell some analytical 'political economy' stories for these different 'types' of export economies which will seek to sort out the different effects over time of the interactions between interests and ideas in explaining their development policies and outcomes. A major purpose of the paper is also to show how the new political economy can be used to analyse some important aspects of long-run development. Thus the countries chosen also typify three different types of 'polity' – what I label respectively the predatory, factional and oligarchic state – in terms of the differing objectives subserved by the controllers of the 'polity'.

Our core analytical model is the so-called specific factors Ricardo–Viner model of trade theory (see Jones, 1971; Snape, 1977; Ruffin and Jones, 1977) and its extensions in analyses of: (a) the Dutch Disease (see Corden and Neary, 1982); (b) the political economy of tariffs – where the political process which yields protection is endogenised – (see the series of models by Findlay and Wellisz, 1982, 1983, 1984 and by Mayer, 1984); combined with the emerging literature on the political economy of fiscal policies (see Brennan and Buchanan, 1980; Findlay and Wilson, 1987; Lal, 1984). Another purpose of this paper is to show how an analytical framework devised from the above can be represented by three simple diagrams which can be used in analysing various aspects of the political economy of long-run development.[5]

Section 2 provides some stylised facts about the five economies. Section 3 deals with the cautionary tale based on the Thai, Ghanian and Tanzanian experience of the predatory state. Section 4 with that of Argentina and the factional state, and Section 5 with Peru and the oligarchic state. As with all cautionary tales it is for the reader to draw the relevant moral. Hence it would be presumptuous to append any conclusions!

2   FIVE EXPORT ECONOMIES – SOME STYLISED FACTS

For a number of developing countries Lloyd Reynolds (1985) has dated the beginning of what he labels intensive growth – when, after a period of population and output growing at the same rate, there is a sustained rise in per capita incomes. For our five countries Reynolds' dates for these turning points are:

    1850 – Thailand
    1860 – Argentina
    1880 – Peru
    1895 – Ghana
    1900 – Tanzania.

The great world-wide boom associated with the establishment and spread of the nineteenth-century liberal trading order – from 1850 – drew these primary producing economies into an expanding world economy. Their export-led growth was based in Peru on a combination of mineral and agricultural products, in Argentina on temperate zone products such as wool, wheat and meat, in Tanzania on sisal and coffee, and in Thailand and Ghana on the expansion of smallholder peasant agriculture producing respectively rice and cocoa for export.

In both Peru and Argentina there was both a sequencing and impressive diversification of primary product exports. Except for some foreign-owned Peruvian mineral exports, much of the value added from the expanded production of primary commodities was retained within the country. This was particularly true of the peasant smallholder economies, where the spread effects of this export-led growth on mass levels of living were also more favourable.

For Argentina Carlos Diaz–Alejandro (1970) estimated that, in the 50 years before the First World War, GDP grew at about 5 per cent per annum, population at about 3·4 per cent, leaving a substantial improvement in per capita income. The domestic capital and labour markets were increasingly integrated with world factor markets, and there was also growth in 'natural' import-competing manufacturing based on processing primary products as well as from the introduction of light industry with the expansion of the domestic market. By 1929, 19 per cent of Argentinian GDP originated in manufacturing.

In Peru, Webb (1986) has estimated that between 1913 and 1941, real GDP grew at about 3·8 per cent per annum and population at 1·5 per cent per annum, yielding a per capita growth rate of about 2 per cent. Exports grew at about 3·8 per cent per annum between 1900 and 1930 and manufacturing output by 4·8 per cent per annum between 1918/19 and 1950.

In Thailand there was a steady rise in population and an even greater rise in rice exports from 1850. There was also a steady rise in per capita income (see Ingram, 1971; Reynolds, 1985, p. 158). Population grew from 6 million in 1850 to 18·15 million in 1950, while rice exports increased from 990 000 piculs (1 picul = about 60 kgs) in 1958–9 to 25 370 000 piculs in 1935–9. The State shared in this prosperity through export taxes. Peasant producers on average received only half the export price. There was very little manufacturing before the Second World War and most of it was in handicrafts. Thus in 1937 only 1·6 per cent of the labour force was employed in manufacturing. The country was ruled by an absolute monarch until 1932, when the king became an influential consti-tutional ruler, and the country has since been ruled in effect by an oligarchy.

Ghana was a British colony from 1874. Exports primarily of small-holder cocoa and gold expanded rapidly, the average rate of growth being 9·2 per cent per annum between 1882 and 1913 (Reynolds, 1985, p. 219). The colonial government's main economic function was to provide improved infrastructure.

Tanzania developed as an export economy from 1900, first as a German and later as a British colony. The major exports were sisal grown on plantations, and coffee, rubber and cotton grown both on settler farms and by peasant smallholders. There was virtually no growth in manufacturing during the colonial period. In all our countries the growth of the export economy was also associated with a rise in public expenditures on infrastructure (see Birnberg and Resnick, 1975).

Table 12.1 provides summary statistics on various aspects of socio-economic performance in our five countries in the post-Second World War period. As is apparent from Table 12.1(A), the growth performance has diverged sharply as between the 5 countries and for all except Thailand over time in each country. Argentina's postwar performance has been much worse by its own pre-war standards, as has Peru's since the mid-1960s, Tanzania's since the early 1970s and Ghana's since the early 1960s.

Each of these 'slumps' in economic performance was associated with the pursuit of policies of 'hot house' industrialisation, by governments keen to break out of the 'colonial' pattern of trade and development. In Argentina this 'turning-point' can be associated with Péron, in Ghana with Nkrumah, in Tanzania with Nyerere's Arusha Declaration in 1967.

Manufacturing as a share of GDP rose in all our countries (seeTable 12.1(B)) the largest change being in Thailand which alone of our five countries industrialised relatively 'naturally' in the postwar period after a brief flirtation with import substituting industrialisation in the mid-1960s. Thus Meesook *et al.* (1986) estimate that, between 1960 and 1972, the sources of growth in domestic industry were: domestic demand, 77·9 per cent; export expansion, 14·3 per cent; and import substitution, 7·8 per cent. For the period 1972–5 the figures were: domestic demand, 90 per cent; export expansion, 9·0 per cent; and import substitution, 1·0 per cent.

Except in Thailand and Argentina, food availability per capita declined (Table 12.1(C)), and except for Thailand and Peru so did the share of exports to GDP (see Table 12.1(D)). There was an increase in the share of public consumption in all our countries, the largest increases being in Tanzania and Peru, while domestic investment collapsed in Peru and Ghana – in the latter country spectacularly.

Ghana and Tanzania also saw a large increase in public employment. In Ghana, Ansu (1984) estimates that 64·8 per cent of the total work force was in public employment in 1964, and this rate rose to 77·8 per cent in 1978. In Tanzania there was a rapid growth in parastatals from 1969. All the growth in regular wage employment of 137 000 between 1969 and 1974, was in parastatals and the public services (see Coulson, 1982, Table 23.2). Public servants accounted for 72 per cent of the total of 363 000 in regular wage employment in 1974. There were improvements in social indicators in all five countries (Table 12.1(C)), the most dramatic being the increase in primary school enrolment in Tanzania.

3 THE PREDATORY STATE

In our first cautionary tale the government is assumed to be controlled by a single ruler – a monarch, a dictator, or a charismatic leader. In the first two forms of government, the monarch or dictator may change, but the form of government is not altered, as we assume the changes result from mere palace coups, and not because of any change in the 'interest groups' controlling the State. Put differently, in this model, the constellation of domestic interest groups has little direct effect on the policies of the sovereign who is more autonomous therefore than in the models in the two following sections. The objective of the State is net revenue maximisation. This is thus a model of the *predatory* State (Lal, 1984). The model will also apply to countries ruled by a charismatic leader who may often also be a dictator; but the model will be applicable only during his/her lifetime, unless a quasi-monarchical dynastic succession can be assured. The model would also apply to a country ruled by a colonial power, which is not beholden to the interplay of domestic interest groups.

The State can be identified in this story with an absolute ruler, who provides the public goods of law and order, and possibly some directly productive inputs such as irrigation, roads, and so on. The cases we have in mind are Thailand since 1850 and Ghana and Tanzania from colonial times. In Thailand the absolute monarch was replaced in 1932 by an oligarchy. The king became a constitutional ruler but with considerable influence. In Ghana and Tanzania the colonial rulers were replaced by charismatic leaders – Nkrumah and Nyerere.

All three are also peasant economies where family-'owned' peasant farms produce the major export commodities. Consider a traditional peasant economy with a very favourable land–man ratio. With traditional techniques, the existing labour force in agriculture is L_A

Table 12.1 (A) Per capita GDP growth rates 1950-80

	Real per capita GDP			Average of decades
	50-60	60-70	70-80	
Thailand	3.3	5.1	4.2	4.2
Argentina	1.2	2.8	1.0	1.7
Tanzania	1.4	5.0	2.0	2.8
Peru	2.9	1.9	0.4	1.7
Ghana	2.4	0.0	-2.1	0.1

(B) Output by sector of origin (% of GDP)

	Agriculture			Industry			Manufacturing			Services		
	50	80	△	50	80	△	50	80	△	50	80	△
Thailand	58	25	-57	16	29	+81	10	20	+100	26	46	+76
Argentina	14	12	-14	38	41	+8	29	33	+14	48	39	-19
Tanzania	63	54	-14	16	13	-18	6	9	+50	22	33	+54
Peru	35	8	-77	24	45	+88	15	27	+82	41	47	+15
Ghana	35	n.a.		24	n.a.		15	n.a.		41	n.a.	

(C) Change in welfare indicators

	Food availability (per capita calories/day)			Primary school enrolment (% of age going)			Life expectancy at birth (years)		
	1964–6	1978–80	Δ	1950	1980	Δ	1960	1980	Δ
Thailand	2 220	2 301	+81	52	96	+44	51	63	+12
Argentina	3 241	3 386	+145	66	112	+46	65	70	+5
Tanzania	2 140	2 025	−115	10	104	+94	42	52	+10
Peru	2 256	2 166	−90	43	112	+69	48	58	+10
Ghana	2 160	1 862	−298	19	69	+50	40	49	+9

(D) Export performance

	Growth of Merchandise Exports (% p.a.) 1950–80	Exports/GDP 1950–52	1978–80	Δ% of GDP
Thailand	10.1	18.2	18.8	+0.6
Argentina	7.9	15.8	10.8	−5.0
Tanzania	5.7	26.0	10.9	−15.1
Peru	9.0	18.0	25.6	+7.6
Ghana	5.4	32.2	10.4	−21.8

Source: Reynolds (1985).

(E) Output by end uses (% of GDP)

	Gross domestic investment			Public consumption			Private consumption			Resource balance	
	51–60	80	%△	51–60	80	%△	51–60	80	%△	51–60	80
Thailand	14	27	+93	10	12	+15	77	66	−15	−2	−5
Argentina		n.a.			n.a.			n.a.			n.a.
Tanzania	14	22	+57	9	14	+56	72	78	+8	+5	−14
Peru	24	16	−33	8	13	+55	70	68	−3	−3	+3
Ghana	15	5	−66	8	9	+18	75	86	+14	+2	0

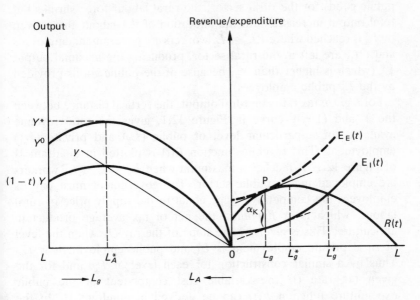

Figure 12.1

working on a fixed quantity of land N ($N < \bar{N}$ the total land available) and through equal work and income sharing each worker receives the (net of tax) average product of labour y in agriculture as his income. There is a sovereign who imposes a fixed proportionate tax at the rate t on rural output to finance his court, army, and law and order institutions. Thus, part of the revenue the sovereign receives is used to hire public servants providing public goods – the police, judges, army, engineers. The rest is used for the sovereign's own purposes – courtiers, palaces, mistresses and the accumulation of 'royal' treasure. Following Findlay and Wilson (1987) we assume that the provision of public goods raises the productivity of the economy above the level that would exist without the State – viz. in anarchy.

Thus in Figure 12.1 we depict the total agricultural output curve of the economy with respect to the given total labour force OL, working on a given fixed acreage. If there are no government employees (L_g) then the total population is in the rural private sector (L_A) and produces output LY^o. This is the 'anarchy' level of output. With some government employees being hired to provide public goods for the rural sector, the rural labour force shrinks but total output increases until the allocation of the labour force given by L_A^* is reached where $LL_A^* = L_g^*$ workers are government employees and OL_A^* are left in the rural sector, producing the maximal output Y^* (which is higher than Y_o, because of the public goods provided by the L_g^* public employees).

For a *given* tax rate t on rural output, the vertical distance between the Y and $(1-t)y$ curve in Figure 12.1, gives the total revenue available for a particular level of public (L_g) and private (L_A) employment. This revenue function $R(t)$ is plotted in quadrant II of Figure 12.1. It reaches a maximum when $L_g^* = L - L_A^*$ workers are employed in the public sector. The government must pay its employees the competitive wage equal to the supply price of rural labour, which is *ex hypothesi* the net of tax average product in agriculture. This is given by the slope of the ray Oy when the level of rural private employment is L_A^* and public employment is L_g^*. Thus by a similar construction for each level of L_g, and for the given tax rate (t) the variable cost component of the public expenditure function $E(t)$ can be derived in quadrant II. In the absence of any fixed costs (on which more below), the variable cost function and $E(t)$ function will be the same. Let us assume that this is so.

The sovereign we have also assumed is a net revenue maximiser. This means – for any given tax rate (t) – that he will seek to maximise the distance between the $R(t)$ and $E(t)$ functions, that is, equate the marginal cost of L_g public employees with the marginal tax revenue from the output produced by the remaining L_A rural workers. It is clear from the shapes of these functions that, irrespective of the tax rate t chosen, the net revenue-maximising sovereign will provide less public employment than the socially optimal level L_g^*.

The net tax revenue will rise as t is raised, as the $R(t)$ and $E(t)$ curves shift outwards. The net of tax income of labour declines with rises in t as the $(1-t)Y$ curve shifts downwards. But there is an upper limit to t, given by the level at which the net of tax average product of labour is equal to subsistence income. Even a revenue-maximising predatory state is unlikely, however, to raise taxes to the level which reduces peasant incomes to the subsistence level, as well before that the current controllers of the multiproduct natural monopoly providing the public goods of 'law and order' and 'security', which is the State, will find that their industry is contestable (in the sense of Baumol *et al.*, 1982. See Lal, 1984, for this interpretation of the limits on the behaviour of the predatory state). The contestants could be either internal or external rivals. The level of taxes which will be sustainable depends upon the barriers to entry – including physical (geographical), technological (military) as well as ideological (including religious) – which allow the maximum 'natural' rent to be extracted by any controller of the State (see Lal, 1984).

These ideas can be formalised as follows. A large part of the costs incurred by an incumbent sovereign in capturing his/her estate will be sunk costs. Say these fixed capital costs are K, and the variable costs of providing the public goods and maintaining the sovereign in power are V. If α is the proportion of the fixed capital costs which are sunk, then the 'advantage' the incumbent has over a new entrant is that whereas its total costs TC_I

$$TC_I = f((1 - \alpha) K, V)$$

that of the new entrant (who has access to the same military and civil technology, say)

$$TC_E = f(K, V)$$

and as $\alpha < 1$, TC_E will lie above TC_I by the fixed amount αK.

Assume that the total variable costs V, are incurred entirely on hiring public employees (these are the same for the incumbent and the entrant) then V for a given tax rate t are (as in Figure 12.1)

$$V = y(L_g) \cdot L_g$$

where y is the net of tax *average* product in agriculture = public sector wage rate, and L_g are the number of public employees hired. Then the total expenditure function for the new entrant $E_E(t)$ for a given tax rate t, can be drawn in Figure 12.1, quadrant II, as a vertical displacement by αK of the total expenditure function of the incumbent $E_I t$.

The maximum profit the incumbent can then earn is π and given by

$$\pi = (V + K) - (V + (1 - \alpha K)) = \alpha K.$$

The optimal tax rate (t) for the net revenue-maximising predatory state will be determined by the tangency of the *entrants* expenditure function $E_E(t)$ with the revenue function $R(t)$ for this optimal rate, as at p in quadrant II of Figure 12.1. For suppose the tax rate were higher ($t' > t$), then the incumbent's and entrant's expenditure functions ($E(t')$) would shift downwards and the revenue function ($R(t)$) upwards (not drawn). The incumbent's monopoly would no longer be sustainable as the entrant could charge a marginally lower tax rate and still make a net profit. Similarly, if the tax rate were lower ($t'' < t$) then the revenue function would shift downwards and expenditure functions would shift upwards and the incumbent would not be maximising net revenue. Thus there will be a unique tax rate, and fiscal cum public employment equilibrium, determined by the underlying production function, and the net barrier to entry costs facing a new entrant. That is, in Figure 12.1, the vertical distance at the sustainable and surplus-maximising point between the $E_E(t)$ and $R(t)$ curves when the $E_I(t)$ curve is tangential to the $R(t)$ curve must equal αK. Thus in the general equilibrium model of the fiscal and employment decisions of a predatory state depicted by Figure 12.1, quadrant II, the surplus-maximising sovereign will set the tax rate t, such that the surplus generated at the public employment level L_g, where the marginal costs and marginal returns (to the sovereign) from public employment are equated, is equal to the net 'barrier to entry' costs facing a new entrant coveting the State.

Suppose this economy has been conquered by a colonial power. Being foreign it will face higher internal costs in terms of its legitimacy than potential internal rivals. This means that, as compared with the indigenous rulers it replaces, the colonial power will only be able to extract a smaller net surplus, as in terms of Figure 12.1, the net 'barrier to entry' costs for its potential contestants will be lower. The $R(t)$ curve in Figure 12.1 quadrant II will be lower and the $E(t)$ curve higher than for the indigenous ruler it displaces, and hence its surplus-maximising tax rate (where the marginal revenue and expenditure are equal, and the surplus is equal to ($\alpha'K$, with ($\alpha' < \alpha$)) will be lower. More importantly the level of public good provision and public employment will be higher than for the indigenous 'predatory' state. This prediction of the model seems to conform to the stylised fact, noted in Section 2, that there was a marked expansion of public expenditures in colonial export economies.

Over time, this economy expands with population growth and the extension of export crop agriculture onto new lands, as in various vent for surplus-type models (see Myint, 1958; Caves, 1965). The foreign exchange earned by the economy will be used to import consumer goods. Depending upon transport costs, there may be – as a result of the increased demand associated with the rise in national income – a viable market for the domestic manufacture of some imported consumer goods. Such 'natural' import substitution can be expected to accompany the growth of the primary producing export economy. Our main concern, however, is to provide some political economy type of reasons why the government might wish to promote industry, particularly in the public sector, beyond these natural limits.

Suppose at some stage the absolute ruler is replaced by a government subject to more popular pressures. This can be said to have happened in Thailand with the 1932 coup and the conversion of the King from absolute to constitutional monarch, and in Ghana and Tanzania with the ending of colonial rule. To the extent that these changes increase the legitimacy of the new incumbents controlling the state, they will *ceteris paribus* increase the costs of rival entrants seeking to capture the State. In Figure 12.1, the $R(t)$ curve will shift upwards and the $E(t)$ curve downwards till a new equilibrium at a lower level of L_g is reached where the 'surplus' is equal to $\alpha^1 K$ with the higher 'net barrier to entry' costs as ($\alpha^1 > \alpha$).

However, unlike the absolute ruler, the new 'constitutional' rulers – albeit dictators – will find it difficult openly to appropriate the net surplus for themselves. They may seek to expand their patronage instead by hiring more retainers. If in addition, as in post-independence Ghana and Tanzania, the new leaders seek to 'modernise' their countries by social engineering through a technocracy, they may have ideological reasons for expanding the bureaucracy beyond the net revenue-maximising point L_g in Figure 12.1. The objective of this post-independent predatory state would be 'bureaucrat maximisation'.

Thus, as is argued by the recent rent-seeking literature (see Krueger, 1974 and Buchanan *et al.*, 1980) the professional bureaucracy and its hangers-on will themselves seek to garner the State's surplus by exerting pressure to expand government expenditure. Findlay and Wilson (1984) describe this as the Parkinson–Niskanen law that 'Government expenditure expands to absorb all the resources available to finance it'. Public employment will expand to $L_g{}^1$, well beyond the socially optimal level L_g^* in Figure 12.1.[6] But in this process, with the increase in the provision of public goods, output could be higher than when the State is run by an absolute monarch or colonial power.

So far we have implicitly assumed that the relative prices of the commodities in our model economy have remained unchanged. Now suppose export prices and that portion of the government's revenue derived from export taxes fluctuate. Once it has hired public servants *pari passu* with the past rise in its revenues, it will be very difficult for the government either to cut current wages or the numbers of public employees when revenues fall. It is thus likely to face a fiscal crisis with every fall in export prices (as R_t shifts downwards and $E(t)$ remains unchanged in Figure 12.1).[7]

One way for the government to insulate itself from the incipient fiscal crises that the periodic collapse in export prices generates is to put some of the revenues at good times in foreign financial assets (reserves) to be used to finance fiscal expenditures when times are bad. But for most third-world states this has proved virtually impossible because of the pressures that arise for the State to spend the windfalls, most often by hiring the relatives of its retainers. To the extent that this increase in public employment also exerts upward pressure on the economy-wide wage rate, the benefits from such spending could be quite wide and hence popular. But the dangers of succumbing to these pressures is the fiscal crisis during the downside of the export cycle. Furthermore during the downside of the cycle as peasant earnings have also fallen, there will be pressures from them to get the State to spend any reserves it has accumulated to stabilise peasant incomes. The state may thus not be able to use the surpluses, accumulated during the upswing of the export cycle and held as publicly visible reserves, to fulfil its objective of stabilising public employment.

An alternative policy for the government to escape its fiscal bind and subserve its bureaucrat-maximising objective would be to insulate the financing of public employment from fluctuating export price-induced changes in revenues. It could use the export tax proceeds in good times to import capital goods to set up import substitute industries (beyond the 'natural' extent that has occurred because of the income growth associated with export led expansion). As long as the domestic demand for the products of these industries is relatively stable, and the products can be sold at a domestic price sufficient to cover *variable costs* (including, above all, those of the public labourers employed), the government will have succeeded in providing a stable means of financing public employment from the fluctuating export tax revenues. It being noted that as efficiency *per se* is not a goal of this net revenue or bureaucrat-maximising state, there is no presumption that the government will choose to maximise the profits of these public enterprises. As far as it is concerned the capital imports financed by the export taxes may well be a sunk cost, and as long as the public employees are paid out of the net revenues (taking account of other variable costs), the State would have achieved its predatory objectives, though by conventional or social accounting criteria most of these public enterprises could well be making losses.

Alternatively, the government may seek to augment its revenues by providing tariff protection to private sector manufacturers. The revenue from the tariff supplements that from the export tax. As long as there is a subsistence sector in the economy which fixes the supply price of labour to the rest of the economy, the introduction or expansion of import substituting industries will merely mean a reduction in output and employment in the subsistence sector, with no change in the wage rate (or in the rents accruing to landlords in the export sector – if agriculture is commercially organised rather than being based on peasant household labour) (see Findlay and Wellisz, 1984). Thus the State may face no 'costs' in the short run from this policy of promoting some 'hot-house' import substituting industrialisation through a combination of both public and private enterprises and the institution of some non-prohibitive revenue tariffs.

This seems to be the story (by and large) of the economic development of Thailand since 1850, of Ghana till about 1961 during the Nkrumah regime, and of Tanzania from colonial times to Nyerere's regime until the Arusha Declaration in 1967. Though introducing well-known inefficiencies in production, the mild protection to promote (in particular public sector-based) industrialisation could have been justifiable from a net revenue and public employment maximising government's viewpoint. This is true even if account is taken of the indirect effects on government revenue from the well-known Lerner symmetry theorem whereby an import tariff is equivalent to an export tax. The revenue tariff is likely to affect export output and hence export tax revenue adversely. But this loss in mean export revenues (in the face of fluctuating export prices) has to be balanced, from the public employment maximising government's viewpoint, against the stability (reduction in the variance of tax revenues) thereby bought in the financing of public employment – essentially by substituting a more stable form of 'revenue' generation through public enterprise-based industrialisation. There will be some optimum level of public enterprise-based industrial employment provision at which these costs and benefits will be equal.

Suppose, however, that on the basis of current ideas (Ghana under Nkrumah)[8] or ideology (Nyerere's Tanzania after the Arusha Declaration)[9] the State seeks to promote public sector-based industrialisation beyond this 'optimal' level: that is, in terms of Figure 12.1, it seeks to increase public employment beyond the level L_g'. As tariffs on final consumer goods become prohibitive and most intermediate and capital goods are allowed into the country at low or zero tariffs to provide high effective protection to public sector industries, tariff revenue is likely to fall, as is the revenue from export crops, with the increase in the direct and indirect tax burden on the sector.

Then, given the interrelationship between export taxes, export output, the rural–urban terms of trade, and the subsistence based supply price of peasant household labourers, there could be a complete elimination of the peasant export crop, as the peasants move to the untaxable subsistence sector. They may still be willing to exchange domestically produced manufactured import substitutes for some subsistence output. But this reduced domestic demand for import substitutes may no longer be sufficient to employ all the existing 'entitled' public sector workers. Furthermore the collapse of domestic export supply following its increased direct and indirect taxation, will have led to a reduction in the supply of foreign exchange required to finance even the imported intermediate inputs required by domestic industry. The State will have a fiscal, foreign exchange and domestic output crisis. The predator will have a problem of surviving as it has virtually destroyed its prey! This seems very much to be the story of Ghana after 1961 and Tanzania in the 1970s and 1980s (see Ansu, 1984; Collier *et al.*, 1987). But this denouement is not inevitable as the more favourable outcome in Thailand illustrates, although this requires a pragmatic and non-ideological State![10]

4 THE FACTIONAL STATE

The second analytical story is roughly based on the Argentinian case. It is of a land-abundant economy *without* a subsistence sector. Agriculture produces for both domestic consumption and exports, and is conducted on medium- or large-scale commercial farms making use of hired labour. In addition there may be a small import-competing manufacturing sector, as well as a non-traded goods services sector.

Unlike the 'absolute' rulers who controlled the State in the story in Section 3, we now have a State which serves the interests of that coalition of pressure groups which succeeds in its capture. The method of capturing the State need not be majoritarian democracy, even though this form of government would be compatible with our story. The interests served are narrowly defined to be the economic self-interests of the constituents of the government. The income effects induced by the economic policies adopted and hence of concern to a particular government will depend upon the returns to the primary factor endowments of its constituents. A recent model of endogenous tariff determination in a voting polity due to Mayer (1984) is helpful in providing an analytical framework for the behaviour of what we may call the factional State.

The basic idea can be explained fairly simply. Suppose that there are only two factors of production, capital (K) and labour (L) and that all individuals in the economy can be described by their respective capital labour ($k_i \equiv K_i/L_i$) endowments. The *mean* of the distribution of these individual k_i endowments will be the aggregate capital–labour endowment $K/L = \bar{k}$ of the economy.

Next we define the set of individuals who are *decisive*, in the sense that they can compete for the capture of the State and thus the determinants of economic policies subserving their interests. Suppose initially that *all* economic agents in the population form part of the decisive set of the polity and the political mechanism is democratic – with 'one man one vote', and the majority capturing the State. All voters vote their economic interests. Then from the well-known median voter theorem, the median voter's capital/labour endowment (k_m) will determine the interests that will be served by the coalition of majoritarian interest groups who capture the state. If the distribution of individual factor endowments is symmetric so that its median and the mean are the same, the median endowment will be identical to the average for the economy as a whole ($\bar{k} = k_m$). Then from the law of comparative advantage we know that the income of the median individual will be maximised by free trade. If, however, the median individual endowment is more (less) capital intensive than the average, the median voter's income-generating interests will be in a tariff (subsidy) on capital intensive imports or a subsidy (tariff) on labour-intensive imports. Thus in this form of the pressure group model what we need to know is the mean of the national factor endowment and median of the distribution of the income-generating factor endowments of the set of decisive individuals.[11]

The economic model we use to tell our story of the factional state is the simple Ricardo–Viner version of the Heckscher–Ohlin model of trade theory with three goods: an agricultural export, non-traded services, and import-competing manufactures. Initially the output of the latter is negligible. We are interested in medium- and long-term changes, and so we assume that all three goods use mobile labour and 'capital' for their production. The land which is in surplus and is specific to the production of the agricultural good (X) can be made 'effective' only with complementary capital (see Kenen, 1965) and hence the output of the agricultural commodity too depends upon the mobile capital and labour used in its production.[12] The agricultural sector is the most capital intensive. The capital–labour ratio in manufacturing (M) is higher than that in services S. A large part of the latter consists of government services. (This stylised economic structure seems to correspond pretty well to Argentina's. See Diaz-Alejandro, 1970, Essay 1.)

This 3 factor-3 commodity model can be depicted in Figure 12.2 (see Corden and Neary, 1982), where L_S is the demand curve for services L_M for manufactures, and the difference between the L_T (the curve for both the traded goods) and L_M the implicit curve for agriculture L_X. These curves in quadrant I are drawn for a given set of relative prices between services, agriculture and manufacturing, and for given stocks of land 'cum capital' in agriculture and capital in the manufacturing and services sectors. We take the domestic price of manufactures as the numeraire.

Initially, the State levies export taxes which it uses to finance non-traded government services. Apart from this trade cum fiscal intervention there is free trade. The economy is linked to both world capital and labour markets, such that (apart from a given constant risk cum transport premium) there is a perfectly elastic

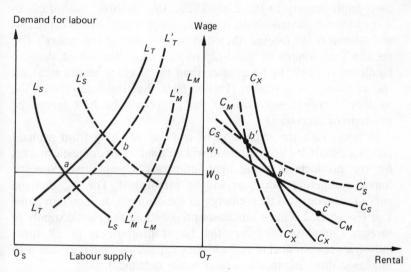

Figure 12.2

supply of both capital and labour at given world interest (r) and wage (w) rates to the economy. Full employment at the given world wage rate of w is constantly maintained through immigration (and emigration), whenever aggregate domestic labour demand exceeds (falls short) of supply. Thus the domestic labour supply O_sO_T in Figure 12.2 varies with the level of aggregate demand for labour.

We start our story in the heyday of the nineteenth-century's liberal trade regime. There is no manufacturing sector. Agricultural export-led growth shifts the L_T schedule to the left. This increased demand for labour is met at the unchanged wage rate of w_o by an expansion of the labour supply by OT' (not drawn). As both the wage and rental rates are *ex hypothesi* constant, the factor proportions in producing both services and agricultural goods remain unchanged, and hence there will also be a capital inflow into the economy, which will lead to an expansion in the outputs of both sectors. With factor prices fixed, the domestic relative price of services and agriculture (the real exchange rate – e in our model) is also fixed. Thus the requisite amounts of foreign capital and labour flowing into the economy will be such as to shift the production possibility frontier between the tradable-agriculture, and non-traded service sectors in a balanced manner.[13]

During this period, corresponding to the second half of the nineteenth century to the early 1920s, the 'decisive' individuals in Argentina are the landlords. As a large proportion of both capitalists and labourers are foreign, they do not form part of the 'polity'. The median endowment of 'land-capital'/labour of the set of decisive landlords is likely to be greater than the average endowment for the economy as a whole. This implies that the interests of the median 'decisive' individual in the polity will be best served by maintaining free trade.

In time, with the expansion of incomes resulting from primary product export-led growth, there will be a sufficient domestic market for the products of some light industries. Competitive domestic import-competing industries will be established. The L_M demand curve for labour will then emerge in the economy as shown in panel I of Figure 12.2. Given our assumptions about the elastic supply of foreign capital and labour, the factor proportions of all three industries remain unchanged and they expand *pari passu* in line with increased domestic incomes (and hence demands).

During the succeeding decades of primary product-induced growth there will also be an increase in the economy's endowments of manufacturing specific capital as 'natural' import-substituting industrialisation begins. Some of this capital will be owned by the landlords, and some by domestic capitalists who will increasingly also become part of the 'decisive' set of individuals whose interests may need to be taken into account by the State.

Now suppose there is a collapse in the world price of the country's export good, and the economy also gets delinked from world labour and capital markets. This happened to Argentina during the Great Depression. We use Figure 12.2 to analyse the outcomes. The second quadrant of this Figure shows the unit cost curves of the three industries drawn in wage-rental space. As exportables (X) are assumed to be the most 'capital'-intensive good the slope of their unit cost curve (which shows the capital–labour ratio) at every wage–rental ratio is steeper than for importables (M) which are of intermediate capital intensity and services (S) which are the least capital-intensive commodity. The initial equilibrium is depicted for given commodity prices and factor supplies by points a and a' in the two quadrants.

With the fall in the price of exportables the C_X curve in quadrant II shifts downwards, as does the L_T curve in quadrant I as labour demand in exportables (L_X) falls while that in importables (L_M) remains unchanged.

For factor market equilibrium the new equilibrium must be at the intersection of the C_X' and C_M curves, viz. b'. This must imply that the unit cost curve for services C_s must shift upwards to intersect the other two curves at b'. Hence the price of services and the real exchange rate (the relative price of non-traded to traded goods) must *rise*. The real wage rises, and the rental on capital falls. In quadrant I, employment and output in the agricultural export sector will fall and in the import-substituting manufacturing sector and services will rise, as will the real wage (see Corden and Neary, 1982 for a formalisation of such a model). Thus, in this process of what may be termed neoclassical adjustments to the collapse of agricultural export prices, further 'natural' import-substituting industrialisation will be promoted as part of the adjustment. This happened in Argentina during the Great Depression (see Diaz–Alejandro, 1970). The only 'losers' from this adjustment are the landlords, but as protection does not serve their interests, they will not oppose the continuation of free trade.

Over time, however, the set of decisive individuals in the economy has been expanding with individuals who have non-traded (services) sector-specific capital and/or labour as their primary endowment increasingly entering the political process. At some stage the median of the distribution of endowments (of 'land-capital' to the other factors), of this expanded set of 'decisive' individuals is likely to become less than the economy-wide average. The state will then seek to subserve the interests of the landless, particularly those with 'non-traded' good capital as they will increasingly have become the 'median' voters. This sector might also come to include those import-competing industries which have succeeded by using arguments based on economic nationalism to obtain the imposition of either import quotas or prohibitive tariffs to convert their outputs in effect into non-traded goods.

With the median of the distribution of the endowments of decisive individuals shifting towards those employed in home goods production there would be political pressures for a squeeze on tradables and in particular on export agriculture. The resulting pressures for a relative expansion of non-traded goods will require an appreciation of the real exchange rate. Diaz–Alejandro provides some estimates which suggest that the combined effect of various domestic policies was a sustained real exchange rate appreciation from about 1929 to well into the postwar period with the extent of 'overvaluation' varying over time.

If, however, the fundamentals of the macroeconomic situation do not require such an appreciation of the real exchange rate there would be a balance of payments problem. As noted above, given the factor intensities of the three goods, the full adjustment to the collapse of primary product prices during the Great Depression would have required some real exchange rate appreciation. However, now consider the situation in the late 1940s or early 1950s when with another turn in the primary product cycle, there is a *rise* in primary product exportable goods prices. The whole process of adjustment analysed in Figure 12.2 goes into reverse.

We continue to examine the medium- to long-term adjustment pressures that arise. In Figure 12.2, given that exportables are the most capital intensive, and services the least with import-substituting manufactures in between, the rise in the price of exports shifts the C_X curve upwards (not drawn). Its new intersection with the C_M curve, at c', is the new long-run equilibrium point. For factor market equilibrium the C_S unit cost curve must also pass through this point, which means that the price of services must fall, that is, there needs to be a *real depreciation*. The money and real wages will fall in the new long-run equilibrium.

This required cut in real wages accompanying the real exchange rate depreciation, will obviously be resisted by those whose factor endowments are dominated by labour, and also by the owners of capital in the import-competing (or tradable) manufacturing sector. For, with the postulated factor intensities, the new equilibrium will entail an expansion in the output of exportables and non-traded goods at the expense of importables.

Given the shift in the distribution of factor endowments of decisive individuals towards a median value which is biased towards labour and non-agricultural capital, the state will be captured by those whose interests lie in preventing the real exchange rate depreciation and hence the real wage cut. This seems to provide an explanation of the rise of Péronist populism, which interestingly, as our model suggests, should have been expected to occur as it did when Argentina's external terms of trade *improved* in the late 1940s, and not when they collapsed during the Great Depression!

However the attempt to maintain an overvalued real exchange rate is not sustainable. With given reserves, the ensuing balance of payments deficit will need to be cured. This inevitably requires the usual expenditure – switching and reducing remedies, and the accompanying distributional shifts in real incomes. If the latter are not however accepted by the workers, then after stability is restored they would seek to restore their *status quo ante* real wages. Domestic price inflation which raises the domestic price of non-traded goods would validate this for a while, but as the resulting real exchange rate appreciation once again leads to a crisis, it is not sustainable. We then get the post-Second World War cycles of Argentinian economic history where devaluation becomes the major focus for the distributional deadlock which is due in our stylised model to a polity which is in inherent conflict with the consequences of its comparative advantage.[14]

This dynamic distributional conflict can be depicted in Figure 12.3[15] in which *LL* shows the combinations of the real tradable wage (that is, the money wage deflated by the price of traded goods – which is a composite of the importable–exportable goods) and the real exchange rate (which is the relative price of non-traded to traded goods) which equates the demand for labour. It must be upward sloping as a rise in the real wage at a constant real exchange rate will generate unemployment while a rise in the real exchange rate at a constant real wage will lead to excess demand for labour. The slope of the curve must be less than unity (the slope of a ray from the origin). For suppose there is a movement along the ray from the origin, this means an equiproportionate rise in both the *tradable* real wage and real exchange rate (say with the nominal wage and price of non-traded goods rising in equal proportions). The real product wage in non-tradable production remains unchanged and hence its output remains unchanged, but traded-good producers face a rise in their real product wage and will reduce their demand for labour, creating excess supply, and these points must then lie below the equilibrium *LL* locus.

The *NN* locus shows the combinations of the real tradable wage and real exchange rate for which the non-traded good market is in equilibrium. This curve will slope upwards as a rise in the real exchange rate (keeping the real tradable wage constant) leads to excess supply of the non-traded good, which is cured by a rise in the real wage to discourage production and thereby restore equilibrium in the non-traded good market. The *NN* curve must have a slope steeper than a ray from the origin (greater than unity), as an equiproportionate rise in the real tradable wage and the real exchange rate leaves output of the non-traded good unchanged but leads to a reduction in its demand and hence to excess supply. These points must therefore lie above the *NN* locus.

The intersection of the *LL* and *NN* loci determines the equilibrium values of the real tradable wage and real exchange rate. The arrows show the direction of movements in the two variables when the economy is not in equilibrium.

With the rise in the price of exportables, there will be excess supply of labour at the initial equilibrium point *a*, as the labour use per unit of output falls in all three sectors, with the capital intensive sector – exportables – expanding. Hence *LL* will shift downwards.

Furthermore, as depicted in Figure 12.2, panel II, the relative price of services must fall in the new equilibrium, implying that there will be excess supply of non-traded goods at the old equilibrium point *a* in Figure 12.3, and hence the *NN* curve must shift to the left (see Corden and Neary, 1982, p. 836). At the new equilibrium point *b* both the real tradable wage and the real exchange rate will be lower.

However, suppose that labour resists the real wage cut. Then there will be a short-run equilibrium at *c*, with the real exchange rate appreciating. This appreciation will lead to a worsening of the

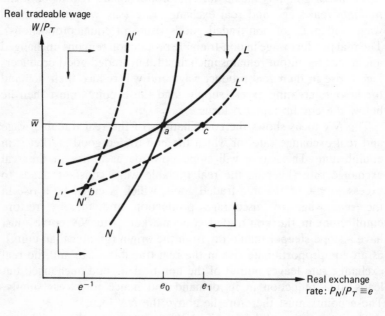

Figure 12.3

balance of payments, and at some stage as part of a package to resolve the stabilisation crisis real wage cuts and a devaluation (to lower the real exchange rate) will become inevitable. The economy will then move towards *b*. However, if subsequently an attempt is made to restore the old real wage, the economy will move back towards *c*, and the crisis will be resurrected.

We thus get the paradoxical result that a combination of the natural industrialisation induced by export led growth; the successful neoclassical adjustment during the Great Depression with the further natural growth of both non-traded good services and import-substituting industries; and the delinking from world capital and labour markets, has created a polity in Argentina where the interests of the median 'decisive' individuals no longer coincide with those which would subserve development along the lines of its comparative advantage.[16] Equally important, our model illustrates how a polity entirely determined by the changing interplay of factional interests may be worse for the social weal than a different form of polity where, as in our previous model of the predatory state, there is a non-ideological 'absolute' ruler with autonomous self-serving ends.

5 THE OLIGARCHIC STATE

Our third story is based on the Peruvian case. The State is controlled by an oligarchy, directly or indirectly representing resource intensive export interests.[17] The general outline of the story can be told in terms of the growth of the export sector between 1830 and 1980 (see Figure 12.4). The economy consists of a subsistence and relatively untouched peasant sector in the Andes (*S*), export agriculture on wage based farms (on the coastal plain) and mining (*X*), and an urban sector which provides various non-traded goods and services (*N*) as well as some import-competing manufactures (*M*). We assume labour is mobile between all four sectors while capital (including that complementary with land used in export agriculture) is mobile between non-traded services, import-competing manufacturing and export agriculture. In the peasant subsistence sector there is equal income and work sharing, and it provides a fairly elastic supply of labour to the other sectors at the subsistence income equal to the average product of labour in peasant agriculture (y_s).

The model can be depicted by Figure 12.5, which is identical to Figure 12.2, except that there is $L_N L_s$ of labour in the subsistence

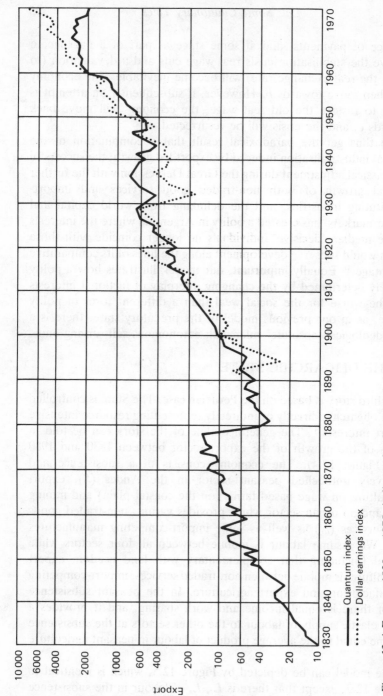

Figure 12.4 Exports 1830 to 1975: indices of volume and dollar value (1900=100)

Source: Figure 1.1, Rosemary Thorp and Geoffrey Bertram, *Peru 1890–1977 Growth and Policy in an Open Economy*, (New York: Columbia University Press, 1978, p. 5).

sector, and the wage (expressed in terms of importables) is determined by the subsistence sector's average product y_s.

The Peruvian story since 1830 (see Thorp and Bertram, 1978) is of a series of export booms in natural resource-intensive commodities (including land), which collapse after about 20 to 30 years (see Figure 12.4). Thus there was the guano boom[18] from 1830 to 1870 with export quantities growing at about 7 per cent per annum; an export boom of a diversified set of commodities – sugar followed by copper, cotton, rubber and petroleum – extending from 1890 to 1929, with exports growing in both value and volume by about 7 per cent per annum; and the most recent boom from the 1940s to late 1960s with extractive industries and sugar, cotton and fishmeal providing the major exports, which together grew in value terms at the rate of 10 per cent per annum from 1942 to 1970.

The periods when exports were booming were also those 'of greatest political stability and conservatism in Peru's history. . . whilst the years of political flux – 1882 to 1895, 1930 to 1948, and since the late 1960s – correspond to periods in which the export economy had entered into crisis and ceased to generate clear guidelines for policy' (Thorp and Bertram, 1978, p. 4). During these periods of crisis, populist voices advocating protection were raised at the same time as some natural import substitution of manufactures (in the 1940s behind tariff walls which were subsequently dismantled and more recently under quantity restriction (QR) regimes which are still in place) always occurred.

Towards the end of each export boom, governments tried to keep the domestic boom going by increasing public expenditures – most often financed by foreign borrowing. This happened in the 1870s, 1920s and in the period from the mid-1960s to mid-1970s. This foreign-financed public pump priming ended in defaults on the foreign debt in the 1870s and 1920s, and arguably too in the current cycle, with President Garcia playing a 'cat and mouse' game with his foreign creditors. But foreign investors' memories seem to be short and foreign direct investment has come in during the middle of each new boom, as memories of past defaults fade and economic recovery is evident. Thus 1901–29 and 1950–68 were high periods of foreign investment of Peru.

The effects of the boom and subsequent slump on the incomes of 'decisive' individuals in the polity can be illustrated by Figure 12.5. We assume that the peasants – mainly Indians – are not part of the 'decisive' set. As they are also, in large part, the mobile migrant labour used in the other sectors, the only 'interest' that will be represented in the polity is that of mobile 'capital', which coincides with the requirements for development in line with the country's comparative advantage. This seems to have been the case in Peru till fairly recently (see Webb, 1986). Over time, with the growth of the export economy and the absorption of labour in the 'modern' sector, the average product and hence incomes and supply price of labour in the subsistence sector will rise (y_s in Figure 12.5 will shift upwards). With the tradable wage and the relative price of importables to exportables fixed exogenously, the internal adjustments required during the export cycles will come about through changes in the rental rate on capital and the price of non-traded goods.

Thus with an export boom, the C_x curve in quadrant II of Figure 12.5 shifts outwards. As the wage is fixed, a differential is opened up in the rental rates in capital used in the export sectors (point b) and the import competing manufactures and non-traded good sectors (still given by point a). As the price of the import competing sector is fixed, C_M cannot shift; so at the given real wage y_s capital will begin shifting from the import competing sector into exportables. As the import-competing good cannot be produced at its exogenously fixed price with the same real wage and higher rental rate, the industry will shut down. (The curve L_M disappears in quadrant I.)

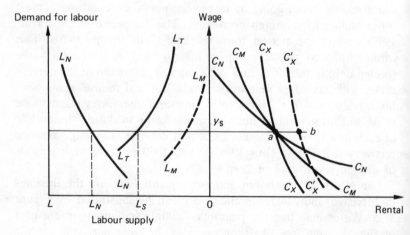

Figure 12.5

What of the non-traded good? The rise in real income and hence in the demand for the non-traded good, as well as the factor price changes represented by point b, imply that the C_N curve will have to shift upwards to intersect the C_x^1 curve at b. The price of the non-traded good must rise, and the real exchange rate appreciate. This seems to have happened in each of the Peruvian export booms (see Thorp and Bertram (1978) for the evidence on real exchange rate movements).

There will thus be a rightward shift in the L_T and L_N curves in quadrant I, with the L_M curve disappearing, and its labour being partly absorbed by the expanding exportable and the non-traded good sector. As the rental rate has risen, the 'decisive' capitalists in the polity will be content with export-led growth, as will labour to the extent that there is an increase in the demand for labour of the modern sector which, by reducing the labour force in the subsistence sector, raises y_s.

With the collapse of the export boom the above process will go into reverse, but if the 'slump' is not long-lasting the next export cycle can begin without any damage to the process of export-led growth. The main difference between the most recent 'slump' of the Peruvian economy and earlier ones is that it seems (see Thorp and Bertram, 1978; Webb, 1986) that the sources of future primary product-based export-led growth seem to be drying up as a result of the exhaustion of natural resources that could be exploited relatively cheaply, as well as the limits being reached for extending irrigation and hence the extension of the land frontier on the coast (which has produced most of the agricultural exports). Taken together with the growth of population, the factor endowments of the economy could be altering, so that the incremental comparative advantage of the country may lie in manufactured exports. However, if this is so, the import-substituting bias of the industrialisation induced during past downturns of the export cycle as well as the rise of economic nationalism and the recent appeal of the 'dependencia' ideology, could militate against the adoption of the appropriate policies which would be needed to foster labour-intensive manufactured exports. As manufactured export-led growth would greatly benefit labour, bringing the subsistence sector into the 'decisive' set which determines the polity may be important for the future growth of the Peruvian economy. However, the effects on economic performance of the rise in populism[19] that the integration of 'labour' might entail – as outlined in the second of our cautionary tales: that of the factional state – could give one cause to pause!

Notes

*   The research on which this paper is based forms part of an ongoing comparative study of 'The Political Economy of Poverty, Equity and Growth', which the author is co-directing with Hla Myint, for the World Bank under RPO 673–73. Comments by participants at seminars at Duke University and the University of Texas at Austin have helped to improve the paper. The World Bank does not accept responsibility for the views expressed herein which are those of the author and should not be attributed to the World Bank or to its affiliated organisations. The findings, interpretations, and conclusions are the results of research supported by the Bank; they do not necessarily represent official policy of the Bank. The designations employed, the presentation of material and any maps used in this document are solely for the convenience of the reader and do not imply the expression of any opinion whatsoever on the part of the World Bank or its affiliates concerning the legal status of any country, territory, city, area, or of its authorities, or concerning the delimitation of its boundaries, or national affiliation.

1.   See Little (1982); Lal (1983) for summaries of the evidence.

2.   In Lal (1985) I have attempted to analyse the political economy factors underlying the contrasting industrial policies and outcomes in two labour-abundant economies – India and Korea.

3.   Three of these countries are part of a larger set being studied in an ongoing multi-country comparative study of 'Poverty, Equity and Growth' in developing countries, which I am co-directing with Hla Myint for the World Bank. I owe Hla Myint a particular debt for the origin of some of the ideas which are common to the analytical framework underlying the comparative study and this paper.

4.   See Reynolds (1985) for a good summary account of the evolution of these economies since the 1850s. The stylised facts used in telling the tales in the next 3 sections are based on the following economic histories of the countries: Argentina: Diaz–Alejandro (1970); Mallon and Sourrouille (1975); Peru: Levin (1960); Thorp and Bertram (1978); Webb (1986); Thailand: Ingram (1971); Meesook *et al.* (1986); Ghana: Killick (1978); Roemer (1984); Ansu (1984); Tanzania: Coulson (1982); Lele (1984); Collier *et al.* (1987).

5.   Though in this paper we have not included monetary aspects, they can be readily incorporated into Figure 12.3, as is shown in Lal (1986a). To have included them in this paper would have led to unnecessary complications without providing any further useful insights.

6.   Thus Coulson writes of the adverse effect on economic performance of the recent expansion of the bureaucracy and its *de facto* takeover of the State in Tanzania: 'The contradiction which has not been recognised is that of implementing a radical programme with a "bureaucratic bourgeoisie" – the servants of the State (with an obvious interest in expanding its services) in the paradoxical position of controlling the State. Either a section of the bureaucracy will

have . . . to pursue a more ruthless capitalist accumulation or else the workers and peasants will have to use Nyerere's ideology to take control of the State through democratic organisations . . .. By 1980 it was clear that Nyerere and the Tanzanian leadership would countenance neither alternative, and that the contradictions and stagnation of the 1970s were likely to continue' (Coulson, 1982, p. 33).

7. See Levin (1960) for a detailed discussion of this aspect of the export economy.

8. See Killick (1978) for an interpretation of irrational dirigiste economic policies under Nkrumah which emphasises that they were influenced by and based on the development economics current at that time.

9. See Coulson (1982) for a discussion of the ideological factors underlying Tanzanian policy.

10. Not seeking to expand public employment beyond the 'sustainable' level L_g' in Figure 12.1 (quadrant II).

11. In this paper the set of decisive individuals and the distribution of their factor endowments is taken to be given exogenously. However, it should be possible using simple growth economics and results from the literature on changing wealth distributions to generate the distribution of individual factor endowments endogenously.

12. See Lal (1986) for the application of a similar model to explain postwar real wage movements in the Philippines.

13. This implies that the tangency between the new production possibility curve and the highest attainable indifference curve occurs at the same unchanged real exchange rate e_o.

14. A recent historian has summarised this deadlock which focuses on devaluation as follows: 'At best devaluation was a short-term expedient, one that invariably prompted urban recession and increased political friction. After each devaluation food and import prices rose and consumption fell, which caused manufacturing output to fall and urban unemployment to increase. Recession, in turn, provoked a decline in government revenues, as the tax base narrowed and tax evasion spread. Government spending then declined, helping to hasten and deepen contraction throughout the economy. When spending did not drop quickly enough, the economic depression was accompanied by inflation. As events in 1954 first showed, political responses to devaluation were usually most potent in the aftermath of recession, once the balance of payments was improving, manufacturing again reviving, and unemployment falling. At this point, as the labour market tightened, the trade unions led strike campaigns to restore the predevaluation wage share in national income. But then as wages rose, so too did production costs and soon prices. The mounting inflation again channelled exportables into the home market. While manufacturers increased production, imports were also rising, which renewed the balance-of-payments crisis and required another devaluation. Through this chain of intersectoral income shifts, changes in relative prices, and inflation, each

devaluation thus carried the seedling of its successor' (Rock, 1985, pp. 327–8).

15.   See Neary (1985), Prachowny (1981), Lal (1986a) for further details about this diagram.

16.   The model also illustrates how the changing structure of the polity impinges on the precommitment of the State to free trade. Thus in the post-1942 period in Argentina the State's earlier precommitment to free trade can no longer be taken for granted.

17.   The earlier phase of the Argentinian study can also be taken to be one of the 'oligarchic state'.

18   See Levin (1960) for a detailed discussion.

19.   It could be argued that populism has already captured the State in the form of President Garcia. But it is doubtful whether the Andean peasants have been integrated into the polity by APRA, whose 'populism' is therefore likely to be rhetorical, and similar to the rhetoric which has been dominant at each downturn in past Peruvian export cycles.

References

Ansu, Y. (1984) 'Comment' in Harberger, A. C. (ed.).

Baumol, W. J., Panzar, J. C. and Willig, R. D. (1982) *Contestable Markets and the Theory of Industry Structure*, (San Diego: Harcourt Brace Jovanovich).

Birnberg, T. B. and Resnick, S. A. (1975) *Colonial Development* (Yale University Press).

Brennan, G. and Buchanan, J. M. (1980) *The Power to Tax* (Cambridge University Press).

Buchanan, J. M. *et al.* (eds) (1980) *Towards a Theory of the Rent-Seeking Society* (Texas A and M University Press).

Caves, R. (1965) ' "Vent For Surplus" Models of Trade and Growth', in Baldwin, R. E. *et al.*, *Trade Growth and the Balance of Payments* (Amsterdam: North Holland, 1966).

Collier, P., Bevan, D. and Gunning, J. (1987) 'East African Lessons on Economic Liberalization', Thames Essay No. 48, Trade Policy Research Centre, London.

Corden, W. M. and Neary, J. P. (1982) 'Booming Sector and De-Industrialisation in A Small Open Economy', *The Economic Journal*, December.

Coulson, A. (1982) *Tanzania – A Political Economy*, (Oxford: Clarendon Press).

Diaz–Alejandro, C. (1970) *Essays on the Economic History of the Argentine Republic* (Yale).

Findlay, R. and Wellisz, S. (1982) 'Endogenous Tariffs, the Political Economy of Trade Restrictions and Welfare' in Bhagwati, J. N. (ed.) *Import Competition and Response* (University of Chicago Press).

Findlay, R. and Wellisz, S. (1983) 'Some Aspects of the Political Economy of Trade Restrictions', *Kyklos,* Vol. 36, Fasco 3, pp. 469–81.

Findlay, R. and Wellisz, S. (1984) 'Protection and Rent-Seeking in Developing Countries' in Colander D. (ed.) *Neoclassical Political Economy* (Cambridge, Mass: Ballinger).

Findlay, R. and Wilson, J. (1987) 'The Political Economy of Leviathan', in Razin, A. and Sadka, E. (eds) *Economic Policy in Theory and Practice* (New York: St Martin's Press).

Harberger, A. C. (ed.) (1984) *World Economic Growth* (San Francisco: Institute for Contemporary Studies).

Hopkins, A. G. (1973) *An Economic History of West Africa* (Columbia University Press).

Ingram, J. C. (1971) *Economic Change in Thailand, 1850–1970* (Stanford University Press).

Jones, R. (1971) 'A Three Factor Model in Theory, Trade and History' in Bhagwati, J. *et al.* (eds) *Trade, The Balance of Payments and Growth* (Amsterdam: North Holland).

Kenen, P. B. (1965) 'Nature, Capital and Trade', *Journal of Political Economy*, October, Vol. 73, no. 5, pp. 437–60.

Killick, T. (1978) *Development Economics in Action – A Study of Economic Policies in Ghana* (London: Heinemann Educational Books).

Krueger, A. O. (1974) 'The Political Economy of the Rent-Seeking Society', *American Economic Review*, June.

Lal, D. (1983) *The Poverty of 'Development Economics'* (IEA, London, 1983, American Edition, Harvard, 1985).

Lal, D. (1984) 'The Political Economy of the Predatory State', DRD discussion paper no. 105, mimeo, World Bank.

Lal, D. (1985) 'Ideology and Industrialisation in India and East Asia' in Hughes, H. and Riedel, J. (eds) *Industrialisation in East and Southeast Asia*, proceedings of a conference at ANU, Canberra, September 1985, to be published by Cambridge.

Lal, D. (1986) 'Stolper–Samuelson–Rybczynski in the Pacific: Real Wages and Real Exchange Rates in the Philippines 1956–1978', *Journal of Development Economics*, April. Vol. 21, no. 1, pp. 181–204.

Lal, D. (1986a) 'A Simple Framework for Analyzing Various Real Aspects of Stabilization and Structural Adjustment Policies', mimeo, VPERS, World Bank, September, *Journal of Development Studies* (forthcoming).

Lele, U. (1984) 'Tanzania: Phoenix or Icarus?', in Harberger, A. C. (ed.).

Levin, J. V. (1960) *The Export Economies* (Cambridge, Mass: Harvard University Press).

Little, I. M. D. (1982) *Economic Development – Theory, Policies and International Relations* (New York: Basic Books).

Mallon, R. D. and Sourrouille, J. V. (1975) *Economic Policymaking in a Conflict Society: The Argentine Case* (Cambridge, Mass: Harvard University Press).

Mayer, W. (1984) 'Endogenous Tariff Formation', *American Economic Review*, December. Vol. 74, no. 5, December, pp. 970–85.

Meesook, O., Tinakorn, P. and Vaddhanaphuti, C. (1986) 'The Political Economy of Poverty, Equity and Growth – Thailand', draft mimeo paper presented to the Lisbon workshop July 7–16, 1986, VPERS, World Bank, June.

Myint, H. (1958) 'The "Classical Theory" of International Trade and the Underdeveloped Countries', *Economic Journal*, vol. 68, no. 270, June, pp. 317–37.

Neary, J. P. (1985) 'Theory and Policy of Adjustment in an Open Economy', in Greenway, D. (ed.) *Current Issues in International Trade: Theory and Policy* (London: Macmillan).

Prachowny, M. (1981) 'Sectoral Conflict Over Stabilization Policies in Small Open Economies', *The Economic Journal*, vol. 91, no. 363, September, pp. 67–84.

Reynolds, L. G. (1985) *Economic Growth in The Third World 1850–1890* (New Haven, Conn.: Yale University Press).

Rock, D. (1985) *Argentina 1516–1982* (California).

Roemer, M. (1984) 'Ghana 1950–80: Missed Opportunities' in Harberger A. C. (ed.).

Ruffin, R. and Jones, R. W. (1977) 'Protection and Real Wages: The Neoclassical Ambiguity', *Journal of Economic Theory*, Vol. 14, no. 2, April, pp. 337–48.

Snape, R. H. (1977) 'Effects of Mineral Development on the Economy', *Australian Journal of Agricultural Economics*, vol. 21, no. 3, December, pp. 147–56.

Thorp, R. and Bertram, G. (1978) *Peru 1890–1977* (Columbia University Press).

Webb, R. (1986) 'The Political Economy of Poverty, Equity and Growth – Peru 1948–1985', draft paper for the Lisbon workshop, June 1986, mimeo, VPERS (Washington, DC, World Bank).

13 Industrialisation, Primary Commodities and Exports of Manufactures

Simón Teitel*
INTER-AMERICAN DEVELOPMENT BANK

1 INTRODUCTION

This paper explores the commodity composition of Latin America's recent exports of manufactures with a view to identifying main products and groups of products exported. Problems of classification are discussed, and an attempt is made at reconciling trade and industrial-based export statistics.

The proportions of world exports in various manufactures accounted for by the region are determined, and apparent sources of revealed comparative advantage are proposed. A distinction is made between: (i) manufactures based on agricultural and other primary inputs, (ii) 'traditional' manufactured exports, and (iii) manufactures developed during more recent import substitution (IS).

Policy conclusions about the sequencing of primary exports and industrial development, including the development of manufactured exports in Latin America, are advanced, trying to bridge the apparent gap between import substitution (IS) and export promotion strategies (EP) portrayed in some of the recent development literature.

2 THE COMMODITY COMPOSITION OF LATIN AMERICA'S MANUFACTURED EXPORTS: CLASSIFICATION PROBLEMS

There are problems of definition about manufactured exports. Some of them bias the statistics against Latin America. Simply put, the international trade classification (Standard International Trade

315

Classification, SITC) does not include as manufactures a number of industrial products, prominent in Latin America's exports, and which are so considered in the classification by industrial origin (International Standard Industrial Classification, ISIC). Although some prior studies already recognised this fact, generally they were not focused on Latin America (Cline, 1984). World Bank (1981) and Inter-American Development Bank (1982) constitute exceptions in this respect.

The importance of classification becomes immediately apparent when note is taken that according to the SITC classification the region only had about 20 per cent of its exports classified as manufactures, while on the basis of a revised classification more than 50 per cent of its total exports were considered to be manufactures (Inter-American Development Bank, 1982, p. 113). This result is corroborated in United Nations Industrial Development Organization (1985), and by recent work on Argentina and Brazil (Teitel and Thoumi, 1986).

To deal with the classification problem, the SITC export data available as of 1985 for the Latin American and Caribbean countries were cross-referenced to the ISIC, using the United Nations tabulation linking the two classifications (United Nations, 1971). Care was taken to include only products whose manufacture involved processing in industrial facilities.

The addition of various food industries (based on agricultural and livestock resources with which the region is well endowed), several non-ferrous metals and metal products, as well as the products of petroleum refineries, are the most important changes in the composition of exports that results for Latin America.

While the products of petroleum refineries and food industries clearly represent manufactured products, the failure to include non-ferrous metals and metal products is the most astounding. It seems quite arbitrary that when metalworking processes are applied to iron and steel inputs the results should be considered manufactured products,[1] but when similar processes are effected on non-ferrous metal inputs they should not.

To compare the results of using both classifications we prepared tabulations of the most important manufactured products by value exported from Latin America based on the SITC, traditional or 'narrow' classification, and also of the products to be *added*, if a 'broad' classification were to be used. The results are shown in Table 13.1.

The additional manufactured exports obtained following the 'broad' definition include some very substantial exports of natural resource-based products such as feeding-stuff for animals, copper, and petroleum refinery products.

There is much less concentration by value of exports among the products included in the 'narrow' definition, although they also include among the main exports by value some natural resource-based goods such as pig-iron and leather.

3 THE REGION'S INTERNATIONAL TRADE PERFORMANCE

Owing to the emphasis placed until recently on IS policies, compared to other developing areas, Latin America is generally considered to have followed less open trade policies and to have lagged in terms of the relative size of its exports (Syrquin, 1986). A subset of this generalisation is the fact that Latin America's exports of manufactures, particularly labour-intensive consumer products, represent a much smaller proportion of total exports than those of Asian Semi-industrialised Countries (World Bank, 1981; Ranis, 1981).

Although the above assertions must be qualified by recognising that (i) the region includes some fairly large countries that, *ceteris paribus*, would be expected to have a smaller degree of openness to international trade, and (ii) that it is also better endowed in natural resources than developing countries in East Asia, the criticisms voiced, as well as the data on which they are based, may still correctly reflect the presence of an anti-export policy bias in the region.

Merely to illustrate that substantial differences in resource endowment indeed exist, in Table 13.2 we show the population density for a group of Latin American and East-Asian countries. With a mean population density of 20 inhabitants per square kilometre for the Latin American countries compared to 163 inhabitants per square kilometre for the East-Asian countries, *ceteris paribus*, there is a presumption of higher natural resource intensity in Latin America and of higher labour intensity in the Asian countries.[2]

Given then its generous natural resource endowment, and the classification problems discussed in Section 2, we contrast below

Table 13.1   Latin America's manufactured exports with largest shares of world manufactured exports – 1983

N°	SITC code	Product	Share of world exports (per cent)	Value (millions US dollars)
		Narrow definition		
1	532	Dyes n.e.s. tanning products	22.9	68.4
2	671	Pig iron, etc.	19.5	606.8
3	611	Leather	13.9	468.9
4	612	Leather products	11.1	104.7
5	851	Footwear	10.2	988.7
6	522	Inorg. elements, oxid, etc.	6.6	415.3
7	831	Travel goods, handbags	6.1	128.1
8	762	Radio broadc. receivers	6.0	309.8
9	512	Alcohols, phenols, etc.	5.7	216.6
10	713	Internal combust. piston eng.	5.7	887.2
11	511	Hydrocarbon n.e.s. derivs.	5.5	500.3
12	846	Undergarments knitted	5.2	189.2
13	674	Iron, steel univ. plate sheet	5.1	890.6
14	651	Textile yarn	5.0	580.3
15	771	Elec. power mach. n.e.s.	4.8	175.1
16	551	Essential oils, perf. etc.	4.8	75.7
17	634	Veneers, plywood, etc.	4.7	200.0
18	585	Plastic materials, n.e.s	4.6	29.6
19	673	Iron, steel, shapes, etc.	4.5	466.4
20	764	Telecom. equip. pts. & acces.	4.2	878.6
21	693	Wire products non-elec.	4.2	76.3
22	658	Textile articles n.e.s.	4.1	130.4
23	652	Cotton fabrics women	3.9	240.0
24	635	Wood manufact. n.e.s.	3.9	105.4
25	664	Glass	3.6	131.3
26	848	Headgear & non-textile cloth.	3.6	121.0
27	642	Paper, etc. precuts, arts	3.6	187.2
28	665	Glassware	3.5	94.0

Latin America's overall and manufactured exports performance with that of the rest of the world.

Table 13.3 shows that in the years 1965, 1970, 1975, 1980 and 1983, Latin America's share of *total* world exports ranged between 4.6 and 6.8 per cent, and the unweighted average for these five years was 5.5 per cent. In comparison, the region's share in world

Table 13.1   Continued

N°	SITC code	Product	Share of world exports (per cent)	Value (millions US dollars)
		Additional products with broad definition		
1	0712	Coffee extract, essences	40.7	316.6
2	081	Feeding stuff for animals	33.3	3 992.5
3	0723	Cocoa butter and paste	28.6	337.2
4	058	Fruits preserved, prepared	24.7	984.2
5	014	Meat prepd., preserved, etc.	23.9	527.1
6	682	Copper excl. cement copper	20.6	2 096.1
7	0612	Refined sugar, etc.	19.1	539.5
8	423	Fixed veg. oils, soft	18.2	651.0
9	265	Veg. fibres, excl. cotton jute	16.9	55.3
10	687	Tin	15.5	296.0
11	682	Silver, platinum, etc.	15.3	946.8
12	334	Petroleum products, refineries	12.2	8 855.7
13	268	Wool (excl. tops), animal hair	8.5	322.4
14	685	Lead	7.9	68.6
15	686	Zinc	7.7	138.4
16	251	Pulp and waste paper	6.3	498.4
17	684	Aluminum	6.1	758.5
18	335	Residual petrol. prod. n.e.s.	5.4	215.0
19	037	Fish, etc. prepd., preserved	5.3	131.7
20	424	Fixed veg. oil, non-soft	5.3	142.2
21	062	Sugar candy non-chocolate	5.1	39.8
22	0722	Cocoa powder, unsweetened	4.8	8.4
23	073	Chocolate and products	4.5	72.4
24	056	Vegetables, preser., prepared	3.5	89.0

Source: United Nations, *1983 International Trade Statistics Yearbook*, New York, 1985.

exports of *manufactured goods* was substantially lower, ranging for the years 1970, 1975, 1980 and 1983 between 3.2 and 3.9 per cent approximately, with a mean of 3.64 for these four years.

The above difference in performance reflects differences in exports composition between the world and Latin America. While for the world, exports of manufactures represented almost two-thirds of

Table 13.2 Population density for selected Latin American and East Asian
countries

Country	Population[1] (millions)	Area (1000 km²)	Density (inhabitants/km²)
Latin America			
Argentina	30.1	2 767	10.9
Brazil	132.6	8 512	15.6
Chile	11.8	757	15.6
Colombia	28.4	1 139	24.9
Mexico	76.8	1 973	38.9
Peru	18.2	1 285	14.2
Mean	49.65	2 739.8	20.02
Standard deviation	46.63	2 916.1	10.36
East Asia			
Indonesia	158.9	1 919	82.8
Korea	40.1	98	409.2
Malaysia	15.3	330	46.4
Philippines	53.4	300	178.0
Thailand	50.0	514	97.3
Mean	63.54	632.2	162.74
Standard deviation	55.35	734.3	145.93

Note: [1]Mid-1984.
Source: Computed from data in World Bank, *World Development Report
1986*, Washington, DC, Table 1. Annex.

total trade (average of 63 per cent for the four years 1970, 1975,
1980 and 1983), for Latin America it amounted to less than 45 per
cent (average of 44.3 per cent for the same four years) (see Table
13.4).

Table 13.4 also shows a trend towards an increase in the share
of narrowly defined manufactured exports (that is, SITC 5–9
excluding the two digit group 68) with a parallel decline in the share
of more broadly defined manufactured exports (that is, foodstuff
and other agricultural and mineral industrial products). While for
the world the share of such manufactures in total exports of
manufactures has varied narrowly around a mean of 81.7 per cent
during the years 1970, 1975, 1980 and 1983, for Latin America, a

Table 13.3 Latin America's share of world exports, selected years
(per cent)

Year	Of total exports	Of manufactured exports		
		Total	Narrow definition	Additional products broad definition
1965	6.77	n.a.	n.a.	n.a.
1970	5.01	3.88	1.00	17.07
1975	4.64	3.75	1.44	15.14
1980	5.16	3.20	1.86	8.76
1983	6.15	3.73	2.16	10.49
Mean	5.55	3.64	1.62	12.87
Standard deviation	0.88	0.30	0.51	3.89

Note: n.a.: not available.
Source: United Nations, *1983 International Trade Statistics Yearbook*,
New York, 1985, and selected issues for other years.

Table 13.4 Latin America's and world share of manufactured exports in
total exports and of narrowly defined manufactured exports in total
manufactured exports, selected years (per cent)

Year	Share of manufactures in total exports		Share of narrowly defined manufactures in total exports of manufactures	
	Latin America	World	Latin America	World
1970	51.2	66.1	21.0	82.0
1975	49.9	61.7	32.0	83.1
1980	38.1	61.2	46.8	80.5
1983	38.2	63.0	46.9	81.1
Mean	44.35	63.0	36.68	81.68
Standard deviation	7.18	2.2	12.58	1.13

Source: See Table 13.3.

Table 13.5 Manufacturing export performance of selected Latin American and East Asian countries

	Annual growth rate (1973–81 per cent)	Share of manufactures in total exports[3] (1979–81 per cent)	Per capita exports (1980 US dollars)	Share of world exports (1980 per cent)	Proportion of capital and durable goods in export manuf. (1979–81 per cent)
Latin America					
Argentina	11.1	57.8	176[4]	0.40	12.1
Brazil	22.7	70.9	111	1.14	26.3
Chile	19.4[1]	78.8	325	0.29	3.3
Colombia	13.9	32.3	44	0.10	14.2
Mexico	7.4[2]	32.2	42[5]	0.27	27.2[5]
Peru	8.5	58.7	106	0.15	4.0
Mean	13.83	55.12	134	0.39	14.52
Standard deviation	6.11	19.37	106	0.38	10.41

East Asia					
Indonesia	23.5	13.7	19	0.24	5.1
Korea	27.3	93.2	430	1.32	28.7
Malaysia	20.0	47.4	402[4]	0.47	25.6
Philippines	18.8	55.0	51[5]	0.24	5.6
Thailand	25.8	58.3	85[4]	0.35	10.3
Mean	23.08	53.52	197.4	0.52	15.06
Standard deviation	3.65	28.38	201.2	0.46	11.27

Notes: [1] 1973–80.
[2] 1973–9.
[3] Broader, UNIDO definition.
[4] 1981.
[5] 1979.

Source: United Nations Industrial Development Organisation, (UNIDO), *Handbook of Industrial Statistics – 1984*, United Nations, New York, 1985.

trend towards increasing the proportion of these manufactures in total manufactured exports is clearly noticeable, with their much lower share (mean of 36.7 per cent for the same four years) more than doubling between 1970 and 1980. Of course, a parallel decline in the share of broadly defined manufactured exports in the total of manufactured exports for the region is taking place. This share went from 79 per cent in 1970 to approximately 53 per cent in 1980 and 1983. This phenomenon is also depicted in Table 14.3 which shows the share of narrowly- and broadly-defined manufactured exports from Latin America in world manufactured exports.

As to comparison with other industrialising countries, in Table 13.5 the manufacturing export performance of the same group of Latin American and East-Asian countries for which we provided population density data in Table 13.2, is contrasted. Although for such indicators as the rate of growth of manufactured exports and the level of exports per capita, the average of the East-Asian countries is substantially higher, the Latin American countries have a somewhat higher share of manufactures in total exports and a similar proportion of capital and durable goods in manufactured exports.

Above all, with a yearly rate of growth for the period 1973–81 of almost 14 per cent, it is hard to argue that exports of manufactures were not increasing rapidly. This fact is not obscured by the much faster, exceptional growth of such exports among the East-Asian countries.

4 REVEALED COMPARATIVE ADVANTAGE EXPORTS

'Revealed' comparative advantage could reflect real cost differences among countries as well as policy and other factors distorting resource allocation. Balassa (1965), proposed an index of revealed comparative advantage based on comparing a country's export performance in a particular commodity (or set of commodities) with its overall trade performance. Such an indicator is shown below:

$$X_{ij} = \frac{x_{ij}}{\Sigma_i x_{ij}} \cdot / \cdot \frac{\Sigma_j x_{ij}}{\Sigma_i \Sigma_j x_{ij}} \qquad (1)$$

where *xij* is exports of commodity *i* by country *j* to the rest of the world. The indicator *Xij* is the ratio of the share of commodity *i* in the total exports of country *j*, to the share of commodity *i* in the total world exports of all commodities. Thus country *j* is presumed to have a comparative advantage in commodity *i* if its share of world exports of commodity *i* is greater than its overall share in total world exports (Kim, 1983).

Following the above definition, among the manufactured exports in the narrow SITC-based classification, we select those sectors with a share of world exports above 3.5 per cent, which is the approximate average for the years 1975, 1980 and 1983 for the share of Latin American manufactured exports in total exports. This is a stringent test because the average for Latin America in this category (that is, narrowly-defined manufactured exports) for the same three years is approximately 1.8 per cent (Table 13.3).

The list includes 28 sectors at the three-digit level (see Table 13.1). Clearly, the three top sectors in terms of their share of total world exports represent natural resource-based products. Below them there is an intermingling of unskilled labour-intensive, natural resource-based and skill-intensive manufactures.

Manufactured exports to be added when following the broad classification, and meeting the same criterion for revealed comparative advantage, are shown in the lower section of Table 13.1. There are 24 sectors included in this case. The main exports in terms of their share of world exports are, as expected, also natural resource-based: agricultural and mineral processed products, some of them with a major stake by export value.

With a more demanding cut-off point, such as would restrict the selection to those products with a share of the world market above the mean for the broadly-defined Latin American manufactured exports in the years 1975, 1980 and 1983, that is, about 11.5 per cent (see Table 13.1), the list would be cut in half, but the main natural resource-based export products would remain, and the value of exports would be reduced by only about 2.5 billion dollars or around 11 per cent of the total (Table 13.1, lower section).

To examine the apparent sources of revealed comparative advantage we have grouped in classes the main manufactured products exported from Latin America and then tried to relate these classes to an indicator of resource intensity. The indicator utilised is the proportion of direct value added in total value of output.

There are $i = 1, \ldots n$ industries and $j = 1, \ldots m$ countries in each group: less industrialised, Latin America, and industrialised. Within each group, the number of countries for which there are data for a particular industry is equal to $k \leqslant m$.

$$NR_i = \frac{\sum_{1}^{k} \frac{NR_i}{Y_i} \times 100}{k} \qquad \text{and} \qquad (2)$$

$$\frac{NR_i}{Y_i} \times 100 = \frac{Y_i - VA_i}{Y_i}$$

$$= \left(1 - \frac{VA_i}{Y_i}\right) \times 100$$

where Y = value of output
$\quad\quad VA$ = value added.

The coefficient of natural resource intensiveness (NR) is an average of the values of the individual coefficients for the k countries.

Thus a sector with a low degree of value added is assumed to be high in resource intensity.[3] We abstract from possible differences in market structure which could affect components of value added like the wage bill and entrepreneurial profits. Also no consideration is given to the impact of commercial policy. Some countries tax exports of primary commodities while they grant rebates, or do not tax, primary inputs processed as manufactured goods for the domestic market, or export.

Before using the proposed indicator of natural resource-based comparative advantage, we tried to ascertain whether the ordering by such an indicator of the Latin American industries was not peculiar to them. For this purpose, we compared the ranks of the 37 ISIC sectors for which comparable data was available in 18 industrialised countries (ICs), 39 less industrialised countries (LICs), as well as 18 Latin American and Caribbean countries.

Since not all products are being produced in all countries, the number of countries for which data are available varies with the sector. Moreover some variability among countries for the same sector is to be expected given the differences in integration of industrial production that exist. Still the degree of concordance observed among the rankings is remarkable. Pairwise comparisons of Latin America with the ICs yields a Spearman rank correlation coefficient of 0.83, and between Latin America and the LICs of 0.87.[4] Likewise, the Kendall coefficient of concordance for the rankings among the three groups of countries was estimated to be 0.89.[5]

Thus it seems that the direct value added/output coefficient can be safely used as representative of the orderings by direct value added in the manufacturing industries for all countries.

Table 13.6 shows the 37 ISIC sectors for which comparable data were available classified in increasing order of value added/output for the Latin American countries.

Table 13.7 indicates where lies the present strength of narrowly-defined (according to SITC) Latin America's manufactured exports. The main grouping by export value is iron and steel and its products which, as can be seen in Table 13.6, is among the sectors with lowest direct value added as a proportion of total output. The same is true for industrial chemicals that follow.

Among the main groupings by value of exports to be added, if a broad classification were used (see Table 13.8), are also sectors which are at the top in terms of low direct value added in relation to total output. The first grouping is petroleum and gas products (first rank by lowest proportion of direct value added), followed by food industries (second place).

It has been argued that some industries, in some countries, engaged at times in variable cost-pricing to export. We have presently no way of assessing the impact of this phenomenon on our data, and implicitly assume that if such (or other export promotion) policies were important, they were applied in a fashion neutral to our considerations of comparative advantage.

5 SUMMARY OF FINDINGS

By properly grouping the main export products and identifying within each group the exports accounting for more than 75 per cent of the total we are able to extract 11 groups (see Table 13.9). The most important products in the first five groups are clearly resource-intensive, that is, with relatively low proportion of direct value added in relation to output. They are also fairly concentrated and within each group a few product lines account for the bulk of exports by the group. Food Industries and Chemical Products show greatest

Table 13.6 Latin America: ranking of manufacturing industries by index of direct value added/output

ISIC	Industry	Value added/ output (per cent)	Rank	Number of countries with data
353	Petroleum refineries	27.76	1	15
311/2	Food products	30.15	2	18
354	Petroleum, coal products	33.70	3	12
3411	Pulp, paper, etc.	34.12	4	9
351	Industrial chemicals	35.17	5	18
341	Paper and products	36.96	6	18
3513	Synthetic resins etc.	38.26	7	10
371	Iron and steel	39.12	8	15
384	Transport equipment	39.68	9	16
3843	Motor vehicles	40.01	10	11
372	Non-ferrous metals	40.02	11	14
323	Leather and products	40.65	12	17
381	Metal products	42.36	13	18
352	Other chemical products	44.04	14	18
322	Wearing apparel	44.20	15	18
356	Plastic products, n.e.c.	44.80	16	17
321	Textiles	44.81	17	18
355	Rubber products	45.49	18	17
383	Electrical machinery	45.60	19	17
3211	Spinning, weaving etc.	46.42	20	12
3511	Basic chemicals excl. fertilisers	46.68	21	13
3832	Radio, TV etc.	47.01	22	10
331	Wood products	47.13	23	18
332	Furniture, fixtures	47.71	24	18
369	Non-metal products n.e.c.	47.74	25	17
382	Machinery n.e.c.	47.95	26	18
324	Footwear	48.13	27	17
362	Glass and products	48.26	28	16
390	Other industries	49.81	29	17
385	Professional goods	51.04	30	16
3522	Drugs and medicines	53.12	31	13
342	Printing, publishing	55.56	32	17
313	Beverages	56.00	33	18
3841	Shipbuilding, repairs	56.26	34	8
361	Pottery, china etc.	59.49	35	14
3825	Office, computing, machinery, etc.	60.67	36	5
314	Tobacco	65.15	37	18

Source: United Nations, *Industrial Statistics Yearbooks* (1976, 1978, 1982 and 1983).

Table 13.7 Latin America's main manufactured exports product groupings
narrow classification – 1983

SITC	Groupings	Value (million US dollars)	Share %
	I *Iron & steel, steel products and manufactures*	2 476.6	
671	Pig iron	606.8	19.5
672	Iron & steel prim. form.	133.4	3.1
673	Iron & steel shapes	466.4	4.5
674	Iron & steel plate	890.6	5.1
678	Iron & steel tubes and pipes	267.5	2.2
693	Wire products	76.3	4.2
696	Cutlery	35.6	3.1
	II *Chemical products of natural and synthetic origin*	1 995.1	
511	Hydrocarbons	500.3	5.5
512	Alcohols, phenols	216.6	5.7
513	Carboxylic acid	161.1	3.4
522	Inorganic elements	415.3	6.6
523	Other inorganic chemicals	118.2	2.8
532	Dyes and tanning prod.	68.4	22.9
551	Essential oils, perfumes, etc.	75.7	4.8
554	Soap, cleansing etc. preps.	74.5	3.0
562	Fertilisers manufacture	139.0	2.2
585	Plastic materials nes.	29.6	4.6
591	Pesticides, disinfectants	116.3	2.8
592	Starch, insulin, gluten, etc.	40.1	2.4
	III *Footwear, clothing & luggage*	1 859.2	
831	Travel goods, handbags	128.1	6.1
842	Men's outwear not-knit.	158.0	2.7
843	Women's outwear not-knit.	220.9	2.4
844	Undergarments not-knit.	53.3	2.7
846	Undergarments knitted	189.2	5.2
848	Headgear, non-textiles clothing	121.0	3.6
851	Footwear	988.7	10.2
	IV *Mechanical and electrical machinery and parts, equipment, motor vehicles*	1 737.3	
713	Engines	888.2	5.7
737	Metalworking machin. n.e.s.	50.2	2.0
771	Electric power mach. n.e.s.	175.1	4.8
772	Switchgear	456.6	3.4
773	Electric distrib. equip.	116.0	2.2
783	Road motor vehicles n.e.s.	51.2	2.1

Table 13.7   Continued

SITC	Groupings	Value (million US dollars)	Share %
	V *Electronic products and equipment*	1 722.4	
761	TV receivers	120.2	2.6
762	Radio receivers	309.8	6.0
764	Telecommunication equipment	878.6	4.2
776	Transistors, valves, etc.	413.8	2.1
	VI *Textiles*	1 083.1	
651	Textile yarn	580.3	5.0
652	Cotton fabrics	240.0	3.9
657	Textile products	132.5	3.3
658	Textile articles n.e.s.	130.3	4.1
	VII *Leather, leather products, skins, furs*	787.5	
611	Leather	468.9	13.9
612	Leather manufactures	104.7	11.1
613	Furs, skins, tanned & dressed	213.9	2.2
	VIII *Various manufactured goods*	770.5	
625	Rubber tyres, tubes, etc.	141.0	2.1
642	Paper materials n.e.s.	187.2	3.6
882	Photo, cinema supplies	141.8	2.4
894	Toys, sport. goods	225.1	3.2
896	Works of art, etc.	75.4	2.6
	IX *Glass, glassware, clay & lime prods.*	402.7	
661	Lime, cement, building prods.	100.7	2.5
662	Clay, refract. building prods.	76.7	2.4
664	Glass	131.3	3.6
665	Glassware	94.0	3.5
	X *Wood, plywood, and wood products*	305.4	
634	Veneers, plywood	200.0	4.7
635	Wood manufactures n.e.s.	105.4	3.9
		13 098.0	

Source: See Table 13.1.

Table 13.8 Latin America's main manufactured export products groupings, additional products, broad classification, 1983

SITC	Groupings	Volume (million US dollars)	Share %
I	*Petroleum and gas products*	*9 900.6*	
334	Petroleum products, refinery	8 855.7	12.20
335	Residual petroleum and petr. prod. n.e.s.	214.9	5.40
341	Gas, natural and manufactured	830.0	2.90
II	*Food industries*	*8 036.4*	
014	Meat pred. prsvd. and n.e.s., etc.	527.1	23.90
037	Fish, etc. prepd. prsvd. & n.e.s.	131.7	5.30
0422	Rice semi-milled and milled	69.8	2.50
048	Cereal etc. preparation	70.4	2.30
056	Veg. etc. prsvd., prepared	88.9	3.50
058	Fruits prsvd., prepared	984.2	24.70
0612	Refined sugar, etc.	539.5	19.10
062	Sugar candy non-chocolate	39.8	5.10
0712	Coffee extract, essences	316.6	40.70
0722	Cocoa powder, unsweetened	8.4	4.80
0723	Cocoa butter and paste	337.2	28.60
073	Chocolate and products	72.4	4.50
081	Feeding stuff for animals	3 992.5	33.30
411	Animal oils and fats	37.2	2.80
423	Fixed veg. oils, soft	651.0	18.20
424	Fixed veg. oils, non-soft	142.2	5.30
431	Processed animal and veg. oil, etc.	27.5	2.20
III	*Non-ferrous metals & metal products*	*4 304.4*	
681	Silver, platinum, etc.	946.8	15.30
682	Copper, excl. cement copper	2 096.1	20.60
684	Aluminium	758.5	6.10
685	Lead	68.6	7.90
686	Zinc	138.4	7.70
687	Tin	296.0	15.50
IV	*Various natural and synthetic materials processed*	*1 009.4*	
233	Rubber, synthetic reclaimed	70.6	2.50
251	Pulp and waste paper	498.4	6.30
261	Silk	3.0	3.30
265	Veg. fibres excl. cotton, jute	55.3	16.90
266	Synthetic fibres to spin	59.3	2.40
268	Wool (excl. tops), animal hair	322.4	8.50
V	*Beverages & tobacco*	*231.2*	
112	Alcoholic beverages	156.3	2.00
122	Tobacco, manufactured	74.9	2.00
		23 481.6	

Source: See Table 13.1.

Table 13.9 Latin America: main manufactured products exported and their share of product groupings

Groupings	Value (million US dollars)	Share %
I *Petroleum and gas products*	*9 900.6*	
– Petroleum refinery products	8 855.7	89
II *Food industries*˙	*8 036.7*	
– Feeding-stuff for animals	3 992.5	
– Fruits preserved and prepared	984.2	
– Fixed vegetable oils, soft	651.0	
– Refined sugar, etc.	539.5	
– Meat prep. preserved, etc.	527.1	
– Cocoa butter and paste	337.2	
– Coffee extract, essences	316.6	91
III *Non-ferrous metals and metal products*	*4 304.4*	
– Copper, excl. cement copper	2 096.1	
– Silver, platinum, etc.	946.8	
– Aluminium	758.5	
– Tin	296.0	95
IV *Iron & steel and steel products*	*2 476.6*	
– Iron and steel plate	890.6	
– Pig-iron	606.8	
– Iron and steel shapes	466.4	
– Iron and steel tubes and pipes	267.5	90
V *Chemical products*	*1 955.1*	
– Hydrocarbons	500.3	
– Inorganic elements, oxides	415.3	
– Alcohols, phenols	216.6	
– Carboxylic acid	161.1	
– Fertilisers, manufacture	139.0	
– Other inorganic chemicals	118.2	
– Pesticides, disinfectants	116.3	85

variety with seven product lines each.

In Group I, Petroleum Refineries accounts by itself for 89 per cent of the total; in Group II (Food Industries) feeding-stuff for animals is by itself responsible for almost 50 per cent of total exports from the group, and together with six other products add up to 91 per cent of the total exports of the group. Similarly, in Group III

Table 13.9   Continued

Groupings	Value (million US dollars)	Share %
VI *Footwear, clothing and luggage*	1 859.2	
– Footwear	988.7	
– Women's outwear not-knitted	220.9	
– Undergarments, knitted	189.2	
– Men's outwear not-knitted	158.0	84
VII *Mechanical and electrical machinery*	1 737.3	
– Engines (internal combustion piston)	888.2	
– Switchgear, etc. and parts	456.6	
– Electric power machinery n.e.c.	175.1	87
VIII *Electronic products and equipment*	1 722.4	
– Telecommunications equipment	878.6	
– Transistors, valves, etc.	413.8	
– Radio receivers	309.8	93
IX *Textiles*	1 083.1	
– Textile yarn	580.3	
– Cotton fabrics	240.0	76
X *Leather, leather products, skins & furs*	787.5	
– Leather	468.9	
– Furs, skins, tanned and dressed	213.9	87
XI *Various manufactured products*	770.5	
– Toys, sport goods	225.1	
– Paper materials, n.e.c.	187.2	
– Photo, cinema supplies	141.8	
– Rubber tyres, tubes, etc.	141.0	90

Source: Tables 13.7 and 13.8.

(Non-Ferrous Metals and Metal Products) copper accounts by itself for almost half of the group exports, and together with three other metals represents 95 per cent of the total. In Group IV (Iron and Steel and Steel Products) pig-iron represents about 20 per cent, and four product lines account for 90 per cent of the total of this group. In Group V (Chemical Products) we find that hydro-carbons account for about a quarter of total exports, and with six other inorganic and organic products they add up to 85 per cent of the total exports of this group.

It is only when Group VI is reached that we can see the possible importance of factors other than natural resources in determining the comparative advantage of Latin America's manufactured exports. In this group we find footwear (mostly made of leather) accounting for more than half of the total, while the addition of three other apparel and textile products makes the four subsectors account for 84 per cent of the total exported.

In Group VII (Mechanical and Electrical Machinery) – where skilled labour and technology presumably are important factors of production[6] three product lines are responsible for 87 per cent of the total, with one, internal combustion engines, accounting by itself for half of the total exports from this group.

In Group VIII (Electronic Products and Equipment) where, presumably, skills and technology also play an important role, the situation is similar; three product lines represent 93 per cent of the total, and one, telecommunications equipment, is responsible for more than 50 per cent.

Group IX (Textiles) has two product lines accounting for 76 per cent of the total, but one, textile yarn, is responsible for more than 50 per cent. For Group X (Leather and Leather Products) the situation is similar; two product lines account for 87 per cent, and one, leather, accounts for 60 per cent of the total.

Finally, in Group XI, which includes various manufactured products, four product lines represent 90 per cent of the total.

While the first three groupings: Petroleum and Gas Products, Food Industries and Non-Ferrous Metals and Metal Products, are clearly resource-based and with a low proportion of direct value added, Groups IV and V represent a transition, since they are resource-based but also demand skilled labour and access to technical knowledge – albeit fairly well diffused and easily available. In Latin America these industries were established in the second stage of IS.

Group VI (Footwear, Clothing and other Products) requires unskilled and semi-skilled labour plus materials, while Groups VII and VIII (Mechanical and Electrical Machinery and Electronic Products and Equipment) are characteristic of a later IS phase and require not only skilled labour but aso access to relatively new technical knowledge. Groups IX (Textiles) and X (Leather and Leather Products) are traditional industries, based on unskilled labour plus natural resources.

As expected, a majority of the products with highest export market share are natural resource-based (see Table 13.10). Moreover, the first six are clearly dependent on agricultural and livestock inputs. Also, with the exception of tanning products, in sixth place, they all belong to the products to be added if a 'broad' classification of manufactured exports were utilised.

Up to the fifteenth place, all product lines are either agriculture or mineral natural resource-based; only in places 16 and 17, leather products and footwear, do we get to industries in which factors other than (mainly) natural resources could account for revealed comparative advantage.

6 POLICY IMPLICATIONS

The generalisations that could be extracted from this analysis must be preceded by the usual caveat that, although our results represent regional patterns, they would not necessarily apply to any country in particular.

In the first place, it seems that the relationship between primary commodities and industrial exports is best looked upon not as a dichotomy, but, at least for Latin America, as part of a continuum in the development process. This is particularly clear for the agriculture/livestock/fish-based food industries which constitute one of the main export groups. Their linkage with some of the primary commodities – so important in Latin America's exports – requires no further elaboration.

The availability of the natural resources coupled with the growth in domestic demand, stimulated in turn by growth in population and income per capita, has led to the development in several Latin American countries of fairly efficient food industries, able not only to serve domestic markets but also to export. There does not seem really to exist a choice between exporting primary commodities or manufactures from these sectors.

In fact it could be argued that, to the extent that local availability of natural resources provides an advantage (because of transportation, storage, and other costs involved in supplying appropriate inputs for local processing industries), some inefficiency in the value added stages could be absorbed by the cost-advantage in resource inputs.[7]

Food industries also provide the best evidence against considering

Table 13.10   Latin America: manufactured exports ranked by export value
and market share – 1983

Rank	Export industries	
	Ranked by value	*Value (million US dollars)*
1	Petroleum refineries	8 855.7
2	Feeding stuff for animals	3 992.5
3	Copper	2 096.1
4	Footwear	988.7
5	Fruits preserved and prepared	984.2
6	Silver, platinum, etc.	946.8
7	Iron & steel plate	890.6
8	Internal combustion engines	888.2
9	Telecommunications equipment	878.6
10	Aluminum	758.5
11	Fixed vegetables oil, soft	651.0
12	Pig-iron	606.8
13	Textile yarn	580.3
14	Refined sugar	539.5
15	Meat prep. preserved, etc.	527.1
16	Hydrocarbons	500.3
17	Leather	468.9
18	Iron and steel shapes	466.4
19	Switchgear, etc. and parts	456.4
20	Inorganic elements, oxides	415.3
21	Transistors and valves	413.8
22	Cocoa butter and paste	337.2
23	Coffee extract and essences	316.6
24	Radio receivers	309.8
25	Tin	296.0

the relationship between natural resources and industrial development as merely one of exploiting a 'staple' or developing an 'enclave'. The number of industries and the variety of products exported in this group are among the greatest of all those with revealed comparative advantage. Moreover, these industries have led in some Latin American countries to a derived demand for machinery and production processes which, in turn, gave rise to the subsequent development of exports of locally developed equipment, and even production technologies, appropriate for the products of these industries. These latter-exports tend to be more skill and technology-

Table 13.10 Continued

Rank	Export industries	
	Ranked by market share	*Share of world exports (%)*
1	Coffee extracts and essences	40.7
2	Feeding stuff for animals	33.3
3	Cocoa butter and paste	28.6
4	Fruits preserved and prepared	24.7
5	Meat prepared and preserved	23.9
6	Tanning products	22.9
7	Copper	20.6
8	Pig-iron etc.	19.5
9	Refined sugar	19.1
10	Fixed vegetable oils	18.2
11	Vegetable oils	16.9
12	Tin	15.5
13	Silver, platinum	15.3
14	Leather	13.9
15	Petroleum refineries	12.2
16	Leather products	11.1
17	Footwear	10.2
18	Wool	8.5
19	Lead	7.9
20	Zinc	7.7
21	Inorganic elements, oxides	6.6
22	Pulp and waste paper	6.3
23	Travel goods, handbags	6.1
24	Aluminium	6.1
25	Radio receivers	6.0

Source: Table 13.1.

intensive than the original food industries (Teitel and Sercovich, 1984).

Other natural resource-based products exported are those based on mineral inputs, in particular, the products of petroleum refineries, and copper and other non-ferrous metals, and their products. Petroleum refineries outputs are used as feed-stocks in petrochemical complexes for the production of hydrocarbons and various other chemicals. The non-ferrous metals case is, in principle, similar to iron and steel and its products; that is to say, various metalworking operations are involved to produce sheet and other flat products, bars and other shapes, tubes and pipes, wires and so on. Obviously these metal products constitute manufactured products, equivalent, from the point of view of the industrial operations involved, to similar iron and steel products.

Besides natural resources, the other important source of industrial exports from Latin America is the IS process. Sometimes also favoured by the availability of natural resource inputs, the initial manufacture for the domestic market led, following the growth of markets and the accumulation of experience, to the mastery of the technologies specific to such industries as footwear and other leather products, textiles, apparel and so on. While resource and labour availability and the growth in market demand were important for the success of this type of industries, no single factor seems to have been of over-riding importance. In terms of the proportion of direct value added to output they are in the middle range. The labour required is, in general, relatively unskilled and in most cases, economies of scale, although present; are not very important.[8] It has also been shown that at the beginning of the 1970s countries in the region had smaller average labour productivity differentials *vis-à-vis* ICs in some of these industries of a more 'traditional' nature, that is, those developed in the initial stages of IS in Latin America (Teitel, 1981).

Two other important export sectors: iron and steel and their products, and chemicals, are obviously also the result of more recent IS stages. Quality steel-sheet, pipes, and other steel products, although only developed in Latin America in the 1970s, have already reached world markets. Moreover, although not yet equally important in value, the development of exports in the mechanical and electrical machinery groups and in the electronic industries – which are of even more recent inception – should also be noted. While the participation of transnational corporations in some of these exports is undoubtedly important, it does not detract from the fact we want to emphasise – the potential supply of manufactured exports arising from IS.

It is also noteworthy that, as shown in Table 13.3, exports of products in the 'narrowly' based classification have been growing fast (they doubled their share of world exports between 1970 and 1983), while the share of the products to be added if a more 'broadly' based classification is used (that is, more resource-intensive exports) has been declining steadily.

Thus, as surmised in Teitel and Thoumi (1986) the Latin American experience has mostly been one of no dichotomy or contradiction between IS and industrial exports.[9] The development of successful manufactured exports has had, as one of its roots, the learning acquired in the domestic market, and only made possible (at least initially) by IS. Natural resource availability also seems to have played a role in some of the later IS cases, but not an excessively important one.

The Latin American experience shows that successful exports of manufactures could emerge from agriculture and mineral processing as well as from the various stages of IS in industry.[10] Much more research about the sequencing and interaction of the various phases of IS and export promotion policies in different countries is clearly needed.

Notes

* Preliminary versions were presented at the 6th Latin American Regional Congress of the Econometric Society, July 22–5, 1986, Córdoba, Argentina, and at a seminar in the Inter-American Development Bank. R. Bautista, C.A.P. Braga, S. Ishikawa, A. Jadresic, E. Londero, A. MacBean, M. Michaely, G. Ranis, H. Schwartz, M. Syrquin, F. Thoumi, and participants at the World Congress, and the above meetings, offered useful comments and suggestions.

    The research assistance provided by S. Block, F. Changanaquí and, particularly, A. Ward is gratefully acknowledged.

    The points of view expressed in this paper are the author's and do not purport to represent the position of the Inter-American Development Bank.

1. For example, SITC 671: Pig-iron; 672: Iron and Steel Primary Forms; 673: Iron and Steel Shapes; 674: Iron and Steel Plate; 678: Iron and Steel Tubes and Pipes, and 693: Wire Products.

2. Disregarding possible scale and technology effects and considering an homogenous production function with three factors: capital, labour and natural resources,

    $$Y = f(K, L, NR)$$

    assuming capital to be the scarce resource in both cases, output per unit of capital would thus be a function of labour and natural resource intensity.

3. This is of course a broad approximation since different primary commodities may, in turn, be more or less natural resource-intensive. Ideally, input–output calculations of indirect value added would be required, but this is beyond the scope of the present study.

4. Using the normal approximation $Z = R \sqrt{N-1}$ the resulting Zs are 4.98 and 5.22 and the probability that the underlying rank correlation is zero is less than 0.0001.

5. Given the relatively large N, we use the F test:
$$F = \frac{(m-1)W}{1-W}$$
where m is number of country groupings and W is the coefficient of concordance estimated. The degrees of freedom are:
$$n_1 = N - 1 - \frac{2}{m}$$

$$n_2 = (m-1)\left(N - 1 - \frac{2}{m}\right)$$
where N is the number of industries ranked.
The resulting F is 16.18 which is significant at the 99th percentile at least.

6. In the United States, Electrical Machinery ranked recently first in number of engineering personnel per 100 employees, R & D personnel per 100 employees and percentage of sales devoted to R & D. For Mechanical Machinery the ranks were 6th, 4th, and 3rd, respectively. (Teitel, 1982, Table 4).

7. As noted above, financial cost differences favourable to industrial producers and exporters could arise in some cases due to the existence of export taxes on primary commodities.

8. In an average ranking of manufacturing industries for a group of ICs and LICs according to three labour-skill indicators, textiles, leather products, and apparel, ranked in the last places (Teitel, 1976, Table 7). For the data on economies of scale, see Teitel (1975).

9. For the phasing of IS and exports in the manufacturing sectors of Korea and Turkey, see Nishimizu and Robinson, 1984.

10. Of course this is not meant to imply that the number (or proportion) of IS industries which have led to exports, or to products which could compete in domestic markets without protection, has been in any sense optimal or even adequate. More research is needed on these matters.

References

Balassa, B. (1965) 'Trade Liberalization and "Revealed" Comparative Advantage', *The Manchester School of Economic and Social Studies*, vol. 33, pp. 99–123.

Cline, William R. (1984) *Exports of Manufactures from Developing Countries*, (Washington, D.C.: The Brookings Institution).

Inter-American Development Bank (1982) *Economic and Social Progress in Latin America – The External Sector, 1982 Report*, Washington, DC, chapter 5.

Kim, C. (1983) *Evolution of Comparative Advantage. The Factor Proportions Theory in a Dynamic Perspective*, J.C.B. Mohr (Paul Siebeck) (Tubingen). p. 12.

Nishimizu, M. and Robinson, S. (1984) 'Trade Policies and Productivity Change in Semi-Industrialized Countries', *Journal of Development Economics*, vol. 16, Nos. 1–2, (September–October), pp. 177–206.

Ranis, G. (1981) 'Challenges and Opportunities Posed by Asia's Superex-
porters: Implications for Manufactured Exports from Latin America', in
Baer, W. and Gillis, M. (eds) *Export Diversification and the New
Protectionism, The Experiences of Latin America,* NBER and University
of Illinois, pp. 204–226.

Syrquin, M. (1986) 'Growth and Structural Change in Latin America Since
1960: A Comparative Analysis', *Economic Development and Cultural
Change,* vol. 34, number 3, (April), pp. 433–54.

Teitel, S. (1975) 'Economies of Scale and Size of Plant: The Evidence and
the Implications for the Developing Countries', *Journal of Common
Market Studies,* vol. XIII, nos. 1 and 2, pp. 92–115.

Teitel, S. (1976) 'Labor Homogeneity, Skill Intensity, and Factor Reversals
– An International Comparison', *Journal of Development Economics,*
vol. 3, pp. 355–66.

Teitel, S. (1981) 'Productivity, Mechanization and Skills: A Test of the
Hirschman Hypothesis for Latin American Industry', *World Development,*
vol. 9, no. 4, (April), pp. 355–71.

Teitel, S. (1982) 'The Skills and Information Requirements of Industrial
Technologies: On the Use of Engineers as a Proxy', ch. 15 in Syrquin,
M. and Teitel, S. (eds), *Trade, Stability, Technology and Equity in Latin
America* (New York: Academic Press) pp. 333–48.

Teitel, S. and Sercovich, F.C. (1984) 'Exports of Technology by Newly-
Industrializing Countries: Latin America', *World Development,* vol. 12,
number 5/6, May-June, pp. 645–60.

Teitel, S. and Thoumi, F.E. (1986) 'From Import Substitution to Exports:
The Manufacturing Exports Experience of Argentina and Brazil',
Economic Development and Cultural Change, vol. 34, no. 3, April, pp.
455–90.

United Nations (1985) *1983 International Trade Statistics Yearbook* (New
York).

United Nations Industrial Development Organization (1985) *Handbook of
Industrial Statistics – 1984* (New York: United Nations).

United Nations Statistical Office (1971) *Classification of Commodities by
Industrial Origin. Links Between the Standard International Trade
Classification and the International Standard Industrial Classification* (New
York: United Nations).

World Bank (1981) 'Differences Between the East Asian and Latin American
Export Performance in Industrial Country Markets in the 1970s' (mimeo),
by Vasilis Panoutsopoulos, Washington, DC (paper presented at the
International Economics Study Group Conference, Isle of Thorns,
University of Sussex, England).

World Bank (1986) *World Development Report 1986* (Washington DC).

14 Industrialisation through Full Utilisation of Foreign Trade: The Case of Some East Asian Economies

Ippei Yamazawa
HITOTSUBASHI UNIVERSITY, TOKYO

1 INTRODUCTION

This paper examines the development experience of Japan, and its implication for contemporary developing countries in Asia. Japan achieved rapid industrialisation by full utilisation of foreign trade. Through foreign trade she not only obtained raw materials unavailable domestically, but also introduced new products and technology and developed modern industrial production through import substitution at home and exportation abroad. As a late-starting industrial country in the late nineteenth century, Japan's industries typically followed the 'catching-up product cycle' (CPC) process of development.[1] She started as a primary exporter at the take-off stage and then succeeded in achieving export substitution, first in labour-intensive manufactures and later in capital- and technology-intensive ones. This pattern is relevant for developing countries with similar resource endowments in Asia after the Second World War. We will first examine the different stages of Japan's development and then take a comparative look at recent experience of the Asian developing countries.

2 THE ROLE PLAYED BY RAW SILK EXPORTS IN ECONOMIC TAKE-OFF

For the 30 years after her opening up to foreign trade in 1858, Japan's trade pattern was similar to that of typical primary export

343

economies, exporting raw silk, tea, copper and coal and importing cotton and woollen fabrics and various machinery. Raw silk was the most important commercial item both in terms of export value and for its prospect for long-term growth. For this reason, many writers have come to view this commodity as Japan's version of a 'staple export', and the one which initiated the country's sustained economic growth.

This view is supported by the following facts. Raw silk was one of the speciality goods that were indigenous to the resource-poor Japan. Because of the limited domestic market for this luxury item, Japan's raw silk production was destined for overseas markets. Export expansion was enhanced by such favourable conditions as the development of the weaving industry in the United States and the effect of silkworm disease in Europe. Raw silk export became an important source of foreign exchange which was used for essential imports during the initial stage of economic growth. During the first three decades following 1858, raw silk made up one-third of Japan's total exports.

2.1 Factors Supporting Raw Silk Export

However, closer examination reveals that raw silk export did not perfectly conform to the staple theory of growth, and that export growth did not come about merely as a result of the growth in foreign demand. Even within the growing US market, Japanese raw silk export took an increasing share of the market from Italian and Chinese exporters because of her lower export prices. At the time, there was only a small amount of unused resources available in the already densely populated country of Japan, and even these had to be wrested from grain cultivation which was already developed. Thus, in order to compensate for this shortage of natural resources, the Japanese promoted technological progress and increased labour productivity in the sericulture and silk reeling industries, which in turn led to further export expansion. Because of these dynamic effects, this industry may be considered as the forerunner of the 'export-oriented industrialisation' strategy based on semi-processed primary products in contemporary developing countries.

Japan's export of raw silk was stimulated as a response to a strong demand from the European silk weaving industries, themselves plagued by insufficient raw material supply due to the ravages of silkworm disease. In the latter half of the 1870s, the United States became a major raw silk importing country owing to the rapid development of its silk weaving industry. Japan's market share rose to 42 per cent during the first half of the 1880s and to 57 per cent thereafter, reaching 71 per cent in 1901. Japan's silk export to the USA continued, mainly in the form of semi-processed raw silk. Although exports in the more processed form of silk fabrics began to grow rapidly in the latter half of the 1880s, they amounted to only a quarter of the total value of Japan's silk exports owing partly to the US tariff structure at the time which exempted raw silk from the imposition of duties, but which imposed a 50 per cent tariff on fabrics.

Expansion of Japan's share in the US market was the combined effect of a number of factors. The opening of the continental railway in 1879 gave Japanese and Chinese exporters easier access to the US market on the East Coast. The silver devaluation in the 1880s, which caused the depreciation of the currencies of silver standard countries such as Japan and China against gold standard currencies in Europe and the USA, also increased Asian shares in the US market. The shift of American consumer demand to broad fabrics and the shift from hand loom to power loom techniques called for raw silk of better and more standardised quality. European steam filature (raw silk reeled by machines and steam engines) was best suited to meet these requirements, but an increased export supply could come about there only at rising labour cost. Japanese producers quickly changed from the traditional hand filatures to steam filatures by the end of the 1880s. In contrast, Chinese producers continued to rely on traditional hand looms and thus were late in introducing the steam filature technique. Furthermore the Japanese supply of cheap raw silk, partly assisted by the silver devaluation, contributed to a lower price for and increased consumption of silk fabrics in the US market. An increased demand for silk resulted.

2.2 The Contribution to Economic Take-off

How did the growth of raw silk exports contribute to Japan's economic growth? In answering this question, attention should be given to the following four major aspects.

First, the contribution of raw silk export growth is most evident in its capacity for generating foreign exchange earnings. Between 1868 and 1881 raw silk export earned approximately 107 million yen, which constituted 35.4 per cent of total export earnings. From

1881 to 1893 exports were valued at 253 million yen, and the share of total exports rose to 36.2 per cent. Import demand during the initial period of economic growth was large. During the first period, in particular, total Japanese imports reached a value of 273 million yen, and thus a huge deficit resulted. This was fully financed by an outflow of gold and silver coins which had been accumulated during the previous period. Under these conditions, it is evident that the contribution of raw silk exports was not inconsequential.

Secondly, the growth of raw silk exports stimulated rapid expansion in the sericuture and reeling industries. The share of the sericulture industry in agricultural output was 8 to 9 per cent during this period and contributed some 11 to 16 per cent of the income from agricultural production. However, since sericulture competed with wheat production for available resources, when the decline in wheat production which resulted from the growth of sericulture is taken into account, the final contribution of sericulture was 4 per cent lower than the figures cited above. The silk reeling and weaving industries' shares of total manufacturing output as well as their rates of contribution to growth of that output, were even larger than sericulture's contribution to agricultural output. From the 1880s to the second half of the 1890s, they were responsible for approximately 21 to 25 per cent of the increase in total manufacturing output.

Thirdly, being highly labour-intensive, the silk reeling industry generated much labour employment. In the 1900s, employment in this industry constituted 27 to 29 per cent of total manufacturing sector employment. Moreover, since these reeling factories were usually located in rural areas, they were able to make use of the rural labour, who would have had few employment opportunities otherwise.

Lastly, however, the linkage effect, in terms of stimulating the development of other industries, was limited. Silk reeling had no major input industry except sericulture, since production was based on traditional techniques, and due to the limitations on economies of scale, the possibilities for technological innovation and productivity improvements were also limited. In contrast, it was the cotton spinning and weaving industry which applied modern production techniques and realised economies of scale from the outset.

To conclude, primary exports played an important role in the take-off of Japanese economic development. These primary exports were based on Japan's meagre endowment of natural resources and their international competitiveness resulted from intensive use of labour (the single abundant factor), and sustained effects in productivity improvement. The last two factors were common to the subsequent development of modern industries in Japan. However, the development of the silk industry took a form different from CPC development, and had only a limited direct inducement effect on the CPC development of modern industries.

3 THE CATCHING-UP PRODUCT CYCLE DEVELOPMENT PROCESS

The development of modern industries in Japan following its late start took the form of the typical catching-up product cycle (CPC): the importation of a new product, followed first by import-substituting production and later exportation of that product. The introduction of the new product creates its own domestic demand. The expansion of domestic demand is first met by increases in imports, but when imports increase to a certain level, domestic production begins, partly in order to substitute for imports and partly to meet the growing demand at home. Exporting is an extension of the substitution of domestic product for foreign product in the foreign markets. However, as countries having started even later than Japan begin to catch up, Japan's export stagnates and eventually is exceeded by resumed imports.

The cotton textile industry achieved a typical CPC development. Domestic production exceeded imports in 1879(tl) and import substitution was completed when export exceeded import in 1910(t2). During the 1920s, 1930s and 1950s cotton fabric was the most important export item from Japan. But since the early 1950s both production and exports have decreased steadily and imports have increased once again, eventually exceeding exports in 1972.

3.1 Underlying Mechanism

What mechanism underlay the CPC development of the Japanese cotton textile industry? Firstly, it should be noted that the import substitution and export expansion were the successive phases of a single process of the substitution of foreign products for domestic ones, first at home and then abroad. The substitution was made possible by the improved cost competitiveness of domestic producers relative to their rivals abroad. It was also assisted by non-price competitiveness such as quality improvement and the offering of a greater variety of production items. The major source of price competitiveness was the long-run decreasing cost of the industry which was realised through economies of scale, new technology and skills accumulated as the domestic production expanded.

Japanese cotton textile producers were at first handicapped by high cost of imported raw cotton and machinery. But they were able to compensate for this handicap through the use of improved technological methods of mixing different varieties of raw cotton imported from various parts of the world and through the intensive operation of machinery. The increase in labour productivity exceeded wage increases and reduced the labour cost. An increase in productivity was achieved through the process of production expansion. In particular, economies of scale and the introduction of new technology were realised through investment in equipment and machinery, and this type of investment needed to be encouraged by the existence of a sizeable domestic demand and the prospect of further growth. It is estimated that domestic consumption of cotton textile in Japan was as large as 40 000 tons in 1880 and increased annually by 2.5 per cent on average in the pound 1880–1940. The demand growth was assisted by good export prospects. Japan was the first to industrialise in East and South-east Asia and she could extend her cotton textile exports gradually from concentration on her neighbours of Korea and China to South-east Asia, and eventually to the rest of the world.

However, the CPC development of cotton textiles in neighbouring Asian countries after the Second World War had a stagnating effect on Japan's cotton textile production. The industry shifted to maturity stage in the early 1960s. The accelerated wage increases surpassed productivity increases and weakened cost competitiveness. Furthermore the newly invented synthetic textile was substituted for cotton textile in the domestic market and many Japanese textile firms relocated their cotton textile production in South-east Asian countries. These changes occurred simultaneously and accelerated the shift to the re-import stage.

Thirdly, the CPC development can be promoted by the government's protective measures such as tariffs and quantity restrictions. However, the Japanese cotton textile industry started through the initiative of private firms and was given little governmental support. It achieved import substitution under tariffs of 5 per cent or less before the recovery of tariff autonomy (1889). It was further handicapped by an import duty on raw cotton and an export duty on cotton yarn until 1895. In contrast, steel, chemical and machinery industries received heavier governmental support including production subsidy and state enterprise.

3.2 Diversification of the Industrial Structure

Many modern industries repeated the CPC development in Japan. Figure 14.1 depicts changes in production/consumption ratios over time for major industries. As is typical of CPC development, the ratio follows a hill-shaped curve, starting from zero, increasing steadily to exceed unity and then turning downward to below unity again. Four curves represent key industries of Japan at different stages of development. The cotton textile industry started first, and is already finishing its life cycle. Steel started around 1900, exceeded unity (became a net export) in the early 1930s, became a major export in the 1960s and 1970s but has started to decline since the late 1970s. Its production/consumption ratio was as low as 1.43 in 1985. In contrast automobiles and industrial machinery were late in exceeding unity and are still on the rise.

Other modern industries would follow a similar path to the curves shown and the sequence of the CPC development of many industries one after the other resulted in the diversification of the industrial structure of Japan. Some factors explain time lags in CPC

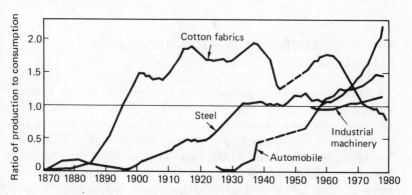

Figure 14.1 The CPC development of major industries of Japan
Note: Production/consumption calculated from seven-year moving averages of the two variables.
Source: I. Yamazawa (1984) Nihon no Keizai Hatten to Kokusai Bungyo (Japan's Economic Development and International Trade) (Toyokeizai Shimpo-sha)

development between industries. Firstly, the state of capital accumulation of Japan limited the number of new industries introduced at any one time, beginning with labour-intensive industries and then extending to capital- and technology-intensive ones. Secondly, forward and backward linkage effects explain the inducement by the CPC development of one industry to that of others. The CPC developments of synthetic dyestuff and textile machinery in the 1910s and 1920s were typical examples of backward linkage in the expansion of cotton textile production. The CPC development of shipbuilding and automobiles was the forward linkage of the steel industry development.

No less important than these factors was the availability of enterpreneurs who correctly foresaw the potential comparative advantage of Japan and the future growth of domestic demand and bore the risk of investment in the new import-substituting industries. Japanese general trading companies should be given credit for this. Through their world-wide operations they acquired information on new products and on both potential market demand for and supply condition of these products at home and abroad.[2]

Successive CPC development of major industries enabled export substitution from primary products to labour-intensive and then to capital- and technology-intensive manufactures. It has brought about the steady improvement of balance of trade and Japan has been freed from the balance of payment constraint to growth since the mid-1960s.

4 CPC DEVELOPMENT IN ASIAN DEVELOPING COUNTRIES

The promotion of industrialisation and the introduction of modern industries began in the East and South-east Asian countries during the 1950s and 1960s. Primary exports played important roles at the early stage of industrialisation in those Asian developing countries. In the early 1960s, more than two-thirds of total exports from Taiwan and South Korea were primary exports, mainly agricultural products from Taiwan and agricultural, marine and mineral products from South Korea. However, because of limited natural resources, those primary products were exported in semi-processed form thus utilising abundant labour, and both countries shifted quickly to exports of labour-intensive manufactures. The share of manufactured exports was around 50 per cent in 1965, amounted to 80 per cent by 1970, and exceeded 90 per cent by 1980. Raw silk was one of the most important primary exports from Korea but its share in its total exports never exceeded 5 per cent. The contribution of primary exports to the economic growth was more limited in Taiwan and Korea than in Japan 80 years ago.

On the other hand, resource-abundant ASEAN countries (excluding Singapore) have relied more on primary exports. Their share in total exports was still over 70 per cent for Thailand and Philippines and nearly 90 per cent for Indonesia and Malaysia in 1980, although the proportion of exports in semi-processed form has increased steadily in all countries. The natural resource base of primary exports is larger in those countries and there seems to exist greater room for their linkage effects on the development of modern manufacturing industries.[3]

4.1 Spread of Industrialisation to Asian Developing Countries

The textile industry was again the first modern industry in those countries, owing to their potential comparative advantage in labour-intensive production and their high domestic demand for imported textiles. Taiwan and Korea introduced their textile industries in the 1950s and by 1970 had achieved import substitution and started export expansion. In the 1970s they initiated the CPC development of heavy industries such as shipbuilding and steel. ASEAN countries started industrialisation in the 1960s. In Thailand and the modern textile industry, first cotton and then synthetic, started in the mid-1960s, achieved import substitution and then started export expansion in the 1970s. Indonesia started its modern textile industry in the late 1960s and achieved import substitution in the 1970s. The heavy industrial production has expanded in some Asian countries since the late 1970s, but it has still remained at a low level.

Figure 14.2 illustrates CPC development of both synthetic textile and steel production for four Asian countries. Production/consumption ratios are measured along the vertical axis and their increase beyond unity depicts the shift from import substitution to export expansion of individual industries. Synthetic textiles developed after cotton textiles. Taiwan began earlier but Korea caught up with Taiwan by the late 1970s. Only in 1971 did the production/consumption ratio exceed 0.5 in Thailand and then remained over unity after 1976. Indonesia's development was lower and seemed to

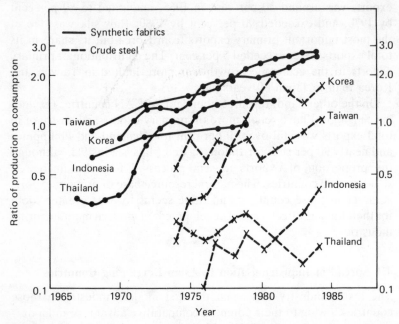

Figure 14.2 Catching-up industrialisation of East and South-east Asian
                countries
Note: Production to consumption ratio of synthetic fabrics and crude steel. Indonesia's
figures for fabrics include cotton fabrics since separate data is not available.
Source: Calculated from the statistics of Japan Chemical Fiber Association and Japan
Iron and Steel Federation.

exceed unity in the 1980s. Steel industry development came in the
mid-1970s for all four countries, five to ten years after the textile
industry. Korea quickly succeeded in the export expansion of steel
by the year 1980, while Taiwan is in the process of achieving import
substitution in the 1980s, and both Thailand and Indonesia are still
far below 0.5.

Both the textile and steel industries have typically followed CPC
development in countries with abundant labour and a sizeable
domestic market. While multinational corporations (MNCs) partici-
pated in the industry development at the early stage, local firms
joined at a later stage and both aimed at import substitution from
the beginning. By contrast, both ready-made clothing and electrical
industries, although more labour-intensive and having been introduced earlier, started export expansion from the beginning without
going through the import substitution stage. There are many such

cases observed in Hong Kong and in the export-processing zones of Taiwan and the Philippines. This particular pattern is made possible by MNCs which bring in capital, technology, packaged parts and materials, use local labour for sewing and assembling, and then export abroad through their marketing channels. Their production technology is standardised so that neither skilled labour nor continued learning of technology is required, and thus export expansion is possible from the beginning.

This is the typical process in the Vernon's Product Cycle (PC) theory of transferring technology and production in developing countries through foreign direct investment. Vernon's theory (Vernon, 1966) explains the transference abroad of assembly operations of a new product, but the theory does not take into account the transference of entire industrial processes capable of accommodating even the innovation of new products. The transplanting of modern industry into Asian developing countries is better explained by a combination of the CPC and PC theories. The CPC development in Asian developing countries has been made possible essentially by technology transfer and improved efficiency but assisted by governmental protection and foreign direct investment.

4.2 Condensed Development

In Korea and Taiwan, the CPC of many industries proceeds through the various stages in a shorter period of time than that of Japan, owing to the quick linkage effect as well as to the quick initiation of exports. This condensed development process is not without its disadvantages. One disadvantage is an intensified need for imports of all kinds at the same time, resulting in acute balance of trade deficits. Korea's trade deficit reflected this structural element and the ASEAN countries will not be free from it if they follow a similar strategy.

However, every industry can pass through the phase of import substitution to export expansion. Many, such as metals, machinery, and chemicals, have not exported after achieving import substitution under protection. Constrained by small-scale production, small domestic markets, and the greater need for technology transfers, these industries can only meet the domestic demand through protection of that industry. The formation of larger regional markets through regional integration agreements will help to promote the CPC development of these industries.

5 CONCLUSION

The CPC development is a rational pattern of industrial development for a late-starting country with a domestic market of a certain size and potential comparative advantage in industrialisation. Indeed there are big differences in international market conditions and initial requirements for industrialisation between late nineteenth century Japan and contemporary developing economies. Nevertheless Japan and developing countries have some basic similarities in their industrialisation processes and mechanisms that are greater than the differences in their initial conditions and the CPC theory may thus have some relevance for developing countries.

The CPC development model provides a framework in which development performance of individual industries can be assessed. If import substitution is slower than expected, it is either because the country lacks comparative advantage in the industry or because improvement in efficiency is obstructed. If expansion of exports does not follow after import substitution is completed, it should be questioned whether import substitution is achieved with improvement in efficiency. An important message of the CPC theory is that the shift from import substitution to export expansion is continuous in the process of industrial development. Therefore a popular discussion on import substitution versus expansion of export strategy should not be regarded as the choice between alternative development processes but merely as the shift of policy emphasis from one to the other in the same development process.

Notes

1. The CPC theory was originally presented by Akamatsu (1943) under the name of 'flying geese pattern' of industry development and later renamed and developed further by Kojima (1973). See also Yamazawa (1984).
2. Yamazawa and Kohama (1985) describe how they initiated the import of new products, the import-substituting production of some of them, and explored the export market abroad for those products.
3. Thoburn (1977) reported the backward linkage effect of tin mining on engineering industry, and that of palm farming on the chemical fertiliser industry in Malaysia.

References

Akamatsu, K. (1943) 'Flying Geese Pattern of Industry Development in Newly Emerging Countries' in *Monographs in Honor of Dr Teijiro Ueda* (In Japanese).

Kojima, K. (1973) 'Reorganisation of North–South Trade: Japan's Foreign Economic Policy for the 1970s' in *Hitotsubashi Journal of Economics*, vol. 13, no. 2, February.

Thoburn, J.T. (1977) *Primary Commodity Exports and Economic Development: Theory, Evidence and a Study of Malaysia* (London: Wiley).

Vernon, R. (1966) 'Industrial Investment and International Trade in the Product Cycle' in *Quarterly Journal of Economics*, vol. 80, May pp. 190–207.

Yamazawa, I. (1984) *Nihon no Keizai Hatten to Kokusai Bungyo* (Japan's Economic Development and International Trade) Toyokeizi Shinpo-sha.

Yamazawa, I. and Kohama, H. (1985) 'Trading Companies and the Expansion of Foreign Trade: Japan, Korea and Thailand' in Ohkawa, K. and Ranis, G. (eds) (1985) *Japan and the Developing Countries* (Oxford: Basil Blackwell).

15 Sudan's Industrialisation after Independence: A Case of Africa's Crisis of Industrialisation

Karl Wohlmuth
UNIVERSITY OF BREMEN

1 THE SUDAN – A SPECIAL CASE OF AFRICA'S CRISIS OF INDUSTRIALISATION?

Is the Sudan a special case? The Sudan is the largest country in Africa with an area of about 2.5 million square kilometres. The population is approximately 21.3 million (mid-1984) with an annual growth rate of about 2.9 per cent. It is classified as a Least Developed Country with a per capita income of 360 US dollars in 1984 (World Bank 1986, Table 1).

The Sudan is an agricultural country with a large irrigated subsector, an expanding mechanised rain-fed farming sector and a neglected traditional rain-fed sector. Out of 200 million feddans of cultivable land (1 feddan = 0.42 hectares = 1.04 acres) in 1985/86 only 20.9 million feddans were actually cultivated; 2.4 million feddans in the irrigated subsector, 8.6 in the mechanised rain-fed farming sector and 9.9 in the traditional rain-fed farming sector. The irrigated subsector of agriculture (producing cotton, groundnuts, sorghum and wheat) with 200 000 tenancies, each cultivating on the average 5 hectares, is employing additionally 400 000 persons as permanent wage labour and 500 000 as seasonal labour; this sector has traditionally provided most of Sudan's foreign exchange earnings via the export of long staple cotton, although in the 1980s the production of medium staple cotton even surpassed the production of long staple cotton.

Cotton has declined from 75 per cent of Sudanese exports in 1950 to 60 per cent in the 1970s. The low share of only 20 per cent in

1981 and 1982 and the return to 50 per cent in 1983 and 1984 reflects the severe crisis of Sudan's cotton production in the late 1970s and the early 1980s. The main source of production is the huge Gezira Scheme with a cultivable area of up to 2 million feddans, out of 3 million feddans which could be cultivated if it were irrigated. The fact that this single project alone is so important for Sudan's export earnings, government revenues, employment situation and market growth (giving a basis for industrialisation) led early to attempts to diversify agricultural production and to integrate its output vertically with local industries. The fact that this sector nowadays supplies only 20 per cent of the net foreign exchange earnings of the country (relative to 50 per cent supplied by the traditional agricultural and livestock sector and 30 per cent by the mechanised farming sector) has led to a re-evaluation of the contributions to development of the three agricultural subsectors, as all three are competing for scarce factors (for example, land, labour, public funds, credit, administrative capacity).

The rapid expansion of mechanised farming (production is only partially mechanised because weeding and harvesting are done manually) implies that around 10 000 large-scale farms employ around 1 million of seasonal labourers to produce sorghum, sesame and some short staple cotton. This sector provides for a marketable food surplus for urban domestic consumption and for exports, but has also contributed to disastrous ecological problems because only 50 per cent of the land used is controlled by the Mechanised Farming Corporation through rotation guidelines and other land conservation measures.

Long neglected in Sudan is the traditional rain-fed farming sector (producing groundnuts, sorghum, sesame, millet) and livestock-raising sector (with an important capacity to export live animals), although this sector has increasing importance as a net foreign exchange earner. It employs 4 million people on 2 million smallholder farms and provides for 2 million seasonal labourers for work in other sectors. Unfavourable prices and insignificant public investments have eroded the potential of the sector in the 1970s to supply food, raw materials, savings, foreign exchange and demand linkages for industrialisation; labour was forced to migrate for longer periods, thereby further increasing the number of urban unemployed and urban informal sector. It can be seen that the role of the traditional sector for Sudan's industrialisation is crucial and that this sector requires more attention from development planners. The mechanised farming sector – although highly subsidised and causing social costs – is a source of food and exportable surplus, whereas the irrigated sector (mostly publicly owned) has become over time a burden for the economy and for industrialisation, with heavy maintenance investment needs that sharply reduces capacity to produce net foreign exchange and absorb industrial consumer goods.

In the 1970s the Sudan became known for its ambitious Bread-basket Strategy (see Oesterdiekhoff and Wohlmuth, 1983; Awad, 1983). The intention was to become a main supplier of food to the Arab neighbouring countries. Supported by Arab funds, the idea was to use the agricultural and livestock resources of the country, which are considered as abundant. To put to use these 'untapped' resources, Arab funds and Western technology were expected to be combined with the Sudan's natural resources for the production of export goods and regional/national import substitutes (such as sugar, meat, textiles, vegetable oils and wheat). The huge agro-industry investment programme of the 1970s may be considered as an aggressive attempt to alter the Sudan's production and trade structures. The ambitous programme is however also considered to be the main cause of the current economic crisis (World Bank, 1985).

As part of this huge investment programme, the Sudan became the location of Africa's largest integrated sugar factory (the Kenana Sugar Company), a venture with investment costs of nearly one billion dollars (compared with the originally planned 150 million dollars). This venture symbolises the Sudan's agro-industrial aspirations; it has become also a symbol of projects disregarding issues of ecology, socioeconomic development, participation, deconcentration of economic activity and efficiency. The project is also a case of extremely weak government intervention into industrialisation (Wohlmuth, 1983).

The Sudan is considered as a case of 'pseudo-development' (UNIDO, 1985c, p. 5) because of the extreme share of services in GDP which increased from 28 per cent in 1960 to 57 per cent in 1981, at 1975 prices. Compared with the shares of agriculture (decreasing from 52 per cent in 1960 to 27 per cent in 1981) and manufacturing (increasing slightly from 6.7 per cent in 1960 to 7.8 per cent in 1981 for modern and traditional manufacturing), and the other subsectors' share (mining, utilities, construction) decreasing from 11.9 to 7.5 per cent, this very high share of services at such a low level of development implies grave distortions.

The Sudan is highly indebted (at around 10.5 billion dollars) and an export figure of as low as 310 million dollars is estimated for 1986 (African Business, August 1986, p. 19). The country belongs to the group of African countries classified by the World Bank as having a prolonged debt crisis (World Bank, 1986a, pp. 9–10 and 46) for which the present rescheduling arrangements are no longer adequate. Among the African group the Sudan has in fact the worst position regarding projected debt service requirements. However, huge potential remittances are available to the country. With sound macroeconomic policies 3 billion dollars per annum could be mobilised (of which at the moment only a small share is officially recorded. In this light the debt and balance of payments situation of the country gets much more positive (see Choucri, 1985). However, the economic crisis of the country has reached extreme proportions. The Government's adjustment policy since 1977/8 has followed IMF/World Bank prescriptions but present rescheduling arrangements are no longer adequate (on the causes of the failure of policy reforms in the Sudan see Wohlmuth and Hansohm, 1984 and 1986). All these factors have contributed to the crisis of industrialisation. The Sudan as a country rich in its history of cottage industries and crafts (Oesterdiekhoff, 1984), the foundations of which had already been destroyed in colonial times, has now also a weakened modern industrial base.

Is the Sudan a typical case of Africa's crisis of industrialisation? Yes, if the industrial structure and performance of modern manufacturing are considered. This is true with respect to the sources of industrial growth (mainly branches producing food, beverages, textiles, clothing and shoes). This is true for the ownership patterns (high/increasing public share), the market structure (highly monopolised industrial sectors), the poor export performance of the manufacturing sector (a negligible share of exports in manufacturing value added), the poor performance of industrial strategies (lack of clear objectives and capacity to implement), the failures of indigenisation (lack of technological adaptation capacity) and also the disastrous consequences of African industrial import substitution policies on the balance of payments (ODI 1986; UNIDO, 1985a and 1985b). However, industrial activity has been affected more negatively since 1977 in the Sudan than in those of other African countries. Despite huge agro-industrial investments since 1973, its industrial output has been on the decline since 1977 (ODI, 1986, Table 2; UNIDO, 1985c, p. 15); only a few branches have been recovering in recent years.

Especially disastrous for Africa's and the Sudan's path of industrialisation is the virtually unchanged dependence on imported inputs. There has been on the average no progress in providing basic and intermediate inputs to key productive sectors, particularly to the agricultural sector (ODI, 1986, p. 3). Therefore, Africa's low share of global industry is not surprising: its very low share in global manufacturing value added has slightly increased from 1970 to 1980, but the even lower share of Africa in manufactured exports declined over this period.

This leads to the causes of problems of industrialisation in Africa. Literature on Africa's crisis of industrialisation is scarce (see Fransman, 1982; Rweyemamu, 1980; Steel and Evans, 1984) and does not show a consensus on the factors responsible for the crisis. There is an accumulation of many paradigms rather than a choice of any one paradigm in this context. Much more work has been done on the crisis of Africa's agriculture (see especially Lele, 1986), but the interwoven problems of the crisis of industry and of agriculture are not tackled adequately. Various external factors (role of export prices, donor policies, inadequate IMF policies) and internal factors (policy distortions, weak state, large and inefficient public sector, neglect of agriculture, deformations of capitalist development, urban–rural bias) are considered in policy-oriented studies. However policy recommendations are also very divergent and a common denominator for prescription of industrial policies as regards objectives, policies of resources use, constraints and instruments has not been found so far. Especially important is the debate on what the engine of industrial growth in the near, the medium and the long term may be: exports, regional import substitution or internal market growth (see Gulhati and Sekhar 1982). The World Bank's Africa Reports still think in terms of option 1 (identifying agricultural crops for exports), whereas option 2 (regional import substitution) is the basis for the Lagos Plan of Action and the Industrial Development Decade for Africa (1980–90). Many authors are sceptical about both options for Africa's industrialisation and recommend option 3, which Adelman (1984) calls Agricultural Demand-Led Industrialisation (ADLI).

The ADLI Strategy requests a shift of public investments towards agriculture first, to maximise linkages (via the creation of a domestic mass market for industrial products – intermediate as well as final products – in rural areas) and secondly, to improve income distribution parallel to changing production structures (by producing more wage goods such as food and textiles and by improving the incomes of the rural poor). The ADLI Strategy is simultaneously a programme to accelerate growth, employment, investments and industrialisation, a programme to improve income distribution, basic needs provision and food security, and also a programme to realise foreign exchange savings and to improve the overall balance of payments situation. In the Sudan this means an improvement of economic conditions for small- and medium-scale peasants and livestock holders, because these segments have a higher labour intensity and a higher use of locally-produced consumer goods and domestic implements for production. With this achieved, employment prospects and markets for industrial products would improve, mainly through policies towards traditional agriculture. In the context of ADLI the raising of agricultural productivity means improving the physical and institutional infrastructure, the incentives for food and livestock production, the land tenure regulations to make incentives work and channelling direct production subsidies to the traditional sector to employ surplus labour, for example, in off-farm activities. At the macro level ADLI implies neutral incentives which are biased neither in favour of exports or imports, nor in favour of manufactures or agricultural and livestock products. As the Sudan's economic incentives are heavily biased against agriculture, policy reforms at the macro level are part of an ADLI package.

In the following sections various aspects of the Sudan's industrialisation after independence (1956) are covered: in Section 2 the origins of the Sudan's industry, in Section 3 the structure of industry by inputs and outputs, in Section 4 the industrial policies and strategies, and in the concluding Section 5 the role of the state in Sudan's industrialisation.

2 ORIGINS AND EVOLUTION OF SUDAN'S INDUSTRY: FROM COLONIAL PRIMARY PROCESSING TO LARGE-SCALE AGRO-INDUSTRIAL PRODUCTION

Six distinct periods may be distinguished:

1. the pre-independence period until 1956 (with cottage industries and colonial-type processing of exported primary products);
2. the period 1956–60 (with indirect public intervention and the start of modern manufacturing);
3. the period 1960–9 (with direct public intervention in industrialisation parallel to the support of private industrial investments);

4. the period 1969–73 (with socialist orientation of government, nationalisation and confiscation of private industries in 1970, but a policy reversal already in 1971);
5. the period 1973–8 (with huge agro-industrial investments, mainly by the public sector);
6. the period from 1977/8 up to the present (of economic crisis affecting industry more and more).

Common to these various periods is the outstanding commitment towards industrialisation by all governments, irrespective of political orientation. However, objectives, strategies and instruments used have changed considerably.

2.1 Pre-independence

In the first period cottage industries prevailed (Oesterdiekhoff, 1984) and some of the products (based on cotton and wood) could even be sold on foreign markets. The sharp increase in the demand for raw materials in the British textile industry led to intensified cotton production in Sudan, enforced by the colonial government. The Sennar dam, built in 1925, made large-scale cotton cultivation in the Gezira possible and the Gezira Scheme, a large-scale export enclave, was created (Awad, 1973). This led to the first stage of manufacturing as represented by cotton-ginning factories. Expansion of this industry encouraged the development of edible oil industries based on cotton seeds. However the step producing yarns and textiles was not possible before independence. Colonial interventions into production and liberal import policies were responsible for this failure to reaching higher stages of raw material processing. The Gezira Scheme as a producer of important primary agricultural products in general and cotton in particular has always been considered the basis for industrialisation of Sudan's primary export economy.

This colonial production pattern in the Sudan has led to the prevailing location of industry around the three towns of Khartoum, Khartoum-North and Omdurman and also the Gezira Province. About 62 per cent of total industrial value added, 62 per cent of industrial labour force and 44 per cent of manufacturing industrial establishments are concentrated now in Khartoum Province (Fadlalla, 1986, p. 17). This is a very important colonial heritage affecting Sudan's industrial development.

2.2 The Years 1956–60

The second period may be characterised as a period of indirect public intervention. Private investment was considered as the main vehicle of industrialisation. The idea was to move quickly from import substitution of consumer goods to import substitution of intermediate and capital goods. Even exports to neighbouring countries were contemplated at that time (Affan, 1985, p. 13). Not only were foreign exchange savings expected from this industrialisation policy, but also a diversification from the dependence on a few primary export products which have shown a high degree of price and volume fluctuations. The Approved Enterprises (Concessions) Act, 1956 was an important step in promoting private investments in the Sudan. In this period, a clear-cut division of economic spheres existed: the state invested in large-scale agricultural and infrastructural projects, whereas the private sector concentrated on industry and housing, mainly in the Khartoum/Gezira regions. Some structural change of industry towards textiles, shoes, paper products and chemical products took place. The second period may therefore be considered as the starting-point of modern manufacturing in the Sudan. However, the limited market size already constrained further industrialisation, leading to small production units, excess capacities and concentration within industrial sectors.

2.3 The Years 1960–69

The third period is crucial to Sudan's industrialisation. Direct public intervention took place. The Ten Year Plan of Economic and Social Development of the Sudan 1961–1970/1 was influential. At the end of the plan period, the Sudan was expected to have transformed its industrial structure as concerns production of intermediate and capital goods, as well as manufactures for export. A considerable share of planned industrial investments was allocated to the public sector, although private (including foreign) capital was expected to remain the leading sector. The creation of the Industrial Bank of Sudan in 1961 was an attempt to give additional assistance to private industries.

The nine public factories built in the spheres of agro-industries did not affect the position of the private sector as the leading one, but resulted in some regional deconcentration of industry, because of the lack of co-ordination between industrial planning and agricultural development, thus leading to periodic raw material shortages. The basic aim of public sector investments in agro-industries, for example, saving foreign exchange on sugar imports, was not realised. These difficulties led to the Organisation and Promotion of Industrial Investment Act, 1967, which stressed the role of the private entrepreneur (Affan, 1985, p. 20). Also in the third period there was a distinct division of economic spheres: the public sector concentrated on local raw materials-based productions, whereas the private sector moved more and more into sectors producing non-essential goods, with excess capacities because of the limited market size.

2.4 The Years 1969–73

In the fourth period, following Numeiri's May 1969 Revolution, nationalisation and confiscation of private industries (including foreign capital) took place, but as early as 1971 a policy reversal occurred. The political changes after the coup d'état against Numeiri in 1971 were important; the co-operation with socialist countries came to an end; these countries also could not really fill the external resource gap envisaged in the Russian-inspired Five Year Plan of 1970/1 to 1974/5 (see on this period Hansohm and Wohlmuth, 1985b). An expression of the policy reversal was the Development and Encouragement of Industrial Investment Act, 1972.

2.5 The Years 1973–77/8

The fifth period marks the intensified direct public intervention in industry under the label of the so-called Breadbasket Strategy. Various forms of capital participation of the state were used and institutional innovations (like the establishment of the Sudan Development Corporation as a catalyst for foreign, Arab and national private and public capital) took place (see Wohlmuth, 1979 and 1983). The government moved more and more into capital-intensive projects (mainly in the branches of sugar and textiles). The sharp increase of the average capital–labour ratio in this period reflects not only a built-in bias towards capital-intensive technologies, but also the growth of excess capacities (Affan, 1985, p. 164). This attitude of the Government was reflected in the establishment of the one billion dollar Kenana sugar project (the story of Kenana is itself a lesson in industrialisation failures in Africa; see Wohlmuth, 1983).

2.6 The Years 1977/8 to the Present

The sixth period is a period of industrial decline; only a few industrial sectors have recovered in recent years. The great number of public sector investment projects (most of them delayed by years) led to overspending and pressure on infra-structure and human skills. Public investments rose by nearly 50 per cent in real terms between 1972/3 and 1973/4, and doubled in real terms by the end of the next year. Large foreign capital inflows that financed this programme inflated aggregate demand; demand pressures; increasing inflation and a worsening of the balance of payments starting in 1976 were the result (World Bank 1985, p. 2). On the surface, this explanation of the crisis is convincing, but more important for an understanding of the real causes of the crisis is the observation that there was no consistent agricultural development strategy beyond the irrigated agricultural subsector and non industrial development planning to the effect of maximising linkages between industry and agriculture (Wohlmuth and Hansohm, 1984; Oesterdiekhoff, 1980 and 1983). Beyond this, there was no serious attempt after independence to design a governmental income and wealth redistribution policy (Mirghani, 1980) in order to create the preconditions for a 'wage goods' strategy, as analysed by de Janvry (1983), aiming at expanding internal markets via broad-based productivity and income increases. According to Mirghani (1980), government policies, consistently since 1956, have ignored equity objectives.

The type of development policies pursued since 1973 have accelerated unequal developments and have restricted the basis for industrial growth. The fact that since 1977/8 all the major branches of manufacturing industry have been on the decline (UNIDO, 1985c, p. 15) may therefore not only be attributed to austerity policies (depressing the demand for goods and the supply of imported inputs), but is basically the result of the inability of industrial policies to remove the basic constraint: market size.

These six periods show the increasing role of the public sector, the increasing limits to import substitution and the increasing level of 'state assistance' necessary to motivate industrial capitalists to stay in the sector.

3 THE STRUCTURE OF THE SUDAN'S INDUSTRY: WEAK LINKAGES AND SOCIAL DISARTICULATION

Classifying the Sudan's industry from the input side by dominant inputs and the extent of linkages and from the output side by the use of output and the social characteristics of the output, one can get better insights into the character of the Sudan's industrialisation process. The scarcity and the weakness of data (as covered in Industrial Surveys) allow only an illustrative analysis. The methodology developed by Oesterdiekhoff (1979 and 1983) will be used utilising data mainly from the Industrial Survey 1970/1 and some other surveys and studies of the 1970s. The still provisional data of the 1981/2 Industry Survey are reflected in the interpretation of results.

The linkages at the aggregate level are considered as very weak, although the backward linkages of industry are more important than those of other sectors. Industry more than other sectors induces primary and secondary demand in other sectors (Oesterdiekhoff, 1979, pp. 34–40). Data based on an input–output table for Khartoum Province reveal that the following sectors are relatively strong in terms of backward linkages: food industry, metal works (a sector which is however quantitatively unimportant), textiles and leather industry. The overall weak linkages of industry with agriculture, with the exception of the food industry, indicate the high import dependence of so many industries. An example is the textile industry, which still depends to a large extent on imported yarns, although import substitution has taken place with the aim of reducing such imports. Concerning linkages within the industrial sector, the chemical industry is strongest in this respect, followed by metal works and basic metals. As food and textiles industries depend more on inputs from outside the industrial sector (agriculture, trade and transport), the most important industrial sectors have very little intrasectoral demand for industrial products (Oesterdiekhoff, 1979, p. 39).

The agro-industrial expansion of the 1970s in sugar and textiles could not modify this pattern of limited inter- and intrasectoral linkages, because of the type of capital-intensive technologies used and the specific demands in terms of imported raw materials. A good example of even weaker linkages is the textile industry; the modern installations were designed to process short staple cotton although the Sudan is known to be a major producer of long staple cotton (Affan, 1985, p. 70).

A more detailed analysis of linkages is necessary however. Classifying industries by the type of dominant input we may distinguish four sectors (see Oesterdiekhoff, 1979 and 1983):

1. Agricultural Food Processing (AF), consisting of ISIC 31 (important products being sugar, oil and flour);
2. Agricultural Non-Food Processing (ANF), consisting of ISIC 32, 33 and 3412 (represented by textiles, leather and paper industries);
3. Non-Agricultural Manufacturing (NAM), composed of ISIC 35, 36, 37 and 38, except 3813 (important products being glass, cement and metal ware);
4. Services (S), covering some workshops and the printing industry (ISIC 3420 and 3813).

Within the four sectors some few subsectors are dominant, as oil mills and sugar in sector AF, textiles and clothing in sector ANF, metal industries in sector NAM and the printing industry in sector S. The sectors may be ranked according to the use of local raw materials and other intermediate products (packing materials and spare parts) as follows: AF relies most on local inputs, followed by ANF, NAM and S; the reliance on imported raw materials has the reverse ranking. The structural change in the 1960s and 1970s has on the whole increased the import dependence. This is the result of diversification of private sector investments (in producing for small markets of higher income groups), and also of the type of products and technologies chosen for the public investments. This import dependency and the lack of a growing internal market for industrial products is constraining the development of input-producing industries. The products produced by the chemical and the engineering industries are only to a small extent relevant to industrial production itself (see UNIDO 1985c, pp. 56–8). Also intersectoral demand is very limited. Sectors AF and ANF take not more than 7 per cent of the agricultural output, so that the agricultural production capacity is used only marginally for industrial production (Oesterdiekhoff, 1979, pp. 47–8).

Paradoxically, in a country with huge agricultural and livestock resources, the raw materials shortage has been an acute problem during the short history of industrialisation. Consequences are excess capacity and the use of capital-intensive and import-dependent technologies to escape this bottleneck. Lack of any co-ordination between agricultural and industrial development planning, such as locational planning is the main cause. Changes from a tenant system to a wage labour system, as in sugar production, have been an early reaction (as early as the 1960s) to the raw materials shortage problem in order to increase control over raw materials supplies. The increasing import dependence made the foreign trade sector become more and more a determinant of the industrial production, quite contrary to the expectation of the late 1950s that accelerated import substitution would reduce foreign sector-induced instabilities. Assembly-type industries were promoted, not only in the NAM sector (chemical industry, metal industries), but also to some extent in the ANF sector (shoes and clothing industry).

Concerning the output side, the theory of social disarticulation (de Janvry, 1983) may be taken as a starting-point for analysis. Social disarticulation is a structural condition in an economy where the key economic sectors (in the Sudan modern agriculture for exports and modern manufacturing for import substitution) are oriented to the production of export and/or luxury goods, so that the balance between production and consumption can hold without a balancing of the shares of profit and wage in national income. In the Sudan this is obviously the case, because the key sectors produce either unprocessed export goods or consumption goods mainly for higher income groups. In an articulated economy, the key sectors produce wage goods, so that the macroeconomic equilibrium implies a balance between profits and wages and between growth and equity. The empirical findings of Oesterdiekhoff (1979 and 1983) may help to qualify the output structure in Sudan more precisely under the framework of this theory. Taking a different group of four sectors which cover: sector I – intermediate goods; sector II – mass consumption goods; sector III – luxury consumption goods; sector IV – exports, and classifying output accordingly, one can draw conclusions on the degree of social disarticulation (assuming that the overwhelming share of modern sector agriculture is export-oriented). Sector I (intermediate goods) is unimportant and had been seriously affected by the crisis since 1977/8 (see Bank of Sudan, 1984, pp. 25–34). The agricultural sector receives very few industrial inputs such as sacks and trailers and only for modern agriculture (Bedri, 1979). However, intermediate industrial products for further processing and for other industries also show a very low degree of diversification, and an inherent inability regularly to meet domestic demand. This is true for yarn, leather, inputs for the packing industry, and also for construction inputs such as cement.

For sectors II and III, Oesterdiekhoff (1979 and 1983) compares industrial luxury goods production versus industrial mass consumption goods production using a careful analysis of consumption patterns, markets for industrial products, incomes (rural and urban) and prices of goods in terms of labour input. The pattern reflects the uninterrupted decline of real wages in urban areas since 1974 (Oesterdiekhoff, 1979, p. 9; see also ILO, 1984, pp. 139–83) and the decline of rural incomes because of worsening internal terms of trade (ILO, 1984). The results are revealing: mass consumption goods amount to only 27 per cent of total industrial value added and to only 38 per cent of fixed assets. This is nearly the situation described by de Janvry and Sadoulet (1983, p. 278) as 'pure social disarticulation' in the sense of key sectors producing mainly luxury goods and export goods. The overwhelming share of industry has no relevance for the majority of the population.

Sector IV (exports) has also shown a weakening performance. Figures from UNIDO (1985c, pp. 41–2) show that the share of manufactures in exports has declined since 1981 in the widest possible definition (covering 148 items) and in the narrowest definition (covering only SITC 5–8 minus 68). The share in the wide definition (including all types of slightly processed goods) has declined because the crisis in the irrigated sector of agriculture has affected the exports of ginned cotton; the share in the narrow definition has declined because of the inability to export textile products and yarn on a regular basis. The traditionally strong position of edible oil exports has also weakened; the Sudan began some years ago to import palm-oil from Singapore. It is therefore left with a fundamentally unchanged export structure (consisting of primary goods such as cotton, sesame, sorghum, livestock, groundnuts). Neither the import substitution targets (for sugar and textiles), nor the 'export substitution' targets (yarn for cotton, leather for hides and skins) could be realised.

All these factors must have consequences for the role of the state in industry and the motivation of industrialists to stay in the industrial sector. Recent data by the World Bank (1985, vol. 22, p. 31) show negative real rates of return on industrial activities as compared to high real rates of return for commodity trading, residential construction and the holding of legal and illegal foreign exchange assets. The shift towards non-tradables in the Sudan is pronounced and also has consequences for stabilisation policies.

4 INDUSTRIAL POLICIES AND STRATEGIES:
RESOURCES, INCENTIVES AND CONSTRAINTS

It is obvious that 'industrial policy' has completely failed; even the realisation of plan objectives has been unsatisfactory (Affan, 1985, pp. 74–100). Most importantly, the share of agricultural resources used in industry as well as the use of industrial inputs in agriculture has remained small. Industrial policy has failed to develop and stabilise private industrial capital, and has led to widespread corruption and inefficiency. Public sector industrialisation has not led to efficient and effective regionalisation and cannot support a viable industrial structure. Industrial policy has failed also with respect to the promotion of small industries/traditional industries and crafts, and even the viability of rural industries is now eroding.

This state of affairs has to be contrasted with the assumed huge agricultural and livestock resources of the Sudan, which give plenty of room for active industrial policies to exploit this potential. Other resources, such as energy, finance and manpower as well as technological capacity are, however, more constrained (see UNIDO, 1985c, pp. 30–6). Some labour shortages have even been reported, because of the very low wages and migration to Arab countries (see ILO, 1984). Although the labour shortages may be more apparent than real, the consequences for industry, in terms of absenteeism and fluctuations, are marked. However, more serious constraints to industry seem to be lack of infrastructure, notably power and transport, of local and imported inputs, adequate financial support and of foreign exchange (World Bank, 1983, pp. 46–55; Affan, 1985, pp. 101–25).

The basic constraint is, however, market size. In this respect the industrial policies have failed completely. Neither the capacity to export manufactures nor the capacity to supply regional markets (of Arab and African countries) has increased; in fact export and regional import substitution prospects have become even worse (see Wohlmuth, 1980; Hansohm and Wohlmuth, 1985b). The only way out of the market size constraint is internal market size growth (via the creation of final demand linkages, and of intersectoral and intrasectoral demand). However, the neglect of the traditional agriculture, the crisis of irrigated agriculture and the uncontrolled activity of the mechanised farming sector limit the agricultural market expansion.

Adelman's ADLI strategy is highly relevant for the Sudan. A structural adjustment concept for the Sudan based on ADLI has been outlined elsewhere (Wohlmuth and Hansohm, 1984 and 1986). A new policy for the main production sectors is required, bringing into balance agricultural subsectors and industry (see ILO 1986). Current policies of rehabilitating agriculture in the Sudan concentrate almost exclusively on irrigated farming but not on the systematic restructuring of rain-fed agriculture. This means that neither a transition towards more articulated growth nor an effective removal of the market size constraint can be expected. Complementary to an ADLI strategy is the promotion of small industries, rural industries and crafts. The advantages of supporting these industries are obvious as regards local resource utilisation, technological skill acquisition, employment and income effects, and regionally balanced development (see Hansohm and Wohlmuth, 1985a).

The nearness to the agricultural resource base and various other production characteristics (flexibility, adaptability to local markets, resilience against economic crisis factors) should make small industries and crafts a favoured sector for governmental support. However, all the Industrial Acts since independence have excluded this sector from any assistance. A recent study on the performance of small-scale industries in Wad Medani, Gezira comes to promising conclusions: given a little public support, this sector could really 'take off' (Anand and Nur, 1985, p. 157). Such a strategy could contribute to local capital formation in rural areas, thereby supporting further rounds of linkages.

A complete reversal of industrial incentive policies on the above lines is necessary in the Sudan. The incentive policies and the Investment Acts have led to distorted structures. The criteria for investment incentives were vague; systematic social profitability appraisals did not take place; criteria such as maximisation of linkages, employment creation and foreign exchange savings were not explicitly used. The system of approvals made directly by the Minister led to political biased decisions and to corruption. Dependence on state assistance increased as well as the expectations of industrial capitalists for favour; the infant industry argument was perverted by the whole system, making industry structurally dependent on protection and financial assistance (Affan, 1985, pp. 44–5). Escalation of incentives in relation to the level of investments led to a preference for large-scale capital-intensive ventures, foreign capital and urban-based investments. As a consequence, industrial policies led to inappropriate products and techniques (World Bank, 1983, pp. 51–3).

These failures of industrial policies obviously stem from policy constraints at the level of the government. How to overcome the policy constraint? The answer of the World Bank (1986a) is to intensify the policy dialogue with African governments primarily on three issues; first, correcting overvalued exchange rates; second, correcting the urban–rural bias and third, rationalising the public sector. Will such propositions help the Sudan to come to a sound basis for industrialisation? In the concluding part of this paper it is argued that the World Bank prescriptions are appropriate only on the surface. In order to become operational, the role of the state in Africa's industrialisation process has first to be considered.

5 CONCLUDING REMARKS: THE STATE AND SUDAN'S INDUSTRIALISATION

In terms of the World Bank's (1986a) prescriptions for Africa the Sudan's economic policies in the 1970s and 1980s have failed to reverse either the overvaluation of the exchange rate bias. After nine devaluations and various agricultural rehabilitation programmes the results are very disappointing and the Sudanese economy is showing aggravating imbalances. The public sector displays crucial inefficiencies and the growth of public sector employment in areas like general administration and defence has been spectacular as has also the decline of real wages in the public service, thereby heavily affecting its overall performance (see ILO 1986). There has been a consistently increasing involvement of the state in the Sudanese economy (see Shaaeldin, 1984, for the colonial period and Aguda, 1973, for the post-colonial period). However, in terms of economic functions, the state has been very weak and become even weaker.

Langdon (1979) considers three functions of the African state: first, *embourgeoisement* or the strengthening of the middle classes; second, meshing of the modes of production; and third, transnationalisation. Taking his theory as a framework one finds that none of these functions were adequately fulfilled with respect to industry. The failure of *embourgeoisement* is evident from the weak position of industrial capital in the Sudan (see Collins, 1976, and Ahmed, 1984) and the eroding position of the industrial petty bourgeoisie in crafts, traditional and small industries, or when analysing the dependence of industry on state assistance and protection. The second function – meshing of modes of production – was not realised, as can be seen from the uncoordinated activity of the state in agricultural and industrial development. The third function (transnationalisation) implies the orientation of production and trade structures according to comparative advantages, so that foreign capital, including remittances, finds adequate and attractive conditions in the Sudan. The irregular support and the weak position of foreign capital in the Sudan signify that this function also was not performed.

Why is the performance of the state in terms of economic functions so poor in the Sudan? The answer requires an analysis of the role of the 'state class', which is composed of the government and the leaders of administrations, parties, army and security, parastatals and social organisations, the relations of this class to other social classes, the revenue base of the 'state class', and the internal and external constraints it faces. Without this analysis it is not possible to say anything about particular segments of the 'state class' view of the industrial sector, nor about the perspectives of those industrial capitalists who might be ready to go along with an ADLI strategy. Those industrialists supplying inputs related to productivity increases in agriculture and those supplying wage goods might benefit especially from such a policy reversal.

What is the meaning of a 'state class' in the Sudanese context? Out of 500 000 persons (in general public administration and in parastatals), only a small share can be considered as belonging to the 'state class'. The 'state class' may be defined as a group professionally concerned with politics that cannot easily be controlled by the masses, can dispose of public funds and can bestow privileges on itself (see Tetzlaff, 1982, on the development and characteristics of the Sudanese 'state class' and its political ideology). Of the total labour force of 6.2 million persons (in 1983) 10 per cent is in formal sector employment (with a half a million being employed in the public sector and in the parastatals), ten per cent is in informal sector employment, 10 per cent is in employment on irrigated tenancies, and 70 per cent of the labour force is employed as smallholders, pastoralists and landless labourers (see ILO, 1986). This employment pattern gives the public sector employees decisive control over production, allocation and distribution of incomes. According to the theory of the state class (see Elsenhans, 1981) various groups representing the central and the regional governments, the parastatals, the army and security system, the political parties and the mass organisations, can intervene in the economic and political process by favouring itself and/or by inducing developmental changes even prior to market demand changes. The lower the level of development, the greater the homogeneity of the various groups of the state class in their interests and the higher the share of their funding from external sources (foreign investments, trade and aid), the greater may be the tendency of the state class to give itself privileges. If there is competition among the groups, if a more diversified economy is already established and if internal sources of revenues are important, the state class as a whole may then lean more towards a progressive role in structural adjustments – even inducing structural changes prior to market demand changes, thereby laying the foundations for industrial progress. In such a context a transition to articulated growth is possible, because changes in the production structure and in income distribution may then coincide. In the case of the Sudan, the tendency for the state class to privilege is obviously dominant; this tendency has even gained momentum during the years of economic crisis (since 1977/8).

What are the revenues of the various groups of the state class in Sudan? Internal revenues come from their relations with other social classes, for example, the commercial, as opposed to the industrial, bourgeoisie, which as a group has gained so much in the 1970s. Revenues from taxing peasants and urban wage earners appear to have declined because of the economic crisis. External revenues from foreign investment, trade and aid have also become constrained, so that the 'state class' as a whole has been leaning more and more on the powerful and prospering commercial bourgeoisie. The increasing pressure from external donors, banks, the IMF and World Bank for policy reforms have even enforced this alliance. An expression is the increasing corruption as a means of accumulation of the 'state class'. Corruption has two aspects: it increases the revenue base of the 'state class', but, through issue of licences, such as import licences, land licences and foreign exchange licences, the scarce domestic factors and foreign exchange funds are diverted into non-productive activities (for example, commodity trading, residential housing, land speculation, speculation with foreign exchange funds) (see Kursany and Kameir 1985). These factors place further constraints on the development of industrial capital in the Sudan. The commercial bourgeoisie became even stronger in the 1970s through alliances with foreign and Arab capital, so that it is not easy to identify a 'national' industrial capitalist class which is ready to go along with an ADLI strategy. The debates on this issue (in ROAPE, 1983, and Mahmoud, 1984) reveal that there are controversies over the existence of a 'national' industrial capitalist class in the Sudan. Elements of a strategy to support a national industrial capitalist class in the Sudan were worked out by Kursany (1983), Hansohm and Wohlmuth (1985a) and by Wohlmuth and Hansohm (1984 and 1986). These were based on a shift of resources towards traditional agriculture to increase productivity and to extend markets, the promotion of small industries in the rural and urban areas and a more balanced development of industry and agriculture.

Conditionality as applied by international organisations can actively support an ADLI strategy and also those industrial capitalists who can sustain such a strategy. However, a new set of conditions related to structural changes is required. Because of the insignificant and disappointing role of industrial capital in all industries in the Sudan, the state has an even stronger role to play in the process of industrialisation (this is also the argument of Schmitz (1984) and Singh (1982) in a more general context). Conditionality should first of all promote the productive use of funds by the state class. A strengthening of the role of the state parallel with a rationalisation programme is required, not symbolic privatisation policies as pursued in the Sudan at the request of IMF and World Bank. The type of conditionality needed has to relate to structural and social factors in order to have an impact and create viable industrialisation patterns.

The approach in this chapter of examining the colonial heritage, weak linkages, social disarticulation, policy process and the state class may be useful not only to understand the prospects for industrialisation in the Sudan, but also in highlighting issues for Africa. It is obvious too that the times of economic crisis should be used for a transition to viable patterns of industrialisation.

References

Adelman, I. (1984) 'Beyond Export-Led Growth.' *World Development*, vol. 12, no. 9 pp. 937–49.

Affan, B.O.A. (1985) Industrial Policies and Industrialization in the Sudan, Khartoum: Graduate College Publications No. 16, University of Khartoum.

African Business (1986) August, 'IMF deal creeps closer', p. 19.

Aguda, O. (1973) 'The State and the Economy in the Sudan. From a Political Scientist's Point of View', *The Journal of Developing Areas*, vol. 7, April, pp. 431–48.

Ahmed, A.G.M. (1984) 'Social Classes in the Sudan: The Role of the Proletariat', Sudan Research Workshop, July 3–5, Institute of Social

Studies, The Hague, Netherlands/DSRC, University of Khartoum, Sudan.

Anand, V. and Nur, T.M. (1985) 'The Role of Small-Scale Enterprises in Developing Countries – A case study of Wad Medani in Sudan', *Asian Economic Review*, vol. 27, nos. 1/2, April/August pp. 137–59.

Awad, H. (1973) 'A Note on Foreign Enclaves and Polarization: Example from Sudanese Agriculture', Seminar paper, United Nations African Institute for Economic Development and Planning, Dakar, Senegal, March, 14 pages.

Awad, H. (1983) 'Why Is the Breadbasket Empty?' DSRC Seminar No. 40, University of Khartoum, 28 pages.

Bank of Sudan (1984) Twenty-Fifth Annual Report, March, Khartoum, Bank of Sudan, Democratic Republic of The Sudan.

Bedri, M.A. (1979) Agricultural machinery industry and rural industrialization in the Sudan, UNIDO, Appropriate Industrial Technology for Agricultural Machinery and Implements (New York: UNIDO) pp. 141–8.

Choucri, N. (1985) A Study of Sudanese Nationals Working Abroad, Final Report, 2 volumes, (Cambridge, Mass.: Massachusetts Institute of Technology).

Collins, C. (1976) Colonialism and Class Struggle in Sudan, Washington/ Cambridge: MERIP report no. 46, pp. 3–20.

Elsenhans, H. (1981) Abhängiger Kapitalismus oder bürokratische Entwicklungsgesellschaft, Frankfurt.

Fadlalla, B.O.M. (1986) Unbalanced Development and Regional Disparity in the Sudan, National Economic Conference Paper, January, 36 pages.

Fransman, M. (ed.) (1982) *Industry and Accumulation in Africa*, (London: Heinemann Educational Books Ltd).

Gulhati, R. and Sekhar, U. (1982) 'Industrial Strategy for Late Starters: The Experience of Kenya, Tanzania and Zambia', *World Development*, vol. 10, no. 11, pp. 949–72.

Hansohm, D. and Wohlmuth, K. (1985a) 'Promotion of Rural Handicrafts as a means of Structural Adjustment in Sudan. With special Reference to Darfur Region', SERG Discussion Paper no. 7, University of Bremen, December, 34 pages.

Hansohm D. and Wohlmuth, K. (1985b) East–South and South–South Economic Cooperation of the Democratic Republic of the Sudan, SERG Discussion Paper no. 3, January, 29 pages.

ILO (International Labour Organisation) (1984) *Labour Markets in the Sudan* (Geneva: International Labour Organisation).

ILO (International Labour Organisation) (1986) Employment and Economic Reform: Towards a Strategy for The Sudan, Report of the ILO/JASPA Mission to the Sudan, August–September (Geneva: International Labour Organisation).

de Janvry, A. (1983) Growth and Equity: A strategy for Reconciliation, in Nobe K.C. and Rajan K.S. *Issues in Third World Development* (Boulder Publisher, Westview) Special Studies pp. 19–33.

de Janvry, A. and Sadoulet, E. (1983) Social Articulation as a Condition for Equitable Growth, *Journal of Development Economics*, vol. 13, pp. 275–303.

Kursany, I. (1983) 'A Strategy for the Transformation of the Precapitalist Part of the Sudanese Society', *Development and Peace,* vol. 4, no. 1, Spring, pp. 167–89.

Kursany, I. and Kameir, E. (1985) 'Corruption as a "Fifth' Factor of Production in the Sudan', in *Development and Peace,* vol. 6, no. 2, Autumn pp. 148–64.

Langdon, S. (1979) 'Multinational Corporations and the State in Africa, pp. 223ff., in Villamil, J.J. (ed.), *Transnational Capitalism and National Development: New Perspectives on Dependence* (Sussex: Hassocks).

Lele, U. (1986) 'Comparative Advantage and Structural Transformation: A Review of Africa's Economic Development Experience', Economic Growth Center, Yale University, 25th Anniversary Symposium, April 11–13.

Mahmoud, F.B. (1984) *The Sudanese Bourgeoisie–Vanguard of Development?* (Khartoum: Khartoum University Press).

Mirghani, H.M. (1980) 'Government Policies and Income Distribution in the Sudan', in Rweyemamu, J.F. (ed.), *Industrialization and Income Distribution in Africa* (Dakar: Codesira) pp. 214–25.

ODI (Overseas Development Institute) (1986) Briefing Paper: Industrialisation in Sub-Saharan Africa, January, 7 pages.

Oesterdiekhoff, P. (1979) Industrial Development and Industrial Structure in Sudan, (in German), Research Report No. 2, University of Bremen, April, 159 pages.

Oesterdiekhoff, P. (1980) 'Agrarpolitische Orientierungen: Phasen, Tendenzen und Alternativen', in Tetzlaff and Wohlmuth (1980) pp. 143–256.

Oesterdiekhoff, P. (1983) 'Industrial Development. Structural Deficiencies, Agroindustrial Prospects and Alternatives', in Oesterdiekhoff and Wohlmuth (1983) pp. 164–93.

Oesterdiekhoff, P. (1984) 'Crafts in Sudan – Technical and Socioeconomic Aspects, SERG Discussion Paper No. 2, University of Bremen, 74 pages (in German).

Oesterdiekhoff, P. and Wohlmuth, K. (1983) 'The "Breadbasket' is Empty: The Options of Sudanese Development Policy', *Canadian Journal of African Studies,* vol. 17, no. 1 pp. 35–67.

Oesterdiekhoff, P. and Wohlmuth, K. (eds) (1983) *The Development Perspectives of the Democratic Republic of Sudan: The Limits of the Breadbasket Strategy* (München/Köln/London: Weltforum Verlag).

ROAPE (Review of African Political Economy) (1983) Special Issue – Sudan, Debates on National Capitalist Class, Number 26, pp. 103–23.

Rweyemamu, J.F. (ed.) (1980) *Industrialization and Income Distribution in Africa* (Dakar: Codesira).

Schmitz, H. (1984) 'Industrialization Strategies in Less Developed Countries: Some Lessons of Historical Experience', *The Journal of Development Studies,* vol. 21, no. 1, October, pp. 1–21.

Shaaeldin, E. (1984) 'The Evolution and Transformation of the Sudanese Economy up to 1950', DSRC, Khartoum: Monograph Series No. 20, August, University of Khartoum.

Singh, A. (1982) Industrialization in Africa: A Structuralist View in Fransman (1982) pp. 24–37.

Steel, W.F. and Evans, J.W. (1984) 'Industrialization in Sub-Saharan Africa. Strategies and Performance', Washington, DC: World Bank Technical Paper Number 25.

Tetzlaff, R. (1982) 'Die Institutionalisierung von politischer Entwicklung im "sozialistischen' Einparteistaat Sudan – ein ungelöstes Problem', in *Verfassung Und Recht In Obersee* (Law and Politics in Africa, Asia and Latin America), vol. 15, no. 1 pp. 25–43.

Tetzlaff, R. and Wohlmuth, K. (eds) (1980) *Der Sudan. Probleme und Perspektiven der Entwicklung* (Frankfurt am Main: Alfred Metzner Verlag GmbH).

UNIDO (1985a) June 7, Final Report (Meeting of High-Level Experts on Africa's External Debt in respect of the Industrial Sector), ID/WG. 439, 17 pages.

UNIDO (1985b) June 20, Summary Report On Industry and External Debt in Africa, IS. 537, 14 pages.

UNIDO (1985c) The Democratic Republic of the Sudan, Industrial Development Review Series, 17 July, UNIDO/IS. 541.

Wohlmuth, K. (1979) International Resources in Sudan: Indebtedness and Foreign Capital (in German), Research Report no. 3, University of Bremen, May, 138 pages.

Wohlmuth, K. (1980) Die Produkt- und Regionalstruktur des sudanesischen Aussenhandels. Potentielle Märkte für traditionelle sudanesische Export-produkte, in Tetzlaff and Wohlmuth (1980) pp. 1–42.

Wohlmuth, K. (1983) 'The Kenana Sugar Project: A Model of Successful Trilateral Cooperation?', in Oesterdiekhoff and Wohlmuth (1983) pp. 195–235.

Wohlmuth, K. and Hansohm, D. (1984) 'Economic Policy Changes in the Democratic Republic of the Sudan', Research Report, University of Bremen, 98 pages.

Wohlmuth, K. and Hansohm, D. (1986) 'Sudan: A Case for Structural Adjustment Policies', SERG Discussion Paper No. 8, University of Bremen, February, 29 pages.

World Bank (1983) Sudan. Pricing Policies and Structural Balances, vol. I: Main Report, Washington DC; November 10, 101 pages.

World Bank (1985) October 7, Sudan. Prospects for Rehabilitation of the Sudanese Economy, vol. I: Main Report, Washington DC; 186 pages, Report No. 5496-SU.

World Bank (1986a) Financing Adjustment With Growth in Sub-Saharan Africa, 1986–90, Washington DC; Report No. 6082, February.

World Bank (1986b) *World Development Report*, Washington DC.

Discussion on Part IV

INTRODUCTION TO THE DISCUSSION

In his introduction to the session, Professor Ishikawa emphasised its focus on primary-export countries, the lack of theory to help define relevant development paths for these countries, and his hopes that the papers and discussion could point the way toward this.

He explained how complicated it is for primary-exporting economies to get on to a steady development track, especially since they often inherit political structures and institutions such as marketing boards that do not always encourage smooth transitions. He saw need for industrialisation patterns that are stylised to particular situations with respect to relative emphasis on processing and servicing industries, and on import substitution and export stimulation.

In Ishikawa's view, country *typologies* are useful starting points. He suggested three criteria for defining such typologies:

1. Differences in *resource endowments* – population size and movements, land, and labour availability.
2. Differences in *technology* – labour/capital-intensive distinction, as well as organisational variations.
3. Differences in *stages of economic development* – stages of industrialisation, key turning-points, and historical events associated with these that are not readily incorporated in analytical models.

He indicated that there are certain models that one can build upon, such as 'Staple Theory', which helps to understand how some Latin American countries become trapped for so long in dependency on exports like coffee before proceeding to industrialisation and import substitution.

PAPER BY DEEPAK LAL

'The Political Economy of Industrialisation in Primary Product Exporting Economies'

Professor Gustav Ranis, the lead discussant, said he liked Professor Lal's paper very much. He saw it as a creative effort to make policy changes endogenous within a neoclassical model – a new institutional economics, so to speak, though it had not been entirely clear *which policies* Lal had it in mind to make internal to the analysis. He saw Lal's typology as useful in its distinction between peasant-dominated (which Lal had called predatory – for example, Thailand, Ghana, and Tanzania), corporate agriculture-dominated (which Lal had called factional – for example, Argentina), and dual (which Lal had called oligarchic – for example, Peru) economies. But Ranis did have some cautionary reactions to Lal's cautionary tales.

For one thing, Ranis felt that there could be the danger of trying to put too much into one model. Trade theoretic models like Ricardo–Viner and various extensions can overreach themselves. The main point to be gained from Lal is that economic analysis can usefully reflect the reality that the state is more than an impartial arbiter – that sometimes it acts on behalf of *itself* or on behalf of certain groups and only sometimes on behalf of all the people.

Referring to Lal's first cautionary tale – the Thailand, Ghana, and Tanzania examples of autocratic states – Ranis related how in Phase 1 the state had been depicted as not being geared to people and making up its own mind about what it will do. Trade policies are often motivated by maximisation of the state's own, or its parastatals', or the sovereign's income. Then, in Phase 2, such economies tend to move from absolute rule to populism, when there is more attention to interest groups, political patronage, and import substitution.

Ranis noted that Lal's depiction did not allow for the imposition of external shocks in a realistic manner and that he had not been clear about what would be a 'natural' rate of import substitution and industrialisation. Also the Lal analysis had neglected monetary and fiscal policy patterns, the question as to who owns the surplus and how it is allocated, and the fact that other characteristics may have affected things (for example, ideologies in Tanzania and bad development ideas in Ghana). For these reasons, Professor Ranis was intrigued by the first cautionary tale but was not completely satisfied by it.

In Lal's second cautionary tale, which depicted Argentina as a factional state, Ranis saw the point that the 'decisive set' changed over time and that the distribution of the resource endowment determines who these decisive individuals are. For example, in the nineteenth century when abundant land was the dominant economic resource, landlords made the decisions. But later, when import substitution was taking place, capitalists joined the decisive set. Ranis also saw the value of tracing the effects of external economic events – terms of trade declines, export price changes, devaluation pressures, wage changes and so on – on decisive factions, but he found Lal's efforts at telling about Argentina in this unconventional way to some extent confusing.

Ranis thought that Lal's third tale – Peru as an oligarchic state – was the sketchiest of the three. He thought that, at the same time, Lal's graphics for explaining the transition from the traditional export domination, the effects on labour and wages, the government's maintenance of expenditures by foreign borrowing and so on were perhaps unnecessarily elaborate; that a lot had to do with the fact that Peru's ability to depend on its natural resource base was coming to an end.

In closing, Ranis reiterated that this was a very interesting paper. He was pleased that Lal had written it. Ranis was sympathetic with the idea of typologies and noted that many people were moving analytically in that direction. He felt that Lal's analysis made very good reading and was suggestive of useful ideas. But he did feel that Lal's work was rather like an unfinished symphony in that there was room to give more careful attention to criteria for grouping countries as well as the demarcation of relevant facts, courses of events, and policy influences.

Professor Lal, in responding to these introductory comments of Ranis, indicated that, in his selection of a typology and grouping of countries, he had been quite conscious of a particular dimension – the type of state. He saw the predatory state as distinct in that it had an autonomous ruler, colonial power or bureaucratic organisation that could accumulate and dispose of economic surplus much as it wished. A ruler might put it all into Swiss bank accounts or devote it to benevolent purposes. If there is an independent bureaucracy, there is often over-provision of public goods and excessive accumulation of revenue. In such situations as Tanzania's, this tendency for individual bureaucracies to maximise their independent ends has resulted in chronic fiscal crises.

In contrast, Lal's factional state had no autonomous objectives of its own. The state tends to serve the *median* decisive voter. In Argentina the decisive set historically coincided with the agricultural set. But, as fluctuating terms of trade and real wage cuts entered the picture in the 1940s and 1950s, the median decisive voter changed and along with him the character of the political leadership.

Regarding Peru, Lal observed that, historically, it had been oligarchic as depicted but that it was tending to move towards a factional situation rather like Argentina's.

Discussion of Lal's paper from the floor began with questions and thoughts about who the decisive individuals were and how to identify them. M. Cocke picked up Lal's point that in 1932 Thailand changed from a monarchy to an oligarchy and asked what he really meant by 'oligarchy' in the case of Thailand. Ranis observed that this had to do with whether the decisive individuals were endogenous or exogenous to government decisions. Ronald Findlay, thinking of Lal's factional state, felt that one should not be too mechanical (for example, as regards analysis of capital–labour balances) and examine the dynamics of the way a median individual becomes a decisive individual. He mentioned some work by Gerald Meier in this direction.

Simón Teitel noted that populism in Peru is not just a recent phenomenon and that the earlier history of the APRA political party reflects such influences. But Teitel's main point was that he felt a more *causal* way of examining these patterns is needed, not just a historical approach. In responding, Lal agreed that APRA reflects populist tendencies but, to be a factional state like Argentina, one would have to have Andean Indians actually in the government. Peru is still dual in that the government talks about the Indian population as 'them'. Lal observed also that many people in Peru feel that the government should promote import substitution and, in fact, for the APRA party at least, that has been almost an ideology.

David Brown asked, when it came to analysing political–economic interventions, how Lal felt his model meshed with the framework suggested by Paul Streeten in his paper in Chapter 3; that is, would Lal internalise such variables or, as Streeten did, would he tend to keep these external to the analysis itself? In response, Lal said he felt that his own was a positive model – one that may be useful to carry around in one's head to explain tendencies. He regarded this as being more flexible than the usual Marxist model, for example.

He would make endogenous to his analysis the means by which decisive individuals actually delivered changes.

Sunanda Sen wondered whether one might not think in terms of some kind of natural openness of an economy – an 'organic nationalism' so to speak – when it came to such matters as import substitution and the theory of the state. Lal's response was that one could assume a natural level of industrialisation as well as a natural level of import substitution against which to judge the effects of artificial export promotion and import substitution. He envisioned a production-possibility curve, with export promotion on one axis and world price ratios on the other as a frame for arriving at optimal departures from 'natural' levels.

Ranis felt that it was operationally significant and useful to think in terms of an organic nationalism. He pointed out that, under certain circumstances of income growth and changes in transport costs, patterns of importing may develop and make it not 'unnatural' to intervene; that is, Ranis did not conceive nationality as a concept saying that the government should do nothing. He went on to place organic nationalism in a broader perspective along with Kuznetsian concepts of secularism and egalitarianism. The basic idea was that, if a state is composed of many ethnic and social groups, the first priority of a government may be to create a sympathetic nationalism in which every citizen views himself as part of the same state. This, Ranis felt, may go a long way toward explaining how nations act in the economic sphere at that early stage of their development.

PAPER BY SIMÓN TEITEL

'Industrialisation, Primary Commodities and Exports of Manufactures'

The lead discussant, Professor Moshé Syrquin, called attention to questions surrounding the classification of manufactured exports. As the author himself had pointed out, many of the semi-manufactured products that are important for Latin America had been left out of the international classification system most used until recently. Lack of inclusion of food products and inconsistencies in the handling of certain commodities – such as ferrous and non-ferrous metals – resulted in a distorted picture.

To the discussant, this suggested a broader question – the need to take a fresh look at the basic rationale for such classifications.

He noted that, once a classification system is in place, it tends to perpetuate itself. He thought that factor intensity would be a useful criterion distinguishing, for example, between labour-intensive goods and those that draw heavily on natural resources (Ricardo-type goods). The latter grouping has been traditionally important in Latin America, but shifts to processing and manufacturing relying on skilled labour were rapidly taking place. If emerging comparative advantages and their sources are to be revealed, a more finely tuned system for detecting relative emphasis on import substitution *vis-à-vis* export promotion, natural resources and labour intensities, as well as technology levels, would be required.

The discussant called attention to, and expressed agreement with, Kuznets' view that individual nations were more appropriate than entire regions as units of economic analysis for such purposes. It was not possible to generalise for all of Latin America about emerging industrialisation and export patterns and their underlying factors.

Concerning the author's conclusion that there is really no dichotomy between import substitution and industrial exports, and that the technological learning that takes place while developing import substitutes for domestic markets may be a prerequisite for such exports, the discussant suggested that the contributions of import substitution to the development of manufactured exports, through training, and the accumulation of experience, should be carefully assessed.

In opening up discussion from the floor, Romeo Bautista noted that export industries are also often subsidised and suggested that one should perhaps abandon the import substitution/export promotion dichotomy and, instead, emphasise distinctions between efficient and inefficient industries, with a view to careful selection of activities to be supported. In a similar vein, the chairman, Deepak Lal, proposed to distinguish between 'natural' import substitutes and 'hot house' industries.

The point was then made by D.C. de Costa that inefficiencies, erosion of competition, and high costs were often associated with the second stage of import substitution, and that this implied the need to link industrialisation strategy to a policy frame which addresses such concerns as external debt, inflation and exchange rate policy. How to achieve such integration was seen as an important matter. To Rajhnam Panthan this raised a question about the Brazilian experience. How could one explain their success in expanding manufactured exports in the face of high inflation?

Turning to the broader question of export success, Gustav Ranis submitted that respectability of performance has to be seen in relation to opportunity. Has a country 'gotten on the boat' at the right time, in the right way? He added that a historical viewpoint could be useful in identifying what a country can do. For example, the early stage of labour-intensive export industries that took place in East Asia seems to have been skipped in Latin America.

Alasdair MacBean observed that manufacturing export success cannot be judged by comparing data based only on *total* value of exports. He asked whether it was fair to compare an export having 80 per cent of local value added with another export having most of its value added stemming from imports to that country.

In responding to various comments about the use of the United Nations Standard International Trade Classification (SITC) and its inadequacies, Teitel mentioned that work was now under way on a new UN trade classification. He reiterated that the SITC tends to underestimate the value of manufactured exports from Latin America, as shown by cross-referencing with the International Standard Industrial Classification (ISIC). World Bank and UNIDO studies, using the latter classification, as well as those done using IMF data, based on the product-by-product approach used in its commodity reporting, show similar results to those obtained in his study.

Regarding the suggestion that a comparative historical viewpoint would be useful, he felt that, had earlier data been analysed, Latin America would have shown a pattern of manufacturing export development that was similar to, but lagged somewhat behind, East Asia's, particularly, with respect to exports of labour-intensive goods such as textiles and clothing. He pointed out that Latin American countries have had relatively lower exports of such manufactures because they were richer in natural resources, and had smaller population density than a majority of the East Asian countries.

Teitel agreed that questions could be raised about his indicator of resource-intensity (direct value added/output). He noted, however, that rankings by his indicator across industries were quite stable for both industrialised and developing countries. To improve on the indicator, detailed input–output studies would be required; this was beyond the scope of his paper.

Concerning the use of regional instead of country data, Teitel noted that the appropriateness of the level of aggregation depends on the analytical purpose of the study. His regional data had helped to reveal some broad patterns of emerging comparative advantage.

Since these data are heavily weighted by a few large Latin American exporters, it could be useful to analyse and compare the performance of individual countries.

Teitel agreed with Bautista that it was difficult to distinguish between import substitution and export promotion, and that efficiency considerations could, instead, be important. However, he cited studies which, after taking into account the effect of promotion policies, had shown no great inefficiencies in Brazil's manufactured exports (Teitel and Thoumi, 1986). Although Latin America may have missed the boat to some extent by lagging behind, particularly in exports of labour-intensive manufactures, he did not feel that there was sufficient evidence to support a sharp dichotomy in which East Asia had been efficient and Latin America not.

Teitel went on to say that there was need now to move into more detailed, less aggregative analysis of emerging export patterns and the factors affecting them. He did not see either inflation or indebtedness as being at the heart of this. He believed that industrial exports mainly reflect such basic factors as resource endowments, economies of scale, technological learning and, broadly speaking, good macroeconomic policies – particularly with respect to the real exchange rate. When making comparisons, one needs to realise that, before becoming successful exporters of industrial products, countries have had different starting-points and different industrialisation experiences.

PAPER BY IPPEI YAMAZAWA

Industrialisation Through Full Utilisation of Foreign Trade: The Case of Some East Asian Economies

The paper by Ippei Yamazawa afforded an opportunity to examine industrial development patterns in Japan since the nineteenth century and make some comparisons with more recent development in Asia. Professor Yamazawa was not present but his paper was introduced and discussed by Professor Shujiro Urata. In his lead comments on the paper, Urata noted that it would be useful (1) to expand the analysis to more commodities and more countries, and (2) to conduct microeconomic studies to examine more closely the influence of scale economies and other factors on the transitions from import substitution to export promotion.

Urata went on to consider whether the catching-up product cycle (CPC) framework emphasised by Yamazawa in fact represented a new basic theory. His conclusion was that it did not. One had to look more deeply for basic explanations. At least two underlying theories could be considered:

1. A dynamic version of Heckscher–Ohlin emphasising that, as Japan developed, capital accumulation was faster than increases in labour use, resulting in an increase in the capital–labour ratio and a pattern of factor endowment giving comparative advantage to more capital-intensive goods than before.
2. Product-cycle theory, a subset of CPC theory, according to which the production of a certain good goes through a cycle of techniques ranging from capital-intensive to labour-intensive. So, even if capital-labour endowment stays the same, a product may be imported first and then later exported. These new technologies are transferred mainly by multinational corporations in conjunction with direct investments.

To Urata this lack of a clear-cut explanation of export expansion and price competitiveness suggested a need for rigorous investigation of how scale economies, new technologies, accumulation of new skills, and other variables entered the picture. He thought that CPC theory may not be appropriate for explaining trade balances; macroeconomic policies, exchange rate policies especially, have to be examined. He did not feel that the amount of evidence presented in Professor Yamazawa's paper was sufficient to support the CPC explanation as a general theory that could be applied, for instance, to large countries like India and China. Hence his call for study of CPC patterns and explanations (1) for more commodities in certain countries like Japan, (2) for certain commodities in a larger number of countries, and (3) to combine the insights gained from (1) and (2). To help gauge the average pace of CPC development for a certain commodity or for a certain country, he suggested use of Chenery–Syrquin type regressions, perhaps using per-capita GNP as a proxy for the capital–labour ratio, if the theory behind it is a dynamic Heckscher–Ohlin type.

Discussion from the floor was opened up by Krishna Murthy who pointed out that India was producing not only primary products but also high-quality manufactured products, utilising labour-intensive methods in an effective manner. He mentioned also that India was preparing an integrated development programme to reinforce this pattern.

Referring to the CPC pattern, David Brown observed that it was not just a matter of some countries condensing the import-substitution stage but that certain products and services were introduced exclusively for foreign buyers – for example, tourism and clothes designed for high-fashion markets abroad. He wondered whether this was an important component and whether this might not be a useful analytical distinction.

Gustav Ranis felt that it was necessary to interpret CPC patterns in terms of whether they had emerged from *natural* efficiencies and resource limitations or from *government-assisted* processes. He observed that Japan's land resource limitations had led to relatively short periods of raw material expansion for primary exports, and early need to turn to other exports to finance new industries. Similarly, Taiwan rather quickly ran out of income from agriculture to finance industry and, having also had foreign aid cut off, was forced to concentrate on new kinds of exports. While he agreed that Japan had had a pattern of export expansion that was 'natural' and different from other countries, there still had been artificial protections of various forms.

PAPER BY KARL WOHLMUTH

'Sudan's Industrialisation after Independence: A Case of Industrialisation'

A glimpse at the varied ways in which agrarian economies of Africa are entering the industrial age, and how one might come to grips with the analysis of their policies and problems, was provided by Professor Karl Wohlmuth's paper on the Sudan.

Professor H.M.A. Onitiri and Dr. J.S. Odama offered the following comments:

'Wohlmuth's paper provides a fairly succinct summary of the problems of the Sudan's industrialisation and the paper also reflects in a general way the problems of industrialisation in many, if not most African countries. Indeed the Sudan case is not just, as the author says, "a special case of Africa's crisis of industrialisation".

It is, in many ways, a typical case, depicting the consequences of small domestic markets, pervasive low productivity arising from inadequate infrastructure and poor management, weak intersectoral linkages and excessive dependence on imported inputs compounded by severe foreign exchange constraints.

'There is little to quarrel about in Wohlmuth's paper regarding the analysis as far as it goes. Later we shall question whether in fact it goes far enough'.

'In the meantime we would like to begin our comments by looking at the central issue of Africa's industrialisation, as raised by Wohlmuth – and we venture to say very aptly – at the end of the first section of his paper: What should be the engine of industrial growth in the *near, short* and *long* term? Should it be *exports, regional import substitution* or *internal markets?* These possibilities are mentioned by the author but unfortunately only one is actually discussed and even then not quite in as much depth as the analysis would demand. Perhaps this is because the author has discussed the details in earlier articles.

'Scepticism about the export and regional import substitution options has led the author to rely almost entirely on the option of the Agricultural Demand-Led Industrialisation Strategy (ADLI) which, in fact, takes up the bulk of the author's analysis. This has invariably limited the scope of the paper and its usefulness as a basis for a balanced discussion of industrial strategy in the Sudan and still less in other African countries. Given the small size of many African economies, it is difficult to go very far in discussing the strategy for a particular African country outside the framework of regional and sub-regional co-operation with its neighbours not only with regard to agricultural development (such as ADLI) but also as regards regional import substitution, which the author has virtually excluded from his analysis.

'While the ADLI development strategy could be a valuable component of industrial strategy in African countries, in particular if it also takes into account the possibilities of regional markets. We can think of two reasons why it cannot go very far without a corresponding programme of regional import substitution.

'Firstly, the ADLI strategy would also entail a large import component in the form of inputs for agricultural production and processing and the equipment for the expansion of infrastructure which cannot be provided nationally or regionally, or which can be produced only with large amounts of imported inputs.

'Secondly, the ADLI strategy, by orienting agricultural productions towards internal regional markets, implies that other means would have to be found (and here we are left with import substitution if export expansion is ruled out) to provide the foreign exchange needed to pay for vital imports of materials and services or to service foreign debts.

'For these two reasons at least, regional import substitution on the basis of the self-reliance programmes of the Lagos Plan of Action cannot be ruled out of consideration in spite of the immense difficulties that African countries have to face in putting such programmes into effect. In this connection, it is expected that the United Nations Programme of Action for African Economic Recovery and Development (UNPAAERD) adopted by the Special Session of the UN General Assembly in June, 1986 should provide a new impetus to regional efforts under which regional programmes will gather increased momentum.

'Among other things, the UN Programme calls for the strengthening and consolidation of existing subregional organisations in Africa "in accordance with the objectives of the Lagos Plan of Action", and the establishment of new subregional organisations as may be necessary.

'It needs to be added that the theoretical arguments in support of such programmes of regional co-operation in Africa are not in doubt. It is the practical problems, such as the equitable distribution of the gains from regional co-operation and how to cope with internal and external agents with vested interests in the existing arrangements that need to be faced. For example, suppose African countries decide to replace the wide variety of models of motor vehicles imported into the continent, or assembled locally with negligible local value added, with a limited number of models whose local production can generate more domestic value added, aside from improving repair and maintenance facilities. The presence of external and internal vested interests in the existing expensive and inefficient arrangements would be incalculable. The same problem would arise if African countries decided to save foreign exchange by replacing existing brands of import-based soda drinks with locally based substitutes. What about 'Africola', for example?

'We are sure that our Indian friends would have much advice to offer in these respects. It is instructive to recall that the UN Programme even looks beyond regional and subregional co-operation and considers that South–South economic and technical co-operation "should constitute a key element in the economic recovery of Africa", and in this connection it proposes a number of action-oriented measures in the priority areas of food and agricultural production that would promote this objective.

'Many African countries have come to realise that they face a bleak future with industrial development unless they take radical measures to harmonise their approaches to industrialisation within the framework of regional and subregional co-operation, rationalise their import-substitution programmes, and curb excessive preferences for imported items for which substitutes produced within the region could be found.

'It is along these lines that future analysis of Africa's strategy of industrialisation can most usefully proceed. Professor Wohlmuth's paper discusses one aspect of this new frontier and to that extent it is a useful contribution to a problem with a much wider scope.'

In his response to the comments of Onitiri and Odama, Professor Wohlmuth explained that he had emphasised an expansion of domestic markets as the main engine of growth because a review had shown that Africa has still a very small manufacturing sector, is producing few inputs, has not made significant progress in import substitution at the regional level, and has made only very limited progress in the creation of industrial exports. However, the support of an ADLI strategy does not mean that regional import substitution and/or export development should be neglected or discriminated.

He suggested that it was useful to analyse Sudan's and Africa's crisis of industrialisation in terms of four levels of analysis:

1. *Historical analysis,* which shows that in the Sudan, and in Africa, colonial and post-colonial patterns have a lasting influence on the industrialisation options now and on the roles of state assistance for the industrial sectors.
2. *Structural analysis,* which shows that linkages between and within sectors, especially between agriculture and industry, are extremely poor. In the context of the Sudan, the answers appear to lie in the promotion of rural industries, the use of domestic resources and the reduction of imports of raw materials, a more rational utilisation of Sudan's agricultural potential and in relating industry to agriculture in a more systematic way by changing the macroeconomic and sectoral policy environment.
3. *Industrial policy analysis,* which focuses on specific policy issues such as industrial sector policy institutions, processes of policy

formation, pricing and incentive policies, sectoral infrastructure and supporting policies.

4. *State policy analysis*, which asks such questions as: What are the roles and what should be the roles of the state in the African industrialisation process? Is the state strong enough in terms of its state functions to generate industrialisation links to the important agricultural subsectors? Can industrialisation be promoted on the basis of policies that give benefits to ruling groups in the government and to commercial interests? What types of reforms at the level of the government are necessary in order to promote industrialisation?

Wohlmuth felt that an analysis on the basis of these four levels can provide valuable guides to mid-term industrialisation strategies. For example, it showed why Sudan's efforts to develop regional import substitution with Arab countries in the 1970s failed, and what the prerequisites for a successful strategy may be. It showed also that there is a need to dwell less on the issue of public versus private ownership, but to focus more on the policy environment and the production incentives.

L.N. Gupta opened the discussion from the floor by seeking clarification about people's participation in the industrialisation of the Sudan. Did it have a pattern of rural and urban pockets? Or was it more one of developed and underdeveloped pockets? What were the population characteristics, notably sex and age distributions, in these pockets? What were the roles of voluntary agencies in overcoming economic and social constraints?

John Page, thinking of the broad question of regional integration, called attention to a paper by Cooper and Massell in the late 1960s which showed that welfare is always increased more by unilateral tariff reductions rather than by having specified common market arrangements. To him this raised questions about the viability of regional marketing arrangements.

He pointed out that the only remaining Latin American regional integration arrangement was in the Caribbean.

S. Ishikawa asked what were the specific roles played in the industrialisation process in the Sudan by each of the agricultural subsectors – irrigated, mechanised rainfed and traditional rainfed?

J.A. Okelo agreed that agricultural subsector analysis is very important in Africa. He observed also that foreign influences had become very significant in both positive and negative ways, and that this was an element that could well be brought out more in an historical light.

S. Mukhopadhya asked about transmission mechanisms – links to global oil development, world economic cycles, and other events outside the Sudan. He felt that one could not assess industrial development entirely in terms of internal inefficiencies, and that one needed to analyse the effect of these external economic influences.

Ms Samanke made the point that in situations like the Sudan 'ad-hocism' seems to be a big factor . . . that there is often no clear development plan. She observed also that the problems of corruption which characterise some underdeveloped situations often stem from lack of knowledge . . . that corruption thrives on ignorance and can be overcome by broader education. She felt that cooperative movements could be an important way to enhance a better understanding of rural development processes.

Pradeep Bhargava wondered whether the Sudan might be analytically similar to Bangladesh and Sri Lanka, where traditional roles of the 'petty bourgeoisie' have been changing relative to the roles of the state and of the commercialisation processes.

Another discussant asked whether World Bank loans for the Sudan could really do more to induce appropriate adjustments. He also questioned the instrument of conditionality in this respect.

In his response to the various observations and questions, Wohlmuth said that an analysis of industrialisation processes in Sudan has to begin with a recognition of three important subsectors of agriculture that now exist: (1) the traditional rainfed crop and livestock subsector, which is where most of the labour is to be found, and which, in contrast to many developing countries, is now the main source of net foreign exchange earnings (more than 50 per cent), and which has plenty of export potential; (2) the mechanised rainfed subsector, which can produce for export in years of good rainfall; and (3) the irrigated cash and food crop sector.

He saw a potential for small industry development in the Sudanese hinterland and felt that all the three agricultural subsectors could provide a base for an industrialisation pattern that would have lower import requirements. But such linkages had not yet evolved and existing policies focused mainly on urban locations and high import-content industries.

He considered policies to help induce small entrepreneurs in the hinterland to produce more effectively as an important step that

Sudan could take towards industrialisation. Until now there has not been much reward for private investors from investing in rural areas in anything beyond simple services. Along with production incentives, there is a need for rural development agencies that have stronger roles related to infrastructure, marketing, storage, etc. There is now a greater awareness of this in the ministries concerned, but the outcome in terms of policy reforms and implementation is likely to depend greatly on political developments.

Regarding regional integration among African countries for encouraging large-scale industry development, Wohlmuth was less optimistic about prospects for the near future. National industrial policies, to the extent that they exist in Africa, tend to be orientated towards protected domestic markets. There is still a need for policies that lay the foundations for the kinds of cooperation called for under the Lagos Plan of Action and other regional undertakings.

Wohlmuth felt that capital from the World Bank and other external sources had important roles to play, but that one must be careful to avoid more of the type of 'technological dualism' that has characterised foreign investment in Africa. As an example, he mentioned the huge Kenana sugar factory, which is producing only at costs far above world market prices.

CHARACTERISTICS OF TRADE IN THE CARIBBEAN

Discussion of analytical challenges associated with export transitions taking place in the small open economies of the Caribbean was stimulated by referral to a model that was being developed by Dr DeLisle Worrell.[1] Dr John M. Page explained how the Worrell model, using the Solow–Swan tradable/non-tradable distinction, had disaggregated exports into four types: (1) tourism, the local demand for which is very sensitive to relative prices elsewhere; (2) manufactured goods for which demand is boundless relative to the insignificant amounts produced by these small island economies; (3) mineral and manufactured items produced by multinational enclaves that have to compete cost-wise with alternative sources or substitutes elsewhere; and (4) agricultural products, which have considerable lags in supply response to world market changes. It was noted that these export characteristics exposed the island economies to severe disturbances from world economic fluctuations and that it was necessary for them to devise policies to cushion the impacts. Accordingly, the Worrell model was intended to help guide policies related to exchange rates, tariffs, direct taxes, government spending and interest rates.

The parameters of this model had not yet been finally established. Preliminary results for Barbados suggested very low elasticities of demand for tourist services (which implied that Barbados could act to some extent as a monopolist regarding hotel rates) but low coefficients of export responsiveness to local policy interventions. It was noted also that the model would be addressing questions related mainly to *short-term* policy adjustments and not long-term export strategies. But the model was expected to help answer such questions as whether to concentrate on high-priced/low-volume tourist services or cheaper facilities aimed at attracting large numbers of tourists.

In explaining his work further, Worrell indicated that he hoped to incorporate data for non-tradables and for other Caribbean nations, as well as estimate elasticities for longer time-spans.

Regarding responses to changes in hotel rates, Alasdair MacBean noted the extent to which special holiday packages and other discounts were being offered to attract travellers from the USA, Canada and elsewhere. He wondered how this might be taken into account. Worrell said that he had used standard fares and rates in his initial estimates. He agreed that efforts would have to be made to disaggregate further so that percentages of tourists coming under discount arrangements could be reflected. He observed that discount packages were more common for Canadian visitors than for Americans.

Gustav Ranis asked about possibilities of scale economies through co-operation among the Caribbean nations. Worrell did not envisage significant potential for economies of size in primary exports such as oil and bauxite refining. In connection with bauxite, he noted how energy-intensive aluminium processing was and also the fact that many substitutes for aluminium had been appearing in automobiles and other products. He felt that future trade opportunities in the Caribbean would be affected less by *natural* resource bases than by *human* resource exploitation, development, and migration patterns.

AGRICULTURAL DEVELOPMENT AND INDUSTRIALISATION IN THAILAND AND OTHER ASEAN COUNTRIES

More specific insight into industrialisation processes and associated changes in Asia was provided through discussion of a draft paper[1] in which considerable descriptive information about changes in Thailand since the early 1960s had been assembled by Professor Medhi Krongkaew of Thammasat University. Based on his preliminary analysis, the author's tentative conclusions were as follows:

'In this paper I argue that the rapid industrialisation of Thailand in the last two and a half decades was helped in large part by contributions from agricultural development in the forms of primary exports of rice and other diversified crops such as maize, cassava and sugar-cane. While this pattern of development has been no different from most other dualistic economies, the situation in Thailand is unique in the sense that the agricultural development has been very land-intensive, involving very little increase (or even a decrease) in yields, and causing very little change in agricultural–industrial employment transformation. Moreover, the apparently successful industrialisation has dwelt too long on the import-substituting stage. This has been brought about mainly by protective policies and defective incentive systems that favoured capital-intensive investments over labour-intensive investments.

Apart from incurring a great cost to the environment and natural resources, this type of industrialisation also implies differential benefits accruing to different segments of the population. The urban, manufacturing and service sectors would benefit more at the expense of the rural, agricultural sectors. The rapid urbanisation of Bangkok and other regional cities is clear testimony to this situation. The social welfare of the rural population, measured in terms of income per capita and the incidence of poverty, has improved through time. This was due partly to the inevitable trickling-down effect. However, the income inequalities across regions in Thailand appear to be worsening also through time. Future policies must aim at a more balanced development between agriculture and industry. This may require changes in the nature of Thailand's agricultural production and exports, as well as adjustments in its industrial structures.'

OBSERVATIONS BY ROMEO BAUTISTA ABOUT THE ASEAN PATTERN

Professor Bautista had been asked by the Session Organiser to prepare some remarks based on Professor Krongkaew's work in Thailand as well as other analyses related to the broader Southeast Asian picture:

'Krongkaew has given us a good news-bad news report on agriculture's contribution to Thailand's economic development since the early 1960s. The good news is that accelerated growth of agricultural output (especially from 1960 to the mid-seventies) was accompanied by rapid industrialisation, growth in per capita rural and urban incomes, substantial alleviation of both rural and urban poverty, and a markedly high growth rate of real GDP that averaged about 7.4 per cent annually during 1960–80 – a remarkable overall growth performance indeed which few, if any, heavily agricultural economies could match. The bad news is that the development process was not of the employment-generating type due to the land-using pattern of agricultural growth and the protected import-substituting character of industrial development; this resulted, among other things, in an uneven regional development, a significant degradation of the environment, and excessive depletion of natural resources. In fact there has been a deceleration of Thai economic growth during the 1970s which was slowed further in the first half of the 1980s by the unfavourable conditions in the external economic environment. Agriculture, in particular, has been suffering from slow growth, down to an average annual rate of 3.5–3.6 per cent during 1975–85 from the 5.1–5.5 per cent annual rate from 1960 to 1975.

'Thailand at present is by no means in a situation of economic crisis. None the less, according to Professor Krongkaew "the development problem of Thailand is now taking on a new dimension". One gets the impression that the Thai experience is the classic case of agriculture-led development process gone wrong. Some general policy suggestions to deal with the problem include efforts to increase agricultural productivity, rationalisation of industrial incentives that would remove the bias against labour-intensive industries, and direct poverty redressal programmes in the rural areas of low-growth regions.

'The analysis and prognosis of Thailand's agricultural and industrial development raises several issues that are worth pursuing, in the context also of the three other heavily agricultural ASEAN economies (which is what Professor Ishikawa originally asked me to cover). There are in fact some similarities in the sectoral development patterns among Thailand, Indonesia, Malaysia and the Philippines. At least during the two decades from 1960 to 1980, these four ASEAN countries registered significantly higher rates of agricultural, industrial and overall GDP growth, compared to most other agricultural economies. Since the early 1980s, however, there has been a marked reduction in these growth rates. The external debt of these countries has also become a major constraint to economic growth, as represented in the extreme case by the Philippines – although it should be remembered that the Philippines debt-service crisis was preceded by a chain of political events initiated by the Aquino assassination in August 1983. None the less, well before that time, there were signs of an impending economic crisis.

'I think it is difficult to deny that the slowdown in ASEAN economic growth since the early 1980s has been influenced by the deterioration in the international economy and an accompanying drastic reduction in world prices of the major primary products of the ASEAN countries. More importantly, however, the ASEAN countries have been unable to compensate for the reduced foreign demand by effectively raising domestic demand. This is not to say that so-called countercyclical macroeconomic policies were not adopted. Such expansionary measures, however, led only to rapid inflation rates and failed to sustain rising production levels for the simple reason that the increased purchasing power did not boost significantly effective demand for domestically produced goods, especially labour-intensive consumer goods. This can be attributed to factors that differ among the ASEAN countries. In the Philippines case, the infamous 'crony capitalists' and large businesses have been the principal beneficiaries of the profligate demand management from the mid-1970s to the end of the Marcos regime. In various degrees the economic structure and policies adopted in Malaysia, Indonesia, and Thailand have also not been fully supportive of segments of their population with a high marginal budget share of food and other labour-intensive goods. The employment and income multipliers of the initial increase in the purchasing power afforded by the expansionary policies were therefore low, preventing a sustained growth of output and employment in the domestic economy. I would suspect that the differential economic performance of the ASEAN countries in the 1980s has been influenced by the relative extent to which the broadly based policy measures promoting domestic production were adopted to offset the decline in foreign demand.

'In reference to Krongkaew's analysis of the contribution of agriculture to Thailand's economic development since the early 1960s, I would like to have seen a systematic examination of the final demand effects of the rapidly rising rural incomes due to the observed rapid growth of farm output in the 1960s and the improving agricultural terms of trade in the 1970s. Within the rural economy, who were the principal beneficiaries, and what were their consumption patterns and saving propensities? Was the land-intensive agricultural growth pattern not complementary to the growth of small-scale production and labour absorption that would have resulted in more favourable final demand effects through higher consumption of food and labour-intensive industrial products?

'In the industrial sector it is presumably the case that the foreign trade restrictions that supported the import substitution drive of the 1960s and 1970s had discriminated against small- and medium-scale producers who have little capacity for rent-seeking activities compared to the larger industrial enterprises and businesses. Again, the employment and output multiplier from the final demand effects of the observed rapid industrial growth would have been lowered by the bias of the import-substitute industrialisation against small producers.

'In the light of the foregoing and in relation to the policy suggestions made toward the end of Krongkaew's paper, it is perhaps necessary to orient policy efforts to assist small producers in both agriculture and industry, ensuring, for example, that they gain access to infrastructure facilities and improved technologies. In the process the linkages between agricultural and non-agricultural activities in both rural and urban sectors will be strengthened. This would seem as crucial to long-run economic growth (not only in Thailand but also in the other labour-abundant ASEAN countries) as it is necessary for the participation of the poor in that growth. 'As a final point, one peculiarity of the Thai development experience has been the significant role of agricultural *food* exports – traditionally rice and, more recently, cassava. Other ASEAN countries have their primary product exports in the form of industrial raw materials such as rubber and tin in Malaysia, crude oil and logs in Indonesia, and copra and copper in the Philippines. Related to this, some questions can be raised concerning those countries' development experiences and future prospects. What socio-economic classes and income groups were favoured by the expansion of exports of such primary products? Are their consumption and saving patterns conducive to self-sustaining growth of domestic production?

'On the supply side it is frequently advocated, most significantly by self-styled economic nationalists, that the government of these countries should actively promote the domestic processing of such primary products for exports, viewing increases in domestic value added and expansion of processed exports as an additional means of promoting industrialisation. There are problems, however, with this industrial development strategy. I can only briefly indicate them here. One is that in some cases, the very high capital-, scale-, and energy-intensities of such processing industries under existing technologies could completely offset, in terms of net social benefits, the country's comparative advantage of already producing the primary commodity. Moreover the need to import intermediate inputs could significantly reduce the net foreign exchange gain from exporting processed rather than primary products. Also the setting up, under heavy protection, of uneconomic domestic processing industries producing internationally uncompetitive intermediate products would effectively hinder rather than stimulate production in downstream industries. Finally, questions might also arise concerning market prospects, considering the higher tariff and non-tariff barriers observed in developed country markets for imports of more highly processed primary products. Following the terminology of Professor Ishikawa, there can be a 'domestic processing trap' for natural resource-rich developing countries.'

Krongkaew responded by agreeing with Bautista that one must be cautious about the extent of promoting operation of one's own processing industries. He cited the example of fertiliser production in Thailand: there were proposals to build a huge fertiliser plant, even though only a low rate of return was expected and it probably would have been better to use Thailand's limited funds in other ways.

Krongkaew went on to elaborate how Thailand's rice exports had been based on large land areas using low-yield practices and that serious soil erosion problems had been one result. He talked also about the vast deforestation process taking place in Thailand, within the previous 20 years especially, and how the land that had been cleared was not being used effectively.

Professor Krongkaew then told how another primary industry – fisheries – had been declining as an income source. He said that, whereas Thailand had been one of the top ten fishing countries in the world, it was now among the top 30 only and, also, fishermen were having to spend 80 per cent more than before in order to catch a given quantity of fish.   Krongkaew indicated that, although most of Thailand's employment was still in the farming sector, this was declining. It had fallen from 82 per cent in the 1960s to 66 per cent in the 1980s. To him, emerging patterns of GDP growth suggested the need to shift emphasis to urban sources of employment. Along with this, he foresaw important welfare implications – a widened rural-urban gap – this disparity increasing at a greater rate as time went on.   He concluded that, while Thailand was not all that unique among ASEAN countries, it did represent a situation where natural resource depletion should be taken especially into account when analysing agriculture–industry growth strategies and balances.

Gustav Ranis, addressing the problems of agricultural intensification and deforestation, cited the example of Taiwan and its success with intensive vegetable production. He noted that Thailand was much more resource-rich than Taiwan and wondered whether one might not foresee a similar shift to high-value crops in Thailand. He saw high-value crops as a way to finance export crops.

Shigeru Ishikawa observed that in many countries like Thailand there had been too much pessimism about the potentials of small-scale industry. He cited two examples. One was how, when Japanese exports of small tractors to Thailand had completely stopped, it was found that many indigenous tractor plants had been set up to imitate Japanese tractors. Though poorer in quality than Japanese tractors, these indigenous tractors worked satisfactorily and sold at only half the price of the Japanese tractors. His second example was how, in downtown Bangkok, many factories which made component parts for cars had rapidly sprung up. Here again, though inferior in quality to parts from Japan and elsewhere, they worked reasonably well and were cheaper. Professor Ishikawa had come to believe that small-scale metalworking industries had become well established as a result of such import substitution.

Ishikawa observed also that the management capabilities of these small-scale industries tend to grow side by side with large-scale export industries. He cited the example of the needs of tin mines and plantations in South-east Asia for local equipment repairs having led to the establishment and improvement of metalworking skills in the region.

Matti Palo of the Forest Research Institute at Helsinki said that a number of countries have had problems of deforestation when industrialisation first began but have since then been able to return much land into well maintained forests. He cited the example of Finland, which now has more forested areas than before, and also Japan, which has much of its area forested despite high population density and much industrialisation. Palo felt that land tenure patterns had much effect on deforestation. This was now apparent in the Philippines, where deforestation was harming the productivity of agriculture itself. He saw the need for positive incentives in land tenure arrangements if forests are not to be destroyed. Professor Krongkaew agreed with these observations about the importance of land tenure for forestation. He said that the problem was serious in central Thailand near Bangkok, where absentee ownership was very common. Elsewhere, as in the northern highlands, there were more smallholders who owned their land and had more incentive to think of the long run, but even there pressures on the land for more production and income were creating problems.

In concluding the discussion of the Thailand case, Professor Krongkaew observed that the import-substitution process there had taken too long and had resulted in too much import protection. However, the next development plan would be giving emphasis to export promotion and, he felt, would probably do away with some of the defective import-substitution measures.

CHAIRMAN'S SUMMARY OF SESSION 15

In concluding the Session, Dr Simón Teitel made some summary comments. He felt that several themes had emerged from the day's discussions. One was that the dynamic processes involved in moving from exports of primary commodities to industrialisation and manufactured exports really constitute a continuum. There are successive stages and, in evolving a typology, one has to look at individual country differences – resources, history, external shocks, policies and so on.

A second theme noted by Teitel was that differences between East Asian and Latin American countries had not been very striking, but that Africa appears now to be a different case. Primary industries have played important roles in both East Asia and Latin America but, as pointed out by Ranis, important differences may be found in *how* one moves from exporting primary commodities to industrial products.

Thirdly, Teitel noted that it was clear from both the East Asian and Latin American data that the contribution of agriculturally-based commodities and labour-intensive products to manufactured exports was declining.

Teitel acknowledged that while the session had only skimmed the surface, the discussion had pointed out some useful leads towards an agenda for further research. The role of policies in promoting efficient exports of manufactures, and their timing, were questions deserving further study. He also saw need to move beyond the mere description of statistical patterns to an examination of the underlying causality.

In closing, Teitel suggested that there was need to restate the economic efficiency objective in terms of the balancing of the benefits to be derived from a certain measure of protection of selected infant industries against the costs involved. The determination of the optimum level of nurturing activities involved detailed consideration of specific candidate industries, and of the potential benefits to be derived from the externalities generated by their development.

Note

1. Unfortunately this paper was not available for publication in its final form.

Reference

Teitel, S. and Thoumi F. (1986) 'From Import Substitution to Exports: The Manufacturing Exports Experience of Argentina and Brazil', *Economic Development and Cultural Change*, vol. 34, no. 3, (April), pp. 455–90.

Index of Names

Index of Subjects

411